平 成 美 術
うたかたと瓦礫（デブリ）
1989－2019
Bubbles/Debris

Art of the Heisei Period

ごあいさつ

京都市京セラ美術館では、この度、「平成美術：うたかたと瓦礫（デブリ）1989–2019」を開催いたします。

令和への改元から今年で3年目となりますが、思い返せば平成年間（1989–2019年）とは、バブル経済の崩壊を経験し、未曾有の災害に繰り返し見舞われた時代だったと言えるでしょう。本展は、美術評論家の椹木野衣を企画・監修に迎え、美術を通して平成年間をここ京都の地から振り返る試みです。

椹木は、先立つ明治・大正・昭和の美術と比較し、「そのような輪郭だった美術の容貌（精神）を、果たして「平成」の美術は持っているだろうか」と私たちに問いかけます。そして災厄が多発した平成期の美術を「複数の美術家たちによる「密」な集合的活動の集積」と捉えて、鴨長明の『方丈記』と磯崎新の近著『瓦礫（デブリ）の未来』に倣い、「うたかた」と「瓦礫（デブリ）」という2つの言葉に喩えて表現しました。

本展では、平成年間を3つに区分し、14のアーティストグループおよび集合体による代表作約100点が、時代背景を解く鍵となる16メートルに及ぶ年表「平成の壁」とともに一堂に会します。30年あまりに及ぶ時空のなかで、あたかも仮設住宅にもなぞらえられる「方丈」の庵のように点在する作品群を回遊しながら、平成年間の美術や社会について思索を巡らせる機会となれば幸いです。

最後となりましたが、本展に参加されたアーティストグループの皆様、企画・監修の労を執ってくださった椹木野衣氏に心より御礼申し上げます。また、本展開催にあたり、貴重な作品や資料を快くご出品くださいました機関、所蔵家の皆様、そして、ご協賛・ご協力くださいました関係各社をはじめ、お力添えを賜りました多くの皆様に深く感謝申し上げます。

京都市京セラ美術館、朝日新聞社

本書は下記の展覧会に関連して出版されました。

平成美術：うたかたと瓦礫（デブリ）1989–2019

2021年1月23日（土）— 4月11日（日）
京都市京セラ美術館　新館「東山キューブ」

主　　　催：平成美術展実行委員会（京都市、朝日新聞社）
企画・監修：椹木野衣
協　　　賛：株式会社サンエムカラー、ミネベアミツミ株式会社

Foreword

The Kyoto City KYOCERA Museum of Art is proud to present *Bubbles/Debris: Art of the Heisei Period 1989–2019*.

From the vantage point of 2021 (the third year of the new Reiwa Period), it is easy to recall the preceding Heisei Period (1989–2019) as a time when Japan's economic bubble burst and unprecedented disasters occurred one after another. However, it was also a significant period for art in Japan. This exhibition, planned and directed by art critic Sawaragi Noi, looks at the Heisei Period through art, with a Kyoto-based perspective.

The art of the Meiji, Taisho, and Showa Periods represented the spirit of those times. What about Heisei? Challenging us to consider whether the art of the Heisei Period also had an appearance or spirit representative of its time, Sawaragi focuses on Heisei art as an accumulation of close collective activities by multiple artists during a time of calamities. Taking cues from Kamo no Chomei's *Hojoki* (The Ten Foot Square Hut) and Isozaki Arata's *Deburi no mirai* (The Future of Debris), he interprets the art of this period as "bubbles" and "debris."

The exhibition divides the Heisei Period into three sections and brings together approximately a hundred representative works by fourteen artist groups and collectives. These are displayed along with the "Heisei Wall," a 16-meter timeline created to provide overall historical context by marking the major events in society and in the art world during the Heisei Period. In the exhibition area, groups of works encompassing thirty years of time and space are arranged like ten-foot-square huts, reminiscent of temporary housing. Touring around them provides the opportunity to ponder art and society during the years of the Heisei Period.

The organizers would like to thank each of the artist groups for participating and thank Sawaragi Noi for planning and directing the exhibition. We would also like to express our gratitude to the institutions and collectors who graciously consented to the exhibit of precious works and materials from their collections, and to everyone who provided assistance in realizing the exhibition.

The Kyoto City KYOCERA Museum of Art, The Asahi Shimbun

This book was published in conjunction with the exhibition:

Bubbles/Debris: Art of the Heisei Period 1989–2019

Jan. 23 (Sat) – Apr. 11 (Sun), 2021
Higashiyama Cube, Kyoto City KYOCERA Museum of Art

Organizer: Heisei Art Exhibition Executive Committee (The City of Kyoto, The Asahi Shimbun)
Curatorial Supervisor: Sawaragi Noi
Corporate Sponsors: SunM Color Co., Ltd., MinebeaMitsumi Inc.

目　次

Contents

平成美術
うたかたと瓦礫デブリ 1989－2019

椹木野衣

美術の時間をどうとらえるか

　ちまたでは平成の終わりくらいからにわかに1980年代の美術をめぐる展覧会が開かれるようになり、このところでは早々に90年代の美術の回顧へと着手する動きもあるようだが、10年を単位に美術の動向を括ろうとするこうした思考の枠組みは、はたして今後も有効なのだろうか。仮に有効だとすれば、私たちはこれからも00年代の美術や10年代の美術、さらには20年代の美術といった切り口で美術をめぐる短期決済に次々と追い立てられることになる。だが、そんな先の見えた決めごとが美術にとってひどく無粋に感じられるのが私だけとは思えない。おそらく、そうした10年単位で文化や芸術の動向を切り取ろうとする志向のあり方は、時間についての機械的な、ほとんどカレンダー的と呼んでよい、順調でも省察を欠いた惰性から営まれている。

　けれども、私たちは今まさに苦く長い経験を余儀なくされているパンデミックでもう十分に痛感させられていると思うのだけれども、時間は人間にとってそんなに都合よく前へ前へと進んでくれるものではない。私たちの生活に甚大な影響を及ぼすような出来事がひとたび起これば、時間は岩を割るようにその前後で真っぷたつに裂けてしまい、結果として生じる深い断裂は容易には回復することができない。2011年／平成23年に起きた東日本大震災では被災地でしばしば発震の直後で止まった時計の様子が記録されている。時計は機械だから外部からの強い衝撃があれば止まるのは当然のことだが、私たちがなんの気なしに80年代とか90年代とか呼んでいる時間の根拠は突き詰めれば時計にあるのだから、大きな外的要因があれば、時間はこのように文字どおり動きを止めるのである。

　時計が外的な衝撃で一斉に止まってしまうような事態が生じれば、その周囲で日々を暮らしていた私たちの生活にも不可逆的な影響が及ぶであろう。そんなことは容易に想像がつく。ましてや、身内を失ったりからだに大きな怪我を負ったり深

いトラウマ（心的外傷）を抱えるようなことがあれば、心理的にも身体的にも、時間はもう前のようには流れてくれない。時間の機械的な運用からなる日常的な思考を失調させ、その一方向的な流れや形式的な計測可能性そのものを不可逆的に無効にしてしまうような別の時間が発生する。私はここでそれを機械的な時間に対して「傷ついた時間」と呼ぶことにする。

　ただちに連想できるように、ここで傷と呼ぶのは心理学で使われるトラウマによる。むろん、心理学の用語としてのトラウマが臨床的には個人の体験に属するものであり、それを非人格的な時代の特性にまで敷衍するのに無理があるのはわかっている。だが、トラウマ（trauma）はもともと古代ギリシア語では端的に「傷」を意味した。私がここで使うのも、時間もまた機械で計測されるような物理的な特性を根に持つ以上、ひとたびなにかあれば回復不可能なほど深い傷を負うという一般的な類推にもとづく。80年代の美術とか90年代の美術とかいうように、頼まれもしないのに課せられた仕事のように時間を先へ先へと進めようとする機械的な時間の運用者は、こうした傷ついた時間の持つ人間への、そしてその人間が存在をあらわにする営みとしての表現活動全般、ここでは美術の時間への根源的な影響を度外視している。

平成元年から戦後が終わった

　おそらく、私たちがよく見知ってきたそうした10年区切りの美術への展望は、傷ついた時間を免れることができた時代の幸福な産物であり、今となってはほとんど残骸、瓦礫＝デブリなのではないだろうか。私がこれから組み立てるのは、そうした10年ごとに美術をとらえようとする泡沫（バブル）的な思考の枠組みが、根源的に「戦後」という、より大きなメタ概念に支えられていたのではないかということだ。

　ところで、戦後という括りもまた、10年ごとの機械的な区切りと同じように、次の大きな戦争が私たちの時代と時間を本源から傷つけ、その前後にわたり2つに裂かない限り、無限に延長することが可能な曖昧な概念ではある。だから、惰性に乗る限り、それは無際限に続けられ、運用されていく。2020年は戦後75年の年でもあったわけだが、そのような区切りにまったく意味がないとは言わないけれども、ヒロシマやナガサキのような人類史的な悲劇であってさえ、切りのよい単位をもとに計られてしまうのだから、そのような機械的な時間が儀礼的な催しごとに回収されてしまうのも無理のないことではあるのだ。そこでは傷ついた時間の持つト

ラウマ性、つまり加算される時間ではなく、何度でも回帰し、循環し続ける時が持つ重苦しい悪夢（トラウマ=トラウム）が消し去られている。しかし、それでも機械的な時間がとくに大きな問題にさらされることもなく長く運用されてきたことの背景にあるのが、先に触れた戦後の無際限さなのではないか。

戦後の時間とは、基本的に焼け跡からの復興、その後の高度成長とさらなる加速、持続からなる。それは、計測することが容易とされた機械的な時間の尺度で評価され、先へ先へと進められてきた。このかん、戦争の残滓としての社会的底辺におけるさまざまな理不尽な出来事や、高度成長の歪みとしての開発＝環境破壊や、大規模な公害事件など悲惨な出来事が絶え間なく起きていた。けれども、それらは 1964 年の東京五輪や 1970 年の大阪万博といった国家的＝国民的事業であり祝祭でもある催しによってその都度消し去られ、傷ついた時間から機械的な時間へと引き戻されてきた。それが戦後（復興と高度成長）ということでもあるからだ。もしそうなら、戦後という機械的な時間の運用は、すでにとっくの前に耐用年数を過ぎていたのかもしれない。気がつけば、私たちの時間はもう長いこと停滞し、先に進んでいないからだ。では、そのような戦後の時間が淀むほどの深い傷を負ったのは、いったいいつのことなのか。

私にはそれが、1989 年＝平成元年という年であったように思われるのである。別の言い方をすれば、戦後は平成元年に終わり、この時点で戦後が携えていた復興と高度成長という機械的な時間の順調さは深い傷を負い、そうした傷を治癒し、長期にわたって修復する国家的＝国民的事業もないまま、ただ傷ついた時間だけが断続的に露呈する時代としての平成へと移行した。言い換えれば、10 年ごとに時代を括る思考の有効性も失効した。そうしてそこから、さながら泡（バブル）の挙動のように振る舞う美術家たちの、個ではなくうたかた（現れては消えゆく泡沫）を思わせる離合集散が生まれるようになった。そして、その結果として瓦礫のように密で非中心的な物質の凝集（かつて「作品」と呼ばれた）が残されるようになったのである。

元号が蓄積した時間を破産（リセット）する

だからと言うべきか、この文章は美術家らによる集合的・集団的活動の歩みを、過去へと遡って網羅的に調査して発表する研究成果のようなものでは始めからない。それどころか、そうした持続的な歴史を支える軸が狂ってしまったのが平成年間なのだとさえ言えるだろう。ならば、できるのはせいぜいがもう少し焦点を絞って考

えてみることくらいかもしれない。たとえば私たちは80年代の美術であるとか90年代の美術とか呼ぶときの枠組みの原型となる1950年代の美術、1960年代の美術といった括りを自明のものとする一方で、1940年代の美術というような言い方をすることは滅多にない。同じように、1920年代の美術、1930年代の美術というようなとらえ方をすることがある一方で、1880年代の美術、1890年代の美術、というような括りを見ることは一般にはほとんどない。なぜだろうか。前者では「大東亜戦争」が、後者では明治維新というように、機械的な時間を深く傷つけるトラウマ的な出来事がその渦中で起きており、その前後で時系列が切断され、持続的に10年単位で文化の様相について語ることを不可能にしてしまっているからだ。

　逆に、そのような傷ついた時間にもとづく時の不連続の様相をとらえるための仮説的な代理として使いうるのが、元号を援用した「明治の美術」「大正の美術」「昭和の美術」といった呼称であり、これらの括りはそもそも、西暦で区分するような機械的な時間に沿っていない。第一にそれは天皇の在位期間（つまりひとりの人間の命）に由来する。同時に、その在位期間のあいだに起きた出来事にもとづき、具体的には「明治の美術」とは実質的に明治維新という傷ついた時間が美術にどのような影響をもたらしたか、ということであり、「大正の美術」とは大正デモクラシーの時代が関東大震災という未曾有の大災害の前後で美術にどのような影響を及ぼしたか、ということであり、「昭和の美術」では戦前・戦中・戦後の美術に分けられるように、「大東亜戦争」が美術にどのような傷と忘却をもたらしたかという、やはり傷ついた時間にもとづいて美術への接近が企てられている。

　そう考えてみたとき、戦後という時間軸にもとづく戦後の美術という枠組みは、大きくは昭和の美術の一環としてあり、なおかつ戦争が終わって「復興・成長・成熟」がこの国にもたらされ、そのなかで機械的な時間も回復されたという前提のもと共有されていたことがわかるはずだ。言い換えれば、復興や成長、成熟が限界に突き当たれば、戦後も戦後の美術も、さらにはそのなかで守られてきた10年を単位に時代を回顧する堆積的で機械的な時間の運用もまた、その役割を終えるのである。

　そういうこともあって、本展／本書が「平成」を掲げるからといって、それは80年代の美術や90年代の美術があるのと同じように、さらに広い射程で明治の美術や昭和の美術と同じく平成の美術が時系列に沿ってあるはずで、ならば西暦に代えてそれを捕まえようというわけでは決してない。むしろ逆だ。日本では、かえってそうした時系列の連続性を断裂させる失意と祈りとしての元号という非西暦的な時間の交代がある。それは近代以前の改元がしばしばそうであったように、災害や

災難の悪気を払拭し、また近代以後でも同様に天皇が亡くなるという喪の時間から始まるという逆立ちを際立たせる兆候となる。天皇の生前退位によって、令和の始まりは例外的にそのよう（崩御）にならなかったわけだが、私たちが改元早々、疫病の蔓延という別の意味で喪の時間（時の崩落）を生きていることに変わりはない。

　そこから振り返り、時系列に沿った機械的な時間の内部でとらえられる「平成の美術」とは異なる意味での「平成美術」を呼び覚まし、新たに固有名詞化して凝集（デブリ）化することを試みようというのが本展／本書のねらいのひとつである。この点で「平成美術」展は、かつて西暦が 1999 年から 2000 年へと移り変わる局面で私自身が企画・監修した展覧会「日本ゼロ年」（水戸芸術館）での企てを継ぐものでもある。同展は 90 年代や 00 年代という機械的な時間の括りをカレンダー的に接続する以前に、日本の美術にはそうした時間のリレーでは容易に埋められない悪い特性（歴史がない、市場がない、受容者がいない）があり、その躓きの可視化を通じて、日本の戦後美術を蓄積・発展へと向けるのではなく、いっそ「リセット（破産）」しようと目論んだものであった。それで言うなら、平成年間とは、西暦の構成要素としては 80 年代末、90 年代、00 年代、10 年代からなり、その約 30 年の中心近くに 2000 年から 2001 年への移行という、西暦的に見ても世紀（センチュリー）の転換よりさらに巨大で、にわかにはその意味をとらえがたいリセット（ミレニアム・イヤー）を挟んでいた。また、そこから派生して日本ではとりわけ「ノストラダムスの大予言」の爆発的・持続的流行によって人類の破滅にまつわる予言年としてきわめて象徴的な意味を持った世紀末＝ 1999 年も含み込んでおり、これらの時間の積層を、こと美術に関してだけ言っても均等に 10 年単位で切り分けるのは、無意味とは言わないが、射程として有効ではない。時が方々で大小に異なる角度で傾いているのだ。

平成の美術になにが起こったか

　とはいえ、傷ついた時間で躓き続けた「平成美術」が孕んだ断続的な時勢と、その跛行した蠢きについて立ち入る前に、平成年間の美術にどのようなことが起きたかについて概観だけはしておこう。以下は、平成が終わるにあたり、雑誌『新潮』から平成の美術をめぐるベストテンを挙げてくれと届いた依頼に、私が少し角度を変えて 10 の項目を挙げ返答したもの［椹木　2019］に一部手を加えた文章である。

1・新世代の美術家の登場。平成の前夜、1968年／昭和43年前後に端を発する「もの派」から「ポストもの派」へのメインストリームの交代劇が仕立てられるなか、そうした動きを度外視する新しい世代、昭和30年代後半生まれの美術家たちが活動を始める。かれらはその頃、旧東京五輪（1964年／昭和39年）をきっかけに全国を同時刻／同番組で結ぶようになるテレビの影響下にあった。舞台となったのは東京、大森東に1991年／平成3年、巨大な倉庫を改装してオープンした日本最大級のギャラリー・スペース、レントゲン藝術研究所だった。ここから飴屋法水、村上隆、ヤノベケンジ、会田誠、小沢剛、八谷和彦、曽根裕、中山ダイスケらが名乗りを上げ、従来のアカデミック、もしくは前衛的な美術と、大衆文化、ポップカルチャーの境界を無化するような初期の代表作をいち早く発表する。

2・新しい美術館の建設ラッシュ。1990年／平成2年に弾けるバブル経済の余韻がまだ残るなか、日本各地に現代美術（アート）に対応する美術館が次々に開館する。現代美術に特化した展示を行う水戸芸術館現代美術ギャラリー（設計＝磯崎新アトリエ、1990年／平成2年）、東京都現代美術館（1995年／平成7年）、森美術館（2003年／平成15年）、金沢21世紀美術館（設計＝妹島和世＋西沢立衛／SANAA、2004年／平成16年）、青森県立美術館（設計＝青木淳建築計画事務所、2005年／平成17年）などは、これまでにない形態と機能を求められた美術施設であり、おのずとポストモダン以降の建築家の果たす役割が比重を大きくするようになった。建築が単なる器ではなく、アートの主役になったと言ってもいい。

3・キュレーター、ギャラリストの台頭。こうした美術館の建設ラッシュに対応するかたちで、従来は学芸員と呼ばれ脇役的な存在であった職能が、海外からの影響もあり、キュレーターと呼ばれ、大きな力を持つようになる。従来どおりの調査・研究だけでなく、展覧会のためのコンセプトを練り、それに応じて美術家の人選を行い、バイリンガルの図録を執筆・編集し、世界を飛び回るかれらには、かつてない役割が期待されるようになり、ビエンナーレやトリエンナーレといった国際現代美術展でコミッショナーとして活躍する者も出てくる。1998年／平成10年には、小山登美夫ギャラリーをはじめとする9つのギャラリーが集まって、事実上のマニフェストとも言える新たなアートフェア「G9　ニューダイレクション展」を開催（スパイラル）。新しい世代の台頭や国際市場との連携に対応すべく、みずからを作品の販売だけに注力する「ディーラー」ではなく、そのための展示に力点を置く「ギャラリスト」と呼ぶ新しいギャラリーが登場し、大きな牽引力を発揮する。

ギャラリストとの協働は、現在では美術館にとって必須のものとなっている。

4・写真や映像のアート化。それまで絵画や彫刻に次ぐ領域とされ、美術館での展示や収集の対象とは積極的に考えられてこなかった写真や映像が、アートにとって中心的な役割を果たすようになる。とりわけ写真は、それまで写真集や写真雑誌（つまり複製、印刷）が主な発表媒体であったのに対し、ギャラリーや美術館での展示に重きを置く展示芸術として扱われるようになった。日本国内では写真家とみなされていた荒木経惟、森山大道らが海外では美術家として評価される逆転は、その象徴的な現象である。写真を最初から美術を制作するうえでの手段・方法とみなす美術家、森村泰昌、杉本博司らも高い評価を受ける。写真や映像に焦点を絞った東京都写真美術館（1990年／平成2年に第一次開館、1995年／平成7年に総合開館）、新興のメディア・アートの拠点となったNTTインターコミュニケーション・センター（1990年／平成2年に設立、1997年／平成9年に施設オープン）などが活動を始めたのも平成年間である。

5・芸術祭の成功。2000年／平成12年に新潟県の山間部で幕を開けた「大地の芸術祭　越後妻有アートトリエンナーレ」は、従来は考えられなかったアクセスが困難な里山一帯を広域にわたって展示場とみなし、土地の住民と交渉のうえ観光客に対して大きく開き、それまで一部にとどまっていたアートの需要層を一気に拡大した。当初は継続を危ぶむ声もあったが、回を重ねるにつれ、非日常的な体験がアートの持つ脱現実性とマッチし、飛躍的に来場者を増やし、平成における美術事業のうち最大の成功モデルとなった。2010年／平成22年からは、過疎にあえいでいた瀬戸内の島々を繋いで開催される「瀬戸内国際芸術祭」が開幕。ベネッセアートサイト直島による意欲的な美術館の立ち上げと相まって、インバウンド上でも大きな効果を上げた（総合ディレクターはいずれも北川フラム）。なかでも、産業廃棄物問題で苦しむ豊島に開館し、風評をほぼ払拭するに至った豊島美術館（設計＝西沢立衛、展示＝内藤礼）は、世界を見渡しても類例のないものであり、平成を代表する美術館＝展示空間となった。

6・アートのグローバル化。1989年／平成元年の冷戦構造解体後、世界が米国の主導によるグローバライゼーションの波にさらわれると、美術家たちも活躍の機会を国内から大きく転回し、主な活動の機会は海外へと移った。なかでも草間彌生、オノ・ヨーコら、これまで国内外で認知が遅れていた女性の美術家への再評価の機

運が高まり、ニューヨークで大きな回顧展が組織されると、日本へと逆輸入される
かたちで評価が定着し、美術史の一部を書き換えるに至った。川俣正、宮島達男、
大竹伸朗、奈良美智、村上隆らも海外で高い評価を受けるが、なかでも村上隆が一
からコンセプトを作り上げた「スーパーフラット」展三部作（2000年「スーパーフ
ラット」展～2001年「SUPER FLAT」展、「ぬりえ」展、2005年「リトルボーイ」展）が欧
米を巡回し、アートワールドでの村上の評価を決定づけた。

7・藤田嗣治と岡本太郎の復活。太平洋戦争中に軍部に協力し、多くの作戦記録画
を残したエコール・ド・パリのスター、藤田嗣治は、これら戦争画の責任を追及さ
れ戦後、日本を捨ててパリに戻り、国籍も離脱、カトリックの洗礼を受けて名もレ
オナール・フジタに変え、二度と母国の土を踏むことなく世を去った。これらの経
緯から藤田＝フジタの研究や調査、展示機会は国内で限られたものとなっていた。
だが、戦中の日本の美術は藤田＝フジタの一連の戦争画を抜きには語れぬものであ
り、戦争画への関心の高まりと並行するかたちで藤田への注目は増し、2006年／
平成18年、戦争画も含む生誕120周年の回顧展が東京国立近代美術館で開催され
るに至る。一方、1996年／平成8年に他界した岡本太郎は、晩年にマスメディア
に登場するなどタレント的な活動を辞さず、結果として美術界での評価を落とし、
亡くなる頃には美術界からほぼ忘れられた存在となっていた。だが、長く秘書を務
め、養女となった岡本敏子の尽力により、岡本太郎の著作は蘇り、太陽の塔も大阪
万博当時を超える時代のアイコンとなり、長くメキシコで行方不明になっていた巨
大壁画《明日の神話》も発見され、修復のすえ東京、渋谷駅の一角に飾られた。太
郎は縄文土器、沖縄、東北の新たな発見者でもあり、核時代のアートにいち早く着
手するなど、日本画と洋画を独自の方法で統合した藤田＝フジタとともに、平成に
活躍する美術家たちを触発する力を十分に備えていた。

8・日本美術＝奇想の系譜。今では信じられないことかもしれないが、長く伝統的
な日本美術は、一部の浮世絵などを除くと概して人気がなく、展覧会にも人が入ら
ず、雑誌で特集されても売り上げに窮していた。ところが、従来の日本美術史では
キワモノ扱いされていた伊藤若冲、曾我蕭白、長沢蘆雪、岩佐又兵衛らを「奇想」
の美術家としていち早く扱った辻惟雄『奇想の系譜』（初出は『美術手帖』、1968年／
昭和43年）への注目がにわかに高まり、これを継承する時宜を得た展覧会が次々に
開催されると、美術館には嘘のように長蛇の列ができるようになり、アートにとっ
ても大きな着想源となった。昭和に種が播かれ、平成と新しい元号の発表をまたぐ

かたちで開催された「奇想の系譜　江戸絵画ミラクルワールド」展（2019年／平成31年、東京都美術館）は、その集大成で、1996年／平成8年に美術史家の山下裕二と前衛美術家、赤瀬川原平が止むに止まれぬ気持ちで結成した異色の組み合わせ、「日本美術応援団」の地道な啓発活動が実ったと言える。

9・アウトサイダー・アートの衝撃。1993年／平成5年、世田谷美術館に「パラレル・ヴィジョン──20世紀美術とアウトサイダー・アート」展が海外から巡回すると、精神を病んだ者、霊能力者の幻視、引きこもりの老人らが描いた長大で常軌を逸した絵や表現は、従来の美術では決して得ることのできない衝撃をもたらした。もとはジャン・デュビュッフェが第二次世界大戦後に着想した「アール・ブリュット」に遡るが、正規の教育を受けない者が手がける表現というと、おもに知的障害者施設の利用者が福祉活動の一環として描く絵などに限定されていた国内では想定外のものばかりで、そもそもアートとはなんなのか、なんのために作るのかといった根源的な問いを掘り起こした。新東京五輪を目前にアール・ブリュットが政策的に恰好のパラ・アートとして解釈されるなか、アウトサイダー・アートは下火となっているが、早晩本来の力を取り戻し、平成以後のアートにとっての起爆力となるだろう。

１０・震災とアート。平成年間は、「平らに成る」（スーパーフラット？）という語の含みに反して、昭和のように大きな戦争こそなかったものの、1993年／平成5年の冷夏による大飢饉級の米の記録的不作をはじめとして、1995年／平成7年の阪神・淡路大震災、2011年／平成23年の東日本大震災という二度の大震災のみならず、九州や北海道でもかつてない規模の大地震が相次ぎ、ほかにも集中豪雨や大規模な土砂崩れなどで日本全国が被災地と化すような、いつ、誰が被災者となるとも知れぬ生活環境の激変を余儀なくされた。これに加え東京電力福島第一原子力発電所での史上最悪級の原子力災害はなお緊急事態宣言下にあり、予断を許さない。そうしたなか、2005年／平成17年に結成されたChim↑Pomのように、震災下の状況に対応する、従来にない美術家たちによる集合的・共働的な活動が活性化しつつある。美術館や芸術祭のような既成の制度や成功モデルに依存せず、未知の事態に対して複数の頭脳、見る力、分散した動きで発表の機会を自主組織し、フレキシブルに行動するこうした態度は、アートにおける平成の動向を象徴するものでもあり、次代へと引き継がれていくだろう。

依頼がベストテンだったので 10 の項目となっているが、今ならここにソーシャル・メディア（おもにツイッターやフェイスブックによる社会的な波及力）の影響力を加えて 11 項目としておくのがよいかもしれない。

　１１・ソーシャル・メディアとアート。東日本大震災では、被災者の救助や生存確認、必要物資の打診といった緊急時の情報共有で、ツイッターをはじめとする SNS（ソーシャル・ネットワーキング・サービス）がたいへん大きな役割を果たした。大規模な停電や浸水により、中央集権的な役所機能が正常に働かないなか、家にいながらにして情報を受信・発信できる、分散的なネットワークゆえの強みであった。こうしたインターネットを活用したプラットホームは、1995 年／平成 7 年の阪神・淡路大震災以降、Windows 95 の急速な普及や、それに歩を合わせての携帯電話、およびその後のスマートフォンの登場によって飛躍的に機能を拡大し、今では社会基盤としてなくてはならないものとなっている。こうしたネットの登場は美術の世界にも少なからぬ影響を及ぼした。もともと美術は、展示という物的・実空間的な基盤に多くを負うため、音楽のデータ配信のようなネット環境への適応は久しくむずかしかったのだが、ネットの内外をほぼ対等なものとし、同時多発的に、特定の物理的な展示会場と非場所としての仮想空間を往還する新しいアートフォームが、日本でも東日本大震災の前夜くらいから目立って登場するようになった。その典型例と言えるのが、黒瀬陽平、梅沢和木、藤城嘘らによるユニット、カオス*ラウンジが 2010 年／平成 22 年に発した「カオス*ラウンジ宣言 2010」である［楳木　2016］。

災難が平らに成る

　ところで、あたりまえと言えばあたりまえのことなのだが、平成の美術に起きたこのような出来事は、満遍なく順序立てて現れたわけではない。このように整理してみることができるのは、まがりなりにも平成が終焉を迎え、新たに令和が始まったからにほかならない。言い換えれば、平成をめぐる美術のこのような整理は、令和の到来を、あるいはその前提としての昭和との差異化を暗黙に含んでいる。それで言えば、私たちはまだ令和という時代がどのような美術を生み出すのかについて知らない。私たちにとって令和の美術がどのような顔を持つかがわかるには、令和のその先の時が傷つき、満ちるのを待つほかないからだ。このように、西暦におい

ては累積が時を重ねる前提となるのに対し、元号では外傷と切断のほうが重んじられる。そして、この離散する時の根拠となっているのが、天皇の存在にほかならない。つまり、私がかつて「悪い場所」と呼んだ時の停滞の背後には、日本列島の地質学的不安定に加え、天皇と改元の影があり、両者は実は忘却と反復によって密接に結びついている。したがって、そのとき天皇がどのような立ち居振る舞いで国民の前に現れていたかは、元号によって始まりと終わりに分断されるそれぞれの時代の相貌に決定的な影を落とすことになる。言い換えれば、先に整理したような平成の美術をめぐる項目の列挙は、実際にはその背後に、いや根底に、同じ平成という時代に固有の顔つきを共通して備えている。

　そのことで言うと、私は1962年／昭和37年に生まれている。1964年／昭和39年に開催された東京五輪の2年前のことだ。だから、五輪の記憶ははっきりせず、昭和天皇の姿を初めて目に焼きつけたのは、その五輪から6年が経過した1970年／昭和45年、テレビの画面から届けられた大阪万博の開会式でのことだった。今あらためて思い起こすに、そこまでの国家的な大事業ではないにせよ、昭和天皇について思いを馳せるとき、その姿はほぼ例外なくそうした晴れの式典と結びついていて、式典であるからには大勢の国民が同じ場所に集まっており、天皇がそれに手を挙げて応える、といった原イメージがあることに気づくのである。日本国の発展と国民の安寧、そしてそのための努力をねぎらう晴れの式典とともにあるこうした昭和天皇の姿は、裏返せば戦後という昭和の明るい側面を象徴する場面ということにもなり、言い換えればそれは戦前から戦中にかけて現人神として戦争とともにあった天皇の存在と表裏一体ということになる。どんなに晴れがましい式典とともにあっても、昭和という時代が長い戦争をくぐり抜けてきたことは消えない。昭和という時代はこうした明暗とともに私たちがいま思う陰影に富んだ顔を作り出した。この明暗を端的に示す言葉があるとしたら、それこそが戦争と平和にほかならない。つまり、昭和という時代は戦争と平和をめぐる明暗とともにあった。それならば昭和の美術にも、たとえどのような型どおりの整理をするにせよ、この陰影が刻まれていないはずがない。

　平成はどうか。平成の天皇の在位期間に昭和の戦後における東京五輪や大阪万博に匹敵する国家的祭典・事業はない。その意味で平成という時代は、ほかでもない「平らに成る」と書くとおり、国民がひとところに束ねられるような晴れがましさやその裏返しとしての総動員体制、つまり戦争と平和が作り出すような明暗や陰影を欠いている。その意味で、美術家の村上隆にならって言えば、平成とはスーパーフラットと、とりあえず呼ぶことができるかもしれない。そこに昭和のような光と

影が織りなすダイナミズムは感じられない。そのかわり、私が平成の天皇と国民の姿という点で強く心に刻んでいるのは、相次ぐ自然災害の被災地での天皇と皇后の立ち居振る舞いだ。そこで平成の天皇が対面するのは、昭和天皇の記憶とは異なり、晴れの式典であるどころか、大規模な災害で住み慣れた家を離れ、学校の体育館などにブルーシートを敷き、仮設の仕切りを立てて当面の難儀をしのごうとする緊急の避難者たちである。そのような場所を飾り気のない佇まいで訪ね、膝を突き合わせるようにして皇后とともに同じ高さの目線で励ます天皇の姿がある。その意味でも天皇の視線は見下ろすものではなく「平らに成った」。緊急事態である災害下の環境が天皇と被災者との目線を平らなものとしたと言えるかもしれない。

　言い換えると、平成という時代は、それほど自然災害が多かった。いや、自然災害だけではない。平成には大きな国家的事業が見当たらない反面、戦後でもあまり例を見なかったような事件、事故、カタストロフが立て続いて起きていた。それらは多くの場合、前触れもなく突発し、動機や因果関係が不明瞭で、昭和の事件や事故のような――多くの場合、その根を深く掘ると戦争まで行き着く――物語性を欠いていた。自然災害はその典型だろう。昭和が戦争をめぐる明暗とともにあったとすれば、平成という時代は、理由や動機といった陰影を欠いたまま、引きも切らず続く災難の常態化（平らに成る＝起こる）とともにあった。言い換えればそれは、災害下の非日常が日常化しつつあるということであり、さらに言えばそれが普通になった、特別なことではなくなった、もっと言えば忘れる速度に拍車が加わった、それどころかなんにも起きていないように見える、ということでもあるだろう。だが、それでもそのようななかでとりわけ突発性が高く、ゆえに無防備でもあり、そのことで平成という時代に亀裂を入れ、その後に長く余波を及ぼしている３つの、ないしは４つの大きな罅割れた「悪い時」が存在する。そして、これらの年が生む傷ついた時間によって、平成の年間は所々でこぼこと縫合されている。それは明暗とは違う。

1989 年／平成元年

　1989 年／平成元年は、前年からずっと体温や心拍数、下血の量といった生理学的な数値に置き換えられ、晴れの姿を国民の前からかき消していた昭和天皇が新年早々に崩御し、国の全体が喪に服し、新たな天皇が即位した原点となる、まさしく平成の始まりにあたっている。だが、それだけではない。今から振り返ると、この

年の持つ意味は想像以上に大きかった。その後に起きることの兆候をこの年から拾い上げれば（ポーランド、ハンガリー、東ドイツ、ブルガリア、チェコスロヴァキア、ルーマニアに及ぶ一連の東欧革命、そして中国での天安門事件など）そのことは即座に理解できよう（本書177頁の片山論考も参照）。そのうちもっとも象徴的で、なおかつ時代を一変させるきっかけとなったのが、ベルリンの壁の崩壊である。

　ベルリンの壁の崩壊は、のちに平成さえ飛び越え、令和のいま蔓延している新型コロナウイルス感染症によるパンデミックに及ぶほど大きな時代の転換点をもたらすことになる、文字どおり大きな事件であった。その年の暮れ近くになって東ベルリンと西ベルリンとを隔てる物理的な壁が壊され、人々が自由な往来ができるようになったのは、それ自体としては出来事としての規模が大きいわけではない。のちの1995年／平成7年や2001年／平成13年、2011年／平成23年のように破局的であったわけでもない。だが、ベルリンの壁が市民たちの手で壊されたということは、第二次世界大戦後に世界を二分して支配したアメリカとソ連という超大国のうち、ソ連の鉄の守りがいともたやすく無効化したことを意味する。それはまもなく、誰も想像していなかったソ連の消滅と東西冷戦体制の解体という世界体制そのものの大転換にまで及ぶことになる。そしてこのことをきっかけに、グローバリズムという資本主義とも共産主義とも異なるイデオロギーなきメカニズムが地球の全体を覆うようになった。グローバリズムとは、壁とはまったく反対に、ヒト、モノ、コトの流動性を極限にまで高め、世界をひとつの市場のなかで加速化しようとするシステムのことを指す。超国家共同体EUの登場やそのなかで実現した国境の簡略化（ヒト）や通貨統合（モノ）はそうした動きの典型であるし、これらをめぐる情報（コト）の流動性を高める最大の転機となったのが、時間や空間に縛られないインターネットの爆発的な普及であるのは言うまでもない。そしてこれを機に、世界は同じ価値の尺度にもとづく大量動員と利益誘導からなる欲望の熱狂のなかに包摂されるようになっていく。

　日本もその例外ではない。戦後、それまでソ連と対立するアメリカの核の傘の下で守られ、奇跡の復興・高度成長を達成してきた日本は、ついに前代未聞のバブル経済に突入する。だが、それも急激にグローバル化しつつあった新たな世界秩序のなかにあっては冷戦下の国内的な沸騰の最後の熱にすぎず、1990年／平成2年、ついにバブルが弾けると、日本は長く出口の見えない不況に突入し、多くの金融機関や大企業が次々に倒れ、合併吸収を繰り返し、外資が大規模に進出し、その余波は今なお完全に消えたとは言えない。戦争や震災のようにものが物理的に一瞬にして破壊されたわけではないかもしれない。だが、バブル経済は急激なスクラップ＆

ビルドによって戦争や震災のように日本の風景を一変させたし、その意味では限りなくカタストロフの一種に近かった。経済だけではない。その風景の溶融はむろん、上部構造としての文化や芸術にも多大な変化を迫ってきた。

　美術で言えば、国内に閉じることで守られていた画壇がグローバル化のもと急激に実質を失い、美術家たちは生計を立て制作を続けるため進んで国外へと出るようになり、世界のアート・マーケットと接続された新興のギャラリストたちがこれを支えた。これは美術の話だが、そうした抜本的な変化があらゆる業種や産業でいっせいに起きた。地球は 1989 年／平成元年を境に、ヒト、モノ、コトをめぐる大攪拌の時代へと突き進み始めたのだ。現在の地球環境をめぐる最大の問題とされ、もはや誰の目にもあきらかな気候変動や、平成年間に繰り返し現れた未知のウイルス（SARS や MERS）による致死的な感染症の蔓延や大流行もまた、地球上でヒト・モノが爆発的に移動するようになり、それまで放置されていた未踏の地までもが開発や観光の対象となったことが一因と考えられる。ヒトやモノだけでなく、長く固有の生態系から移動することのなかったウイルスまでもが人間の環境とシャッフルされ、輸送や旅客を通じて世界へと拡散されていくことになる。その最初のきっかけとなったのが、旧体制にとって臍のような機能を果たしていたベルリンの壁という一大障壁の崩壊であった。それが起きたのが 1989 年、すなわち平成元年でもあったのだ。

1995 年／平成 7 年　戦後 50 年

　1995 年／平成 7 年は、冷戦の終わりをきっかけに幕が切って落とされたグローバリズムの始まりが、日本国内でその負の姿を最初にあらわにした年だった。奇しくもこの年は、日本にとって戦後 50 年という大きな節目にあたっていた。本来であれば敗戦から占領を経て復興し、高度成長を経てグローバル化に適応しようとするところまでたどり着いた半世紀の歩みを、それこそ平成の天皇とともに国民的に寿ぐ平成でも稀な晴れの局面であったはずだ。ところが 1 月早々に阪神・淡路大震災が勃発。それまで戦災にせよ震災にせよ、少なくとも私自身、神戸という日本を代表する近代都市のひとつがあっというまに根こそぎ破壊され、瓦礫と灰塵に帰してしまうような出来事は、これまで映画やマンガ、テレビのなかでしか体験したことがなかった。まさかそれが唐突に、戦後 50 年の年初に起きるとは、誰も想像だにしていなかった。だが、現実に私たちが目の当たりにしたのは、街の方々が無残

に崩れ、随所から火の手が上がり、家を失った人たちが避難所に押し寄せ、食糧や暖を求めてその日の命をつなぐ、まるで戦時下・敗戦直後に戻ったような景色だった。だがそれも、その後に日本の各地で立て続くことになる震度7級の大地震によって、少しずつ見知った風景となっていく。先に触れた、避難所で国民を励ます平成の天皇の姿は、まさにその渦中で象徴的な意味を持つようになっていく。

　そしてこの年にはそれからまもない3月、早朝から東京の都心へと通勤するための主要鉄道網を走る満員電車のなかで化学兵器サリンが散布されるという衝撃的な事件が起きた。実行犯はオウム真理教の一部急進派の信徒で、首謀者は教団の導師、麻原彰晃と特定され、判決の結果死刑囚となったかれらはいずれも平成のうちに刑を執行されている。計画によるとかれらは首都の上空からヘリコプターを使ってサリンを散布し、大量殺人と国家転覆＝クーデターを実行することを考えていたとされる。目で見るための美術にとって凶兆と言うほかない。「目には見えないもの」がとうとう水面へと浮上したのだ。そしてこの水面を揺らす姿の見えない無生物（バブル）は、サリンから放射能へ、放射能からコロナ禍へと平成、令和を通じて段階的に様態を変えていく。そしてグローバリズムがかれらの通路を世界へと張り巡らしたのだ。

　先に1995年／平成7年はグローバリズムの負の側面が国内で姿を現した年にあたると書いたが、富士の麓に位置するサティアンと呼ばれる教団の拠点で密かに行われていた集団的な武装や化学兵器の精製に至る技術や知識、資金源は、解体した旧ソ連が残した負の遺産との地下ネットワークにあったともいわれている。冷戦の解体は膨大な量の余剰兵器を生み、グローバルなネットワークを通じて売買の対象となり、のちの対テロ戦争を招く闇の背景を作り出していく。その最初の萌芽が、世界で一番安全だとされた平成の日本で、都心の地下鉄網を利用し、車両内で前代未聞の化学兵器を散布して日本人が日本人を殺すという不気味な顔を見せることになったのは、今なおその意味について考えるにあまりある。またこの事件をきっかけに、日本では当時まだ聞き慣れなかった「セキュリティ」と呼ばれる監視体制——目に見えないものを目に見えるようにする——の強化が市中の各所で急速に推し進められていく。そしてそのことで、それまで路上を積極的に活用し、集合的にゲリラ的な活動を繰り広げていた新世代の美術家たちも、刻々とその行動を可視化されることで否応なくその活動の機会を狭められることになる。

２０01 年／平成 13 年　9・11

　2001 年／平成 13 年、ニューヨーク、マンハッタンの金融街にそびえるグローバル経済の象徴、WTC（ワールドトレードセンター）と呼ばれた白亜で一対の超高層ビルに、ジェット旅客機が燃料を満載したまま相次いで突っ込み、炎と黒煙を上げる姿が世界中に中継されながら、直後に 2 棟とも地面へと向けて一気に崩落する。私もたまたま同時刻にテレビの報道番組を見ていたが、急遽カメラが現地からの中継に切り替わり、その一部始終を目の当たりにした。これに前後してバージニア州のアメリカ国防総省の本庁舎、通称ペンタゴンにも旅客機が自爆攻撃で突入し、首都ワシントン D.C. も攻撃対象となっているなどの未確認情報が流れた。のちにアメリカ同時多発テロ事件と呼ばれることになるこの事件は、その時点ではなにが起きているのかまったくわからなかった。ただ、信じられないようなことがたったいま目の前で起きているという切迫感だけが伝わってきた。

　ただちにイスラム原理主義者、アルカイダのオサマ・ビンラディンによる反アメリカ的なテロ攻撃と断定されたこの事件は、1 カ月も経ずに関与が疑われるタリバンの支配するアフガニスタンへの空爆へと発展する。こうして拡大した宣戦布告も国際条約も度外視した見えないテロリストたちとの世界中に拡散した新しい戦争（なのだろうか?）は、大量破壊兵器の秘匿をめぐってイラク戦争にまで発展し、首都バグダッドは総攻撃により灰燼に帰す。やがてその報復テロは戦場と特定されない街中での自爆、乗用車による突入へと拡大し、ソフトターゲットと呼ばれるコンサートホールやスタジアム、レストランまでが標的となり、日常の場所が潜伏的にいつ、どこでも戦場と化す「対テロ戦争」と呼ばれるグローバリズムの負の側面を象徴する奇怪な様態へと変貌していく。従来の中央集権的な戦争に対し、テロリストたちは進んでコレクティヴ化していったと言ってもいい。それをもう少し飾ってテロリストのマルチチュード化と呼ぶとしても、それはせいぜいが言葉の綾にすぎない。

　ところで、戦争をめぐるこうした新しい事態も、元を正せば 1989 年、すなわち平成元年という平成の始まりまで遡ることができる。ある意味、平成年間とは、平成元年に播かれた種が発芽し、奇妙な枝を伸ばし、見たこともないような密林へと変貌を遂げる道筋であったとさえ言えるかもしれない。この年の末に起きた、米ソ冷戦の象徴であったベルリンの壁が崩壊し、それから数年のうちにソ連という超大国が消滅するという異例の出来事は、自由主義、民主主義を掲げたアメリカのイデオロギーが、共産主義を理想とし社会主義の体制を維持するソ連に最終的に勝利し

たことを意味する。唯一のものとして残されたイデオロギーは、もはや二者択一の闘争状態になく、結果としてイデオロギー闘争は消滅し、したがってイデオロギーではなくなった。自由主義、民主主義は地球にとっての正義となったのだ。

だが、東西の対立がなくなると、今度はイデオロギー闘争によって見えにくくされていた別の対立軸が浮上して、世界を別種の混乱へと陥れる新たな火種となっていく。それがイスラム圏との原理主義的な対立であった。そして、その最初の具体的な顕在化が、1991年／平成3年に起きたアメリカにとってベトナム戦争以来となる湾岸戦争であった。湾岸戦争はのちにアメリカ同時多発テロ事件が起きる平成で最初の伏線となり、フセインとの軋轢はのちにイラク戦争を招く大きなきっかけとなった――というより、イラク戦争は湾岸戦争の規模を拡大した反復形態のように見える。たとえば、バグダッドを攻撃する様子がCNNによって世界中にライヴで中継されるような、新しいテクノロジーを擁する戦争という点において、それはアメリカ同時多発テロ事件で崩落するWTCの模様が実況される事態を先取りしていた。そして、これらのすべてが平成美術に影を落とし、同時に平成美術によってその後に起きることを先取りされてもいた。

事実、湾岸戦争での実戦への投入を経て、モバイル・テクノロジーは一気にその実効精度を上げ、そのフィードバックは私たちの生活へと欲望を喚起する商品として反映されていく。たとえば刻々と連絡と応答を積み上げ続けなければならないソーシャル（ソーシャリー・エンゲイジド？）・メディアをはじめとする今日の情報テクノロジーは、いつでもどこでも自分の位置を確かめ、共有し、ただちに作戦（オペレーション）を開始することができるための戦場の心理を生み出す。そうして私たちは、心休まるはずの日常にいながら、絶え間なく着信と応答の不安によって扉を叩かれ続ける非日常にさらされて際限なく疲弊する。たとえ銃を構えなくても、日常が戦場化しているのだ。戻りたくても私たちに残された日常はもはや存在しない。私たちの日常が情報の絨毯爆撃による「砂漠の嵐作戦」（湾岸戦争での多国籍軍によるイラクへの爆撃の作戦名）と化しているからだ。

2001年／平成13年のアメリカ同時多発テロ事件は、こうして1989年／平成元年以降、水面下で流れるようになった反グローバル主義の火種が、蒼く晴れ渡ったアメリカの空へとキノコ雲を思わせる噴煙として立ち上り、巨大な2基の火焰へと姿を変え、グローバルな情報ネットワークを通じて世界へと配信された瞬間であった。そしてこれ以降、2001年／平成13年という傷ついた時間による私たちの平成という時代もまた、可視化と不可視化、日常と戦場の論理の相対化に巻き込まれ、「平らに成った日常＝平坦な日常」という消耗戦を無目的に闘うことを余儀なくさ

れることになったのだ。

2011年／平成23年　3・11

　それから10年が過ぎた2011年／平成23年3月11日午後2時46分、日本列島をマグニチュード9.0という未曾有の超巨大地震が襲う。東北を主に、東日本の太平洋沿岸は数百キロにわたり巨大な津波に急襲され、数えきれないほど多くの人が犠牲となり、今なお行方知れずとなっている。生き延びた多くの人も住み慣れた街と家を失ってやむなく故郷をあとにせざるをえなくなった。さらには地震と津波の影響で東京電力福島第一原子力発電所が全電源を喪失、冷却水を失った圧力容器が核燃料の崩壊熱で空焚きとなり、ただちに3基の核燃料がメルトダウンする前代未聞の事故へと発展した。原子炉下方へと溶け落ちた核燃料の行方はいまだにわかっていない。事故を起こした施設からは膨大な量の放射性物質が風に乗って拡散し、東日本の随所を放射能で汚染した。そのなかにはいまだに放射線量が十分に下がらず、住民の帰還が長期にわたりできずにいる場所もある（帰還困難区域）。
　このように、技術をめぐる様相が複雑に絡み合った現代では、自然災害と人為の災害とをはっきりと分けることはできない。地震は避けることができない地球の生理であり、原発（核発電）は人間の行いのひとつとひとまず言うことはできる。けれども、そもそも原発が列島の沿岸に乱立と言っていいほど建てられた背景には、急激に温暖化する地球環境に対し、持続的に二酸化炭素の排出量を削減するという方便、すなわち戦後という時間の延長があった。とすると、核発電という人為は地球の自然環境と密に結びついていることになる。「地球にやさしい」という標語には誰もが聞き覚えがあるはずだ。ところが1989年／平成元年以後のグローバリズムは「地球にきびしい」地球温暖化のアクセルをむしろさらに加速して推し進めた。国際会議で削減目標などが議論され京都議定書が採択され一定の合意に達したあとも、片道だけでも大量の二酸化炭素を大気中に排出する大小の飛行機は世界の空を休みなく飛び続けた。昨今の凶暴と呼んでいい気候変動を呼び込む働きの一助にも確実になっただろう。未踏の地に隠れていた未知のウイルスの拡散や旧知のウイルスの再流行にも大いに寄与したはずだ（AIDS、SARS、MERS、ジカ熱、デング熱、エボラウイルス病など）。むろん、核発電という技術が巨大地震を誘発したわけではない。だが、私たちが地球環境との接し方を根本から見直さなかったことが地震や津波の人的被害を大きくしたことは否めない。

地震や津波だけではない。本展では会場に「平成の壁」と名づけた巨大な年表を立てたが、本図録所収の年表でも見られるとおり、すでに平成が始まった直後から日本列島の各地で火山の噴火や天候不順による農作物の不出来（1993年／平成5年）、過去に例を見ない核発電所や核燃料工場での過酷な事故が起き、身近なところで被害が出始めていた。とりわけ後者のうち戦後初めて国内の核関連施設による事故で2名の死者を出すことになった1999年／平成11年の東海村JCO核燃料加工施設で起きた臨界事故はそのことを端的に示す出来事だった。その後に起きた2011年／平成23年の東日本大震災は超巨大な複合的甚大災害として過去に例を見ないものとなったが、その前兆と呼べる事象や見えにくい社会的な後遺症、あるいはさらなる大災害が起こる予兆はそれ以降もずっと続いている。たくさんの被災者たちが家を離れ体育館などの公的な施設の床に座をとり難を凌いでいる風景は、もはや全国、いつでもどこでも起きうる事態となった。

明日、誰が避難者になるともわからない。象徴的に言えば、2011年／平成23年以降、私たちはそのような事故や災害が引きも切らず起き、慣れた生活を根本から覆されてしまいかねない不安を抱えて生きていく時代に入っている。こうした自然と人為による地球の不調の延長線上に、平成が終わり、令和になった途端に私たちが見舞われた新型コロナウイルス感染症によるパンデミックがあることは言うまでもない。平成と違い、もう今上天皇が被災地を訪問することさえままならない。目に見えないウイルス感染のリスクが双方にあるからだ。こうして2011年／平成23年以降の事態は、平成の終わりを不吉な高揚感へと導くとともに、次なる令和の暗い始まりを予告する性質を持っていた。

災害文学／反建築の書『方丈記』

ところで、災害の多発と不穏な日常の持続ということで言うなら、かつて日本でこれとよく似た事態を抱え、日本における災害文学の始まりと呼びうる随筆がひとつ存在する。平安末期から鎌倉へという政治的にも大変な転換期を生きた隠遁者、鴨長明による高名な『方丈記』がそれである。

実際、長明が生まれ育ち暮らしたのは、それまで並ぶもののない栄華を誇った平氏が新たに勃興した源氏による武士勢力によって覆され、ついには壇ノ浦に沈んで一切の命運が尽きる時代にあたっていた。権力の担い手が貴族から武家へ、その中枢も京都から鎌倉へと一気に移る、いわば極地移動（ポールシフト）が起きていたことになる。また

この時期、京都は相次ぐ自然災害、人災に見舞われていた。「ゆく河のながれは絶えずして、しかも、もとの水にあらず。よどみに浮かぶうたかたは、かつ消え、かつむすびて、久しくとどまりたるためしなし」で始まる誰もが一度は耳にしたであろう『方丈記』の書き出しは、権力の座が移ろい、それに従い都の豪奢な家も姿を変え、加えて災難が大火、旋風（竜巻）、遷都、飢饉（疫病）、大地震と引きも切らず、なすすべなく都が荒れて見慣れぬものとなっていく様変わりを、ひとときも同じところにとどまらず、現れては消えゆく泡（うたかた＝バブル）の離合集散に見立てたものである。

　それを「無常」と一言で呼んでしまえばそれまでだが、こうした無常観は思慮を重ねた者の悟りや諦念の結果というより、災害や被災という物理的な現実から距離をとる避難（ディスタンス）の精神から生まれている。だからこそ長明はそうした災いの渦中にある京の都を離れ、日野の山へと逃れ、仮に被災しても簡単に組み直すことができ、土地にも縛られず転居もたやすい、いわばモバイルハウス＝方丈（一辺が約3.03メートル）を構え、その内に籠って、都とは異なる傷ついた時間のなかで現世とその移ろいを観想する機会を設けたのではなかったか。方丈と呼べば趣もあるが、むしろそれは災害仮設住宅のようなものだったかもしれない。しかし、そういう場所でなければ生まれない想念というものは確かにある。長明はそれを狭い庵のなかで書きつけることを選んだ。『方丈記』が災害文学であるというのは、そういうことだろう。『方丈記』とは、動乱する中世日本の無常観を生々しく記した名随筆であるだけでなく、災害避難者の文学であり、さらに言うとそのための仮住まいをみずから構えた（決して建築ではなく）住宅のための文学でもある。

　事実、浅見和彦の校訂・訳による『方丈記』（ちくま学芸文庫）の「はじめに」に、「おそらく日本の文学史上、災害というものを正面から取り上げた最初の文学作品は『方丈記』なのではなかろうか」（8頁）とはっきり記されている。ところで、その直前にある「日本人と建物」と区切られた節を読むと、次のようなくだりが目に飛び込んでくる。

　　　「大臣」は「だいじん」とも読むが、一方「おとど」という読みも存在する。「おとど」の語源は「おほとの」、すなわち「大殿」ではないかといわれている。
　　　天皇は「みかど」ともいう。「みかど」はすなわち「御門」で立派な大きな門をさす。現代、天皇に使われる「陛下」という尊称の「陛」は宮殿に登る立派な階段を意味する。似た言葉に「閣下」という表現があるが、「閣」も天

守閣などと使われるように、立派な高い建物をさす。

　「大臣」にしても「天皇」にしても「陛下」も「閣下」も、すべて立派な頑丈な建物を直接、間接にさし示す言葉で、それがだんだんとその立派な建造物に住む住人をさす言葉として転用されていったのである。

　大きくて立派な建物はその所有者、居住者の地位と権力を象徴する。逆に小さな家、粗末な建物は地位からも権力からも無縁であることを表象した。建物や家は人間の評価基準となった。それゆえ日本人はハコモノにこだわる。マイホームにこだわるのである。

　しかし、長明は宏大な家を嫌った。地位、権力、財力とは無縁の人物が山の中の小さな庵にあって、時代と社会を静かに眺め、そして思いを綴った。それが『方丈記』という作品の輪郭である。（同書、6-7頁）

　これはつまり、『方丈記』とは一種の反建築の書だということでもあるだろう。その際、建築とは権力の象徴でもあり、その頂点には大殿や天皇がいる。長明はそれを避けた。だが、最初からそのような立場にいたわけではなく、権力闘争に巻き込まれておのれにふさわしい居場所（由緒ある寺社）を失ったのが遁走のきっかけではあった。だが、どのような動機があったにせよ、長明が「立派な建造物」とそこに住む住民の「地位と権力」を厭い、冷めた目で距離を持ち眺めるために、それらに対し「庵」にすぎない「方丈」を置いたのは疑いようのないことである。そのように考えたとき、2011年／平成23年以降、原発に象徴される大きくて堅牢な建築としての大殿を失い、方々で被災してはそれと対照的な避難所や仮住まいを転々としながら暮らすこととなった平成末期からの私たちにも、『方丈記』は教養を養うための古典などではなく、目の前の現世を生きる不安へと直に訴えかけてくるものがあるのではないか。逆に「小さな家、粗末な建物」に仮の居を定めることに、地位や権力に翻弄されず、ということはつまり、大きな建物や設備、技術の犠牲になることなく現世を生き延びるための態度を見ることができるのではないか（これと正反対な震災後の事実上の標語となったのが「国土強靭化計画」であるのは言うまでもないだろう）。

　なにも建物に限った話ではない。大臣とはつまり、美術に言い換えれば「巨匠」のことであろう。巨匠が激動する時代を乗り越えて個人の名で名作、代表作を世に残す。だが、そういうことがはたして、このような時代に可能なのであろうか。むしろ平成という巨大な建屋のもとに巨匠や大臣という大きな物語を誘発する建物を継ぎ足して権威の根拠とするのではなく、小さな方丈を寄せ集め、うたかたのよう

に離合集散を繰り返し、その都度起きる「よどみ」に即応しながら、作品ともプロジェクトとも呼びえないうたかたの持続を生きることを集合的に試し続けてみせたのが、10年ごとに整理された建築物の部分（パーツ）としての平成の美術史ではなく、傷ついた時間とここで呼ぶ事態の断層を境にジグザグと動く「平成美術」の様相なのではなかったか。

　もしそうなら、本展で美術家にとどまらず多くの人たちが、巨匠の代表作の掲出によって時代を象徴する平成の歴史化に意識してか無意識のうちか逆らって、それぞれの「方丈」にその都度集い水面下で淡々と持続的な活動を続けてきたことのほうに目を向けるべきだろう。それは決して、平成の始まりの頃に「コラボ」や「越境」というふうに、そして平成の終わりには「コレクティヴ」や「ソーシャリー・エンゲイジド」というかたちで耳にするようになった学習的な知識整理のための便利なキーワードや用語のたぐいではない。アーティストたちはどういうかたちであれ肩を寄せ、対面し、声をかわして結集せざるをえなかった（ネットも同様だろう）のであり、これらの集結の形態は、そのようでしかありえなくなった時代をおのずから鏡のように映しとる。

未来都市は瓦礫（デブリ）である

　けれども、泡のようになにより軽く移ろい、めまぐるしい出入りを繰り返していたかれらも、引きも切らぬ非常事態のなかで、しだいに瓦礫（デブリ）へと接近していく。瓦礫とは東日本大震災以降、大津波被災地を描写する際に私たちがもれなく聞くことになった不気味な言葉であり、同時に福島第一原発事故で溶け落ちた核燃料の様相をも示している。激烈化し続ける豪雨災害や洪水などでは必ず大量の瓦礫が出る。巨大な建築物に逆らう無重力のうたかたのような実体のなさとは対極だが、うたかたにせよ瓦礫にせよ、それがバブル経済やその崩壊、および大震災で私たちが住み暮らし活用した大きな建築物が破壊されたすえ現れた文明の残骸である以上、表層でけたたましく離合集散するうたかたであると同時に、地下で溶融し分離できないほど凝り固まった瓦礫（デブリ）でもあるのが私たちの似姿なのだ。本展でもたびたび召喚されるその響きは、本展を「うたかたと瓦礫」と呼ぶ際に鴨長明と並び着想の源となった建築家、いや反建築家と呼んだほうがよいだろう──磯崎新の2019年／令和元年の著作『瓦礫（デブリ）の未来』に多くを負う。

　ところで、磯崎は鴨長明と誰よりも縁の深い建築家＝反建築家でもある。『瓦礫（デブリ）

の未来』より前の2016年／平成28年に出され、第Ⅰ部に「瓦礫と隊列」と名付けられた書き下ろしの第3章を含む『偶有性操縦法──何が新国立競技場問題を迷走させたのか』は、あとがきにかえて末尾に「磯崎新私譜」を持つ。そこには磯崎が誕生し満州事変が勃発した「1931年（0歳）」から東日本大震災の起きた「2011年（80歳）」までが、戦争や動乱、震災などの災難とともに個人のものである年齢と併せて10歳おきに短く列記されている。

　これによると磯崎は、「物心ついてすぐに、我が家の先祖は慶長大地震の際、別府湾の海中に沈んだと伝えられる瓜生島から流れ着いた、と聞いた」と記している。朝鮮戦争の渦中にあった「1951年（20歳）」には「両親を亡くし、自宅は焼失、家財はのこらず処分されて上京。住所は転々と変り、東京流民となる」とあり、キューバ危機の影が迫る「1961年（30歳）」には「グランド・ツアーとしての世界の旅に出た。建築は現場に立って考えるものだと悟り、仕事場をアトリエと呼んだ。各地を渡り歩く「流れ」職人を、モデルにする」と述懐する。これは海中に沈み、火で焼かれ、そのあげくに常なる家を捨てて旅に出て、大殿＝建築から距離をとり、手に職を持つ流浪の流れ人になることを選んだ磯崎の、鴨長明を思わせる若き日の記述でもあるだろう。そしてこの鴨長明との時を超えた二人同行は、「1971年（40歳）」で「世界文化大革命」について触れ、「旅先で「方丈記」を英訳でよんで、はじめてこれが災害の書であったことを思い知る。仮設の小屋こそが「建築」なのではないか」と気づくことで決定づけられる。反建築家としての磯崎にとっての建築＝仮設の小屋は、いわばこのときに成ったと言ってもいいかもしれない。

　ここを起点に磯崎の私譜はさらに10年ごとに刻まれる動乱や震災とともに齢を重ね、「1981年（50歳）イラン革命」では「「時は飛去する」とする道元の言葉を手がかりに「有時庵」を構想した。この頃、マンハッタンとサンタ・モニカのホテルが仮の栖であ」り、「1991年（60歳）ソ連崩壊」には「還暦を機に、「無所有」を私の人生の信条と決めた。つまり流民のままでいること」を心にとどめ、「2001年（70歳）9・11」には「近代住宅の名作をえらんで『栖十二』をメールアートの形式で発行した。自邸はふくまれていない。誰もが「流れ」建築家だった。さしあたり私はパラサイト」と振り返り、そして「2011年（80歳）3・11」には「まれびとが「うつふね」に乗って訪れる民話から移動演奏会場 ARK NOVA のアイディアがうまれた。「方丈」が大八車で運ばれたように、これは折りたたまれてコンテナーに収まっている。いまでも次の寄港地をさがしている」と書き、ここでもまた鴨長明『方丈記』の「方丈」が、地中の基礎なく海上を移ろう流浪船に喩えられて海の

なかから姿を現す。

　こうした大殿（建築）の対極にある磯崎にとっての方丈（小屋であり船でもある）には、建築＝反建築のみならず、その磯崎が1960年／昭和35年の日米安保闘争のころ力を注いだ反芸術をめぐる活動の根底に横たわる「未来都市は廃墟である」とのテーゼが幾重にもこだましている。この廃墟がかたちを変え、いま大震災と核事故を経て「未来都市は瓦礫（デブリ）である」と言い換えられる事態を迎えた。そう、水上のうたかたは繰り返される平成の事件や事故、震災を経てしだいに凝集し、距離なく密接する瓦礫（デブリ）とほぼ一体化した。こうして、かつては大殿＝巨匠だった権威の象徴は今、そのことごとくがいつ、うたかたのように消え失せ、残骸の集積へと転ずるとも知れぬ、処理することが難しい「瓦礫（デブリ）＝粗大ゴミ」となった。

　令和になってからのことになるが、2019年／令和元年、大水で9つの収蔵庫が一気に水没し、22万9,000点に及ぶ収蔵作品・資料が被災した川崎市市民ミュージアムの例を見れば、美術館とてその例外ではありえない。もしも廃館となるようなことがあれば、たちまち壮大な「粗大ゴミ」と化すだろう（磯崎は都市の巨大建築を「粗大ゴミ」と呼んで物議を醸したことがある。いわば「未来都市は粗大ゴミである」ということだろうか）。このように、すべてがうたかたと消え、瓦礫となりうる世界のなかでは、美術館も地に足をつけた大殿ではもはやなく、嵐で方々に白波の立つ大海に行方知れずの船出をする方舟（アーク）のようなもので、そこにはつねに難破と沈没の危機（デブリ化の予感）が同居している。

うたかたと瓦礫（デブリ）

　そう、平成の時代を通じて、折ごとに越境とかコラボレーションとかコレクティヴとかソーシャリー・エンゲイジドとか呼ばれて有望視された美術家たちの結集は、潜在的にはいつもよどみに浮かぶ「うたかた」であり、堅牢な御門を有する大殿としての美術館にも、つねに不可視な未来の「瓦礫（デブリ）」が大量に潜伏していたのだ。そして、今こうして京都に立つ装いも新たな美術館で、「うたかたから瓦礫へ（バブルからデブリへ）」と移り変わる平成年間を通じての事態の推移のなかで、美術家たちの離合集散と凝集をあらためて眺め直し、平成を3つの傷ついた時間に沿って分割し、歴史化することが不可能な固有名としての「平成美術」として振り返ってみたとき、それが同時に、潜伏的な瓦礫（デブリ）のなかにしつらえられた方丈の結集からなる「うたかたと瓦礫」——つまり、やがて禁じられることになる予兆として

の「密の美術」（密閉・密集・密接）でもあったことに気づくのだ。

振り返れば、本展の会場となった京都市京セラ美術館（京都市美術館）は、1933年／昭和8年に開館した、現存する日本で最古の公立美術館として知られる。そのきっかけとなったのは、1928年／昭和3年に京都で行われた昭和天皇の即位の礼を記念してのことだった。ゆえに、当初の名称は「大礼記念京都美術館」であり、京都市美術館と改称されたのは、敗戦後の駐留が解かれてからのこととなる。つまり、美術館の成り立ちそのものが、天皇のあり方や元号の推移と根底で深く結びつくという由来を持つことになる。そして、その点で、本展が昭和から平成へ、平成から令和へという時代の区切りを扱う以上、本展の企画はこの美術館の出自そのものとも切り離せない連続性／非連続性を兼ね備えることになる。

そして、元号とはとりもなおさず、天皇というひとりの生命の内部でのみ可能になる呼称である。実際、「一代」を意味する「世」の文字は、もともと「十」を3つ合わせて「三十」の意味を持つという。これが平成の30年と重なるのは偶然だろうか。とすると、「平成美術」をうたうこの展覧会もまた、天皇というひとりの生命を内に宿しているという意味で、一種の体内性を持つことになる。言い換えれば、展覧会の会場の外はその体外となり、そこはすでに令和という時空のなかで時が刻まれている。本展／本書第Ⅰ部で3章に分けて追っていく「平成美術」をめぐるアーティストらの「うたかた」と「瓦礫（デブリ）」を思わせる離合集散も、その意味では、一種の内部性のなかに閉じ込められている。しかし、この離合集散は、同時に令和の時代へと「橋渡し」される点で、展覧会の外へと開かれた結集（バブル）と凝集（デブリ）でもあるに違いはない。この外部と内部が隣接する境界線の先で、まだ知らぬ「令和美術」では、美術家たちはいったいどのような離合集散を起こし、はたしてそれはなんと呼ばれるだろうか。

付記1　京都市京セラ美術館（京都市美術館）では、1973年／昭和48年の「1973京都ビエンナーレ」で「集団による美術」を主題にグループ展が開催され、計6つの集団が参加している。そこでは「確々の美術団体や単なる共同制作による美術を意味するものではなく、いくつかの新しい課題に対して接近・離合をくり返す一時的な集団による美術」（「開催にあたって」より）を扱うものとされ、「それぞれに〈現代美術〉が当面していることがらの複雑さと難かしさを具体的に示しつつ、今後美術はいかなる機能を担うかが質されるはず」とねらいが記されている。図録では平野重光「〈集団による美術〉とは何か？」が寄稿され、6つの集団（五人組写真集編集委員会＋5、Equivalent Cinema、「知ってる人＋知ってる人＋知ってる人」、ニルヴァナ資料集積－究極表現研究所、THE PLAY、JAPAN KOBE ZERO）に向け「あなたがたにとって集団とは何か」の質問が投げかけられて

いる。その意味では、京都市京セラ美術館で美術における集団（接近・離合＝うたかた・瓦礫？）に特化した企画展が催されるのは、まったく初めてのことではない。だが、本文で記したとおり、本展はこうした歴史的な系譜を扱わない。ただ、このビエンナーレ展に参加した THE PLAY が会場で「吊り橋」状の《BRIDGE》を設置したことが偶然、今回の展示における「突然、目の前がひらけて」へと「架橋」しうる別の潜在的な意味がありうるので特記することとした。

付記 2　それで言うと、本展／本書において「集団による美術」（1973 京都ビエンナーレ）にあたるのは、「アーティストらによる集合的活動」である。「集団（group）」ではなく「集合（set）」としたのは、14 組の「参加作家」の集合性に基づく「活動」（本書では「うたかた」、「瓦礫」による離合集散の性質がこれにあたる）のほうをより強く念頭に置いたからで、これらの集合をかたちづくるのが「要素／元（element）」としての「メンバー」となる。メンバーは原則として 2 人以上を基準としたが、それが 1 人の場合、または 0 人の場合もありうる（解散の状態）。その意味では、本展／本書における主要な概念としての「うたかた」、「瓦礫」も集合の一種である。さらに言えば、本展／本書におけるもっとも包括的な概念としての「平成美術」は、これら複数の多様な「集合」による活動の総体を、平成年間（1989 年〜 2019 年）を通じて「集合の集合」として捉えるメタ概念ということになる。

（さわらぎ・のい）

【参考文献】

磯崎新『偶有性操縦法——何が新国立競技場問題を迷走させたのか』青土社、2016 年

磯崎新『瓦礫の未来』青土社、2019 年

鴨長明『方丈記』（浅見和彦 校訂・訳）ちくま学芸文庫、2011 年

椹木野衣「私的＝史的叙述　一九九一―二〇一五」『日本美術全集』第 20 巻、小学館、2016 年、177–185 頁

椹木野衣「平成の美術　1989 － 2019」『美術評論家連盟会報』19 号、2018 年 11 月 9 日公開、美術評論家連盟公式ウェブサイト　https://www.aicajapan.com/ja/no19sawaragi01/（最終閲覧日：2021 年 1 月 5 日）

椹木野衣「平成アートベストテン」『考える人 Web マガジン』2019 年 6 月 16 日公開　https://kangaeruhito.jp/article/7711（最終閲覧日：2021 年 1 月 5 日、初出は『新潮』116 巻 5 号、新潮社、2019 年、164–166 頁）

年　　表

平 成 美 術

1989–2019

A History of Heisei

（1989–2019）

Bubbles/Debris

凡 例

・平成年間の社会と美術にかんする出来事をベースに、本書第Ⅰ部でとりあげる、本展の参加作家（資料展示を含む）にかんする動向を中心にアーティストらによる集合的活動を一覧する試みをおこなった。

明朝体：社会にかんする出来事
　　　　　████　自然および人為による災害（戦争を含む）

・とくに甚大な影響を及ぼしたものは新聞記事の画像を掲載した。

・被害状況の詳細を（　）内に記載した。死＝死者数、不明＝行方不明者数、負＝負傷者数、M＝マグニチュード、メートル＝津波高（被害が顕著な場合のみ記載）。

ゴチック：美術にかんする出来事
　　　　　参加作家にかんする事項（グループ結成前・解散後の事項を含む。ただし、その場合は項目の頭にグループ名を付していない）

　　　　　参加作家以外のアーティストらによる集合的活動は、活動を開始した元号の下に配置し、五十音順（欧文表記の場合はアルファベット順）に記した。

・書籍の刊行情報は、各年の末尾にまとめて著者名の五十音順に記した。

―：年全体に及ぶ事象や、月が特定できない事項

・同じ月に分類の異なる事項が複数並ぶ場合、社会にかんする出来事、美術にかんする出来事の順に記載した。参加作家にかんする事項は美術にかんする出来事の末尾に記し、参加作家の順序は、本書第Ⅰ部の掲載順に従った。

・参加作家にかんする事項は、平成以前・以後の項目も例外として掲載した。

・氏名の敬称は略した。

・年表作成にあたっては以下を主に参照した。『朝日新聞』（1989~2019年）、総務省「令和元年版　情報通信白書」、消防庁国民保護・防災部「平成30年　災害年報」（「令和2年　地方防災行政の現況」所収）、消防庁ウェブサイト「災害情報」、気象庁ウェブサイト「気象庁が名称を定めた気象・地震・火山現象一覧」、『日本美術全集』第19・20巻（小学館、2015年、2016年）、『美術手帖』71巻1076号（美術出版社、2019年）。

昭和 62 年 _1987_

— Complesso Plastico **Complesso Plastico 結成**

昭和 63 年 _1988_

2 月 Complesso Plastico **個展「愛と黄金」** ギャラリー白（大阪）

— IDEAL COPY **IDEAL COPY デビュー**

1989 昭和 64 年 / 平成元年

ダイアモンズ・アー・フォーエバー Hi et H

1 月 **昭和天皇崩御、皇太子が即位。8 日に「平成」改元**

1989 年 1 月 7 日 朝日新聞 夕刊

3 月 女子高生コンクリート詰め殺人事件発覚

Complesso Plastico 《Love and Gold》「メタリズム」展、スパイラル（東京）

4 月 消費税導入（3%）

P3 art and environment 設立

5 月 広島市現代美術館開館

「大地の魔術師たち（Magiciens de la Terre）」展、ポンピドゥ・センター（フランス）

IDEAL COPY 《Channel: Great Painter in New Face》「ニューフェイス」展、ギャラリー VIEW（大阪）

6 月 リクルート事件、竹下内閣総辞職

天安門事件

「アゲインスト・ネイチャー──80 年代の日本美術」展
（キュレーター：キャシー・ハルブライヒ、トーマス・ソコロフスキ、河本信治、南條史生）、
サンフランシスコ近代美術館を皮切りに全米を巡回。日本では ICA 名古屋で開催

7 月 **伊豆半島東方沖で群発地震、伊東市沖で海底噴火**

Complesso Plastico 個展「What's NEWLIFE」モーリー・ギャラリー（大阪）

8 月 東京・埼玉連続幼女誘拐殺人事件

「アゲインスト・ネイチャー」展
カタログ

ソニーが米国のコロンビア・ピクチャーズ・エンターテインメントの買収を発表 **9**月

Bunkamura ザ・ミュージアム開館

「ARMS──芸術の腕」展、ハイネケンヴィレッジギャラリー（東京）

個展「Transmedia Work」ギャラリー COCO（京都）

三菱地所がロックフェラーセンターを買収 **10**月

セゾン美術館（旧西武美術館）リニューアルオープン（1999年閉館）

《Channel: Merchandise》「saga art forum '89　飛来するさかな」展、
嵯峨美術短期大学（京都）

坂本堤弁護士一家殺害事件 **11**月

横浜美術館開館

ベルリンの壁崩壊

冷戦終結宣言（米ソ首脳会談） **12**月

東京証券取引所で日経平均最高値（3万8,915円87銭）

飴屋法水による「M.M.M.」が SKIN シリーズを随所で発表 **―**

北澤憲昭『眼の神殿──「美術」受容史ノート』（美術出版社）刊行
中ザワヒデキ『近代美術史テキスト──印象派からポスト・ヘタうま・イラストレーションまで』（トムズボックス）刊行

東独、国境を開放

ベルリンの壁、実質撤廃

数万人、直ちに西へ

首脳会談を急ぐ
ポーランド訪問は中断

1989年11月10日 朝日新聞 夕刊

平成2年 **199**

Doo+Doo+Doo

株価急落、バブル崩壊開始 **1**月

「キリンプラザ大阪コンテンポラリー・アワード」設立、最優秀作品賞：ヤノベケンジ

テクノクラート結成

「企業メセナ協議会」発足 **2**月

大蔵省（当時）が不動産融資の総量規制通達 **3**月

水戸芸術館開館

「プライマルスピリット──今日の造形精神」展、
ハラミュージアムアーク（群馬）を皮切りに北米を巡回

ゴッホの《ガシェ博士の肖像》を大昭和製紙名誉会長の斉藤了英が、 **5**月
当時史上最高額の8,250万ドルで落札

川村記念美術館開館

テクノクラート 個展「War Bar」246club（東京）

《Love and Gold/Amore e Oro》第44回ヴェネツィア・ビエンナーレ「アペルト'90」展 **6**月

「脱走する写真──11の新しい表現──」展、水戸芸術館（茨城）、 **7**月
出展作品に Complesso Plastico《Everybody knows NEW LIFE》、IDEAL COPY《Faces of 10 Artists》ほか

「手塚治虫展」東京国立近代美術館

「ファルマコン'90　幕張メッセ現代の美術」展、幕張メッセ（千葉）

イラクによるクウェート侵攻 **8**月

ダムタイプ《pH》公演、スパイラル（東京）

ワタリウム美術館開館 **9**月

日経平均株価が一時2万円を割る **10**月

東西ドイツ統一

天皇即位の大嘗祭 **11**月

水戸芸術館 全景
撮影：田澤純
提供：水戸芸術館

任天堂、「スーパーファミコン」発売

「アート・ナウ——関西の 80 年代」展、兵庫県立近代美術館

IDEAL COPY 《Channel: Peace Cards》「観念の刻印——1990 日本の版画・写真・立体」展、栃木県立美術館

12 月 テクノクラート 《人はパンのみにて生きるにあらず》「SANYO POW WOW TIME」トークイベントシリーズ、スパイラル（東京）

1991 年 1 月 17 日 朝日新聞 夕刊

1991 平成 3 年

大阪 3D 協会　カウンシル　相談芸術（大学）　パルパス H プランツ　SMTV

1 月　**湾岸戦争勃発**（日本は多国籍軍に戦費 90 億ドルの追加拠出を決定。総額 130 億ドル）

3 月　日比野克彦、タナカノリユキ、関口敦仁「X デパートメント——脱領域の現代美術」展、
伊勢丹美術館（東京）

テクノクラート 《ジャパニーズ・ソング》「NTT インターコミュニケーション '91——電話網の中の
見えないミュージアム」展（キュレーター：浅田彰、伊藤俊治、彦坂裕）、電話回線内（関東一都七県）

4 月　牛肉・オレンジの輸入自由化

自衛隊によるペルシャ湾への掃海艇派遣。初の海外派遣

6 月　**雲仙・普賢岳噴火で大火砕流**（死 41 人、不明 3 人、負 10 人）

1991 年 6 月 4 日 朝日新聞 朝刊

レントゲン藝術研究所オープン

キヤノン・アートラボ設立

Complesso Plastico 《REALIZE——すべては成就する》「アートラボ第 1 回企画展——ARTLAB」
TEPIA（東京）

IDEAL COPY 個展「Channel: S.P. 1988–1990」ギャラリー NW ハウス（東京）

7 月　IDEAL COPY 《Channel: ICAM（IDEAL COPY Art Museum）》「ピエール＆ジル写真展」
なんば CITY シティホール（大阪）

8 月　DIVINA COMMEDIA 《DIVINA COMMEDIA》神戸ジーベックホール（兵庫）

9 月　内藤礼個展「地上にひとつの場所を」佐賀町エキジビット・スペース（東京）

Complesso Plastico 《REALIZE——すべては成就する》「ジャパン・フェスティバル '91：過激分子」展、Old Library Gallery（イギリス）

10 月　クリストとジャンヌ＝クロード「アンブレラ 日本＝アメリカ合衆国、1984–91」
カリフォルニアと茨城に 3,100 本の巨大傘を同時に立てたプロジェクト。日本での大規模地域芸術祭の先駆けとなった。
カリフォルニアでは突風により観客が死亡する事故が、茨城では撤去作業にあたっていた作業員が感電死する事故が発生

12 月　ソビエト社会主義共和国連邦崩壊、ロシア連邦に

— 東高現代美術館閉館

椹木野衣『シミュレーショニズム——ハウス・ミュージックと盗用芸術』（洋泉社）刊行

椹木野衣『シミュレーショニズム』

内藤礼個展「地上にひとつの場所を」
の展示風景、1991 年
撮影：畠山直哉

クリストとジャンヌ＝クロード
「アンブレラ 日本＝アメリカ合衆国、1984–91」
の展示風景、1991 年
© Wolfgang Volz/laif/amanaimages

アトリエ・ワン　現代美術工等兵　スモールヴィレッジセンター　東京ガガガ
中村と村上　LSX (light speed institute)　Mission Invisible　THE OK GIRLS

改正大規模小売店舗法施行	1月
村上隆個展「Wild, Wild」レントゲン藝術研究所（東京）	2月
新幹線に「のぞみ」誕生	3月
第1回 NICAF、パシフィコ横浜（神奈川）	
東北芸術工科大学開校	4月
国家公務員の週休2日制始まる	5月
ベネッセハウスミュージアム開館	7月
「アーバナート #1」渋谷パルコ（東京）、パルコ賞：かわいひろゆき	8月
自衛隊をカンボジアに派遣	9月
「アノーマリー」展（キュレーター：椹木野衣）、レントゲン藝術研究所（東京）、 出展作家に伊藤ガビン、中原浩大、村上隆、ヤノベケンジ	
都市銀行などの不良債権 12兆3,000億円となる	10月
東京佐川急便事件で金丸信の罰金刑が確定	
愛知芸術文化センター開館	
「水戸アニュアル '93　アナザーワールド・異世界への旅： あるいはヴァーチャル・リアリティからの逃走」展、水戸芸術館（茨城）	11月
スモールヴィレッジセンター（小沢剛＋村上隆＋中村政人＋中ザワヒデキ）「大阪ミキサー計画」 JR大阪駅・阪急梅田駅界隈、「中村と村上」大阪展の関連企画	12月
個展「Dutch Life vol. 1 コンタミネイテッド」レントゲン藝術研究所（東京） テクノクラート	
キヤノン「第1回写真新世紀」年間グランプリ：木下伊織	—
ソニー・ミュージックエンタテインメント「アートアーティストオーディション」開始、翌年に明和電機が第2回大賞受賞	—

「アノーマリー」展の展示風景、1992年
撮影：黒川未来夫

「中村と村上」展カタログ

ザ・ギンブラート《宇治野宗輝パフォーマンス》1993年
撮影：中村政人
提供：3331 Arts Chiyoda

アフロサイサイ　加瀬大周宇乙プロジェクト　カワイオカムラ　キキとララ
ザ・ギンブラート　なすび画廊　明和電機　ROGUES' GALLERY

釧路沖地震（M7.5、死2人、負967人）	1月
「fo (u) rtunes」展（キュレーター：西原珉）、レントゲン藝術研究所（東京）	
《Dutch Special 私もかわいいアライグマ》「第1回マラリア・アートショー―2月1日祭―」テクノクラート 原宿マラリア・アートショウ（東京）	2月
《Dutch Life vol. 2 ジャンキーフード》テクノクラート 「マラリア・アートショウ（第2回）」原宿マラリア・アートショウ（東京）	
ワークショップ「trobar clus」DIVINA COMMEDIA 水戸芸術館（茨城）、「水戸アニュアル '93　アナザーワールド・異世界への旅」関連プログラム	
《Channel: Exchange》「ハラ・ドキュメンツ2　IDEAL COPY―IDEAL COPY Channel: Exchange」展、原美術館（東京）	3月
富山県立近代美術館の大浦信行作品売却と図録焼却処分が発覚	4月
個展「Everybody knows NEWLIFE / Nobody knows NEWLIFE」Complesso Plastico なんば CITY シティホール（大阪）	
Jリーグ開幕	5月
ゼネコン汚職事件	6月

『世界最初の移動式画廊「なすび画廊」の活動録 1993–1995』

Nasubi Gallery

皇太子徳仁親王が小和田雅子と成婚

第 45 回ヴェネツィア・ビエンナーレアペルト部門に椿昇、中原浩大、柳幸典が参加

^{テクノ}^{クラート} ライブ「Dutch Life vol. 3 ドナ・ドナ」吉祥寺バウスシアター（東京）

7 月 東京サミット（主要先進国首脳会議）

北海道南西沖地震（奥尻島地震）（M7.8、死 202 人、不明 28 人、負 323 人）

^{テクノ}^{クラート}「都市の未来型 [I] Colony in the City」発表
（NTT 出版『InterCommunication』1993 Summer No. 5 誌上）

^{テクノ}^{クラート} 個展「Dutch Special ヒューマン・ジュース」レントゲン藝術研究所（東京）

8 月 細川連立内閣の発足により 55 年体制が崩壊

鹿児島水害（死 71 人、不明 1 人、負 142 人）

1993 年 9 月 29 日 朝日新聞 朝刊

9 月 　　記録的冷夏・米不足によりタイ米などを緊急輸入

「再制作と引用」展、板橋区立美術館（東京）

「パラレル・ヴィジョン——20 世紀美術とアウトサイダー・アート」展、世田谷美術館（東京）

村上隆《タイムボカン》「ART TODAY '93　ネオ・ジャパノロジー考：日高理恵子、アズビー・ブラウン、村上隆、尹煕倉」展、セゾン現代美術館（長野）

10 月 ^{テクノ}^{クラート} 個展「Dutch Life vol. 4 カミングアウト」レントゲン藝術研究所（東京）、同年 12 月には阿倍野 SOHO（大阪）に巡回

11 月 EU（欧州連合）発足

12 月 法隆寺、世界遺産に（国内初）

— 失業者急増、就職氷河期

村上隆《タイムボカン》
セゾン現代美術館（長野）での展示風景、1993 年
© 1993 Takashi Murakami/Kaikai Kiki Co., Ltd. All Rights Reserved.

— 宇川直宏キュレーションによるギャラリー「Atomage」
（クラブ Automatics に併設）が始動

木下直之『美術という見世物——油絵茶屋の時代』（平凡社）刊行

「昭和 40 年会」結成記者発表、1994 年
左から会田誠、大岩オスカール、松蔭浩之、小沢剛、開発チエ、曽根裕、パルコ木下
提供：長谷川仁美（MIACA）

ダムタイプ《S/N》1994 年
撮影：福永一夫

1994 平成 6 年

昭和 40 年会　新宿少年アート　スタジオ食堂　灰塚アースワークプロジェクト

1 月 ^{IDEAL}^{COPY}《Channel: OPEN #2》「亜細亜散歩」展、資生堂ギャラリー（東京）

2 月 ^{IDEAL}^{COPY}《Channel: Catalogue》「21 世紀・的・空間」展、セゾン美術館（東京）

^{テクノ}^{クラート}《Dutch Life vol. 5 セックス・アパルトヘイト》「人間の条件」展
（キュレーター：南條史生）、スパイラル（東京）

3 月 小選挙区制導入などを盛り込んだ関連法が成立

「第 1 回 VOCA 展」上野の森美術館（東京）、VOCA 賞：福田美蘭、世良京子

4 月 名古屋空港で中華航空 140 便が墜落事故

奈義町現代美術館開館

P-HOUSE オープン、「岡崎京子」展

フロッピー・アート・マガジン
「JAPAN ART TODAY-14」
P-HOUSE「岡崎京子」展

「909 アノーマリー2」展カタログ

松本サリン事件 **6月**

古橋悌二「アートラボ第4回企画展 LOVERS──永遠の恋人たち」ヒルサイドプラザ（東京）**9月**

「Japanese Art after 1945: Scream Against the Sky」展、グッゲンハイム美術館（アメリカ）

テクノクラート《Dutch Life vol. 6 メガネ・ドラッグ》「Open Air '94 "Out of Bounds"─海景の中の現代美術展─」
直島コンテンポラリーアートミュージアム（香川）

大江健三郎、ノーベル文学賞受賞 **10月**

北海道東方沖地震（M8.2、津波10メートル、負437人）

ファーレ立川オープン

サントリーミュージアム開館（2010年閉館）**11月**

ソニー・コンピュータエンタテインメント、「PlayStation」発売 **12月**

三陸はるか沖地震（M7.6、死者3人、負788人）

Complesso Plastico《Love and Gold》
「第6回アートの広場──
90年代・日本・メディア・アート・シーン」展、
ふくやま美術館（広島）

平成7年

岡画郎　時の蘇生／柿木プロジェクト
反重力音楽グループ／河田田／みかんぐみ
メガ日記　PUZZLE PUNKS

1995年1月17日 朝日新聞 夕刊

阪神・淡路大震災（M7.3、死6,434人、不明3人、負43,792人）**1月**

ダムタイプ《S/N》公演、スパイラル（東京）（日本初演）

東京都写真美術館総合開館

「909 アノーマリー2」展（キュレーター：椹木野衣）、レントゲン藝術研究所（東京）、**2月**
出展作品に Complesso Plastico《NOMAN》、テクノクラート《Dutch Life vol. 7 公衆精子計画》ほか、
映像協力：宇川直宏

オウム真理教による地下鉄サリン事件 **3月**

警察庁長官狙撃事件

東京都現代美術館開館

特集「モダニズムのハード・コア──現代美術批評の地平」
『批評空間』第2期臨時増刊号（太田出版）

1996年に開催予定の世界都市博覧会中止が決定 **5月**

IDEAL COPY《Channel: Exchange》「芸術祭典・京」展、元龍池小学校（京都）

DIVINA COMMEDIA《Gravity and Grace》「neuFundland II」展、ZKM
（Zentrum für Kunst und Medientechnologie, Karlsruhe）（ドイツ）

第46回ヴェネツィア・ビエンナーレにて千住博が名誉賞受賞 **6月**

テクノクラート《Dutch Life vol. 8 公衆精子計画》第46回ヴェネツィア・
ビエンナーレ「トランスカルチャー」展（キュレーター：南條史生）

アトラス、「プリント倶楽部」（通称「プリクラ」）を市場投入 **7月**

Complesso Plastico《NOMAN》「アートは楽しい6：機械帝国」展、
ハラミュージアムアーク（群馬）

戦後50年を受けて「村山総理大臣談話」が植民地支配と侵略を謝罪 **8月**

沖縄米兵少女暴行事件 **9月**

1995年3月20日 朝日新聞 夕刊

「水の波紋 '95」展（総合監督：ヤン・フート）、ワタリウム美術館（東京）

IDEAL COPY 《Channel: Exchange》「The Age of Anxiety」展、Power Plant（カナダ）

10月 庵野秀明『新世紀エヴァンゲリオン』放送開始（テレビ東京系列）

ダムタイプ・古橋悌二がエイズによる敗血症のため逝去

養老天命反転地オープン

11月 マイクロソフト、「Windows 95」日本語版発売

千葉市美術館開館

豊田市美術館開館

12月 **高速増殖原型炉「もんじゅ」ナトリウム漏洩事故**

住専（住宅金融専門会社）処理で公的資金 6,850 億円の投入決定

— ネットカフェブーム

— Complesso Plastico 活動休止

— 飴屋法水がアニマルストア「動物堂」（東京・東中野）を開店、のちにふくろう専門店「Owl Room」に

美術と美術館のあいだを考える会編『あいだ　美術と美術館のあいだを考える会』Vol. 1（桂書房）刊行

『あいだ　美術と美術館のあいだを考える』
Vol. 1、1995 年 2 月 8 日刊
「富山県立近代美術館問題を考える会」が「美術と美術館のあいだを考える会」へと発展し、桂書房より刊行された

森村泰昌《セルフポートレート（女優）／バルドーとしての私・2》1996 年
所蔵：島根県立石見美術館

1996 平成 8 年

 エキソニモ　キュピキュピ　グラインダーマン　日本美術応援団

1月 岡本太郎逝去

2月 菅直人厚相、薬害エイズ訴訟で血友病患者に謝罪

任天堂、ゲームボーイ用ソフト「ポケットモンスター赤・緑」発売

4月 らい予防法廃止

東京三菱銀行が発足、金融機関の再編が進む

普天間基地の返還で合意（橋本首相とモンデール駐日大使）

「Yahoo! JAPAN」開設

「森村泰昌展　美に至る病——女優になった私」横浜美術館（神奈川）

「TOKYO POP——新しい美術のイメージ」展、平塚市美術館（神奈川）

5月 水俣病和解成立（関西訴訟を除く）

「第 1 回フィリップモリス・アートアワード」グランプリ：曽根裕

6月 会田誠個展「戦争画 RETURNS」ギャラリーなつか（東京）

7月 英ロスリン研究所で世界初のクローン羊「ドリー」誕生

8月 「アトピックサイト」展、東京ビッグサイト

IDEAL COPY 《money》「On Camp/Off Base」展、東京ビッグサイト

9月 「ジェンダー——記憶の淵から」展、東京都写真美術館

第 6 回ヴェネツィア・ビエンナーレ国際建築展で日本館「亀裂 Fractures」
（コミッショナー：磯崎新）が金獅子賞、パビリオン賞受賞

IDEAL COPY 《Ideal Copy Archives》「美術家の冒険——多面化する表現と手法」展、
国立国際美術館（大阪）

テクノ クラート 第 5 回メキシコ国際パフォーマンス・フェスティバル関連企画に参加、
エクス・テレサ・アルテ・オルテルナティヴォ（メキシコ）

10月 小選挙区制で初の衆議院選挙・自民勝利

会田誠《紐育空爆之図（戦争画 RETURNS）》1996 年
零戦 CG 制作：松橋睦生 高橋龍太郎コレクション
撮影：長塚秀人

PostPet 2001
© PetWORKS, Sony Network Communications Inc.

「揺れる女／揺らぐイメージ」展カタログ

FLOATING IMAGES OF WOMEN IN ART HISTORY
from the Birth of the Feminism toward the Dissolution of the Gender

ICC オープニング企画展「海市」―もうひとつのユートピア
「シグネチャーズ」の展示風景、1997 年
提供：NTT インターコミュニケーション・センター［ICC］

平成 10 年　1998

8月　北朝鮮の弾道ミサイル「テポドン1号」が三陸沖に着弾

　　　秋吉台国際芸術村オープン

9月　高知豪雨（死6人、負12人）

　　　高知県立美術館が浸水、水没

　　　IDEAL COPY 《Channel: Exchange》「Donai yanen!」展、パリ国立高等美術学校（フランス）

10月　日本長期信用銀行が破綻、一時国有化ののち売却

　　　「マンガの時代展——手塚治虫からエヴァンゲリオンまで」展、東京都現代美術館

11月　戦後最悪の不況に政府が24兆円の緊急経済対策を決定

　　　「ラヴズ・ボディ：ヌード写真の近現代」展、東京都写真美術館ほか

12月　日本債券信用銀行が破綻、一時国有化ののち売却

　　　椹木野衣『日本・現代・美術』（新潮社）刊行

「G9　ニューダイレクション展」
フライヤー
資料提供：
スパイラル／株式会社ワコールアートセンター

softpad

椹木野衣『日本・現代・美術』

平成11年

1月　EU、11カ国で単一通貨ユーロ導入

　　　「MOT アニュアル1999——ひそやかなラディカリズム」展、東京都現代美術館

2月　NTT docomo、「i-mode」開始

　　　「時代の体温——Art/Domestic」展、世田谷美術館（東京）

3月　大手15行に公的資金約7兆5,000億円投入

　　　福岡アジア美術館開館

　　　第1回福岡アジア美術トリエンナーレ、福岡アジア美術館ほか

4月　整理回収機構（RCC）発足

　　　東京藝術大学先端芸術表現科設立

　　　「荒木経惟　センチメンタルな写真、人生。」展、東京都現代美術館

　　　「草間彌生　ニューヨーク／東京」展、東京都現代美術館

5月　「2ちゃんねる」開設

　　　「東京ガールズ・ブラボー」展（キュレーター：村上隆）、NADiff（東京）

6月　ソニー、「AIBO」限定受注販売を開始

　　　男女共同参画社会基本法施行

　　　西日本豪雨（死39人、不明1人、負69人）

7月　IDEAL COPY 《Channel: ICAM #3（IDEAL COPY Art Museum）Max Ernst》
　　　「共同制作の可能性——コラボレーション・アート展」福島県立美術館

　　　DIVINA COMMEDIA 《歴史の天使》「恋スル身体——A SENSE of REALITY」展、宇都宮美術館（栃木）

8月　国旗・国歌法成立

9月　茨城・東海村JCO東海事業所での国内初の臨界事故（死2人）

　　　東京オペラシティ アートギャラリー開館

10月　自民・自由・公明で連立政権組閣

　　　川崎市岡本太郎美術館開館

「時代の体温」展ポスター

1999年10月1日 朝日新聞 朝刊

「日本ゼロ年」展（企画・監修：椹木野衣）、水戸芸術館（茨城）、**11月**

出展作家に岡本太郎、小谷元彦、成田亨、大竹伸朗、できやよい、会田誠、横尾忠則、ヤノベケンジ、東松照明、村上隆、飴屋法水

日本におけるインターネットの人口普及率 が21.4%に ―

大竹伸朗『既にそこにあるもの』（新潮社）刊行

「日本ゼロ年」展ポスター

平成12年 2000

クリエイティブサポートレッツ　ゐるさんちまん　gansomaeda　ICANOF

《Channel: Exchange》「Worthless（Invaluable）」展、**2月**
リュブリアナ近代美術館（スロベニア）

有珠山噴火 **3月**

介護保険制度開始 **4月**

小渕内閣総理大臣入院、森内閣発足

「スーパーフラット」展（キュレーター：村上隆）、パルコギャラリー（東京）を皮切りに、規模を拡大して「SUPER FLAT」展としてロサンゼルス現代美術館（アメリカ）ほか米国各地を巡回

京都精華大学芸術学部にマンガ学科開設

「スーパーフラット」展カタログ

金融庁発足 **7月**

九州・沖縄サミット開催

三宅島雄山噴火（M最大6.5、死1人、負15人）

第1回大地の芸術祭　越後妻有アートトリエンナーレ（ディレクター：北川フラム）、新潟

「Google」日本語版サービス開始 **9月**

東海豪雨（死10人、負98人）

鳥取県西部地震（M7.3、負182人）**10月**

「没後200年　若冲」展、京都国立博物館

長島有里枝、HIROMIX、蜷川実花が第26回木村伊兵衛写真賞受賞

「村上隆 & HIROPON FACTORY「最終回―ガチンコゼロ年―」」水戸芸術館（茨城）、「日本ゼロ年」展関連プログラム **11月**

「芸術道場・原宿フラット」ラフォーレミュージアム原宿（東京）

ヒトゲノムの解析がほぼ完了 ―

コンピュータ2000年問題 ―

赤瀬川原平、山下裕二『日本美術応援団』（日経BP社）刊行

村上隆編著『スーパーフラット』（マドラ出版）刊行

平成13年 2001

地球H爆　カイカイキキ　photographers' gallery　チ十ムラ方

省庁再編、1府12省庁体制に **1月**

せんだいメディアテーク開館

芸予地震（M6.7、死2人、負288人）**3月**

「21世紀アートのエネルギーをみる」展、○美術館（東京）ほか

独立行政法人国立博物館設立 **4月**

小泉内閣発足

takashi murakami summon monsters?
open the door?
heal?
or die?

情報科学芸術大学院大学（IAMAS）開校

「村上隆展　召喚するかドアを開けるか回復するか全滅するか」カタログ

カイカイキキ設立

6 月　大阪教育大学附属池田小学校で児童殺傷事件

宇川直宏《OP RACE 20000000000》「オプ・トランス！」
（プロデュース：椹木野衣、キュレーター：東谷隆司）、キリンプラザ大阪

2001 年 9 月 12 日 朝日新聞 朝刊

8 月　「奈良美智展　I DON'T MIND, IF YOU FORGET ME.」横浜美術館（神奈川）

「村上隆展　召喚するかドアを開けるか回復するか全滅するか」東京都現代美術館

9 月　米国同時多発テロ

第 1 回横浜トリエンナーレ（アーティスティック・ディレクター：河本信治、建畠晢、中村信夫、南條史生）

GEI
SAI　「芸術道場 GP 2001」
東京都現代美術館、「村上隆展　召喚するかドアを開けるか回復するか全滅するか」関連企画

10 月　針生一郎、椹木野衣、楠見清、村上隆「芸術徹底討論会」東京都現代美術館、
「村上隆展　召喚するかドアを開けるか回復するか全滅するか」関連企画、9.11 の米国同時多発テロを受けて開催

磯崎新『UNBUILT／反建築史』（TOTO 出版）刊行

椿昇＋室井尚《インセクト・ワールド、飛蝗》2001 年
横浜トリエンナーレ 2001 の展示風景
撮影：黒川未来夫
提供：横浜トリエンナーレ組織委員会

 平成 14 年

Antenna　ジェイ・チュン＆キュウ・タケキ・マエダ　じゃぽにか
身体表現サークル　トゥキ・ザ・ウッズ　やさしい美術プロジェクト　ART TRACE
KATHEY　MMAC（Mixed Media Art Communications）　morito＋sigi
Port B　SHINCHIKA　The SINE WAVE ORCHESTRA　wah（ワウ）

反戦運動「殺す・な」の題字
ベ平連が『ワシントンポスト』（1967 年
4 月 3 日）に掲載したベトナム反戦広告
に岡本太郎が寄せた手書きの文字をさま
ざまにリミックスし活用したもの

3 月　GEI
SAI　GEISAI#1、東京タワーアミューズメントホール

4 月　ゆとり教育がスタート

5 月　日本経済団体連合会が再編・発足

奈良美智《The Little Judge》2001 年
© Yoshitomo Nara

6 月　日韓共催 2002 FIFA ワールドカップ開幕

「ぬりえ」展（キュレーター：村上隆）、カルティエ現代美術財団（フランス）

8 月　GEI
SAI　GEISAI#2、東京ビッグサイト

9 月　日朝平壌宣言。小泉内閣総理大臣が訪朝し、日本人拉致を公式に認めさせる

10 月　熊本市現代美術館開館

11 月　中国広東省にて SARS（重症急性呼吸器症候群）感染者確認、大流行へ

食糧ビルディング（東京）閉鎖に伴い「エモーショナル・サイト」展開催

「EXPOSE 2002 夢の彼方へ：ヤノベケンジ×磯崎新」展
（キュレーター：椹木野衣）、キリンプラザ大阪

— SuperDeluxe（六本木）オープン（2019 年閉店）

— 宇川直宏が「ULTIMATE TV UNIVERSITY!!!!!」を開始
（東京にあるスタジオと京都造形芸術大学 [現・京都芸術大学] の教室を結ぶ双方向配信の授業）

椹木野衣『「爆心地」の芸術』（晶文社）刊行
松井みどり『アート──“芸術”が終わった後の“アート”』（朝日出版社）刊行

米英、イラク攻撃

バグダッドの拠点爆撃

米大統領が開戦宣言

首相　米の武力行使支持

長期化覚悟を

SARS死者500人超す

トリ・コロナの祖先から分岐?

上海でも初の犠牲

す　な

「YES　オノ・ヨーコ」展カタログ

平成 15 年 2003

イルコモンズ　エレクトリック　ココルーム　殺す・な　たまたま　パラモデル　反戦ハート・ネットワーク　湊町アンダーグラウンドプロジェクト　淀川テクニック　core of bells　YOSHITOMO NARA+graf

2003 年 3 月 20 日 朝日新聞 夕刊

イラク戦争開始　3 月

『千と千尋の神隠し』、米アカデミー賞（長編アニメーション部門）受賞

反戦運動「殺す・な」（発起人：小田マサノリ、工藤キキ、椹木野衣、山本ゆうこ）

GEISAI GEISAI#3、パシフィコ横浜（神奈川）

オウム真理教元代表松本智津夫（麻原彰晃）被告に死刑求刑　4 月

2003 年 5 月 9 日 朝日新聞 朝刊　個人情報保護法成立　5 月

感染症 SARS が大流行

「ヤノベケンジ MEGALOMANIA」展、国立国際美術館（大阪）　8 月

十勝沖地震（M8.0、津波 2.55 メートル、不明 2 人、負 849 人）　9 月

指定管理者制度施行

K.K.《ワラッテイイトモ、》が
キリンアートアワード 2003 審査員特別優秀賞受賞

GEISAI GEISAI#4、東京ビッグサイト

森美術館開館　10 月

「YES　オノ・ヨーコ」展、水戸芸術館（茨城）ほか

『ART iT』創刊（2009 年休刊、ウェブサイトへ移行）

山口情報芸術センター（YCAM）開館　11 月

GEISAI GEISAI ミュージアム、六本木ヒルズ森タワー 24 階特設会場（東京）　12 月

宇川直宏個展「Daily Psychic TV/Emperor's Dead」LADMUSICIAN Gallery（東京）　—

平成 16 年 2004

ふつう研究所　モイズプロジェクト　桃色ゲリラ　四谷アートステュディウム　COUMA　intext　SWAMP

鳥インフルエンザがアジアで流行（日本でも 79 年ぶりに山口県の養鶏場で発生を確認）　1 月

自衛隊のイラク派遣開始

「mixi」「GREE」「Flickr」開設　2 月

GEISAI GEISAI#5、パシフィコ横浜（神奈川）　3 月

ボーダレス・アートミュージアム NO-MA 開館　6 月

IDEAL COPY《Channel: Exchange》「コピーの時代——デュシャンからウォーホル、モリムラへ」展、滋賀県立近代美術館

新潟・福島豪雨（死 16 人、負 4 人）　7 月

福井豪雨（死 4 人、不明 1 人、負 19 人）

「ノンセクト・ラディカル 現代の写真III」展、横浜美術館（神奈川）
高嶺格の映像作品《木村さん》が展示上映中止となり物議を醸す

地中美術館開館

福井県美浜発電所で配管破裂（死 5 人）　8 月

9 月 浅間山が 21 年ぶりの中規模噴火

「アメーバブログ」開設

GEI SAI GEISAI#6、東京ビッグサイト

10 月 台風 23 号（死 95 人、不明 68 人、負 555 人）

新潟県中越地震（M6.8、死 68 人、負 4,805 人）

金沢 21 世紀美術館開館

11 月 国立国際美術館が大阪万国博覧会跡地から中之島に移転

contact Gonzo 結成前の垣尾優と塚原悠也が
「泉北アートプロジェクト」で《公園》を撮影

12 月 スマトラ島沖で大地震（M9.1、死 22 万人、負 13 万人）

― ライブドア旋風

 平成 17 年

清島アパート　芸術の山　素人の乱
トロールチカ　西荻ビエンナーレ

1 月 BankART Studio NYK オープン（2018 年閉館）

3 月 日本国際博覧会（愛・地球博）開幕

福岡県西方沖地震（M7.0、死 1 人、負 1,204 人）

GEI SAI GEISAI#7、東京ビッグサイト

4 月 JR 西日本福知山線で脱線事故

「GyaO」開設

「Gmail」ベータ版開始（2006 年 8 月に日本で招待制からサインアップ制へ移行）

「リトルボーイ」展（キュレーター：村上隆）、
ジャパン・ソサエティー・ギャラリーほか（アメリカ）

7 月 ロンドンで同時爆破テロ

「GUNDAM 来たるべき未来のために」
（キュレーター：東谷隆司）、サントリーミュージアム（大阪）

アヤ ズ「バ ング ント」展
（プロデュース：秋田敬明、展示：飴屋法水、音：大友良英、文：椹木野衣）、P-House（東京）

モエレ沼公園がグランドオープン（デザイン：イサム・ノグチ）

三瀬夏之介個展「日本の絵」gallery neutron（京都）

8 月 「第 1 回アートフェア東京 2005」東京国際フォーラム・展示ホール

Chim↑Pom Chim↑Pom 結成（メンバー：卯城竜太、林靖高、エリイ、岡田将孝、稲岡求、水野俊紀）

9 月 郵政解散選挙で自民圧勝

GEI SAI GEISAI#8、東京ビッグサイト

11 月 耐震強度偽装事件

12 月 出生数が死亡数を初めて下回る

「AKB48」活動開始

村上隆が「エフエム芸術道場」を開設

椹木野衣『戦争と万博』（美術出版社）刊行
白川昌生『美術・マイノリティ・実践――
もうひとつの公共圏を求めて』（水声社）刊行
杉本博司『苔のむすまで』（新潮社）刊行

金沢 21 世紀美術館 外観
撮影：石川幸史
提供：金沢 21 世紀美術館

「リトルボーイ」展カタログ

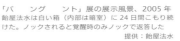

「バ ング ント」展の展示風景、2005 年
飴屋法水は白い箱（内部は暗室）に 24 日間こもり続
けた。ノックされると覚醒時のみノックで返答した
提供：飴屋法水

椹木野衣『戦争と万博』

モエレ沼公園
提供：モエレ沼公園

壁ぎわ　田田の家　ライゾマティクス　CAMP　MIHOKANNO　Nadegata Instant Party

青森県立美術館 外観

平成 18 年豪雪（死 159 人、負 2,145 人）	1 月
「生誕 120 年　藤田嗣治展」東京国立近代美術館	3 月
宇川直宏が「Mixrooffice」をオープン（2008 年閉鎖）	
長野、島根、鹿児島などで豪雨（7 月豪雨）（死 32 人、不明 1 人、負 64 人）	7 月
青森県立美術館開館	
「Facebook」一般開放	9 月
「大竹伸朗　全景　1955–2006」展、東京都現代美術館	10 月
京都国際マンガミュージアム開館	11 月
「ニコニコ動画」プレオープン（2007 年 1 月にβバージョンに移行）	12 月
日本美術オーラル・ヒストリー・アーカイヴ設立	
Chim↑Pom 個展「スーパー☆ラット」無人島プロダクション（東京）	
contact Gonzo **contact Gonzo** 結成（メンバー：垣尾優、塚原悠也）	—
千葉成夫『未生の日本美術史』（晶文社）刊行 村上隆『芸術起業論』（幻冬舎）刊行	

聞き耳　キワマリ荘　西京人　246 表現者会議　Nerhol　SZ　writtenafterwards

「夏への扉——マイクロポップの時代」展フライヤー
提供：水戸芸術館現代美術センター

国立新美術館開館	1 月
contact Gonzo 「吉原治良賞記念アート・プロジェクト 2008 入選展」にて展示、大阪府立現代美術センター	
5,000 万件の年金記載漏れ事件発覚	2 月
「夏への扉——マイクロポップの時代」展（キュレーター：松井みどり）、水戸芸術館（茨城）	
夕張市財政破綻	3 月
能登半島地震（M6.9、死 1 人、負 356 人）	
「Ustream」配信開始（2017 年終了）	
21_21 DESIGN SIGHT 開館、サントリー美術館移転開館	
伊藤一長・長崎市長、暴力団幹部に撃たれ死亡	4 月
宇川直宏「UKAWA NAOHIRO − A Series of Interpreted Catharsis episode 2 − earthquake」展、NANZUKA UNDERGROUND（東京）	
「YouTube」日本語版サービス開始	6 月
Chim↑Pom 「Re-Act 新・公募展 2007」広島市現代美術館賞（大賞）受賞	
新潟県中越沖地震（M6.8、死 15 人、負 2,346 人）	7 月
新潟県柏崎刈羽原子力発電所で火災発生。放射性物質が漏洩し海に流出	
「初音ミク」発売（クリプトン・フューチャー・メディア）	8 月
就任から約 1 年で安倍首相辞任、第一次安倍内閣総辞職	9 月
「pixiv」ベータテスト公開	
郵政民営化	10 月
村上隆回顧展「©MURAKAMI」ロサンゼルス現代美術館（アメリカ）を皮切りに海外 3 カ国 4 都市を巡回	
宇川直宏《A Series of Interpreted Catharsis episode 1 - Hurricane Katrina》	
「六本木クロッシング 2007：未来への脈動」展（共同キュレーター：天野一夫、荒木夏実、佐藤直樹、椹木野衣）、森美術館（東京）	
Chim↑Pom 個展「Thank You Celeb Project—I'm BOKAN」無人島プロダクション（東京）	11 月

12月 [contact Gonzo] 「HARAJUKU PERFORMANCE ＋」にてパフォーマンス公演、ラフォーレミュージアム原宿（東京）

針生一郎、椹木野衣、蔵屋美香、河田明久、平瀬礼太、大谷省吾編『戦争と美術──1937-1945』（国書刊行会）刊行
美術評論家連盟編『美術批評と戦後美術』（ブリュッケ）刊行
松井みどり『マイクロポップの時代──夏への扉』（パルコ出版）刊行

2008 平成20年

針生一郎、椹木野衣ほか編『戦争と美術』

悪魔のしるし　オレたちひょうげん族　NPO法人 swing　銀塩写真家集団 Phenomena
組立　渋家　引込線　Art Center Ongoing　THE ECHO
21st Century Cardboard Guild ＋ MONUMENT FOR NOTHING II

2月 アメリカ兵による少女暴行事件

3月 村上隆が東京にカイカイキキギャラリーを開く

4月 後期高齢者医療制度開始

「Twitter」日本語版サービス開始

2008年9月16日 朝日新聞 夕刊

十和田市現代美術館開館

東京藝術大学大学院映像研究科にアニメーション専攻新設

5月 村上隆《マイ・ロンサム・カウボーイ》が約16億円で落札（サザビーズ・オークション）

[GEISAI] GEISAIミュージアム #2、東京ビッグサイト

6月 東京・秋葉原で無差別殺傷事件

岩手・宮城内陸地震（M7.2、死17人、不明6人、負426人）

[DIVINA COMMEDIA] 《iris/HAKODATE》「函館ルミナート」展、はこだて未来大学（北海道）

7月 北海道洞爺湖サミット開催

米アップルの携帯電話「iPhone」が日本で発売

[Chim↑Pom] 個展「日本のアートは10年おくれている」NADiff gallery（東京）

[contact Gonzo] フィンランドへ遠征。ヘルシンキ市内にある核シェルターでの撮影及び北極圏の街イナリの森にてキャンプ生活

8月 愛知で豪雨（8月末豪雨）（死2人、負7人）

9月 世界金融危機（リーマンショック）

[GEISAI] GEISAI#11、東京ビッグサイト

[contact Gonzo] 南京トリエンナーレ2008にて展示・パフォーマンス公演、南京博物院（中国）

藤城嘘が人力SNS集団を称するポストポッパーズを立ち上げ、GEISAI#11に最初の出展を行う

10月 日本人4人にノーベル賞

横尾忠則『ぶるうらんど』（文藝春秋、2008年）が泉鏡花文学賞を受賞

[Chim↑Pom] 広島市の上空に「ピカッ」という文字を飛行機雲で描き、謝罪会見にまで発展。予定されていた広島市現代美術館での展覧会が取り止めに

[contact Gonzo] Platform Seoul 2008「I Have Nothing to Say and I am Saying It」展にて展示・パフォーマンス公演、ソウル駅（韓国）

11月 岡本太郎の《明日の神話》が渋谷駅（東京都渋谷区マークシティ内）に設置

12月 [GEISAI] GEISAI MIAMI 2008、SOHO studios miami（アメリカ）

[contact Gonzo] 「HARAJUKU PERFORMANCE＋SPECIAL」展にてパフォーマンス公演、ラフォーレミュージアム原宿（東京）

中ザワヒデキ『現代美術史日本篇』（アロアロインターナショナル）刊行
福住廉『今日の限界芸術』（BankArt1929）刊行

渋谷駅構内に掲げられた岡本太郎の《明日の神話》

オル太　美術犬（I.N.U）　わくわくプロジェクト　Artists' Guild　hyslom　parapera（パラぺら）

ビットコイン発行　**1 月**

第 1 回恵比寿映像祭、東京都写真美術館　**2 月**

contact Gonzo　**吉原治良賞記念アート・プロジェクト 2008「the modern house ──或は灰色の風を無言で歩む幾人か」** project MINIMA MORALIA section 1/3 にて展示・パフォーマンス公演、大阪府立現代美術センター

日経平均株価がバブル後最安値（7,054 円 98 銭）　**3 月**

GEISAI　**GEISAI#12**、東京ビッグサイト

Chim↑Pom　**個展「広島！」** Vacant（東京）

カオス ラウンジ　**藤城嘘による「カオス*ラウンジ」** mograg garage（東京）

別府現代芸術フェスティバル 2009「混浴温泉世界」（総合ディレクター：山出淳也）、大分　**4 月**

三瀬夏之介、東北芸術工科大学に赴任

新型インフルンザ世界的大流行　**5 月**

裁判員制度開始

VACANT（原宿）オープン（2019 年閉店）

「ネオテニー・ジャパン　高橋コレクション」展、上野の森美術館（東京）

改正著作権法成立　**6 月**

DIVINA COMMEDIA　**《iris/KYOTO》「out of place」**展、旧嵯峨御所大本山大覚寺（京都）

Chim↑Pom　**個展「にんげんていいな」** 山本現代（東京）

中国・九州北部豪雨（死 35 人、負 59 人）　**7 月**

第 1 回水と土の芸術祭（ディレクター：北川フラム）、新潟

衆議院選挙で民主が圧勝　**8 月**

第 1 回所沢ビエンナーレ美術展 2009──引込線、西武鉄道旧所沢車両工場（埼玉）

鳩山内閣発足　**9 月**

GEISAI　**GEISAI#13**、カイカイキキ三芳工場（埼玉）　**10 月**

政府がデフレ宣言　**11 月**

「'文化' 資源としての〈炭鉱〉展」目黒区美術館（東京）

GEISAI　**GEISAI TAIWAN#1**、華山創意園区（台湾）　**12 月**

contact Gonzo　**「HARAJUKU PERFROMANCE ＋ 2009」にてパフォーマンス公演、** ラフォーレミュージアム原宿（東京）

東北画は可能か？　**「東北画は可能か？」プロジェクトが始動**　**—**

新型インフル

「世界的大流行」を宣言

WHO、警戒度 6 に

WHOの警戒レベル（フェーズ）の定義

フェーズ 6
・人→人の感染が、WHOが定める地域の 2 か国以上で続く
→パンデミック（世界的な流行）の可能性は高い、確実だ
・パンデミック
・フェーズ 6 に加え、人→人の感染がWHOが別の地域の 1 か国で発生

2009 年 6 月 12 日 朝日新聞 朝刊

Chim↑Pom《ヒロシマの空をピカッとさせる》2009 年
© Chim↑Pom
撮影：Cactus Nakao
提供：作家、ANOMALY、無人島プロダクション

思い出横丁情報科学芸術アカデミー　画賊　劇団★死期　写真分離派
新川方法主義　全感覚派　戦闘系アーティストチーム「旅団」
秩父前衛派　天才ハイスクール!!!!　ハシメテン　犯罪ボーイズ　〇〇〇〇　Yotta

日本航空が経営破綻　**1 月**

南米チリで大地震（M8.8、津波 2 メートル以上、死 802 人）　**2 月**

宇川直宏《Dr. Toilet's Rapt-up Clinic》
「リフレクション──映像が見せる "もうひとつの世界"」展、水戸芸術館（茨城）

「平成の大合併」終了　**3 月**

GEISAI　**GEISAI#14**、東京ビッグサイト

contact Gonzo 「六本木クロッシング 2010 展：芸術は可能か？」にて展示・パフォーマンス公演、森美術館（東京）

DOMMUNE 「DOMMUNE」開局（東京）

4月　東北画は可能か？　個展「東北画は可能か？其ノ一」アートスペース羅針盤（東京）

カオス*ラウンジ 「カオス*ラウンジ宣言 2010」発表「カオス*ラウンジ 2010 in 高橋コレクション日比谷」（東京）

5月　カオス*ラウンジ 「破滅*ラウンジ」展、NANZUKA UNDERGROUND 渋谷（東京）

6月　菅内閣発足

3331 Arts Chiyoda オープン

7月　第 1 回瀬戸内国際芸術祭 2010（総合ディレクター：北川フラム）、香川

8月　第 1 回あいちトリエンナーレ 2010（芸術監督：建畠晢）

「田中一村　新たなる全貌」展、千葉市美術館

Chim↑Pom 個展「Imagine」無人島プロダクション（東京）

contact Gonzo 「オールナイト解体」展にてパフォーマンス公演、AD&A gallery（大阪）

9月　尖閣諸島沖で中国漁船が日本の巡視船に衝突

Chim↑Pom 「第 29 回サンパウロ・ビエンナーレ：There is always a cup of sea to sail in」に参加、イビラプエラ公園、シッシロ・マタラッツォ・パビリオン（ブラジル）

10月　鹿児島・奄美大島で豪雨被害（死 5 人、負 139 人）

豊島美術館開館

contact Gonzo 「Out of Place, Out of Time, Out of Performance」展にてパフォーマンス公演、ナム・ジュン・パイク アートセンター（韓国）

contact Gonzo 「新 incubation2: Stelarc × contact Gonzo; BODY OVERDRIVE」展にて展示・パフォーマンス公演、京都芸術センター

11月　「ウィキリークス」が米国外交公電を公開

GEISAI GEISAI TAIWAN#2、華山創意園區（台湾）

・　会田誠『カリコリせんとや生まれけむ』（幻冬舎）刊行
黒ダライ児『肉体のアナーキズム──1960 年代・日本美術におけるパフォーマンスの地下水脈』（grambooks）刊行
村上隆『芸術闘争論』（幻冬舎）刊行

2011 年 3 月 12 日 朝日新聞 朝刊

2011 年 3 月 14 日 朝日新聞 夕刊

2011 平成 23 年

キュンチョメ　ゲルオルタ　小森はるか＋瀬尾夏美
プロジェクト FUKUSHIMA!　堀浩哉＋堀えりぜ
AAG（The Academy of Alter-Globalization）
phono/graph
S.R.L（Survival Revival Laboratory）
XYZ Collective

1月　小沢一郎・民主党元代表が強制起訴（のちに無罪）

中国の国内総生産（GDP）が日本を抜いて世界 2 位に

霧島山（新燃岳）噴火（負 42 人）

カオス*ラウンジ 「荒川智則個展」トーキョーワンダーサイト渋谷（東京）

3月　東日本大震災（M9.0、津波 9.3 メートル以上、死 19,689 人、不明 2,563 人　負 6,233 人）

東京電力福島第一原子力発電所冷却不能。1 号機、3 号機、4 号機の原子炉建屋で水素爆発

東日本大震災を受け、目黒区美術館が 4 月 9 日から 5 月 29 日まで予定していた「原爆を視る 1945–1970」展の中止を発表

「生誕 100 年 岡本太郎展」東京国立近代美術館

contact Gonzo 「風穴　もうひとつのコンセプチュアリズム、アジアから」展にて展示・パフォーマンス公演、国立国際美術館（大阪）

「五百羅漢──増上寺秘蔵の仏画　幕末の絵師　狩野一信」展、江戸東京博物館　**4月**
（震災の影響により1カ月以上延期しての実施）

山本作兵衛の炭坑記録画が世界記憶遺産に登録　**5月**

_{Chim↑ Pom}　渋谷駅に設置された岡本太郎の壁画《明日の神話》に東京電力福島第一原発事故を思わせる
板絵《LEVEL7 feat. 明日の神話》を付け足す。警察により Chim↑Pom の3人が書類送検、その後不起訴に

_{Chim↑ Pom}《気合い100連発》制作

_{Chim↑ Pom}　個展「REAL TIMES」　無人島プロダクション（東京）

_{東北画は 可能か？}　個展「東北画は可能か？──方舟計画」イムラアートギャラリー東京

_{DOM MUNE}「DOMMUNE FUKUSHIMA!」開設

全国で脱原発デモ　**6月**

「LINE」サービス開始

電力使用制限令が発動　**7月**

なでしこジャパン、世界一に

オリンパスが巨額損失の隠蔽を公表

新潟・福島豪雨（死4人、不明2人、負13人）

_{DOM MUNE}「FREEDOMMUNE 0＜ZERO＞A NEW ZERO」東扇島東公園（神奈川）、震災復興チャリティー野外フェス（荒天中止、翌年実施）　**8月**

野田内閣発足　**9月**

台風12号（紀伊半島大水害）（死83人、不明15人、負113人）

灰原千晶《渡れるかもしれない橋》「武蔵野美術大学油絵科コンクール」武蔵野美術大学（東京）

_{GEI SAI}"petit" GEISAI#15、都立産業貿易センター台東館（東京）　**10月**

_{東北画は 可能か？}　個展「東北画は可能か？──方舟計画」大和川酒造 昭和蔵（福島）、「会津・漆の芸術祭2011〜東北へのエール〜」に参加

_{Chim↑ Pom}　個展「Chim↑Pom」MoMA PS1（アメリカ）　**11月**

東京電力福島第一原子力発電所事故の収束宣言　**12月**

_{GEI SAI}　GEISAI TAIWAN#3、華山創意園區（台湾）

_{Chim↑ Pom}　個展「LEVEL7 feat. 広島 !!!!」原爆の図丸木美術館（埼玉）

朝鮮大学校美術科43期グループ展「NOW展」朝鮮大学校（東京）

カオス・ラウンジ「破滅・ラウンジ」2010年
背景に梅沢和木《ネオネオエクスデス☆嫁渦 IIDX》を含む
提供：梅沢和木

村上隆個展「Murakami-Ego」の展示風景、2012年
撮影：GION
© 2012 Takashi Murakami/Kaikai Kiki Co., Ltd. All Rights Reserved.

平成 24年

かセンHトランスプラントＥ 国立奥多摩美術館
ウインドウ 目[mé] AGAIN+ST

村上隆個展「Murakami-Ego」アル・リワーク展示ホール（カタール）、　**2月**
日本では2015年10月に森美術館（東京）にて「村上隆の五百羅漢図展」として開催

「Pandemonium」展、XYZ collective（東京）、参加作家に梅津庸一ほか

_{東北画は 可能か？}《東北八重山景》《方舟計画》《東北山水》「第15回岡本太郎現代芸術賞」展、
川崎市岡本太郎美術館（神奈川）、岡本太郎現代芸術賞入選

_{contact Gonzo}《能動的滑落としての「山サーフィン」の開発》　**3月**
「メディア・ジム　道具をつくる身体をつくる Document Media Gym」展、コーポ北加賀屋（大阪）

_{contact Gonzo}「Double Vision: Contemporary Art from Japan」展にて展示・パフォーマンス公演、モスクワ市立近代美術館（ロシア）

朝鮮大学校美術科43期卒業制作展「CHODEMI Volume 2」朝鮮大学校（東京）

_{GEI SAI}　GEISAI#16、東京流通センター　**4月**

_{Chim↑ Pom}「ひっくりかえる」（キュレーター：Chim↑Pom）、ワタリウム美術館（東京）

「武蔵野美術大学油絵4年袴田クラス＋朝鮮大学校美術科チョデミ合同展」武蔵野美術大学（東京）

5月　東京スカイツリー開業

北関東竜巻（死3人、負59人）

國府理個展「水中エンジン」アートスペース虹（京都）

7月　福井県の大飯発電所3号機再稼働

九州北部豪雨（死30人、不明2人、負27人）

DOM
MUNE　「FREEDOMMUNE 0 ＜ ZERO ＞ ONE THOUSAND 2013」幕張メッセ（千葉）

8月　消費税増税を柱とする社会保障と税の一体改革

「ラッセン展」（キュレーター：大下裕司、原田裕規）、CASHI（東京）
翌年、本展を受けて原田裕規編著『ラッセンとは何だったのか？──消費とアートを越えた「先」』（フィルムアート社）刊行

第13回ヴェネツィア・ビエンナーレ国際建築展「ここに、建築は、可能か」（コミッショナー：伊東豊雄）が金獅子賞受賞

9月　尖閣諸島国有化

GEI
SAI　GEISAI#17、都立産業貿易センター台東館（東京）

Chim↑
Pom　個展「Chim↑Pom」バルコミュージアム（東京）

contact
Gonzo　パフォーマンス公演「Abstract Life《世界の仕組み／肉体の条件》」神奈川芸術劇場

10月　山中伸弥教授、iPS細胞でノーベル医学生理学賞受賞

沖縄にアメリカの新型輸送機オスプレイ配備

Chim↑
Pom　「第9回上海ビエンナーレ：REACTIVATION」に参加、上海当代芸術博物館（中国）

「LOVE LOVE SHOW 2012」展（キュレーター：櫛野展正）、鞆の津ミュージアム（広島）

11月　「会田誠展──天才でごめんなさい」森美術館（東京）

「Tokyo, 1955–1970: A New Avant-Garde」展、ニューヨーク近代美術館（アメリカ）

12月　衆議院選挙で自民が圧勝、第二次安倍内閣発足

『日本美術全集』全20巻（小学館）刊行開始

足立元『前衛の遺伝子──アナキズムから戦後美術へ』（ブリュッケ）刊行
Tsuji Nobuo, *Lineage of Eccentrics: Matabei to Kuniyoshi*, Kaikai Kiki 刊行
（辻惟雄『奇想の系譜　又兵衛─国芳』ちくま学芸文庫、2004年［初版：美術出版社、1970年］）

2013–2014年 宇都宮美術館 館外プロジェクト
「おじさんの顔が空に浮かぶ日」
主催：宇都宮美術館　作家：目［mé］

平成 25 年

芸宿　景風趣情　スパイダーズ　鳥栖喬　原久路＆林ナツミ　蜜の木

1月　「である、しゅとぅるむ」展、名古屋市民ギャラリー矢田（愛知）

3月　Chim↑
Pom　個展「PAVILION」岡本太郎記念館（東京）

4月　日本銀行による「異次元の金融緩和」発表

秋田公立美術大学設立

『めめめのくらげ』（監督：村上隆）公開

GEI
SAI　GEISAI#18、都立産業貿易センター台東館（東京）

6月　**サウジアラビアにてMERS（中東呼吸器症候群）感染者確認、大流行へ**

富士山、世界文化遺産に

第55回ヴェネツィア・ビエンナーレ国際美術展国別参加部門で田中功起の個展「abstract speaking - sharing uncertainty and collective acts（抽象的に話すこと──不確かなものの共有とコレクティブ・アクト）」（主催：国際交流基金、キュレーター：蔵屋美香）を行った日本館が特別表彰受賞

國府理《水中エンジン》「國府理　未来のいえ」展、西宮市大谷記念美術館（兵庫）

^{DOM}MUNE 個展「YCAMDOMMUNE」DOMMUNE ビル、山口情報芸術センター（YCAM）　**7月**

「「在日」は必要だった。」展、朝鮮大学校美術科（東京）

あいちトリエンナーレ 2013「揺れる大地──われわれはどこに立っているのか：場所、記憶、そして復活」（芸術監督：五十嵐太郎）　**8月**

山口晃『ヘンな日本美術史』（祥伝社、2012 年）が小林秀雄賞を受賞

^{contact}Gonzo 展示・パフォーマンス公演《hey you, ask the animals. ／テリトリー、気配、そして動作についての考察》
「アートと環境の未来・山口 YCAM 10 周年記念祭」元・山口県 21 世紀の森

東北画は可能か？ 個展「東北画は可能か？〜まなざしの解放〜」ARTZONE（京都）

2020 東京五輪の開催決定　**9月**

^{GEI}SAI GEISAI#19、都立産業貿易センター台東館（東京）

台風 26 号による伊豆大島土石流（死 36 人、不明 3 人、負 22 人）　**10月**

「絶命展〜ファッションの秘境」パルコミュージアム（東京）

アーツ前橋開館

^{IDEAL}COPY《Money（kyoto）》「公私混同のかたち」展、HAPS（京都）

^{DIVINA}COMMEDIA《sky/sea》「out of place」展、旧嵯峨御所大本山大覚寺（京都）

東北画は可能か？ 個展「東北画は可能か？」リアス・アーク美術館（宮城）

「武蔵美×朝鮮大　この場所にいるということ」展、武蔵野美術大学（東京）

特定秘密保護法成立　**12月**

^{Chim↑}Pom 個展「広島 !!!!!」旧日本銀行広島支店

^{contact}Gonzo パフォーマンス公演「熊を殺すと雨が降る」
（contact Gonzo ×ホンマタカシ）、AI・HALL（兵庫）

梅津庸一が画塾「パープルーム予備校」を設立　──

2020 年東京五輪開催決定の瞬間
提供：共同通信社

平成 26 年

新しい骨董　グランギョョル未来　前田文化　わたしの穴 美術の穴　MaS(T)A

^{Chim↑}Pom「Love Is Over」（エリイの結婚披露宴として行われたパーティ／デモ）、東京　**1月**

「Instagram」日本語版開始　**2月**

ギニアでエボラウイルス病の感染者確認、大流行へ　**3月**

消費税率 8％へ　**4月**

^{contact}Gonzo《黒い家》「六本木アートナイト 2014」展、六本木ヒルズ（東京）

^{contact}Gonzo「様々な困難を伴う作業の痕跡と音」展にて展示、山本現代（東京）

「在日・現在・美術」展、eitoeiko（東京）

「ヤンキー人類学」展（キュレーター：櫛野展正）、鞆の津ミュージアム（広島）

「國府理展 相対温室」展、青森公立大学国際芸術センター青森
作品の調整中、事故により國府理急逝

^{GEI}SAI GEISAI#20、東京流通センター　**5月**

^{カオス}ラウンジ ポストスーパーフラット・アートスクール設立

STAP 細胞論文不正疑惑による取り下げ　**7月**

地裁判決後の会見で「一部無罪」の紙を掲げるろくでなし子
提供：朝日新聞社

ろくでなし子がわいせつ物頒布等の疑いで逮捕。2016 年 5 月、東京地裁は展示作品に対しては無罪を、販売・頒布した作品
に対しては有罪の判決を下す。後者に対して被告側が最高裁に憲法違反として上告、2020 年 7 月に有罪判決を受けている

「グランギニョル未来」公演メインビジュアル
イラスト：ひらのりょう（FOGHORN）

第1回札幌国際芸術祭 2014（ゲストディレクター：坂本龍一）、北海道

8月 ▊広島土砂災害（死77人、負68人）▊

▊デング熱の感染者確認（日本で69年ぶり、160人が感染へ）▊

「これからの写真」展、愛知県美術館
鷹野隆大作品に撤去指導があり、作品の一部を隠す措置が取られる

飴屋法水「グランギニョル未来」公演（作：樅木野衣、共演：山川冬樹ほか）、
YCC ヨコハマ創造都市センター（神奈川）

contact Gonzo「Dance Moves the City」展にてパフォーマンス公演、Koka Riga（ラトビア）

9月 ▊御嶽山噴火（死58人、不明5人、負69人）▊

「反戦──来るべき戦争に抗うために」展（キュレーター：土屋誠一）、SNOW Contemporary（東京）

東北画は
可能か？「山形ビエンナーレ 2014」に参加、東北芸術工科大学 7F ギャラリー、研究棟ギャラリー

DOM
MUNE《THE 100 JAPANESE CONTEMPORARY ARTISTS》
「DOMMUNE University of the Arts-Tokyo Arts Circulation-」3331 Arts Chiyoda（東京）

10月「武蔵美×朝鮮大　孤独なアトリエ」展、武蔵野美術大学（東京）

11月「チームラボ　踊る！アート展と、学ぶ！未来の遊園地」展、日本科学未来館（東京）

「3.11 以後の建築」展、金沢 21 世紀美術館（石川）

パープル
ルーム 梅津庸一《智・感・情・A》「パープルーム大学II」展、熊本市現代美術館

飴屋法水『ブルーシート』（白水社）刊行
北川フラム『美術は地域をひらく──大地の芸術祭 10 の思想』（現代企画室）刊行

御嶽山噴火 10人重体・重

突然、ドー　迫る灰
「ボウリング球大の噴石」

2014 年 9 月 28 日 朝日新聞 朝刊

平成 27 年

会田家　アメクラジ　ミルク倉庫＋田田田津々
Don't Follow the Wind　hanage　MES　Sabbatical Company

1月 IS による日本人の殺害が発覚

「表現の不自由展──消されたものたち」ギャラリー古藤（東京）

2月 GEI
SAI「GEISAI ∞ infinity」プロジェクト開始、Zingaro（東京）。以降毎年開催

3月 ▊ブラジルでジカ熱の感染者確認、大流行へ▊

東京・渋谷区で同性パートナーシップ条例成立

第1回 PARASOPHIA　京都国際現代芸術祭（アーティスティックディレクター：河本信治）、京都市美術館ほか

「Don't Follow the Wind」展（立案者：Chim↑Pom）、東京電力福島第一原発事故に伴う帰還困難区域内（福島）、展示継続中。
出展作品に Chim↑Pom《青写真を描く》、グランギニョル未来《デミオ福島 501》ほか

4月 東芝の不正会計問題が発覚

「世界制作のプロトタイプ」展（キュレーター：上妻世海）、HIGURE 17-15 cas（東京）

DOM
MUNE 宇川直宏《DJ JOHN CAGE & THE 1000 WORLDWIDE DJS》、DOMMUNE《THE 100 JAPANESE
CONTEMPORARY ARTISTS》「われらの時代：ポスト工業化社会の美術」展、金沢 21 世紀美術館（石川）

5月 ▊口永良部島噴火で大火砕流（負1人）▊

東京国立近代美術館が所蔵作品展「MOMAT コレクション 特集：誰がためにたたかう？」で戦争記録画 12 点を一挙公開

「民意軽視の政治 問い続ける」

安保法 成立へ
海外で武力行使に道
自公 違憲批判押し切る

国会前やまぬ「反対」

「Apple Music」サービス開始 **6月**

東京五輪公式エンブレム模倣騒動 **7月**

「おとなもこどもも考える　ここはだれの場所?」展、東京都現代美術館
会田誠(会田家)作品に美術館が撤去要請を行い物議を醸す

contact Gonzo 「知らない都市──INSIDE OUT」展にて展示・パフォーマンス公演、京都精華大学ギャラリーフロール

パープルルーム 「パープルルーム大学物語」展、アラタニウラノ(東京)

Chim↑Pom 個展「耐え難きを耐え↑忍び難きを忍ぶ」Garter Gallery(東京) **8月**

DOMMUNE DOMMUNE UNIVERSITY OF THE ARTS「THE 100 JAPANESE CONTEMPORARY ARTISTS / season 3」展、山本現代(東京)

安全保障関連法(平和安全法制、通称「戦争法」)強行採決 **9月**

2015年9月19日 朝日新聞 朝刊

平成27年9月関東・東北豪雨(死20人、負82人)

「Netflix」日本で配信開始

新国立競技場国際デザイン・コンクールの再コンペ実施(没案:ザハ・ハディド)

DOMMUNE スタジオが集中豪雨により浸水被害を受ける

カオス*ラウンジ 「カオス*ラウンジ新芸術祭2015市街劇「怒りの日」」もりたか屋ほか2会場(福島)

DIVINA COMMEDIA 《Forbidden Colours》「out of place」展、旧嵯峨御所大本山大覚寺(京都) **10月**

contact Gonzo パフォーマンス公演《訓練されていない素人のための振付コンセプト001》「Who Dance?　振付のアクチュアリティ」展、早稲田大学演劇博物館(東京)

パリ同時多発テロ **11月**

東北画は可能か? 個展「東北画は可能か?-地方之国構想博物館-」東京都美術館

突然、目の前がひらけて 「武蔵美×朝鮮大　突然、目の前がひらけて」展、武蔵野美術大学、朝鮮大学校(東京)

contact Gonzo 「HUGO BOSS ASIA ART 2015」にてパフォーマンス公演 **12月**
(写真家・西光祐輔とのコラボレーション)、Rockbund Art Museum
(上海外灘美術館)(中国)

DOMMUNE 「DOMMUNE TAKAMATSU!」
(ゼネラルディレクター、キュレーター、審査委員長:宇川直宏)、高松メディアアート祭、香川

椹木野衣『アウトサイダー・アート入門』(幻冬舎)刊行
椹木野衣『後美術論』(美術出版社)刊行

当初のコンペで選ばれたザハ・ハディドのデザイン案
提供:Zaha Hadid Architects

チームラボ《Nirvana》2013年
「チームラボ　踊る!アート展と、学ぶ!未来の遊園地」
展の展示風景、2014年

2016
平成28年

カオス*ラウンジ INSIDE OUT 牛人の耕平 山形藝術界隈 CANCER
THE COPY TRAVELERS THE EUGENE Studio THE TETORAPOTZ

日本銀行、マイナス金利政策導入を決定 **1月**

マイナンバー制度開始

シャープ、ホンハイ(台湾)への傘下入りが決定 **2月**

北海道新幹線開業 **3月**

「MOTアニュアル2016　キセイノセイキ」展、東京都現代美術館
複数の作品・資料が展示されず、会場の一部が「もぬけの殻」状態となる

藤井光《爆撃の記録》2016年
「MOTアニュアル2016　キセイノセイキ」展の展示風景
撮影:椹木静寧

2016 年 4 月 15 日 朝日新聞 朝刊

4月　**熊本地震**（M7.3、死 273 人、負 2,809 人）

「小泉明郎　空気」展、無人島プロダクション（東京）

「生誕 300 年記念 若冲展」東京都美術館
一大ブームを巻き起こし、入場者数は 44 万 6,242 人を記録した

クシノ
テラス↑　クシノテラス設立、「極限芸術 2 〜死刑囚は描く〜」展

5月　オバマ大統領、広島を訪問

DOM
MUNE　DOMMUNE UNIVERSITY OF THE ARTS「THE 100 JAPANESE
CONTEMPORARY ARTISTS / season 4」山本現代（東京）

AI 美
芸研　「人工知能美学芸術研究会」発足

6月　英国、国民投票で EU 離脱を決定

contact
Gonzo　野外彫刻フェス「Sonsbeek 2016」にてパフォーマンス公演、オランダ

7月　「ポケモン GO」リリース

参議院選挙で改憲勢力が 3 分の 2 を突破

相模原障害者施設殺傷事件

『シン・ゴジラ』（総監督：庵野秀明、監督：樋口真嗣）公開

美術評論家連盟 2016 年度シンポジウム「美術と表現の自由」東京都美術館

Chim↑
Pom　「U.S.A. Visitor Center」プロジェクト、メキシコ

「在日・現在・美術 II」展、eitoeiko（東京）

8月　天皇が退位の意向を表明

「岡﨑乾二郎の認識　抽象の力」展の
展示風景、2017 年
撮影：青木兼治
提供：豊田市美術館

9月　第 1 回 さいたまトリエンナーレ 2016（ディレクター：芹沢高志）

第 1 回 KENPOKU ART 2016 茨城県北芸術祭（総合ディレクター：南條史生）

Chim↑
Pom　《パビリオン》「釜山ビエンナーレ 2016 Project 1 an/other avant-garde china-japan-korea」
（日本側キュレーター：楢木野衣ら）、韓国

東北画は
可能か？↑　《辿望楼（てんぼうろう）》「みちのおくの芸術祭 山形ビエンナーレ 2016」東北芸術工科大学芸術実習棟

DOM
MUNE　アルスエレクトロニカ（オーストリア）にサテライトスタジオを開設

10月　第 1 回岡山芸術交流 2016（アーティスティックディレクター：リアム・ギリック）

「THE PLAY since 1967　まだ見ぬ流れの彼方へ」展、国立国際美術館（大阪）

Chim↑
Pom　《ビルバーガー》ほか、「また明日も観てくれるかな？」展、歌舞伎町商店街振興組合ビル（東京）

contact
Gonzo　《伊吹島ドリフト伝説》瀬戸内国際芸術祭 2016、伊吹島（香川）

東北画は
可能か？↑　《方舟計画》《しきおり絵詞》「つくることは生きること――震災《明日の神話》」展、川崎市岡本太郎美術館（神奈川）

クシノ
テラス↑　「遅咲きレボリューション！」展、クシノテラス（広島）

11月　「パリ協定」で 2020 年以降の地球温暖化対策のための新たな枠組み発効

「目 in BEPPU」（総合プロデューサー：山出淳也）、大分市役所

パープル
ルーム↑　「ゲルゲル祭 2016」パープルームプーポンボン（神奈川）

12月　「震災と暮らし――震災遺産と人びとの記録からふりかえる」展、せんだいメディアテーク（宮城）

contact
Gonzo　パフォーマンス公演「ゴンゾ解體新書」咲くやこの花芸術祭 2016、大阪市中央公会堂

－　國府理「水中エ
ンジン」再制
作プロジェクト　「水中エンジン」再制作プロジェクトが始動

東浩紀編『ゲンロン 3 脱戦後日本美術』（ゲンロン）刊行
荒木慎也『石膏デッサンの 100 年――石膏像から学ぶ美術教育史』（三重大学出版会）刊行
藤田直哉『地域アート＝ Community-engaged art project：美学 / 制度 / 日本』（堀之内出版）刊行

米国でドナルド・トランプが大統領に就任　**1 月**

「Instagram Live」運用開始

森友学園問題　**2 月**

「パロディ、二重の声——日本の一九七〇年代前後左右」展、東京ステーションギャラリー

^{contact}^{Gonzo} 個展「コンタクトゴンゾ展 フィジカ・トピア」ワタリウム美術館（東京）

^{クシノ}^{テラス} クシノテラス×ギャラリー・マルヒ合同企画「空想キングダム」展、ギャラリー・マルヒほか（東京）

「岡﨑乾二郎の認識　抽象の力—現実（concrete）展開する、抽象芸術の系譜」展、豊田市美術館（愛知）　**4 月**

^{クシノ}^{テラス} 「性欲スクランブル」展、クシノテラス（広島）

^{國府理「水中エ}^{ンジン」再制}^{作プロジェクト} 國府理《水中エンジン（再制作）》「裏声で歌へ」展、小山市立車屋美術館（栃木）

第 1 回北アルプス国際芸術祭 2017（総合ディレクター：北川フラム）、長野　**6 月**

^{パープル}^{ルーム} 個展「恋せよ乙女！ パープルーム大学と梅津庸一の構想画」ワタリウム美術館（東京）

^{突然、目の前}^{がひらけて} 第 6 回 都美セレクション「境界を跨ぐと、」展、東京都美術館

北朝鮮による ICBM 発射実験　**7 月**

九州北部豪雨（死 42 人、不明 2 人、負 39 人）

第 1 回 Reborn-Art Festival 2017（実行委員長：小林武史）、宮城

^{Chim↑}^{Pom} 「Sukurappu ando Birudo プロジェクト 道が拓ける」キタコレビル（東京）

^{東北画は}^{可能か？} 個展「東北画は可能か？　地方の国構想博物館」
鶴岡アートフォーラム（山形）、同会場では「三瀬夏之介個展——日本の絵」も同時開催

^{國府理「水中エ}^{ンジン」再制}^{作プロジェクト} 「國府理 水中エンジン redux」展、アートスペース虹（京都）

^{DOM-}^{MUNE} DOMMUNE UNIVERSITY OF THE ARTS「THE 100 JAPANESE CONTEMPORARY ARTISTS / season 5」　**8 月**
札幌国際芸術祭 2017（ゲストディレクター：大友良英）、北海道

「TikTok」国際版リリース　**9 月**

「Reborn-Art Festival 2017」
ポスタービジュアル

日産自動車、完成車試験で不正発覚、他社でも

第 1 回奥能登国際芸術祭 2017（総合ディレクター：北川フラム）、石川

^{Chim↑}^{Pom} 《道（Street）》6th Asian Art Biennial 2017、国立台湾美術館

^{contact}^{Gonzo} 「RAM HIGHLIGHT 2017: DISPLACE」展にてパフォーマンス公演、
Rockbund Art Museum（上海外灘美術館）（中国）

^{東北画は}^{可能か？} 個展「TOHOKU CALLING」3331 Arts Chiyoda（東京）

衆議院選挙で自民圧勝、民進分裂　**10 月**

^{國府理「水中エ}^{ンジン」再制}^{作プロジェクト} シンポジウム「過去の現在の未来 2　キュレーションとコンサベーション　**11 月**
その原理と倫理」関連展示、兵庫県立美術館

^{AI 美}^{芸研} 「人工知能美学芸術展」沖縄科学技術大学院大学

^{DIVINA}^{COMMEDIA} 《winter solstice》「out of place 2017」展、旧嵯峨御所大本山大覚寺（京都）　**12 月**

^{カオス*}^{ラウンジ} 「カオス*ラウンジ新芸術祭 2017 市街劇「百五〇年の孤独」」zitti ほか、泉駅周辺の複数会場（福島）

^{國府理「水中エ}^{ンジン」再制}^{作プロジェクト} 再制作のエンジン 1 台目（3 号機）を國府家の庭に埋める

椹木野衣『震美術論』（美術出版社）刊行

椹木野衣『震美術論』

2018 平成 30 年

（しんかぞく）

3 月 48 年ぶりに岡本太郎《太陽の塔》(1970 年、万博記念公園)
内部の一般公開を開始

contact Gonzo パフォーマンス公演《鹿を殺すと残る雪》
（ホンマタカシ×コンタクトゴンゾ）、京都芸術センター

5 月 コンゴ民主共和国でエボラウイルス病の感染者確認、大流行へ

宇佐美圭司による巨大絵画《きずな》(1977 年、東京大学中央食堂)
の廃棄について、東京大学消費生活協同組合が謝罪文を発表

東北画は可能か？《the gleeman》「Multi Layered Surfaces」展、NICA（東京）

6 月 初の米朝首脳会談

大阪府北部地震（M6.1、死 6 人、負 462 人）

contact Gonzo 「im/pulse: 脈動する映像」展にて展示・パフォーマンス公演、
京都市立芸術大学ギャラリー @KCUA

7 月 松本智津夫らオウム真理教関係者 13 人死刑執行

西日本豪雨（7 月豪雨）（死 263 人、不明 8 人、負 490 人）

「起点としての 80 年代」展、金沢 21 世紀美術館ほか

「没後 50 年 藤田嗣治展」東京都美術館ほか

クシノ テラス S-HOUSE ミュージアム×クシノテラス合同企画展
「越境するミュージアム」クシノテラス（広島）、S-HOUSE MUSEUM（岡山）

8 月 パープル ルーム パープルームギャラリーオープン

9 月 台風 21 号（死 14 人、負 980 人）

平成 30 年北海道胆振東部地震（M6.7、死 43 人、負 782 人）

復興の象徴として JR 福島駅近くに設置されたヤノベケンジの立体作品で、防護服を着た子どもの像
《サン・チャイルド》が、原発事故の風評被害などを懸念した市民からの強い批判を受け撤去される

東北画は可能か？ 山形ビエンナーレ 2018「山のような 100 ものがたり」展
（キュレーター：三瀬夏之介、宮本晶朗）、東北芸術工科大学キャンパス

10 月 東京・豊洲市場開場

朝鮮人元徴用工問題を発端に日韓関係悪化

Chim↑Pom 《ビルバーガー》「にんげんレストラン」展、旧歌舞伎町ブックセンタービル（東京）

DOM MUNE 「SADOMMUNE」さどの島銀河芸術祭、新潟

11 月 日産自動車会長のカルロス・ゴーンを金融商品取引法違反の疑いで逮捕

2025 年国際博覧会の開催地が大阪に決定

「ニュー・ウェイブ　現代美術の 80 年代」展、国立国際美術館（大阪）

Chim↑Pom 個展「グランドオープン」ANOMALY（東京）

パープル ルーム 「パープルタウンでパープリズム」展、パープルーム予備校ほか全 6 会場（神奈川）

12 月 「バブルラップ：「もの派」があって、その後のアートムーブメントはいきなり「スーパーフラッ
ト」になっちゃうのだが、その間、つまりバブルの頃って、まだネーミングされてなくて、其
処を「バブルラップ」って呼称するといろいろしっくりくると思います。特に陶芸の世界も合体
するとわかりやすいので、その辺を村上隆のコレクションを展示したりして考察します。」展
（キュレーター：村上隆）、熊本市現代美術館

— 2012 年以降急増していた訪日外国人旅行者の数が 3,000 万人の大台を突破

岡﨑乾二郎『抽象の力——近代芸術の解析』（亜紀書房）刊行
小田原のどか編著『彫刻 SCULPTURE 1——空白の時代、戦時の彫刻／この国の彫刻のはじまりへ』（トポフィル）刊行

岡本太郎《太陽の塔》内部
提供：大阪府

2018 年 9 月 7 日 朝日新聞 朝刊

「Oh！マツリ☆ゴト　昭和・平成のヒーロー＆ピーポー」展フライヤー

米司法省、中国通信機器大手「華為技術(ファーウェイ)」と同社 CFO を起訴　**1 月**

「Oh！マツリ☆ゴト　昭和・平成のヒーロー＆ピーポー」展、兵庫県立美術館

contact Gonzo　パフォーマンス公演「untitled session」トーキョーアーツアンドスペース本郷（東京）

トランプ米大統領、メキシコ国境の壁建設費用確保のため国家非常事態を宣言　**2 月**

「奇想の系譜展　江戸絵画ミラクルワールド」展、東京都美術館

パープルルーム　「オブジェを消す前に──松澤宥 1950–60 年代の知られざるドローイング」展、
パープルームギャラリー（神奈川）

マリナーズのイチロー選手が引退表明　**3 月**

フランス・ノートルダム大聖堂で大火災　**4 月**

「東京インディペンデント 2019」展、東京藝術大学大学美術館陳列館

東北画は可能か？「TOHOKU CALLING」展に参加、佐藤美術館（東京）

クシノテラス「櫛野展正のアウトサイド・ジャパン展」Gallery AaMo（東京）

「令和」改元、天皇即位　**5 月**

2019 年 5 月 1 日 朝日新聞 朝刊

2025 年大阪万博の開催が決まり
道頓堀で喜ぶ人たち
提供：朝日新聞社

AI 美芸研　個展「S 氏がもし AI 作曲家に代作させていたとしたら」The Container（東京）　**7 月**
2014 年に発覚した佐村河内守のゴーストライター事件を受けて企画

砥綿正之（DIVINA COMMEDIA）逝去　**11 月**

第 Ⅰ 部
３つの時代

Part Ⅰ ,
in Three Chapters

凡 例

・第Ⅰ部は平成年間における3つの時代区分に従い、3章立てで構成されている。参加作家は活動開始時期、もしくは結成時期に従って時系列に掲載した。ただし、その始まりにおいて時期（開始・結成年）を同じくするものについては、作家名の五十音順に従った。

・図版は基本的に過去の参考作品から構成されており、本展の出品作品は主に展示風景写真として本カタログのカバーに掲載した。なお、カバーの図版はミシン目に沿い、個々に切り取ったうえで本文中に貼り込める仕様になっている。

・作品情報は作品タイトル、制作年の順に記し、必要に応じて補足説明（作家のステートメントや作品の詳細など）を記した。

・上記以外の情報と図版未掲載の出品作品については、巻末の作品リストとフォトクレジット一覧に掲載した。

・作家・作品解説は以下が執筆した。
　［NM］野崎昌弘
　［IM］泉川真紀
　［TA］筒井彩
　［TT］土屋隆英

Notes

・Part I is divided into three sections, corresponding to the exhibition's division of the Heisei Period into three periods.

・Artists (art groups) are presented in chronological order based on the start of their career (or date of formation). Where a number of artists started at about the same time (year), they are ordered according to the Japanese phonetic order for their names.

・Catalogue illustrations mainly represent referential works. Exhibited works are mainly shown in installation views on the catalogue cover. The cover plates are perforated, allowing individual works to be separated and pasted alongside the text in the catalogue.

・Artwork data consists of each work's title and date of execution, accompanied where necessary by additional descriptions (such as an artist's statement or description of details of the work).

・Further information and information about exhibited works not included in the plates is given at the end of the catalogue in the List of Works or the Photo Credits.

・Artist profiles and commentaries on the works are written by Nozaki Masahiro ("NM"), Izumikawa Maki ("IM"), Tsutsui Aya ("TA"), and Tsuchiya Takahide ("TT").

第 1 章
う た か た の 時 代

1989年〜2001年、平成元年から平成13年

喜ばしき知恵(コラボ)

　1980年代もそろそろ終わりを迎えようかとする頃から、その直前までの美術の通例とはかけ離れた、個人の作家名（漢字）ではない、どちらかと言えばロック・バンドのような、素性の知れない奇妙な響きのカタカナ（英字）の名を冠した美術家の集団が目立つようになる。この傾向は、先んじて関西を中心に始まり、ついで東京でも複数、見られるようになった。前者については、それまでの禁欲的で観念的、造形主義的な現代美術の主勢力へのカウンターとして登場した、いわゆる「関西ニュー・ウェイブ」の快楽主義的、感覚的、領域侵犯的な流れを汲むものであったと考えられるが、名乗りが個人から集団へと変化したのは、既存の美術を逸脱する、さらに大きな地殻変動からの波及であったと考えられる。

　背景としては、そもそも関西ニュー・ウェイブという呼称自体が、同時期にイギリスを中心に、ロック・ミュージックにおける権威的な旧勢力を全面的に否定したパンク・ロック（当初はニューヨーク）から生まれた、さらに新しい波＝ニュー・ウェイブを連想させるように、ポピュラー音楽の分野における先端的かつ享楽主義的で、消費社会を武器とする対抗主義的な動向があったと言えるだろう。わかりやすく言えば「ひとりで汲々とせずバンドでもやろうぜ」ということで、実際この時期、バブル経済の勢いに乗って、日本でも第二次バンドブームと呼ばれるアマチュア・ロックバンドの大きな流行が見られた。具体的にはBOØWY、HOUND DOG、レベッカ、BUCK-TICK、プリンセス・プリンセスなどの名前が挙げられる。そして、大きな成功を収めたかれらのあとを追う者たちにとっての登竜門的な役割を果たしたテレビ番組に『三宅裕司のいかすバンド天国』（通称「イカ天」、TBSの深夜番組『平成名物TV』の一コーナー、1989年／平成元年2月〜1990年／平成2年12月）があった。

　これらの動向とこの時期に活発化し、今回出展しているグループを直に比較するのは無理があるが、Complesso Plastico（コンプレッソ・プラスティコ）の前身のひとつと考えられるロック・ユニットにPBC（パーフェクト・ボディ・コントロール）があり、イギリスのニュー・ウェイブ・バンド、ワイヤーに「アイデアル・コピー（The Ideal Copy）」（1987年／昭和62年）と題するアルバムが存在し、加えて、テクノクラートの飴屋法水が、もと唐十郎「状況劇場」で音響を担当していたことや、ダンテの『神曲』に由来するDIVINA COMMEDIA（ディヴィナ・コメディア）で、音楽・音響が従来の美術と比べて著しく大きな役割を果たしていたことは、決して偶然ではないだろう。こうして、平成の幕開けに美術の分野で集合的・集団的な美術の動きがにわかに始まった要因として、それまでは美術にとって周辺分野にすぎなかった音楽からの要素の混入があったものと思われる。

Chapter 1
The Bubbly Age

1989-2001 / Heisei 1-13
Auspicious Collaborations

From the end of 1980s, artist collectives started appearing, often sounding more like rock bands than art groups, with bizarre sounding names written in *katakana* (foreign word syllabary) or in the Roman alphabet, something completely outside of art world conventions, which had always very seriously written artist's individual names in Chinese logotype characters. This tendency began in Kansai, historical central-west Japan, then spread to manifest in multiple examples in Tokyo. The former were likely descended from the hedonistic, intuitive, and expansionary movement, the Kansai New Wave, which emerged as a kind of protest against what was then mainstream: ascetic, conceptual, and formalistic contemporary art. But the transformation of the artist's identity from individual to collective, and then an ambiguous one at that, was probably the effect of a larger shift from existing norms.

This Kansai New Wave was reminiscent of the musical New Wave of the 1970s and 80s, beginning with the punk rock movement in New York, traveling to the UK, completely upending rock authority by being edgier, more hedonistic and counter-cultural than the "rock gods" of the day, and conquering the hearts of the youth in the process. Simply put, these new collectives were "art bands" wanting to make it or break it with their friends, rather than aspiring to each be an art maestro in their own right. At the end of the 1980s many interesting musical acts were formed too. Bands with names like BOØWY, HOUND DOG, Rebecca, BUCK-TICK, and Princess Princess rode what the media called the 2nd Japanese band boom (after the 1st in the 70s). This led, in turn, to a TV program called Miyake Yuji's *Ikasu Band Tengoku* (Miyake Yuji's Cool Band Heaven) which served as a precursor to the "XX has got talent" TV shows today.

It's no coincidence that one of the previous incarnation of the artist group Complesso Plastico was a rock unit called PBC (Perfect Body Control), or that the UK new wave band Wire released an album called Ideal Copy (1987/Showa 62), and one exhibited artist group is called Ideal Copy, or that Technocrat's Ameya Norimizu used to be a sound man for Kara Juro's *Situation Theatre*, or that music and sound played an arguably greater role in the work of the art unit Divina Commedia than did traditional art. A contributing factor to the sudden emergence of these collectives in art at the start of the Heisei does seem to be some overflow from popular music, which had only been a peripheral influence before.

もうひとつ考えられるのは、やはり80年代初頭に現代思想の分野で始まった「ニュー・アカデミズム」の余波である。浅田彰や中沢新一といった「知のニュー・スター」を生み出し、旧来の大学中心のアカデミズムの重力から解放され、消費社会を闊歩する「たのしい知識」（ニーチェの「喜ばしき知恵」より）を標榜したこの動向は、自立した主体という考えの相対化を徹底しようとするポスト構造主義や、近代の終わりを前提とするポストモダンとも深く結びつき、自立（自律）した作家・作品という概念を解体し、めまぐるしく流動する関係性のなかに、資本主義の加速化を見据えた「闘争から逃走へ」の活路を見ようとした。こうした背景のなかから、いわゆる分野やジャンルを超えた領域横断性、マルチタレント性、ユニット、コラボ（コラボレーション）での活動などが、バブルによって極限まで活性化した経済活動に勢いを得て、各種メディアを中心に盛んに試みられたことも、この時期の美術の集合的・集団的動向の増加と無縁ではないだろう。

　とはいえ、平成の始まりとは、日本ではいまだネットや携帯電話は一般にはとても手が届かぬ夢のような存在で、格安航空会社はまだまだ遠い未来の話で、ファクスやワープロ（せいぜいがパソコン通信）が私的な先端技術であったような時代のなかでは、海外と国内との情報格差はいまとは比べものにならないほどかけ離れており、これだけ情報環境が整った現在でも、この時期のこうした活動の詳細を調べようとすると、記録や記憶媒体のアナログからデジタルへの移行期ゆえ、ネットからもこぼれて落ち、その実体はなかなか見えてこない。わずかに残されたミニコミやファクス通信などが、その具体的な証左を伝えるのみであって、今回の展示でも、残されたパーツや記憶、写真（本展／本書のタイトルに倣ってあえて言えば残骸、瓦礫＝デブリ）からの再構成が中心となった。

　ここに示した動向は、その後、二度の社会的インパクトによって、大きく後退する。ひとつは、1990年／平成2年に起きたバブル経済の崩壊であり、もうひとつは、1995年／平成7年に首都、東京で起きた、オウム真理教の一部信徒による化学兵器サリンを使った大規模な無差別テロ事件である。前者は、社会を広く包んでいた楽観的で快楽主義的な気分を支えた経済的な後ろ盾を一気に崩壊させ、社会は次第に暗く重苦しい空気に覆われていく。また後者では路上や街頭でのセキュリティ意識が急激に高まり、集団的で不審な行動への警戒が自明のものとなって、社会の隅々までもが可視化される監視社会へと移行していく端緒となった。

（椹木野衣）

Another possible factor is the influence of "new academism," a literary movement which began in early 80s contemporary philosophy, and gave birth to new public intellectual stars including Asada Akira and Nakazawa Shin-ichi, both of whom urged a liberation from the strictures of the academies, in favor of "*the Gay Science*" (Nietzsche) of pop consumer literacy. Born out of a post-structuralist exhortation to put a rift between the discourse and the objects of discourse, and post-modernism, the new academics sought to dismantle the concept of the independent (autonomous) auteur and/or their artwork, and to feed the "from fight to flight" impulses within the ever-accelerating flux of relationships implicit in late-stage capitalism. Thus, cross-disciplinary, multi-talented "units," and collaborations which transcended fields and genres gained momentum, were often celebrated in the media… all on the stage of the overheating Japanese asset price bubble economy: all limits were off.

And yet, the beginning of the Heisei was years before the Internet or smart phones played a part in cultural discourse. Discount airlines were a remote future. The most advanced technologies in common use were the fax machine and dedicated word processing electric typewriter (or for some advanced people, early personal computer ftp telecommunications, at best). The information disparity between the West and Japan was huge. Even today, with such a rich information environment in place, it's hard to obtain substantial reference materials for this period, because it was still a transitional period from analog to digital storage media. In this exhibition the main body of evidence was reconstituted from fragments, memories, photographs (wreckage and debris to borrow from the exhibition/catalogue title) of the few remaining zines and faxes which we were able to uncover.

This movement later suffered setbacks due to two social impacts. The first was the collapse of the asset price bubble economy in 1990/Heisei 2. The second was the Tokyo subway sarin attack, a mass terrorist act perpetrated by Aum Shinrikyo cult members on the Tokyo subways in 1995/Heisei 7. The former collapsed and swallowed the economic backing which had sustained Japan's arguably hedonistic optimism, drawing society down to a darker, heavier mood. The latter quickly raised security awareness in public spaces, making precautions about collective and suspicious behavior common, prefacing the transition towards today's surveillance society.

(Sawaragi Noi)

Complesso Plastico

1987 – 1995 Showa 62-Heisei 7　大阪、東京 | Osaka, Tokyo

Love and Gold
「メタリズム」展の展示風景、スパイラル（東京）、1989 年

Love and Gold
Installation view of *Metalythm*, SPIRAL, Tokyo, 1989

Complesso Plastico

平野治朗（1963– ）と松蔭浩之（1965– ）が大阪芸術大学在学中の 1987 年に結成。ユニット名はイタリアの未来派のバッラやデペロが提唱した新しい芸術である「造形複合体」に由来する。1980年代、「西高東低」と言われていた現代美術シーンのなかで、「関西ニュー・ウェイブ」のもっとも若い世代の一翼として大阪、京都で注目を集める。1989 年には東京に進出し、1990 年には第44 回ヴェネツィア・ビエンナーレのアペルト部門に招聘され話題を呼んだ。ヴェネツィアから帰国した後は、ユニットは継続するも、多忙ゆえに1995 年には解散した。その後も二人はそれぞれ活動を続け、日本の現代美術シーンで継続的な影響力を発揮しつつ現在に至る。

Complesso Plastico

Complesso Plastico was formed by Hirano Jiro (1963–) and Matsukage Hiroyuki (1965–) in 1987 while both were students at Osaka University of Arts. The name derives from the *complesso plastico* (plastic assemblage) art advocated by Italian futurists Giacomo Balla and Fortunato Depero. They gained a reputation in Osaka and Kyoto as part of the youngest generation of the 1980s "Kansai New Wave" artists at a time when the contemporary art scene in Kansai was said to be more dynamic than that of the Tokyo area. They moved to Tokyo in 1989, and made the news the following year when they were invited to present in *Aperto '90* at the 44th Venice Biennale. The unit continued to function after their return from Venice, but eventually broke up in 1995. Hirano and Matsukage continued separate artistic careers, and they remain influential members of Japan's contemporary art scene today.

[上 | above]
愛と黄金
ギャラリー白（大阪）での展示風景、1988 年

Love and Gold
Installation view at GALLERY HAKU, Osaka, 1988

[中央 | right]
Live Together
天野画廊（大阪）での展示風景、1988 年

Live Together
Installation view at Amano Gallery, Osaka, 1988

[下 | below]
Everybody knows NEW LIFE
「脱走する写真―11 の新しい表現―」展の展示風景、
水戸芸術館（茨城）、1990 年

Everybody knows NEW LIFE
Installation view of *Beyond the Photographic Frame
-11 Recent Works-*, Art Tower Mito, Ibaraki, 1990

Love and Gold
「メタリズム」展の展示風景、
スパイラル（東京）、1989 年

Love and Gold
Installation view of *Metalythm*,
SPIRAL, Tokyo, 1989

バブル経済の影響が現代アートにも及んでいた 1980 年代後半は、演劇、音楽その他のジャンルとともに、研ぎ澄まされた感性や、洗練と過激さが表現に強く求められる傾向があったと言えるだろう。そうした先鋭的なオーディエンスの期待を背景にデビューした二人は、当時最新のスタイルだった映像インスタレーションによる作品《Love and Gold》(1988 年 −)を制作・発表した。映像にはポスト・インダストリアルやノイズなどの音源をサンプリング、リミックスして被せ、キッチュでポップな造花の薔薇や十字架などを用いながら、「ギリシャの求道僧を模倣して現世に歯向かう二人の異形のセルフポートレイト」* を配置するなどして、ある種のディストピアの風景を世紀末を迎える都市のなかで繰り広げて見せた。

かれらのデビュー作でもある《Love and Gold》は、大阪バージョン(個展「愛と黄金」ギャラリー白［大阪］、1988 年)以降、スパイラルでの東京バージョン(2 人展「メタリズム」1989 年)、ヴェネツィア・ビエンナーレでの《Love and Gold/Amore e Oro》(1990 年)まで、内容を変えながら続いた初期の代表作である。

本展でのインスタレーション作品は《C + P 2020》(2020 年)と名付けられ、《Love and Gold》東京バージョンの写真を背景に、十字架形テレビモニターを再制作し、他に《Everybody knows NEW LIFE》(「脱走する写真─11 の新しい表現─」展、水戸芸術館［茨城］、1990 年)などの要素を組み込んだものとしておよそ 30 年振りに再構成される。[NM]

* 2020 年 10 月に本展カタログのために実施した松蔭浩之氏へのインタビュー。

In the second half of the 1980s, Japan's bubble economy brought a boost to contemporary art, along with theater, music, and other genres. It was a time when audiences of art refined their ideas and styles, and expectations were growing for a more sophisticated, more radical art scene. Consequently, audiences were already tuned in when Complesso Plastico debuted, producing and presenting *Love and Gold* (1988–), a video installation work in line with the latest styles. The video had a soundtrack including remixes of sampled noise and post-industrial sound sources, along with colorful, kitsch artificial roses and crosses. Including items such as "unorthodox self-portraits of the two artists rejecting the temporal world as Greek novice monks,"* the installation depicted some sort of dystopian scene in a city approaching the end of the century.

Complesso Plastico's debut work *Love and Gold* became representative of the unit's early period, and was created in a number of versions with varying content: an Osaka version (solo exhibition of *Love and Gold* at Gallery HAKU, Osaka, 1988), a Tokyo version (two-person exhibition *Metalythm* at Spiral in Aoyama, 1989), and a Venice Biennale version (*Love and Gold/Amore e Oro*, 1990).

The installation for *Bubbles/Debris* is *C+P 2020* (2020). It uses photographs of the *Love and Gold* Tokyo version as a background, recreating the cruciform TV monitors, and combined with other elements from works including *Everybody knows NEW LIFE* (*Beyond the Photographic Frame -11 Recent Work*s- at Contemporary Art Gallery, Art Tower Mito, Ibaraki, 1990). This combination of elements is the first new configuration in about thirty years. [NM]

* Interview with Mr. Matsukage Hiroyuki for exhibition catalogue in October 2020.

1

本書カバーを切り取り該当する図版をお貼りください

Please detach the corresponding plate from the cover and paste it here.

「平成美術：うたかたと瓦礫 1989−2019」展示風景
京都市京セラ美術館、2021 年

Installation view of *Bubbles/Debris: Art of the Heisei Period 1989–2019*
Kyoto City KYOCERA Museum of Art, 2021

IDEAL COPY

1988 Showa 63 — 京都 | Kyoto

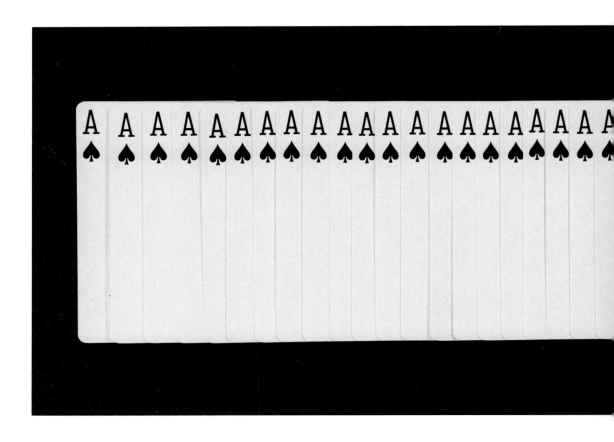

IDEAL COPY

匿名かつ流動的なメンバー構成を 30 年以上にわた
り継続しているアーティストの集まり。それぞれが
専門的なスキルを持つが、それが必ずしも IDEAL
COPY で求められるかれらの役割ではないという。
1988 年、ギャラリー射手座（京都）での作品発表を
皮切りに、東京都写真美術館での個展「Channel:
Documents」（1997 年）、フランスのパリ国立高等美
術学校で開催された「Donai yanen!」展（1998 年）
への参加など、90 年代後半までダムタイプなどと並
び、関西の若手アーティストの代表格として国内外の
展覧会へ数多く招聘された。某有名クリエイターが、
ビートルズや YMO とともに IDEAL COPY に影響を
受けたというエピソードも残る*。かれらのプロジェ
クト名（個展タイトルと作品名を兼ねる）は、《Channel:
Mode》、《Channel: Merchandise》、《Channel:
Documents》など、思考のチャンネルを切り替える
イメージでタイトルが付けられており、コロン（：）
のあとに続くワードは、かれらがターゲットとした
「社会のシステム」を表している。

* 椹木野衣『22 世紀芸術家探訪』エスクァイアマガジンジャパ
ン、1999 年。

IDEAL COPY

Ideal Copy is a group of artists that has remained active for
over 30 years, with an anonymous and fluid membership.
Apparently, each member has his or her own specialist skills,
but those skills are not necessarily relevant to the role that
Ideal Copy expects them to perform. The group's first work
was presented in 1988 at Gallery Iteza (Kyoto). In the late 1990s,
Ideal Copy, like Dumb Type, was seen as representative of
young artists in Kansai and was in demand for presentations
at exhibitions around Japan and internationally, including a
solo exhibition *Channel: Documents* at Tokyo Photographic Art
Museum (1997), and participation in the *Donai yanen!* exhibition
at the École nationale supérieure des beaux-arts in Paris (1998).
One well-known Japanese creator even listed Ideal Copy along
with the Beatles and YMO as a key influence.* The group's
project names (which also function as solo exhibition names and
the names of their works) begin with "Channel:" —*Channel: Mode,
Channel: Merchandise, Channel: Documents,* etc.—maybe to
mark the switch between thought channels. The word after the
colon indicates the social system that the project is targeting.

* Sawaragi Noi, "22nd Century Artist Visit," *Esquire Magazine Japan*, 1999.

トランプは52枚で1セットである。トランプ52セットから、たとえば「スペードのエース」を52枚、「ハートの2」を52枚というような同じマーク・同じ数字のセットがつくられ、プロジェクターにて投射される。その一枚一枚はまぎれもなく「トランプ」のカードなのだが、同じマークと同じ数字からなる52枚のカードのセットはその機能を失っていることからもはや「トランプ」とは呼べないとも言える。

A deck (set) of playing cards contains 52 cards. Taking 52 decks, the cards are rearranged into decks where each card is the same, having the same suit and the same rank: a deck of 52 Ace of Spades cards, a set of Two of Hearts cards, etc. These rearranged decks are displayed using a projector. Each individual card in the deck is unambiguously a playing card, but as they all have the same rank and are all part of the same suit, the deck of cards has lost its function. In a sense, they can no longer be considered "playing cards."

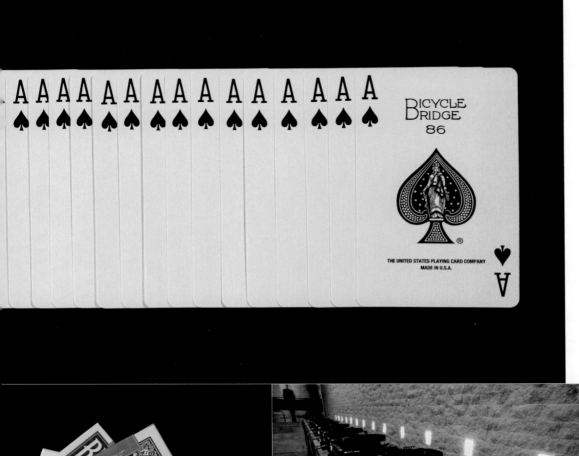

「観念の刻印」展の展示風景
栃木県立美術館、1990-1991年

Installation view of *The Imprinted Ideas*
Tochigi Prefectural Museum of Fine Arts, 1990-1991

Channel: Exchange
Channel: Exchange
1993-

IDEAL COPY は「両替所」を開設する。
IDEAL COPY は広く一般に呼びかけ、
個人が所有する外国硬貨を IDEAL COPY コインと交換する。
IDEAL COPY コインは、1IC/10IC/100IC の3種類がある。
交換レートは、外国硬貨 1 グラム＝1IC である。
このように交換された外国硬貨は、オブジェとして会場に展示される。
このプロジェクトは、地球上のすべての外国硬貨が
IDEAL COPY コインに交換されるまで継続される。
「すべては美学と経済学に要約される」ステファヌ・マラルメ

IDEAL COPY will open an "exchange station"
and call out to the general public to gather all foreign coins.
Coins owned by individuals are available to be exchanged
for IDEAL COPY coins with the rate of 1gram of foreign coins=1 IC.
IDEAL COPY will issue three types of IC coins, 1 IC, 10 IC, 100 IC.
The foreign coins that are exchanged in this way
will be displayed at venues as an installation.
This project will continue until all foreign coins around the world
have been exchanged for IDEAL COPY coins.
"Everything is summed up in Aesthetics and Political Economy"
Stéphane Mallarmé

[左から 2、3、5番目｜2nd, 3rd, 5th from left]
Channel: Exchange
「芸術祭典・京」展の展示風景、元龍池小学校（京都）、1995 年
換金量総計＝ 8,368g

Channel: Exchange – Kyoto
Installation view of "Kyoto Arts Festival," Former Tatsuike Elementary School, Kyoto, 1995
Total amount of coins exchanged=8,368 grams

[左から 4 番目｜4th from left]
Channel: Exchange
「The Age of Anxiety」展の展示風景、
パワープラント（カナダ）、1994 年

Channel: Exchange
Installation view of *The Age of Anxiety*, The Power Plant, Canada, 1994

IDEAL COPY は現代美術を背景に活動するクリエイティヴ・プロジェクトとして 1988 年結成。
アーティストは「作品」と「社会のシステム」の中に存在する。
IDEAL COPY は現代社会の創作物である様々な「社会のシステム」をターゲットに既存の枠組みを
越えた活動を展開している。
IDEAL COPY はメディアを通してワールドワイドな展開の可能性を追求していく。
　　　　　　　　　——《Channel: Documents》にて表明された IDEAL COPY によるテキスト

　IDEAL COPY が何者であるかを問うことは無意味だろう。IDEAL COPY をとりあげるということは、
ある意味そのメンバーになったつもりでコミットすることが必要とされる。かれらがあらゆる解釈を拒む
ことを理解し、精巧な構想に寄り添う。あとは作品がそこにあるのみ。もし、ほんの少しでも何かが感じ
られたのであれば、鑑賞者もすでに IDEAL COPY のメンバーであると言えるかもしれない。
　本展に出品される《Channel: Peace Cards》（1990 年）は、トランプ・ゲームに必ずついてくる「勝
敗」を反故にする試みだ。かれらが得意とする、物そのものには何も「足さず」、機能のみを「引く」手
法を使ったものだが、「勝敗の反故」＝ Peace というタイトルは、それ以前も以後もかれらの作品には見
られない観念的なタイトルである。この作品が展示された 1990 年 11 月とは、かれらが生まれて初めて
戦争を身近に感じることとなったであろう、湾岸戦争勃発直前であったことを記しておきたい。
　もうひとつの作品《Channel: Exchange》（1993 年 –）は、1993 年 3 月から 2004 年まで国内外で繰
り返し展示された代表作である。「ワールドワイド（World Wide）」を掲げたかれらが、世界中どこでも
通じる単純なコンセプトを綿密に練り上げ、場所ごとに展示方法を変えた。日本で初めて World Wide
Web（URL につく小文字の www はこの略称）によるホームページが開設されたのは 1992 年 9 月。その半年
後に発表された作品である。[IM]

IDEAL COPY began its creative projects in 1988 and has been active in the contemporary art
world since then.
IDEAL COPY's projects are based on the belief that each artist exists within his or her "works" as
well as within various "social systems."
IDEAL COPY takes these various "social systems" as its target and aims to expand artistic activity
beyond established frameworks and definitions.
IDEAL COPY aims to expand its projects internationally through the media.
　　　　　　　　　—Text by Ideal Copy presented as part of *Channel: Documents*

It is probably meaningless to ask who Ideal Copy is. In a sense, taking an interest in Ideal Copy
requires the same sort of commitment as becoming a member. It requires an acceptance that the
artists reject any fixed interpretation, and a single-minded focus on their exquisite concept. Apart
from that, the work is everything. As a viewer, if you feel something in these works, however slight,
then perhaps you can already be considered an Ideal Copy member.
　Two works by Ideal Copy are included in *Bubbles/Debris. Channel: Peace Cards* (1990) attempts
to short-circuit the win-lose dynamic that is normally an inseparable part of games involving
playing cards. It exemplifies the group's methodology of subtracting functions from an object while
adding nothing, but it is their first and only use of a conceptual element ("peace") in the title. At the
time when this work was presented in November 1990, the Gulf War was about to erupt, and Japan
seemed to be closer to involvement in war than at any other time in the lives of the artists.
　The second exhibit is the group's best-known work, *Channel: Exchange* (1993–), which was first
exhibited in March 1993 and then presented at a number of Japanese and international venues up
until its most recent showing in 2004. The group's commitment to expanding its projects world-wide
led to the creation of simple concepts that would be understandable anywhere in the world, and
then only modifying the method of exhibition to create a site-specific version for each individual
venue. This world-wide focus can be seen in the fact that this work dates from only six months after
Japan's first page appeared on the World Wide Web (the "www" in internet addresses) in September
1992. [IM]

本書カバーを切り取り該当する図版をお貼りください

Please detach the corresponding plate from the cover and paste it here.

「平成美術：うたかたと瓦礫（デブリ）1989–2019」展示風景
京都市京セラ美術館、2021年

Installation view of *Bubbles/Debris: Art of the Heisei Period 1989–2019*
Kyoto City KYOCERA Museum of Art, 2021

テクノクラート TECHNOCRAT

1990–1996 Heisei 2-8　東京｜Tokyo

テクノクラート

1990 年に舞台出身の飴屋法水（1961–）、および石川成俊（機械製作担当、1965–）、中山大輔（後の中山ダイスケ、美術造形担当、1968–）の 3 名で結成された領域横断的なアートユニット。中心となる飴屋は、1980 年代に演劇界の若手の旗手として注目され、その後、「飴屋法水 × 三上晴子プロジェクト」（1987 年）、「M.M.M.」（1988–1989 年）といった演劇と美術が混淆する表現ユニットでの活動を経てテクノクラートに至る。結成から個展「WAR BAR」開催（246club［東京］、1990 年）までをテクノクラートの第 1 期とすると、その後の第 2 期ではメンバーも入れ替わり、「Dutch Life」シリーズ（1992–1995 年）他を矢継ぎ早に発表した。1995 年には同シリーズでヴェネツィア・ビエンナーレにも招聘された。同年、動物商として「動物堂」を立ち上げた飴屋は、メキシコでの菌のパフォーマンス（1996 年）を最後に「テクノクラート」名義での発表は行っていない。ただし、飴屋自身の中では、テクノクラートは活動休止のまま 1999年の「日本ゼロ年」展（水戸芸術館［茨城］）のころまで続いたという。

TECHNOCRAT

Technocrat was a cross-genre art unit formed in 1990 by performance artist Ameya Norimizu (1961–), along with Ishikawa Narutoshi (mechanical apparatus, 1965–) and Nakayama Daisuke (visual art, 1968–). Ameya was one of the leading young artists in Japanese theater in the 1980s, and before forming Technocrat, was active in projects that brought together theater and art, including Ameya Norimizu × Mikami Seiko project (1987) and projects by M.M.M. (1988–1989). Technocrat's first term includes its solo exhibition *WAR BAR* (246club, Aoyama, Tokyo) in 1990, which was followed by the start of a second term with new members, presenting new works in rapid succession, including its *Dutch Life* series (1992–1995). One of the works in this series was selected for presentation at the Venice Biennale in 1995. Then he started *Dobutsu-do* as an animal dealer in the same year, and *Virus* was performed in Mexico in 1996, the last time the Technocrat name was used. To Ameya, however, Technocrat was only taking a break. He thinks of it as remaining in existence until the *GROUND ZERO JAPAN* exhibition in 1999 (Contemporary Art Gallery, Art Tower Mito, Ibaraki).

WAR BAR
246club（東京）での展示風景、1990 年

WAR BAR
Installation view at 246club, Tokyo, 1990

Dutch Special 私もかわいいアライグマ
映像キャプチャー、1993 年
Dutch Special: I'm a Cute Raccoon, Too
Video Capture, 1993

Dutch Life Vol. 7 公衆精子計画
Dutch Life Vol. 7: PUBLIC SEMEN
「909 アノーマリー 2」展の展示風景、レントゲン藝術研究所（東京）、1995 年
Installation view of *909 ANOMALY 2*, Roentgen Kunst Institut, Tokyo, 1995

動物堂　　*Dobutsu-do*　　1995

Dutch Life vol. 5 セックス・アパルトヘイト
スパイラル（東京）での展示風景、1994 年
Dutch Life vol. 5: SEX APARTHEID
Installation view at SPIRAL, Tokyo, 1994

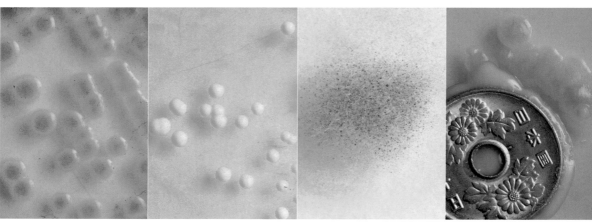

Dutch Special コロニー・イン・ザ・シティ　　*Dutch Special: Colony in the City*　　1993

丸いジャングル
「第5回メキシコ国際パフォーマンス・フェスティバル」、エクス・テレサ・
アルテ・オルテルナティバ（メキシコ）、1996年

Round Jungle
5th Festival Internacional de Performance, X Teresa Arte
Alternativo, Mexico, 1996

Dutch Life vol. 4 カミングアウト
レントゲン藝術研究所（東京）、1993年

Dutch Life vol. 4: COMING OUT
Roentgen Kunst Institut, Tokyo, 1993

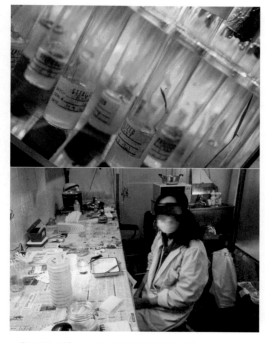

Dutch Life vol.1 コンタミネイテッド
レントゲン藝術研究所（東京）、1992年

Dutch Life vol.1: CONTAMINATED
Roentgen Kunst Institut, Tokyo, 1992

Dutch Special 入れ墨・輸血パフォーマンス
心斎橋ミューズホール（大阪）、1994年

Dutch Special: TATOO & BLOOD TRANSFUSION
PERFORMANCE
Shinsaibashi Muse Hall, Osaka, 1994

テクノクラートの最初の仕事は 1990 年に行った東京・青山のカフェバーの内装だった。カフェに展示する現代アートのインスタレーションを受注したのだが、その後、テクノクラートによる「WAR BAR」という個展の開催ということとなり、テクノロジーと経済と戦争をテーマにした異形のカフェバーとなった。ベルリンの壁崩壊からのちのソ連崩壊へと続く先行き不透明な世界情勢のなか、当時、国内はバブル経済に沸き、世紀末のディストピア感もがないまぜになった 1990 年代の幕開けを迎えていた。

スペース中央には対空ミサイルの砲塔（マシン 1）が据え付けられ、壁一面に積み上げられたモニターでは世界各国の戦争にまつわるニュース映像が放映され、株価ニュースが常に流れる電光掲示板も設置された。さらには回転する二つの椅子（マシン 2）を床面から 90 度立ち上げて設置し、それぞれにアメリカとソ連の国旗を背負わせて回転させた。

第 1 期テクノクラートはこの個展で区切りがつけられ、その後の第 2 期では、飴屋と医療従事者や医学や生物工学を専攻する学生らが協働するかたちで「Dutch Life」という作品シリーズが立ち上げられた。菌類、ウイルス、血液、精液などを用いた生物化学的な対象をテーマに、1992 年から 95 年までの足掛け 4 年間で vol. 1 から vol. 8 までの作品を展覧会などで次々と発表した。

テクノクラートは新自由主義が覆うグローバリズムのデッドエンドを見据えて、機械、戦争、株価、電子工学と情報の加速度的な流通をテーマにする一方で、前述のように体液や菌類、ウイルスの個別的かつグローバルな交換可能性をめぐる問いに取り組んでいた。

本展では、テクノクラートの活動の全容を示す「WAR BAR」、《Dutch Life》シリーズ の vols. 1–8、および《丸いジャングル》（1996 年）、さらには《インプリンツ・オブ・自分》（1999 年）までの記録映像が約 30 台のブラウン管モニターに映し出される。記録映像は、ほぼすべてが美術館では初公開の貴重な一次資料となる。これらに、《動物堂》（1995–2003 年）の資料を含む作品資料と作品パーツを加え、アーカイブ展示が構成される。タイトルは、《Dutch Lives》と名付けられた。[NM]

Technocrat's first project was the interior design and decoration of an Aoyama café-bar in 1990. The original request involved installation of contemporary art in the café, but the project soon turned into a solo exhibition by Technocrat, entitled *WAR BAR*, turning the venue into a highly unconventional café-bar with a technology, economy, and war theme. This was a time of geopolitical instability, with the Berlin Wall having already fallen, and the dissolution of the Soviet Union looking increasingly likely. In Japan, the economic bubble was going strong but at the start of the 1990s the euphoria was mixed with a sense of dystopia as the Millennium approached.

A surface-to-air missile turret (*Machine 1*) was placed in the center of the space, and monitors were stacked to cover a whole wall and show news footage from war zones around the world. There was also a constantly-updated electronic signboard displaying stock and share prices. In addition, two revolving chairs (*Machine 2*) were installed so as to rise from the floor through 90 degrees and rotate, one bearing a Soviet flag and the other an American flag.

This exhibition marked the end of Technocrat's first term. In its second term, Ameya collaborated with healthcare workers and with medicine and bioengineering students to produce the *Dutch Life* series. Working on bioscience themes and using materials such as fungi, viruses, blood, and semen, the collaboration resulted in exhibitions and other productions over a four-year period from 1992 to 1995, presenting its work as *Dutch Life Vol. 1* to *Vol. 8*.

Technocrat assumed that globalism cloaked in neoliberalism would be a dead end. In addition to taking up themes such as machinery, war, stock prices, electronic engineering, and the accelerating flow of information, it investigated issues involving bodily fluids, fungi, and viruses, both individually and in terms of global exchangeability.

For *Bubbles/Debris*, documentary footage of *WAR BAR*, *Dutch Life Vols. 1–8*, and projects from *Round Jungle* (1996), as far as *Imprints: 100 Questions to You* (1999), is displayed on about 30 CRT monitors. Most of this original video has never been presented in an art museum setting, and represents a valuable primary source of information. The footage is complemented by documentation, other materials, and parts of works relating to the projects shown, including materials of *Dobutsu-do* (1995–2003). Overall, this exhibit represents an archive of works of Technocrat and Ameya, and is titled *Dutch Lives*. [NM]

「平成美術：うたかたと瓦礫（デブリ） 1989－2019」展示風景
京都市京セラ美術館、2021年

Installation view of *Bubbles/Debris: Art of the Heisei Period 1989–2019*
Kyoto City KYOCERA Museum of Art, 2021

3

本書カバーを切り取り該当する図版をお貼りください

Please detach the corresponding plate from the cover and paste it here.

DIVINA COMMEDIA

1991 Heisei 3 — 京都、神戸 | Kyoto, Kobe

DIVINA COMMEDIA

1991 年、神戸のジーベックホールで行われたプロジェクト「DIVINA COMMEDIA」を機に作家活動をともに行うようになった砥綿正之（1959–2019）と松本泰章（1958– ）は、もとは京都市立芸術大学にて出会った同級生同士だった。当時、日本画から構想設計へと専攻を変更した砥綿の周辺には、森村泰昌が非常勤講師として写真を教え、石原友明、松井智恵、ダムタイプの古橋悌二など、ほどなく日本の美術界を賑わす学生が多く在籍し、その先端を肌で感じ取る環境にあった。一方、松本は油画専攻（フレスコ画）で、その文脈からはやや距離があったという。だが、二人のコラボレーションにキリスト教的なモチーフが多用されていることは、クリスチャンでもあった松本の影響であり、先端テクノロジーへの関心や哲学的な表現は、その分野を得意とした砥綿の影響であっただろう。日本のメディアアートの黎明期を担った二人である。

DIVINA COMMEDIA

Divina Commedia, presented at Xebec Hall (Kobe) in 1991, was the first project in the collaboration between Towata Masayuki (1959–2019) and Matsumoto Yasuaki (1958–). Towata and Matsumoto first met at Kyoto City University of Arts, where they were contemporaries. Towata originally majored in *nihonga*, but switched to the Concept and Media Planning class, where he joined artists such as Morimura Yasumasa, Ishihara Tomoaki, Matsui Chie, and Furuhashi Teiji, who within a few years were considered to be some of Japan's most exciting contemporary artists. Towata was part of that group, and the environment gave him a feel for the bleeding edge of contemporary art in Japan. In contrast, Matsumoto majored in oil painting (and studied frescoes), so he was further away from that context. In Towata and Matsumoto's collaborations, the abundant use of Christian motifs shows the influence of Matsumoto's Christianity, and the interest in advanced technology and the philosophical discourse probably come from Towata. Both artists played a significant part in the early days of media art in Japan.

DIVINA COMMEDIA
体験型インスタレーション、30分、神戸ジーベックホール

DIVINA COMMEDIA
Installation, 30 min. Xebec Hall, Kobe
1991

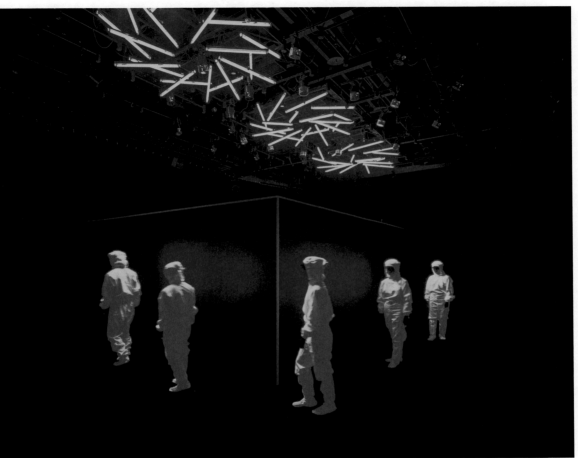

10トンのゼリーで満たされたプール、当時国内に24本しかなかった「データフラッシュ」（60回／秒点滅のストロボ）が24本、ブラックライト54本、防塵服、ドローン系電子音響（藤本由紀夫が制作に参加。ジーベックのスタジオでマルチトラック収録された）。各回5名限定で6日間の開催中に体験できたのはわずか250人。ディレクターとして巽直央、マネージメントとして続木東作が携わった。

Pool filled with 10 tons of jelly, 24 Dataflash strobes
(at a time when there were only 24 of these 60-flashes-
per-second strobes in Japan), 54 black light units, dust
protection suits, drone music (with Fujimoto Yukio,'
multitrack recording at the Xebec studio). Exhibited for
six days, only 250 people had the full experience (five
participants at a time). Tatsumi Naohiro participated as
director, and Tsuzuki Tosaku handled management.

照明プラン《DIVINA COMMEDIA》
ドローイング
Lighting plan, *DIVINA COMMEDIA*
Drawing
1991

axonometric *DIVINA COMMEDIA 1991*

アクソノメトリック《DIVINA COMMEDIA》
コラージュ
Axonometric, *DIVINA COMMEDIA*
Collage
1991

1980年代から90年代、アートにおいてもテクノロジーの進化は、表裏一体をなして「身体」に関する活発な議論を生み出した。《DIVINA COMMEDIA》の体験型展示は、まさにその表裏を扱う作品として当時の美術誌の表紙を飾ったりもしたが、体験者がわずか250人であったため、ほとんど伝説的な作品となった。タイトルは13世紀末のイタリアを舞台としたダンテの長編叙事詩『神曲』の原題である。本作は、そのモチーフである「地獄」「煉獄」「天国」という3つの「死への過程」を擬似体験させるための装置であった。登場人物ヴェルギリウスやベアトリーチェに手引きされて、ブラックライトに照らされた青いゼリーのプールに体を浮かべ、重力から解放される。大量のストロボ・ライトとドローン系電子音楽が徐々に増幅し、最終的には爆音と強烈な光に心身ともに曝される。体験というよりもむしろそのコメディア（劇）の演者となり、トリップとエクスタシーによって昇天することで「死と再生のビジョン」が提示されるのである。もとは湾岸戦争や核兵器が生む「MEGA DEATH」（大量死）を意識して、「ぼくたちは死をどう考えるか」を命題とする企画であったという。松本は、「30年を経た今、震災やコロナなど新たな「MEGA DEATH」の要因があるとは当時誰が思ったであろうか」と語っている*。

　阪神・淡路大震災で被災した松本は「その体験で一挙に眼前の幕が開き、幕の向こう（現実の先にあるもの）を模索するようになった」*と語り、2019年に惜しくも逝去した砥綿が死を目前にしたときの心境に思いを巡らす。死に直面するなか、「死のプラクシス」という副題を持つ本作の出展依頼を受けた砥綿の姿に、松本は、かれらがしばしば言及してきた『神曲』の挿絵を手掛けるボッティチェリの姿を重ね合わせる――「幾度も幾度も描き直し、線を重ねながら、ボッティチェリは天界の場面を描いた。その煩悶する手の跡が、なんと美しいことか」*と。本展では資料として唯一残された8分の記録映像を上映し、当時、実際に行われた展示に近い音響環境での鑑賞を目指す。[IM]

*2020年8月に本展カタログのために実施した作家へのインタビュー。

In the 1980s and 1990s, evolving technology led to fervent debate about the physical body, and art was no exception. The astonishing interactive presentation of Divina Commedia was predicated on this integration of body and technology, and it made the covers of art magazines. Only 250 people actually had the full experience of this work, so it gained an almost mythical status. The title is taken from the Italian title of Dante Alighieri's *Divine Comedy*, a long narrative poem set in Italy at the end of the 13th century. Towata and Matsumoto's Divina Commedia is a mechanism for providing a simulated experience, taking as its motifs the three stages of Dante's journey through death—Hell (Inferno), Purgatory, and Paradise. Participants are led by Virgil and Beatrice, the guides to the journey in Dante's poem, and float in a pool of blue jelly illuminated by black light, freed of the constraints of gravity. There are large numbers of strobes and drone music, which increase in strength and volume, until at the end, body and mind are assaulted by explosive noises and intense light. Rather than just experiencing all this, the participants become *commedia* performers, presenting a vision of death and rebirth, rising to heaven through trips and ecstasy. Towata and Matsumoto originally gave the project a working title of "MEGA DEATH," and focused on the question of "What do we think about death?" which was based on their concerns about the Gulf War and the threat of nuclear weapons. "At the time, no-one had any idea that thirty years later we would be facing new mega-death factors such as earthquakes and pandemics," reflects Matsumoto.*

　Matsumoto was in the disaster zone and directly affected when the Great Hanshin Earthquake hit in 1995. "That experience really opened up my eyes, and I began to explore what was beyond the curtain that had been removed (what lies beyond our current reality),"* he explained, before turning his thoughts to his feelings a few years ago when Towata was told that his life was coming to an end. Facing death himself, Towata received Sawaragi's request to exhibit *Divina Commedia*, which is subtitled *The Praxis of Death*. Matsumoto recollects that the sight of Towata receiving the request reminded him of Sandro Botticelli, who produced the illustrations for Divine Comedy and who Towata and Matsumoto had frequently discussed. Botticelli's drawings retain many traces of lines over lines. In those lines, Matsumoto had seen great beauty as well as Botticelli's anguish. and he also saw this beauty in Towata's last days.*
The exhibition screens an eight-minute documentary that is the only video of the original work, presented in an acoustic environment that attempts to reproduce as closely as possible the audio that the original participants would have experienced. [IM]

*Artist interview for exhibition catalogue in August 2020.

4

本書カバーを切り取り該当する図版をお貼りください

Please detach the corresponding plate from the cover and paste it here.

「平成美術：うたかたと瓦礫デブリ 1989–2019」展示風景
京都市京セラ美術館、2021年

Installation view of *Bubbles/Debris: Art of the Heisei Period 1989–2019*
Kyoto City KYOCERA Museum of Art, 2021

第 2 章
うたかたから瓦礫へ

2001年〜2011年、平成13年から平成23年

新たなる集結

　1990年／平成2年と1995年／平成7年の経済と治安をめぐる大きなカタストロフを経て、美術家たちによる美術館外のオルターナティヴ・スペースや路上、街頭での集合的・集団的な活動が冷え込む一方で、インターネット元年とも呼ばれる95年以降、ネットを通じて誰もが国内外に発信することができる社会インフラが整うようになると、海外と国内との情報格差は一気に縮まり、海外旅行の日常化もあいまって、美術家の多くが気軽に海外に出るようになった。かれらの発表機会として、世界の各所を多国籍的にネットワークでつなぐ新興のギャラリーやアートフェア、国際現代美術展や芸術祭も定着する。本展／本書で第一期／第1章として区分した1989年／平成元年から2001年／平成13年のうち、後半に美術家たちによる集合的・集団的な活動が目立たず、ほとんど空白（ブランク）と呼べる時期があり（本書「年表 平成美術 1989–2019」を参照のこと）、この間に近代における美術の典型とも言える個人の名前での活動をする美術家がふたたび増えて、反対に従来の美術批評や美術市場の枠をはみ出すような奇妙な名付けが減ったのは、そのほうが現在進行形で定着しつつある国際的な現代美術のサーキットやマーケットに乗りやすかったという合理的な事情もあったものと思われる。こうした国際化は、一方で美術が世界に向けて開かれる一方で、国内的にはかつてのような一般的な広がりを失い、国際的なアート・スターと呼べる美術家が登場する反面、かれらは国内で認知される前に、海外で経済的な成功をおさめ、それを担保に逆輸入されるという評価の逆転現象が目立つようになった。

　この機に乗じて拡大する多国籍企業に身を置くビジネスマンがそうであるように、美術家も日々、めまぐるしく世界を移動するようになり、カネ・ヒト・モノ・コトの交錯が国境をもろともせずに広がるようになると、作品も従来の絵画や彫刻のように物理的な実体として存在するのではなく、美術家たちの移動に即して、かれらが身を置いた場所の条件や環境、由来などと分かち難く混淆し、その都度再編成され、複数の異なる主体のあいだで共有されて、一定のかたちを持たない過程や運動として発表されることが多くなった。映像やパフォーマンス、ワークショップは、こうした状況の変化に柔軟に対応できる形式であったから、世界中の国際現代美術展でそのような傾向が広く共有されるようになったのも、当然のことであった。だが、こうした集合的・集団的活動の活性化にもかかわらず、多くの場合、平成の始まりの頃とは違って、美術市場や国際現代美術展の尺度に沿って規格化されやすいこれらの「作品」は、最終的には個人の作家名に帰されることがかえって増えている。

　村上隆の主宰した「GEISAI（ゲイサイ）」は、これらの動向と真逆の方向性を持っていた。村上自身はいわゆるアート・ワールドでもっとも大きな成功を収めた美術家のひとりとして今日、揺るぎない存在となっているが、国内で2001年／平成13年の「東京芸術夏祭り」（東京都現代美術館「村上隆展 召喚するかドアを開けるか回復するか全滅するか」関連企画＝くるり演奏会「東京ミミック」＋芸術道場グランプ

Chapter 2
From Bubbles to Debris

2001-2011 / Heisei 13-23

The New Collectives

After the catastrophes of 1990/Heisei 2 (collapse of Japan's economic asset bubble) and 1995/ Heisei 7 (the Tokyo subway sarin gas terrorist attacks), extra-institutional artistic activities in collectives and alternative spaces cooled. Tim Berners-Lee invented the Web in 1989/ Heisei 1, but it wasn't until 1995 that the Internet as we know it became available to all. This new technological infrastructure enabling anyone to virtually contact anyone else, anywhere, immediately, dramatically alleviated the informational disparity between Japan and the rest of the developed world. International travel was facilitated by what was still a stronger yen, and so Japanese artists' participation in international gallery shows, art fairs, contemporary art exhibitions and festivals became more common. Within the period 1989–2001/Heisei 1–13, classified as the first period in this exhibition and catalogue, this resulted in a collapse of domestic collective artistic activity. Artists more commonly used their birth names again and eccentric stylings decreased. One of the reasons for this was, of course, that using conventional names made it easier for artists to work internationally, still then an emerging phenomenon. The internationalization of contemporary art on one hand opened up art in Japan to the world, and on the other caused it to lose some of its relevance domestically. It created a reverse evaluation phenomenon, in which some Japanese artists became international art stars, were re-imported to Japan from overseas, and then became recognized in Japan.

Predictably, the many opportunities globalization presented to artists were best suited to those who treated their practice like a multinational business, dashing around the world, positioning themselves at key nodes in networks of money, goods, people, and events. Expanding their activities across borders, often maintaining their pace by releasing artworks as process or movement such as moving images, performances, and workshops, rather than as physical objects like paintings and sculptures, these artists mixed conditions, environments, and derivations of locations, and positioned themselves according to their migrations, continually re-organizing, and seeking representation from multiple partners. Latter Heisei saw renewed vitality in collective activities, yet with more of the art reverting back to individual credit for authorship, accommodating both domestic sociological, and international market forces.

One fascinating project which took an opposite orientation was GEISAI, led by Takashi Murakami, an artist unrivalled among Japanese for personally achieving rapid global art world successes. Originally created as part of the *Takashi Murakami: Summon monsters? Open the door? Heal? or die?* 2001 exhibition at MOT, which featured related events *Tokyo Art Summer Festival (=GEISAI)—Quruli Concert "Tokyo Mimic"*

リ）を皮切りに、2001年／平成13年から本格化する「GEISAI」は、同時期に始まる国際現代美術展や国際アートフェアとは根本的に異なって、ドメスティック極まりない美大芸大の「芸祭」や、オタクによる同人誌の展示即売会「コミックマーケット（コミケ）」を範例とし、それをアートの領域に敷衍して、海外に「出稼ぎ」に行くのではなく、並ぶもののないアートの世界的拠点を東京に構築しようとする、きわめて野心的な試みで、先に触れた第一期後半の空白を埋める以上の素地を作ったと言える。

　これらを受け、この時期以降でもっとも代表的と位置付けられるアーティスト集団が、2005年／平成17年に東京で結成されたChim↑Pom（チンポム）である。実際、かれらの初期の代表作《SUPER RAT（スーパーラット）》（2006年／平成18年〜）や《サンキューセレブプロジェクト　アイムボカン》（2007年／平成19年〜2008年／平成20年）は、いずれも、村上隆キュレーションによる展覧会「スーパーフラット」（2000年／平成12年〜）や、今日に至るまで壁画として多用される《タイムボカン》（1993年／平成5年〜）に着想を得たものであり、かれらなりの先行者へのアンサーと考えることができる。アートのグローバル・スタンダードの成功モデルを全否定し、真の意味でアクチュアルな美術の最前線が、ドメスティックなネットのなかに匿名的に存在していることを強く主張したカオス＊ラウンジのメンバーも、「GEISAI」への参加を経て登場する。ここでは、かれらの活動が2001年／平成13年以前とは激変した美術館の外の情報環境や路上を中心に始められたことから考え、美術家たちによる集合的・集団的活動の平成美術での第二期の勃興としている。それは、平成の始まりのようにバブル経済やポストモダンの影響下に始まったものでない。また、一般にこの時期のこうした美術の動向を担うわかりやすい名称として、アーティスト・コレクティヴやリレーショナル・アート、あるいはソーシャリー・エンゲイジド・アートといったものがあるが、それと必ずしも対応するわけではない。ここでとりあげた美術家たちによる活動が、一概にそうしたアートをめぐるグローバル・スタンダードに乗らないノイズ成分を多く孕むだけでなく、そもそもがそうした動きに対抗する要素を多く備えていたからである（加えて言えば、美術家たちが美術の外部と関係を結ぶ集合的・集団的活動自体は、言うまでもなく20世紀初頭のアヴァンギャルドから連綿と続いている）。

　地下鉄サリン事件以後の路上、インターネット元年以後の情報環境だけではない。大学というかたちでの美術教育の現場を再活性化しようとする動き、放送という規格を超えたストリーミングという世界同時情報発信、そしてもっとも情報化の困難な身体の情報環境下での活用という領域でも、グローバル・スタンダードに乗りつつ外れる、もしくはそのことで隠蔽される地域格差というノイズを、むしろ積極的に発現しようとする動きが、やはりこの時期、「東北画は可能か？」「DOMMUNE（ドミューン）」「contact Gonzo（コンタクト・ゴンゾ）」といった異なるかたちで浮上している。

　他方で、2001年／平成13年9月11日に突如として起きたアメリカ同時多発テロ事件以降の目に見えない突発的・分子状の対テロ戦争、そしてAIDSに次いで現れたSARS（重症急性呼吸器症候群、2002年／平成14年〜2004年／平成16年）といった未知のウイルスの不気味なアウトブレイクは、やがて訪れる「令和」という時代にも大きな困難をもたらすことになるだろう。それらは、目に見えないテロリストの「マルチチュード」化や、新型ウイルスの「パンデミック」の兆しを、着々と準備しつつあった。

（椹木野衣）

+ *GEIJUTSU DOJO GP*, GEISAI was fundamentally different from the international contemporary art exhibitions and fairs held in Japan, which also began around the same time. GEISAI mimicked domestic art schools' festivals (art=*gei* festival=*sai*), and transposed the pop culture Comic Market phenomenon of *otaku* (=obsessives) fan conventions into the world of contemporary art. Like all things Murakami, GEISAI was a bold and ambitious project, an attempt at building an unparalleled worldwide hub for art in Tokyo, by and for artists, as an alternative to migrating overseas in search of success, and it more than made up in the second period for the collapse of domestic collective artistic activity mentioned previously.

The group which I think represents late Heisei best is Chim↑Pom, established in Tokyo, in 2005/Heisei 17. In fact, their early representative works *SUPER RAT* (2006–/Heisei 18–) and *Thank You Celeb Project "I'm Bokan"* (2007–2008/Heisei 19–20), both reference Takashi Murakami, the former by the *Superflat* exhibition curated by Murakami (2000/Heisei 12) and the latter by one of his frequent motifs *Time Bokan* (1993–/Heisei 5–). Either can be thought of as a response to these projects. The members of Chaos*Lounge, a group that completely denied the global standard success model of art, and instead asserted that the actual frontline of art exists anonymously in the domestic Internet, also came to prominence after participating in GEISAI. In this exhibition and catalogue, we put Chaos*Lounge in the second wave of artist collectives in the art of the Heisei Period, considering that their activities began centrally in information environments (the Internet) and public spaces, outside of museums, which drastically changed from 2001/Heisei 13. The reasoning is that this second wave didn't start under the influence of the bubble economy or post-modernist philosophy like the Heisei first wave. And while there are generally recognized art movement descriptors such as artist collective, relational art, and socially engaged art, which may also be applied to practices in this period, they do not necessarily correspond to these art groups because their activities not only contained dissonant elements which broke with these global classifications, but also because they were based on many elements specifically opposed to those movements.

The second wave was not only limited to public spaces, despite the impacts of the Tokyo subway sarin attack, or information environments after the first generation of the Internet. In the areas of revitalizing education in the universities, simultaneous worldwide information streaming outside of mass media broadcasting frameworks, and utilizing the informational environment of the body, and movement to actively express the noise of regional disparity, projects including "Is Tohoku-ga (art from a hypothetical State of actually existing Tohoku) possible?" a project which contains the name of a devastated area and has since become a post-disaster challenge in itself, DOMMUNE, and contact Gonzo are emerging bright lights.

The invisible, unexpected, and molecular wars on terror since the shocking events of September 11, 2011/Heisei 23 in the US, and the ghastly outbreaks of unknown viruses which have continued to arrive, including SARS (2002–2004/Heisei 14–16), created a prelude of constant vigilance for proliferation of new forms of terrorists, as well as pandemics by novel viruses, from the very beginning of Reiwa.

(Sawaragi Noi)

GEISAI

2001 - 2014 Heisei 13-26

東京、神奈川、埼玉、台北、マイアミ | Japan, Taiwan, U.S.A.

「GEISAI#11」会場風景、2008 年
Photos from *GEISAI#11*, 2008

GEISAI

GEISAI は、村上隆（1962– ）が「チアマン」を務めるアートフェスティバルである。村上をはじめ複数のアーティストの制作・マネージメント事務所でもあるカイカイキキが実行委員会形式で開催してきた。2001 年秋の東京都現代美術館での「村上隆展　召喚するかドアを開けるか回復するか全滅するか」に際して行われたイベント「芸術道場 GP」をプロトタイプとし、以降 2014 年まで年 2 回を基本に開催。こうした活動は、一方では新進作家へのサバイバル指南を通して作家を育て、もう一方ではマーケットの裾野を広げることをめざし、他ジャンルの要素も加えながら新しいプラットフォームを作る試みであった。14 年間にわたり東京、神奈川、埼玉、台北、マイアミにて合計 28 回、延べ 1 万 8,000 人以上の作家が参加した壮大なプロジェクトとなった。

GEISAI

GEISAI was an art festival chaired by Takashi Murakami (1962–). Kaikai Kiki Co., Ltd., the office handling art production and management of Murakami and other artists, organized GEISAI through the GEISAI Executive Committee. Using as a prototype the *GEIJUTSU DOJO Grand Prix* event held at the time of the exhibition *Takashi Murakami: Summon monsters? Open the door? Heal? or die?* at the Museum of Contemporary Art Tokyo in autumn 2001, GEISAI was generally held twice a year from the time it was established until 2014. These efforts were an attempt to create a new platform, while adding elements from other genres, fostering talent by teaching young artists how to survive while also aiming to expand the market. Over the course of fourteen years, it became a grand project that was held 28 times in Tokyo, Kanagawa, Saitama, Taipei, and Miami with the participation of over 18,000 artists.

「芸術道場ＧＰ」会場風景、2001 年
Photos from *GEIJUTSU DOJO Grand Prix*, 2001

「GEISAI#11」会場風景、2008 年
Photos from *GEISAI#11*, 2008

「GEISAI#13」会場風景、2009 年
Photos from *GEISAI#13*, 2009

「芸術道場GP」会場風景、2001年
Photos from *GEIJUTSU DOJO Grand Prix*, 2001

「GEISAI#11」会場風景、2008年
Photos from *GEISAI#11*, 2008

「GEISAI#13」会場風景、2009年
Photos from *GEISAI#13*, 2009

本展では、過去に開催された GEISAI のなかから 3 つの回をピックアップし、当時の膨大なアーカイブ画像をスライドで壁に投射するかたちでの資料展示として紹介する。

　1 つ目は、「芸術道場 GP」。これは前身となるイベント「芸術道場・原宿フラット」（ラフォーレミュージアム原宿［東京］、2000 年）などの準備期間を経て、カイカイキキが満を持して開催したもので、参加作家約 300 人、本戦審査員に安野モヨコ、椹木野衣、奈良美智、宮脇修一、村上隆、特別審査員に大下健太郎が参加。他に企業やギャラリーによるスカウト審査員もあり、賑やかなイベントとコンペティションを行うなど、その後の展開の雛形となった。

　2 つ目は、回を重ねるごとに認知度を高め、動員を増やし、ミニバブルの時勢を得てひとつの頂点をなした 2008 年秋の「GEISAI#11」である。この回では審査員にマーク・オリヴィエ・ウォラー、アリソン・ジンジェラス、フィリップ・セガロ、ジャック・バンカウスキー、キャロル・イングファ・ルーを迎え、参加作家は約 1,300 人、入場者はおよそ 1 万 2,000 人と、いずれも人数としては最高記録を達成した。

　3 つ目は、リーマン・ショックの余波が本格的に日本経済にもダメージを及ぼすなかで規模の縮小を余儀なくされ、埼玉のカイカイキキ三芳工場で行うことになった 2009 年秋の「GEISAI#13」だ。

　以上の 3 回によって、実質的な立ち上げとなった初回、規模として最大の回、および大幅に縮小した回を振り返ることができる。環境や規模の大小とは別に参加者の熱量は観る者を圧倒するものがあり、また、それぞれの現場の様子を一気に通覧することで、一般的にアーティストたちのサバイバルの方法論や作品性が大きく変化したと言われる平成の時代の変遷を垣間見ることができるだろう。［NM］

Selecting from three past GEISAI events, *Bubbles/Debris* presents an enormous number of archived images from the events by projecting slides on the wall.

The first GEISAI event featured is *GEIJUTSU DOJO Grand Prix*. Held by Kaikai Kiki after careful preparation and after a period of time for the groundwork for events such as its predecessor, *GEIJUTSU DOJO/Harajuku Flat* (at Laforet Museum, Tokyo, 2000), *GEIJUTSU DOJO Grand Prix* had over 300 participating artists, and Anno Moyoco, Sawaragi Noi, Nara Yoshitomo, Miyawaki Shuichi, and Takashi Murakami serving as judges making the final selection and Oshita Kentaro acting as special judge. It also had scout judges from companies and galleries, lively events, and competitions, and became a model for later events.

The second GEISAI featured is *GEISAI#11*, which was held in autumn 2008, and constituted an apex reached through increasing name recognition and turnouts achieved with each event, boosted by a vibrant economy. Marc-Olivier Wahler, Alison Gingeras, Philippe Ségalot, Jack Bankowsky, and Carol Yinghua Lu served as judges, over 1,300 artists took part, and about 12,000 people turned out, the last two of which were all-time records.

The third event, *GEISAI#13* held in autumn 2009, took place at the Kaikai Kiki factory in Miyoshi, Saitama Prefecture, as it was forced to scale down due to the impact on the Japanese economy of the financial shock triggered by the bankruptcy of Lehman Brothers.

Focusing on these three events allows us to review what was effectively the first GEISAI, the largest GEISAI, and a GEISAI that saw a significant reduction in scale. Regardless of the environment or scale, the passion of the participants overwhelms the viewer, and surveying all of these venues together makes it possible to glimpse the transformations that occurred during the Heisei Period (1989-2019), when major changes took place in the general methodology for the survival of artists and for the nature of the works that the artists produced. [NM]

5

本書カバーを切り取り該当する図版をお貼りください

Please detach the corresponding plate from the cover and paste it here.

Chim↑Pom

SUPER RAT -Scrap and Build-
SUPER RAT -Scrap and Build-
2017

Chim↑Pom

2005 年、卯城竜太、林靖高、エリイ、岡田将孝、稲岡求、水野俊紀の同世代 6 人により、東京で結成された。時代のリアリティを追求し、現代社会に介入した批評性の高い作品を次々と発表。広島や福島などの被曝をめぐる事象に当事者意識をもって反応し、議論を巻き起こす。また、消費社会、環境問題、公共性を表象した「都市論」をテーマに、取り壊し直前の東京・歌舞伎町商店街振興組合ビルなどを舞台にした「Sukurappu ando Birudo」（2016-2017 年）、国立台湾美術館における《道（Street）》（2017-2018 年）など、数々のプロジェクトを展開している。2011 年の原発事故による帰還困難区域内の封鎖解除まで一般には誰も観ることができない展覧会「Don't Follow the Wind」（2015 年 -）は、かれらによる発表で自らも作品を出展し、現在も継続中である。釜山ビエンナーレ（2016 年）、リヨンビエンナーレ（2017 年）など、多くの国際展にも参加。現在は新宿の「ホワイトハウス」を拠点に活動している。

Chim↑Pom

Chim↑Pom was formed in Tokyo in 2005 by six members from the same generation—Ushiro Ryuta, Hayashi Yasutaka, Ellie, Okada Masataka, Inaoka Motomu, and Mizuno Toshinori. Responding to the reality of the current period in real time, they have produced a rapid succession of diverse works characterized by highly critical interventions in contemporary society. Tackling radiation issues head-on, they triggered public debate by presenting works at sites such as Hiroshima and Fukushima that have been irradiated or are linked to radiation in some way. They also take up themes that deal with the consumer society, environmental issues, and the public sphere as represented by the city, through projects such as *Sukurappu ando Birudo Project* (Kabukicho Shopping District Promotion Association Building and Kitakore Building in Tokyo, 2016-2017), and *Street* (National Taiwan Museum of Fine Arts in Taichung, 2017-2018). After the nuclear disaster in 2011, they initiated and organized *Don't Follow the Wind* (2015-), an exhibition including their own works inside the Exclusion Zone. The exhibition is still running, but can't be viewed by the general public until the ban on entering the area is lifted. Chim↑Pom has exhibited at many international exhibitions and festivals, including Busan Biennale 2016 and Biennale de Lyon 2017. They are currently based at White House, Shinjuku.

[右 | right]
SUPER RAT ビデオ
渋谷センター街でネズミを捕獲する様子
SUPER RAT Video
Catching Rats at Shibuya Center-gai Street, Tokyo
2006

[上 | above]
SUPER RAT
渋谷センター街で捕獲したネズミの剥製
SUPER RAT
Rats stuffed after being caught at
Shibuya Center-gai Street, Tokyo
2006

[上左 | upper left]
SUPER RAT -Scrap and Build-
SUPER RAT -Scrap and Build-
2017

[左 | left]
SUPER RAT -Scrap and Build-
スタジオでの展示風景（東京）、2017 年
SUPER RAT -Scrap and Build-
Installation view at the artists' studio,
Tokyo, 2017

Chim↑Pom は結成当初から、隠された歴史、原爆や原発などの核、資本主義経済、国境、公共性、都市や環境などをテーマに、批評性とユーモアとをもって観る者の意表を突きながら同時代の現実に斬り込んできた。

2020 年のオリンピック・パラリンピック（2021 年に延期されることとなった）の東京開催が決定された 2013 年から数年が経ち、変わりゆく東京を目の当たりにした Chim↑Pom は、「Sukurappu ando Birudo」プロジェクトを開始し、新宿や高円寺の老朽化したビルで個展を開催する*。震災や再開発で「スクラップ・アンド・ビルド」が繰り返され、刻々と姿を変える日本の都市を背景に、東京がどこへ向かうのか、都市はだれのものか、そこで人がどう生きるのかといった問いを投げかけた。

本展では、この「Sukurappu ando Birudo」、そして「にんげんレストラン」プロジェクト（旧歌舞伎町ブックセンタービル［東京］、2018 年）から生みだされた作品を展示する。前者のプロジェクトで制作された《SUPER RAT -Scrap and Build-》（2017 年）では、ピカチュウのようなスーパーラット（殺鼠剤への耐性を持ったネズミ）が、ビルと一緒に壊された歌舞伎町のジオラマのうえで瓦礫を見つめ、その下にはネズミの巣の痕跡が都市の内臓のように吊り下がっている。一方、《ビルバーガー》（2018 年）では、「にんげんレストラン」の会場となった建物の 3 層分が切り出され、コンクリート床のバンズにビルの残置物が挟まる。このような壊れたジオラマやビルの残置物は、否応なしに、日本に生きる人々のもつ「瓦礫（デブリ）」の記憶を呼び覚まし、可視化する。

さらに、本展ではかれらの原点とも言える、《SUPER RAT -CHIBAOKAKUN-》（2006 年）を、同作のために渋谷・センター街でネズミを捕獲する様子をとらえた映像とともに出展する。そこに映しだされる「人間との歪んだ共生を送る」** ネズミはかれらの肖像だとされるが、平成期の都市文化を起点に生まれた作品の数々は、「焼け野原に身体だけがあった」*** 戦後復興の延長上にある日本の現代都市に他者と「共生」できる空間が残されているか、私たちに執拗に訊く声のようでもある。[TT]

* 「また明日も観てくれるかな？」（歌舞伎町商店街振興組合ビル［東京］、2016 年）、「道が拓ける」（キタコレビル［東京］、2017 年）。

** Chim↑Pom ウェブサイト「スーパーラット Statement」http://chimpom.jp/project/superrat.html（最終閲覧：2021 年 1 月 5 日）

*** Chim↑Pom ウェブサイト「Chim↑Pom による 2 週間限定のレストランが歌舞伎町にオープン！」http://chimpom.jp/ningen/（最終閲覧：2021 年 1 月 5 日）

Since its formation, Chim↑Pom has been baring the realities of contemporary society, astounding viewers with critical, humorous projects that address themes such as hidden histories, nuclear weapons, nuclear power, capitalism, national boundaries, the civic sphere, urban issues, and the environment.

Within a few years of Tokyo's 2013 selection as the host city for the 2020 Olympic and Paralympic Games (now rescheduled to 2021), Chim↑Pom became concerned about how Tokyo was being transformed, and launched the *Sukurappu ando Birudo Project* to organize solo exhibitions in decrepit buildings in Shinjuku and Koenji.* Change is constantly occurring in Japanese cities, where the urban fabric is subject to an ongoing scrap-and-build approach driven by earthquakes and urban redevelopment. In this context, Chim↑Pom's project brought attention to the questions of where Tokyo is going, who owns the city, and how people should live their lives there.

The exhibition, *Bubbles/Debris*, incorporates works that emerged from the *Sukurappu ando Birudo Project* and the *Ningen Restaurant* project (Former Kabukicho Book Center Building, Tokyo, 2018). *SUPER RAT -Scrap and Build-* (2017), created as part of the former project, is a Pikachu-like super rat (a rat immune to rat poison), stretching up to survey the debris in its surroundings, the collapsed buildings in a diorama of Kabukicho. Below ground, traces of rat nests stretch down from the surface as if they were the internal organs of the city. *Build-Burger* (2018) is a burger cut out from three stories of the building that hosted *Ningen Restaurant*. The concrete floor sections act as buns, and rubble from the building provides the filling. The demolished city diorama and the rubble from buildings indisputably stir and visualize memories of debris that are held by everyone living in Japan.

Also exhibited is what can be considered Chim↑Pom's conceptual starting point: *SUPER RAT -CHIBAOKAKUN-* (2006), presented here with video of the members catching the rats in Shibuya's Center-gai. The rats, "maintaining crooked coexistence with human beings,"** are said to reflect the members of the group. Nevertheless, Chim↑Pom's many works that emerged from this birthplace of Heisei Period urban culture also come across as an insistent voice questioning whether there is still any space for living in harmony with others in contemporary Japanese cities—cities that have been under continuous development since the postwar recovery from circumstances where "there were only bodies in the burnt-out ruins."*** [TT]

* *So see you again tomorrow, too?* (Kabukicho Shopping District Promotion Association Building, Tokyo, 2016); *Sukurappu ando Birudo project: Paving the Street* (Kitakore Building, Tokyo, 2017).

** Chim↑Pom. "SUPER RAT Statement," http://chimpom.jp/project/superrat.html.

*** Chim↑Pom. "Chim↑Pom opens a 2-week only 'Ningen Restaurant' in Kabukicho," http://chimpom.jp/ningen/eng.

「平成美術：うたかたと瓦礫（デブリ）1989–2019」展示風景
京都市京セラ美術館、2021年

Installation view of *Bubbles/Debris: Art of the Heisei Period 1989–2019*
Kyoto City KYOCERA Museum of Art, 2021

6

本書カバーを切り取り該当する図版をお貼りください

Please detach the corresponding plate from the cover and paste it here.

contact Gonzo

2006 Heisei 18 — 大阪 | Osaka

contact Gonzo

2006 年、大阪の NPO 法人ダンスボックスに関わっていた塚原悠也 (1979-) は、ダンサーの垣尾優に誘われ、コンテンポラリーダンスの一要素「コンタクト・インプロビゼーション」に初めて取り組む。それを起点に確立していった独自のメソッドである「contact Gonzo」がユニット名となった。一見「めちゃくちゃ (gonzo)」で即興的に行われる「接触 (contact)」は、「押す」「叩く」「体を引く」などの所作に、「重さ」や「速さ」といった力が加わる激しいパフォーマンスである。主に食を中心とした日常や、山にまつわる自然事象など、自分たちを取り巻く環境とのつながりを意識し、制御もままならぬなかで、直感的かつ運良く掴みとるべきものとしての周囲との関係性を拠り所にしたかれらの行為は、インスタレーション・写真・映像作品の制作、雑誌編集などへも展開される。現メンバーは、2020 年に京都国際舞台芸術祭「KYOTO EXPERIMENT」の共同ディレクターに就任した塚原悠也、大阪を中心にアートスペースなどの活動に関わる三ケ尻敬悟 (1980-)、デザイナー／フォトグラファーの松見拓也 (1986-)、立体・平面作品を手がける NAZE (1989-) の 4 人。

contact Gonzo

In 2006, Tsukahara Yuya (1979-), who was involved in the Osaka-based NPO Dance Box, first incorporated the contemporary dance technique of contact improvisation into his work at the invitation of dancer Kakio Masaru. The distinctive method they developed from those beginnings, called contact Gonzo, became the name of their unit. Their impromptu contact style seems very 'gonzo' (wild and crazy) but actually it provides an intense performance conducted by adding force in the form of weight and speed to movements involving things like pushing, hitting, and dragging each other's bodies. Their work, which also includes the production of installations, photography, and videos, as well as magazine editing, is often based on being aware of their daily lives—like eating—and of natural phenomena like mountains. They are concerned mostly about the environment around them. They know their acts and their work emerge from a relationship with their surroundings that assumes that the things around them cannot be controlled, and should be grasped intuitively and with a bit of luck. The unit currently consists of four members—Tsukahara Yuya, who was appointed a member of the collective of directors heading Kyoto International Performing Arts Festival's KYOTO EXPERIMENT in 2020, Mikajiri Keigo (1980-), who is involved in work at art spaces mainly in Osaka as well as other venues, designer and photographer Matsumi Takuya (1986-), and two- and three-dimensional artist NAZE (1989-).

[左頁上 | opposite]

公園
映像
出演：垣尾優　撮影・編集：塚原悠也
* contact Gonzo 結成前、「泉北アートプロジェクト」にて出展
Koen (Park)
Video
Performance by Kakio Masaru　Filmed by Tsukahara Yuya
* First exhibited at "Senboku Art Project" before the formation of contact Gonzo
2005

[上 | above]
Shelters
映像
Shelters
Video
2009

ヘルシンキにて
「the first man narrative」シリーズより
Helsinki
from the series, "the first man narrative"
2008

国内外で多くの展覧会やパフォーマンスを行う contact Gonzo は、「痛みの哲学、接触の技法」を謳うが、15 年間実践されてきたこの「接触」は、「間の取り合い」のようにも見え、だとすればそこには日本的な美意識が垣間見えさえする。私たちが無意識に注視させられているのは「接触」前後に生み出される物理的・心理的空間かもしれない。

本展では「コンタクト・ゴンゾ」とかれらが名付けたパフォーマンスの端緒となった、垣尾優と塚原悠也による「泉北アートプロジェクト」（2004–2005 年）で撮影され、新たに編集された《公園》が初めて正式に紹介される。公園を行き交う人々に声をかける。落ち葉を一緒に受けとめ、芝山を抱き合って転がる。そのような物的・心的「接触」のドキュメントである。

その後、現代美術へと活動を押し広げながらメンバーを増やしたかれらは、「吉原治良賞記念アート・プロジェクト 2008」大賞受賞を機に、以前より関心を抱いていた北欧フィンランドへと向かう。首都ヘルシンキに意外なほど身近に多数あるという核シェルターの存在に誘発され、あてもなく彼の地に降り立ったかれらは、核シェルターへのアクセスを模索しながら、前述の映像作品《公園》を彷彿させるがごとく、歩きまくり、人と話す。こうした「接触」の末、核シェルターに立ち入ることができ、そこで「ゴンゾ」する。一方、ヘルシンキからひたすら北上し、偶然たどり着いた北極圏のイナリの森では、キャンプ生活も行う。

彼の地のふたつの場所でのふたつの行為の対比が、《Shelters》（2009 年）として今回 2 画面で上映され、展示の中心となる。さらにシェルターやイナリ近辺で撮影された「the first man narrative」（かれらが名付けた、使い捨てカメラで無作為に撮影する独自のメソッド）による写真も初めてまとめて展示される。

肉体を用いるかれらの多種多様な身体表現は、単に新しいパフォーマンスとしてではなく、現代のアート表現としても認知され、多方向に予測不可能な展開を続けている。[IM]

Contact Gonzo bases its many exhibitions and performances in Japan and internationally on what it calls the "philosophy of pain, technique of contact." This 'contact,' which they have engaged in for fifteen years now, seems to offer a glimpse of the Japanese aesthetic concept of *ma* (balance between time and/or space). In other words, what our attention is being unconsciously made to focus on is the physical/psychological space produced before and after actual contact.

Koen (Park), performed by Kakio Masaru and filmed by Tsukahara Yuya at the Senboku Art Project (2004–2005), became the start of their performances that they named "contact Gonzo." This video is newly edited, and presented officially for the first time in this exhibition. It documents Kakio's attempts to make emotional and physical contact with the people walking in the park, inviting them to catch falling leaves together, or to roll down a grassy hill locked together, etc.

Subsequently, the unit expanded its activities to encompass contemporary art and increased the number of members. Upon winning the Yoshihara Jiro Art Project 2008 grand prize, it headed to Finland, which had been a focus of interest for the unit for some time due to the existence of shelters as a nearby presence in daily life. In the capital Helsinki, descending upon an area, they walked around talking with people as they tried to get access to these shelters. (The actions made them remember the *Koen* project.) After establishing this 'contact,' they were able to enter a fallout shelter and finally proceeded to perform 'gonzo.' From Helsinki, they headed straight north, and spent time camping in a forest in Inari, a Finnish town within the Arctic Circle that they happened to reach by chance.

For *Bubbles/Debris*, the contrast between their activities at these two locations is shown on two screens as *Shelters* (2009), which forms the core of contact Gonzo's exhibit. Also featured are photos taken in the Helsinki shelter and in the area around Inari using 'the first man narrative'—a term coined by the unit for a unique method in which members take random photos of each other with a disposable camera while performing. This is also the first showing of collected photos of Helsinki in an installation.

The diverse physical expression employing their own bodies is recognizably contemporary art, not just a new form of performance. Even today, they continue to develop 'gonzo' in multiple directions and in unpredictable ways. [IM]

7

本書カバーを切り取り該当する図版をお貼りください

Please detach the corresponding plate from the cover and paste it here.

東北画は可能か？　Is Tohoku-ga possible?

2009 Heisei 21 — 山形 | Yamagata

東北画は可能か？

東北芸術工科大学における学生の課外活動として2009年に始動し、アートシーンの中心から遠く離れた地「東北」でフィールドワークを重ねながら、現在まで継続するプロジェクトである。教員であり京都市立芸術大学の日本画科出身で画家としても活躍する三瀬夏之介 (1973-) と、同じく教員で福島生まれの画家である鴻崎正武 (1972-) によって取りまとめられ、多くの学生が参加してきた。フィールドワークを基礎に、学生たちの個別の制作とともに大型作品の共同制作を行ってきたこともかれらの活動を特徴づけている。「東北画は可能か？」はプロジェクトの名称であるとともに、展覧会のタイトルとして掲げられ、地元山形や東北地方のみならず、東京、京都など、各地で多くの展覧会が開催されている。

Is Tohoku-ga possible?

Is Tohoku-ga possible? is a project that began in 2009 as an extracurricular student activity at Tohoku University of Art and Design, and to this day it continues to engage in field work in the Tohoku area, which is far from the center of the Japanese art scene. The project has involved many students, and it is headed by Mise Natsunosuke (1973-), a professor at the university who studied *nihonga* at Kyoto City University of Arts and is an active painter, and Kozaki Masatake (1972-), an associate professor at the university and a painter who is originally from Fukushima Prefecture. In addition to works by individual students based on field work, the project is characterized by collaborative work on large-scale pieces. "Is Tohoku-ga possible?" also serves as the title of numerous exhibitions resulting from the project, held locally at venues in Yamagata and around Tohoku, and also in Tokyo, Kyoto, and other parts of Japan.

[右頁上 | opposite, top]
東北山水
Tohoku Mountain and Waterscapes
2011

[右頁下 | opposite, bottom]
東北八重山景
Overlapped Tohoku Mountainscapes
2010

方舟計画
Ark Plan
2011

しきおり絵詞
Shikiori-Ekotoba —a Woven Narrative of Seasons—
2013-

　「東北画」は、明治期に創案された「日本画」という概念に対する批評的な態度／概念として生み出された。「東北画は可能か？」と疑問符を加えることで、その態度が持つ政治性も含めて、成立が困難であろうことをあらかじめ示している。まだ見ぬ「東北画」を求めてフィールドワークと制作を続けることが、そのまま新たな概念を創出する運動となるような活動として、かれらの仕事は見なされるべきだろう。

　本展出展作でもある三瀬夏之介個人による作品で、日本地図を逆さに表した《日本の絵》（2017年）には、中心と周縁を逆転させる思考とともに、上記と同様の批評性を垣間見ることができる。

　集団でのフィールドワークに基づいた個人の作品制作とは別に、グループ全体の活動を象徴する意味では、集団制作による複数の大型絵画、および布地の端切れを継ぎ合わせて作る東北の伝統的な防寒着「ドンジャ」の作品《しきおり絵詞》（2013年–）が代表作として挙げられる。

　本展では、大きな壁面に「東北画は可能か？」の活動をクロノロジカルに示すグラフィックをベースに、それぞれ幅約4メートルに及ぶ集団制作絵画《東北八重山景》（2010年）、《方舟計画》（2011年）、《東北山水》（2011年）の3点を並べて展示し、「東北」の自然を題材にしつつ震災を予見するような、緊張感溢れる世界観を伝える。また何年にもわたって集団制作を続けている《しきおり絵詞》は、現在、高さ4メートルを超え、山脈の彼方を見晴るかすように幾重にも作品群が重なる空間に展示される。東日本大震災の発生から今年（2021年）でちょうど10年を迎え、震災と復興をめざした平成の日本に思いをいたすなかで、本展は「東北」をめぐる問いに改めて耳を傾ける機会となるだろう。［NM］

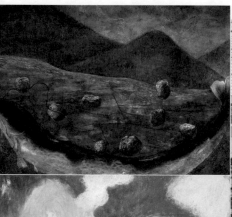

[右上から順に | top right to bottom left]
佐々木綾子
レイヤー
Sasaki Ayako
Layer
2011

多田さやか
色即是空
Tada Sayaka
Void
2011

渡辺綾
山神さま～みちしるべ～
Watanabe Aya
Mountains of Prayer
2010

久松知子
ひと山むこうでなまずが
Hisamatsu Tomoko
The Catfish Raged Across the Mountain
2011

近江谷沙里
強風ハローごはん
Omiya Sari
Gale Hello Meal
2011

佐々木優衣
東北遷都計画
Sasaki Yui
New: Japanese Civil War (2012～)
2010

狩野宏明
天狗飯七
Kano Hiroaki
Tengu's Spoon
2013

海藤千紗音
若木山縁起
Kaito Chisato
Auspicious of Mt. OSANAGI
2010

石原葉
si:
Ishihara Yo
si:
2011

"Tohoku-ga" emerged as a critical attitude/perspective toward *nihonga* painting, a genre of Japanese painting invented during the Meiji Period (1868-1912). By adding a question mark to its name, Is Tohoku-ga possible? indicates in advance the likely difficulty of its establishment, as well as the political nature of the project's stance. The project continues to conduct field work and create art in pursuit of a Tohoku-ga that has yet to emerge, so its work should be viewed as an effort to become a movement that creates a new concept.

Painting of Japan (2017), a work by Mise Natsunosuke shown at *Bubbles/Debris*, depicts a map of Japan flipped upside down, providing a glimpse of the critical nature of this project, as well as of the artist's approach of reversing the center and periphery.

In addition to the creation of works by individuals based on collective field work, multiple large paintings created by the group and *Shikiori-Ekotoba—a woven narrative of seasons—*(2013-), which is a traditional Tohoku *Donja* coat pieced together from scraps of cloth to provide protection from the cold, are representative works by the project in the sense that they symbolize the activities of the entire group.

Highlighting nature in Tohoku but also conveying a worldview full of tension that seems to foresee the 2011 disaster, the exhibition displays three approximately 4m-wide paintings created collectively next to each other—*Overlapped Tohoku Mountainscapes* (2010), *Ark Plan* (2011), and *Tohoku Mountain and Waterscapes* (2011)—presented against a wall graphic conveying the work of Is Tohoku-ga possible? in chronological order. *Shikiori-Ekotoba*, which has been worked on collectively for many years and is now more than 4m tall, is exhibited in a space of overlapping works, creating a vista that resembles a spectacular view of distant mountains. This year, 2021, marks ten years since the Great East Japan Earthquake. As we look back on Heisei Period Japan, which experienced disaster and worked toward recovery, the exhibition provides an opportunity to re-consider questions about Tohoku. [NM]

8

本書カバーを切り取り該当する図版をお貼りください

Please detach the corresponding plate from the cover and paste it here.

「平成美術：うたかたと瓦礫（デブリ）1989−2019」展示風景　京都市京セラ美術館、2021年
Installation view of *Bubbles/Debris: Art of the Heisei Period 1989–2019*　Kyoto City KYOCERA Museum of Art, 2021

会場グラフィックデザイン（東北画は可能か？）：アイハラケンジ
Graphic design for Is Tohoku-ga possible?: Aihara Kenji

DOMMUNE

2010 Heisei 22 — 東京 | Tokyo

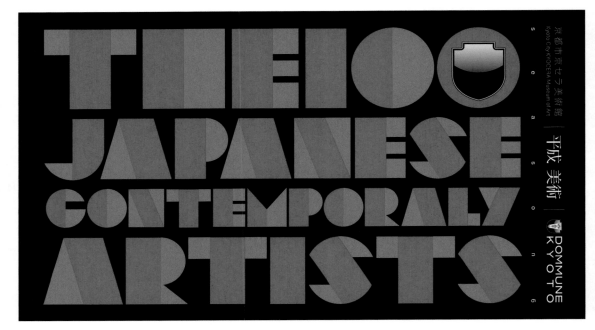

THE 100 JAPANESE CONTEMPORARY ARTISTS/season 6
ロゴ
THE 100 JAPANESE CONTEMPORARY ARTISTS/season 6
Logotype
2020

DOMMUNE

2010 年、宇川直宏（1968– ）が東京・渋谷で開局したライブストリーミング・スタジオ兼チャンネル。「DOMMUNE」とは「commune（共同体）」の次のステップ（Cの次のD）という意味が込められており、ライブでの動画配信を通してスタジオ、番組視聴者、そして視聴者によるタイムラインへのコメントとそれへの応答による新たなコミュニケーションの可能性を開いてきた。宇川は、映像作家、グラフィックデザイナー、VJ、文筆家など、さまざまな領域で多岐にわたる活動を行う「現在美術家」。2001 年「Buzz Club: News from Japan」（MoMA PS1 [ニューヨーク]）、「JAM: Tokyo-London」（バービカン・アート・ギャラリー [ロンドン]）に参加して以降、国内外にて多くの展覧会に出展している。2006 年には前身となる自らのオフィスを改良したクラブ Mixroffice を主宰、密室に集うことで感じられる身体性をオンラインでも共有しようと DOMMUNE を開局する。前半はトーク番組、後半はDJ を迎えたライブ中継にするスタイルで、10 年間に配信した番組は約 5,000（約 10,000 時間、200 テラ）を超え、トータル視聴者数は延べ 1 億人を超えた。2019 年には渋谷 PARCO にスタジオを移転し、「SUPER DOMMUNE」として 5G 以降の最先端テクノロジーとともに未来を見据えた新たな展開を図っている。

DOMMUNE

DOMMUNE is a live streaming studio and streaming channel that Ukawa Naohiro (1968–) launched in Shibuya, Tokyo in 2010. Its name symbolizes being one step on from a commune (with 'c' advancing to 'd'). By streaming video from live events, DOMMUNE opened up new potential for communication between the studio, channel viewers/listeners, and a timeline where people post comments and interaction occurs. "Current artist" (as opposed to "contemporary artist") is how Ukawa describes himself, but his activities have included roles in a variety of genres, including moviemaker, graphic designer, VJ, and writer. Beginning in 2001, when he took part in *Buzz Club: News from Japan* (MoMA PS1, New York) and *JAM: Tokyo-London* (Barbican Gallery, London), he has been featured in many exhibitions worldwide. In 2006, he headed Mixroffice, a club created by converting his own office. That led on to DOMMUNE, which he launched in order to share online the physical experience of gathering together in a closed space. Based on a style of streaming a talk program in the first half followed by live DJ sets in the second half, DOMMUNE has run for 10 years, streaming about 5,000 programs (about 10,000 hours, 200 terabytes worth of programming, and over 100 million views). In 2019, the studio moved to Shibuya PARCO and became SUPER DOMMUNE, securing its future with access to 5G streaming and further new technologies.

[上 | top]
東京・渋谷 PARCO にある SUPER DOMMUNE のスタジオ風景、2020 年
SUPER DOMMUNE studio in Shibuya PARCO, Tokyo, 2020

[下 | above]
宇川直宏
DJ JOHN CAGE & THE 1000 WORLDWIDE DJS
3331 Arts Chiyoda での展示風景、2014 年
所蔵：金沢 21 世紀美術館

Ukawa Naohiro
DJ JOHN CAGE & THE 1000 WORLDWIDE DJS
Installation view at 3331 Arts Chiyoda, 2014
Collection: 21st Century Museum of Contemporary Art, Kanazawa

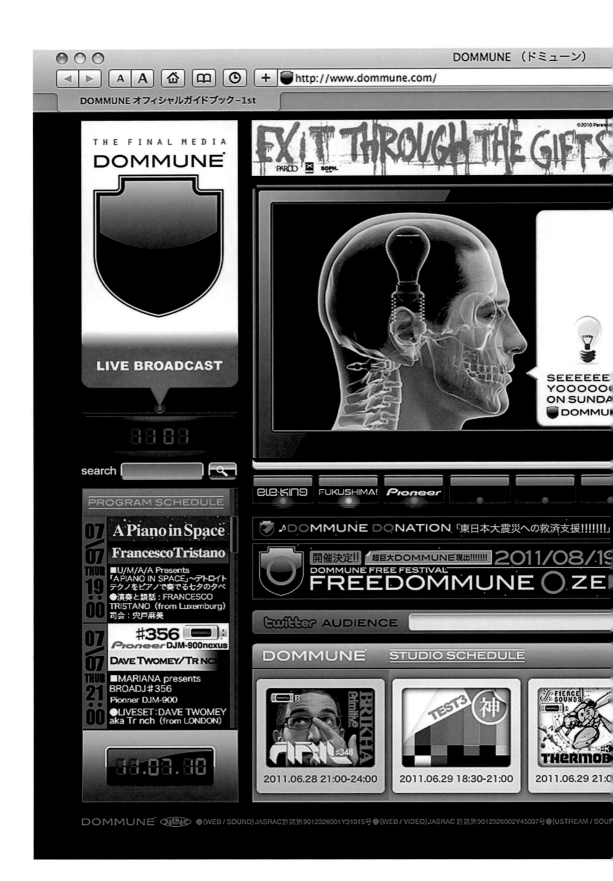

DOMMUNE のウェブサイト画面、2010 年
DOMMUNE website, 2010

「世界は映像によって連帯している」という言葉をもって 2010 年に開局宣言をした DOMMUNE は、ストリーミングの舞台となるスタジオ、視聴者のいる環境、そして SNS のタイムラインという 3 つの現場から構成される。DOMMUNE を通じて宇川は、リアルタイムな美術を示すタグとしての「現代美術」とは異なる、「明日完全に腐ってしまう映像、つまり "今ここに生きている動画"」が持つ一回性にこそ見いだされるべき価値を伝える「現在美術」としての在り方を提起してきた*。

生放送であることで生じる共時性と、現実のスタジオに足を運ぶことで実現する身体性への回帰を重視してきた DOMMUNE は、平成の時代に急速に進歩したテクノロジーを享受するなかで、5 年目を迎えて「THE 100 JAPANESE CONTEMPORARY ARTISTS」と題するシリーズを立ち上げる。そこで宇川は「文化遺産としてのアーカイブを残す意志を再定義」** することを新たに謳い、次のステップに入った。

本展出展作もそのシリーズに連なるもので、代表的な日本現代美術作家を 100 人選出し、インタビュー映像を配信しながら作家の作品展示とともにアーカイブを蓄積していくプロジェクトである。2014 年の 3331 Arts Chiyoda での開始から、金沢 21 世紀美術館（2015 年）、山本現代（2015 年、2016 年）、札幌国際芸術祭（2017 年）での実施を経て、本展では参加アーティストへのインタビュー番組を制作し、プロジェクトの第 6 シーズンとして収録、配信、会場での上映を行う。1 作家につき 1 時間半から 2 時間程度にわたるインタビュー動画では、批評家やアーティストをよく知る人物が聞き手となり、アーティストの半生と仕事をひもといていく。

シリーズの開始から今年（2021 年）で 8 年目を迎え、本展参加アーティストの映像をシリーズに加えることで、動画本数は 50 本を超えた。本展では、映像から流れる全作家の生きた言葉と、会場に展示されている各作家の作品を同時に鑑賞することで、作品のなかに生きる「現在」をより深く感じることが可能になるだろう***。[TA]

DOMMUNE launched in 2010 with the declaration that video brings the world together. It integrates three locations: the studio that provides the stage for streaming, the environment of the viewers and listeners, and the timeline on social media. Through DOMMUNE, in contrast to the "contemporary art" tag for real-time art, Ukawa proposed "current art," to communicate the value produced by the one-time-only nature of "video that will be stale by tomorrow, or in other words, 'video that is currently alive.'"*

DOMMUNE emphasized the synchronicity produced by being a live broadcast, along with the return to physicality experienced by a visit to the actual studio. In its fifth year, taking advantage of the rapid advances in technology during the Heisei Period, it launched a series entitled THE 100 JAPANESE CONTEMPORARY ARTISTS. Through this series, Ukawa took another step forward by bringing in a new approach, "a redefinition of the meaning of archives as cultural legacy."**

DOMMUNE/Ukawa's contribution to Bubbles/Debris includes a continuation of this series, which is a project to select and interview one hundred of Japan's best-known contemporary artists, broadcast the video interviews, exhibit works by the artists, and build an archive. The project began in 2014 at 3331 Arts Chiyoda, followed by the 21st Century Museum of Contemporary Art, Kanazawa (2015), Yamamoto Gendai (2015, 2016), and Sapporo International Art Festival (2017). Interviews with artists exhibiting here are being recorded and broadcast as the project's sixth season, and screened at the exhibition venue. Each artist's video interview includes one and a half to two hours of footage, with the interview conducted by an art critic or someone who knows the artist well, with the aim of putting together an understanding of the artist's work and life to date.

This year, 2021, is the eighth year since the beginning of the series. With the addition of the artists' videos in this exhibition, it has accumulated over fifty videos. Through these videos, viewers can hear the actual words of each of the artists in conjunction with the works that they created, enabling a deeper grasp of "the current time" embedded in and living in the works. *** [TA]

* 宇川直宏『@DOMMUNE：FINAL MEDIA が伝授するライブストリーミングの超魔術 !!!!!!!!』河出書房新社、2011 年、48 頁。
** 島貫泰介「宇川直宏インタビュー——5 年目を迎えた DOMMUNE の次なる目標」『CINRA.NET』2014 年 10 月 20 日公開、https://www.cinra.net/interview/201410-dommune（最終閲覧日：2021 年 1 月 5 日）。宇川は本プロジェクトに取り組む以前から、DOMMUNE について「文化を「現在」として切り取る行為。なのでアーカイブを残すことが重要で〔……〕サブカルチャーにとっての重要な文化遺産だ」と述べている（「ARTIST INTERVIEW 宇川直宏：ファイナルメディア DOMMUNE とは何か？（特集 Chim↑Pom プレゼンツ REAL TIMES）」『美術手帖』64 巻 964 号、美術出版社、2012 年、42 頁）。
*** 本展出展作（season 6）のうち、カオス・ラウンジと人工知能美学芸術研究会は過去の収録に基づく。

* Ukawa Naohiro, @DOMMUNE: The super magic of live streaming taught by final media!!!!!!!! (Kawade Shobo Shinsha, 2011), p. 48.
** Shimanuki Taisuke, "Ukawa Naohiro Interview—DOMMUNE's next target after entering its fifth year," in CINRA.NET (October 20, 2014) https://www.cinra.net/interview/201410-dommune. Even before this project, Ukawa had commented about DOMMUNE that "this is an act of taking a slice of culture to represent 'the current time.' For that reason, it's important to leave archives... it is a key cultural legacy for the subculture." ("ARTIST INTERVIEW Ukawa Naohiro: What is The Final Media DOMMUNE? (Feature: Chim↑Pom Presents REAL TIMES)," Bijutsu Techo vol. 64 no. 964, 2012: 42).
*** For this exhibition (Season 6), the Chaos*Lounge and Artificial Intelligence Art and Aesthetics Research Group interviews are based on earlier recordings.

「平成美術：うたかたと瓦礫 1989−2019」展示風景
京都市京セラ美術館、2021年

Installation view of *Bubbles/Debris: Art of the Heisei Period 1989−2019*
Kyoto City KYOCERA Museum of Art, 2021

9

本書カバーを切り取り該当する図版をお貼りください

Please detach the corresponding plate from the cover and paste it here.

カオス*ラウンジ　Chaos*Lounge

2009 Heisei 21 —　東京｜Tokyo

　インターネットを活動のベースにしたアーティストたちの集合体。2008 年にアーティストの藤城嘘（1990–）がオフラインのイベント企画として「ポストポッパーズ」を立ち上げ、その藤城が 2009 年 3 月に東京・国分寺で行った展覧会のタイトルとして「カオス*ラウンジ」という名称は生まれた。

　2010 年よりキュレーターとして美術家・美術批評家の黒瀬陽平（1983–）が参加し、以降、梅沢和木（1985–）を加えた 3 人が中心となり、活動を展開してきた。当初はインターネット上の言論空間に加え、pixiv など画像投稿サイトのネットワークやそのコミュニティが形成された時期にあたり、ネット空間では新たな世代が技術的なスキルを前提に、すべてをアーキテクチャに還元する工学的な思考とデータベースの蓄積からの引用により、クールな DIY で誰もが制作・発信するようになってきていた。そうしたスキルとネットワークをもつかれらがギャラリースペースなどのリアルな空間に舞台を移し、2010 年 4 月に「カオス*ラウンジ 2010 in 高橋コレクション日比谷」を開催。これまでアートとして可視化されてこなかったネット上の特殊なキャラクター表現と、その担い手たちをギャラリーに召喚した。同年 5 月、ネットワーク上で遊ぶ「ギーク」（ネットの技術的な知識に特化したオタク）が会場に常駐する「破滅*ラウンジ」（NANZUKA UNDERGROUND［東京］）を開催し、ネット上の言論空間でも活発な議論を提起することで、日本の現代美術史に新しい文脈を加えた。

　近年では、福島県いわき市で行った「カオス*ラウンジ新芸術祭 2017 市街劇「百五〇年の孤独」」（2017–2018 年）をはじめとして、東日本大震災の被災地に赴き、「復興」「鎮魂」「巡礼」をキーワードに、現地での活動も行っていた。

　本展では、震災前と後のそれぞれのプロジェクトを橋渡ししつつ回顧するインスタレーションを計画していた。しかし、カオス*ラウンジの組織内のトラブルにより、展示計画の実現のための交渉を継続することが困難となった。この状況を踏まえ、本展では「カオス*ラウンジ宣言 2010」を資料として展示する。［NM］

Chaos*Lounge is a group of artists who made the internet the base for their activities. Artist Fujishiro Uso (1990–) launched *postpoppers* in 2008 as an offline event project, and the "Chaos*Lounge" name first emerged in March 2009 as the title of an exhibition by Fuijshiro in Kokubunji, Tokyo.

　Artist and critic Kurose Yohei (1983–) joined the group as curator in 2010, followed by Umezawa Kazuki (1985–). Fujishiro, Kurose, and Umezawa have since been the core members of the group. Around the time when Kurose and Umezawa joined, online platforms such as pixiv had arisen, databases providing cool do-it-yourself interfaces that gave everybody the opportunity to create and share their work. Online communities were developing around them, predicated on the technical skills of a new generation, with everything feeding back into the architecture. Chaos*Lounge next shifted their venue into real space, presenting *Chaos*Lounge 2010 in Takahashi collection Hibiya*, in April 2010. In May 2010, *Ruin*Lounge* (NANZUKA UNDERGROUND, Tokyo) put the spotlight on the lives of geeks playing with networks, and actual geeks (members of the otaku subculture distinguished by technical knowledge of the Net) were a fixture at the venue. The event triggered animated discussions in chatrooms and forums online, adding a new context to the history of contemporary art in Japan.

　More recently, the group has been visiting areas hit by the Great East Japan Earthquake in 2011, using keywords meaning "recovery," "repose of souls," and "pilgrimage" as the basis for activities such as "CHAOS*LOUNGE New art festival 2017 city play 'One Hundred and Fifty Years of Solitude'" (2017–2018), which they organized in Iwaki, Fukushima.

　Plans for *Bubbles/Debris* initially included a retrospective installation bridging the collective's work pre- and post-disaster projects. Unfortunately, internal issues at Chaos*Lounge made it difficult to arrange such an installation in time for the exhibition. Given these circumstances, *The Manifesto of CHAOS*LOUNGE 2010* is exhibited to illustrate the group's work. [NM]

ゼロ年代と呼ばれたこの10年、日本のアートは何も生み出さなかった。

今、われわれの目の前に広がっているのは、欧米を真似たアートフェアの乱立によってつくられた、ありもしない国内アート・マーケットの表象と、助成金を喰い物にしながら無限に繰り返される慈善事業だけである。この風景は、ゼロ年代の幕開けに突きつけられた、日本のアートについての問い（「日本ゼロ年」、「オタク」、「スーパーフラット」……）を徹底的に無化することによって成立している。

ゼロ年代に入って、ますますわれわれの生活を変容させた情報化の進展は、あろうことかアートにおいて、日本と世界の格差を埋めるものとして、きわめて楽観的に解釈された。日本のアートはアクチュアルな文化であることをやめてしまった。アーティストたちは「物」に充足することで、「情報」から目を逸らし、ナマな文化の営みに身を晒さない。無根拠なアートの神秘性によって身分を保障されると同時に、小器用な職人として囲い込まれている。「悪い場所」は再び隠蔽された。

ゼロ年代の間、カオス*ラウンジは地上に姿を現さなかった。なぜなら地上は、本当は焼け野原であることを知っていたからだ。Google、2ちゃんねる、mixi、Flickr、YouTube、ニコニコ動画、Twitter、Tumblr……、カオス*ラウンジはネットの中で、主にアーキテクチャと呼ばれるインフラストラクチャーの変化とともに存在していた。

そこは常に、膨大に、匿名的な想像力がうずまき、作品未満の作品、コンテンツ未満のコンテンツが現れては消える場所であり、にもかかわらず、作者性に目覚めてしまった有象無象の集う場所である。増殖を続けるアーキテクチャは、アートの神秘性を認めない。そこでは、すべてが可視化され、分類され、操作可能となる。内面などない。知性も感性も、すべてはアーキテクチャ上で、システマチックに組み立てられてゆく。人間の内面は、アーキテクチャによる工学的な介入によって蒸発する。

カオス*ラウンジから生まれたアーティストは、それでもなお、地上に脱出することはなかった。なぜなら、地上で生み出されているものはアートではないと知っていたからだ。彼らは、アーキテクチャによる工学的介入を、一度は徹底的に受け入れる。アートに神秘性などない。人間の知性も感性も内面も、すべては工学的に記述可能である。しかし、彼らは、アーキテクチャによる工学的介入の結果に対し、さらに人為的に介入を試みるのである。彼らは、アーキテクチャによって、自動的に吐き出される演算結果を収集する。そして、自らがひとつのアーキテクチャとなって、新たな演算を開始するのだ。

カオス*ラウンジは今、ようやく、ここに姿を現す。単なる「情報」でも「物」でもない、アーキテクチャ時代のアート、すなわち、一〇年代のアートとして。

In the decade since the year 2000, contemporary art in Japan has produced nothing.

Now, the vista before us is an image of a domestic art market that is mere mirage, one that mimics the rise of western art fairs; just a charity infinitely sustained by a diet of government sponsorship.

This Japanese art landscape is the product of an utter failure to question the Japanese art churned out at the start of the 2000s, that referred to by the terms "Japan Year Zero," "otaku" and "Superflat."

Our lifestyles have been continually transformed by developments in information technology, developments that somewhat surprisingly have been interpreted optimistically in the art sector as having the potential to bridge the gap between Japan and the rest of the world.

Japanese art gave up being a real culture.

By supplying the "objects" of the culture, Japanese artists have turned away from the information sphere failing to expose themselves to the activities of a raw culture. Given status by the unwarranted mystique of art, they are simultaneously pigeonholed as skillful artisans.

Once again, the "bad place" has been disguised.

Chaos*Lounge never showed itself during the last decade, as it was aware that the world was actually a wasteland. Chaos*Lounge existed online alongside the changing infrastructures that we call the architecture of the web: Google, 2 channel, mixi, Flickr, YouTube, Nico Nico Douga, Twitter, Tumbler, and so on.

It was a whirlpool of constant vast, anonymous imagination, a place of non-art art and non-content content appearing and disappearing. Nonetheless, it was also a gathering place for the masses, finally waking up to their authorship.

This continually proliferating world does not recognize the mystique of art. Everything is visualized, classified and operable.

Now nothing is internal; intellect and sensibility, everything is assembled systematically on the digital architecture. Human interiority evaporates through the technological intervention of this architecture.

Still the artists born out of Chaos*Lounge did not break out into the real world, since they knew that the things being created there were not art. They completely accept technological intervention via web architecture. In art there is no mystique. Human intellect, sensibility, and interiority are all describable via technology.

However, they do experiment with intervening further in the results of this digital intervention, collating the computerized results spat out by the web, then becoming architects themselves, and embarking on wholly new calculations.

Now here at last Chaos*Lounge has made its appearance.

It is neither "data" nor "thing," but the art of the internet age, that is to say, the art of the coming decade.

第 3 章
瓦礫の時代

2011年〜2019年、平成23年から平成31年

作家なき作品へ

　2011年／平成23年3月11日に突如として勃発した巨大地震と原子力発電所のメルトダウンは、それまでの価値観を白紙に戻すほどの衝撃を作り手たちにもたらした。

　これほどまでの事態に対し、美術はまったくの無力であったからだ。もとより無力であることで逆説的な効力を持つのがアートでもあったわけだが、そのことを逆手にとることもできないほどの、それは過酷な危機であった。多くの美術家たちが沈黙し、せいぜいが支援といった活動に甘んじるなか、第二期／第2章に登場した集合的・集団的美術家たちの大震災への反応には、そうした紋切り型に収まらないものが当初より見られた。すでに触れたChim↑Pomやカオス*ラウンジ、そして被災地の名を文字どおり含み、いまや大震災後の課題そのものとなった「東北画は可能か？」や、被災地支援のための大々的なフェスティバルを企画したDOMMUNEなどが、本当の意味でその力量を試されたのは、この大震災を契機としてのことであった。言い換えれば、かれらはこのような危機の時代の到来を先取りしていたと言うこともできるだろう。いまや、近代に確立された個人の名を基点とし、「作品」を単位に評価、歴史化される美術が、その有効性を根本から問われていた。

　こうしたなかから姿を現した美術家たちによる集合的・集団的活動は、さらにその離合集散性を高め、一時的な目標のために流動的に集結すると、その後も断続的に持続するものや、美術とは無縁のものも含め、はるかに流動的・複合的な性質を帯びるようになり、あえてわかりやすい言葉に置き換えれば、コレクティヴというよりもプロジェクトへと推移していった。美術家、國府理の不慮の死をきっかけに、かれが遺した作品？ 作家名？ 概念？ タイトル？ 保存？ 再制作？ はいかにして可能かを問う「水中エンジン」再制作プロジェクト」や、壁一枚隔てただけの武蔵野美術大学と朝鮮大学校のあいだに長く存在しなかった交流を美術家たちの手で実現・回復しようとする「突然、目の前がひらけて」などは、アーティスト・コレクティヴとも旧来のアート・プロジェクトとも相当に異なる一回性を持つ。平成の幕引きを予感しつつ、作家なき作品の時代がやってきたのだ。

　また、美術教育や表現ではなく福祉支援活動から発し、「遅咲きレボリューション」「ヤンキー人類学」など、国家の文化政策により日本では主に知的障害者に限定された「アール・ブリュット」では認知されない*、美術界からは疎外されたアウトサイダー・アートを列島行脚的に発掘、連携させることをめざすクシノテラスや、人工知能が美術にもたらす表現そのものの根源的な転回的性質を、展

Chapter 3
The Age of Debris

2011-2019 / Heisei 23-31

Projects without Artists

The massive earthquake, tsunami, and meltdown of the nuclear plant on March 11 2011/ Heisei 23 generated a shock to the Japanese creative community that caused many artists to reassess their practice.

"Art" can seem powerless before a crisis of such magnitude. Art has a paradoxical strength derived from vulnerability, but this became a watershed moment when many artists went silent, or busied themselves with humanitarian support at some level. Right from the moment of the crisis, however, second period artistic collective practices including those of Chim↑Pom, Chaos*Lounge, Is Tohoku-ga possible?, and DOMMUNE, which planned large-scale festivals to support devastated areas, showed that they were ready for this moment. In Japan, at least, it was the artist collective and not the "name" artist, nor the "art work," which forged new artistic paths forward, and which caused many of us to question the way the international art world has come to function.

This new resurgence of collective activities meant an increase in ways of meeting and parting. Gatherings for temporary purposes, some continuing, some leading to activities unrelated to art, each co-evolving a creative network increasingly fluid and complex, a transition towards projects rather than collectives. "Kokufu Osamu's Engine in the Water re-creation project," an attempt to recreate a project by the late artist Kokufu Osamu, raised questions at every level: what? who? concept? title? preservation? reproduction? "Suddenly, the view spreads out before us." was a project to realize and recover exchange between Musashino Art University (a leading Japanese arts university) and Korea University (a University teaching a North Korean curriculum in Korean in Japan), which are located in adjoining buildings, with just one wall in-between. Both projects were one-offs. They were not the result of artist collectives and neither were they traditional art projects. As the curtain fell on the Heisei, we witnessed the arrival of a time of projects without artists.

Art space Kushino Terrace aims to excavate and present outsider art (which should be distinguished from Art Brut, which is limited to developmentally challenged artists in Japan as national cultural policy)* typically excluded from the art world. One might describe their activity as welfare rather than art education. Examples include art by institutionalized persons including death-row prisoners, thugs, and the elderly. The Artificial Intelligence

示や発表、討論、研究会などを通じて模索する人工知能美学芸術研究会（AI 美芸研）も、従来のコレクティヴやプロジェクトの枠に収めることはできない。また、当初から「予備校」を名乗り、相模原という匿名的な場所で近隣的に散在しながら、ツイッターに象徴されるソーシャルメディアを活用し、教育と表現、発表と生活の垣根を共同／共働的に再定義することを試みるパープルームも、従来の美術とそうでないもの、アートとその外部との境界線上を往復する点で、これまでに例を見ない離合集散性（プロジェクト）を持っている。

　概して言えば、平成年間を通じて、このような美術家たちによる集合的・集団的な活動は断続的に続いていた。だが、その傾向はその都度の社会的な背景に応じ、相当に異なる特徴を備え持つ。だが、美術がますます個人——そもそもこの個人という概念の輪郭が見失われつつある——による制作だけでは困難となるさらなる危機の時代を迎えつつある現在、こうした美術のコレクティヴ化、プロジェクト化はその都度、かたちを変えつつ、今後いっそう名付けえぬものへと生成・変化していくことが予測される。だが、繰り返すようだが、こうしたコレクティヴないしはプロジェクトという言葉自体は、あくまで暫定的なものであって、時代の様相に適応できていない既製の仕様であることはあきらかで、それに代わる概念の絶え間のない刷新が必要であることは、改めて強調しておく必要がある。きっと私たちは、依然として旧来の美術やアートからの緊急避難や仮設のまっただなかにいるのだろう。そう思って周囲を見渡せば、そこかしこに「ラウンジ」や「テラス」、「研究会」といった、小さいが遊撃的な室内（方丈？）の比喩が見られることは、タイトルに鴨長明『方丈記』による書き出しの一節からとった「うたかた」を引く本展／本書にとって、来たるべき兆しになるかもしれない。

　「うたかた」と「瓦礫（デブリ）」に引き寄せて言うならば、平成という時代の美術は、つまりは「平成美術」は、前半に「バブル」の余韻を長く引き、後半に「デブリ」が散らばる荒涼とした風景をずっと、心のどこかで「バブル／デブリ」を透して二重に垣間見て来たと言えるだろう。

付記　ここでの 3 章にわたる「作家作品」だけを目にしたなら、本展では、実際の会場での展示もまた、3 つのセクションに分かれて、時系列的に構成されているように感じられるかもしれない。実際にはまったくそのようなことはなく、会場での展示・構成はむしろ、進んで渾然一体（うたかたと瓦礫）となされている。本書は、そのような渾然一体から、各自の「平成美術」をもう一度想起し、組み立て直し、再構成してみることができるための手引きとして活用できるよう編集されている。そのため、尺度としての年表（会場では「平成の壁」と名付けた——思えば平成は壁の解体＝交通から始まったが、ふたたび壁を築き始めること＝分断で終わった）をとくに重視した。総じて展示では、平成という 30 年あまりにおよぶ時間を空間に見立てている。この空間は「方丈（集合）」と「道、もしくは路地」からなり、最低限の公共性を備えた「界隈」と見なされる。端的に言えば、この仮想の「界隈」が平成美術である。

＊椹木野衣「美術と時評 82：批評と評価——障害をめぐるアートをめぐる」『ART iT』2019 年 3 月 9 日公開
https://www.art-it.asia/top/contributertop/198188（最終閲覧日：2021 年 1 月 5 日）

（椹木野衣）

Art and Aesthetics Research Group explores the fundamental invertible nature of expression that AI brings to art through exhibitions, releases, debates, and workshops. Their activities also extend beyond pre-existing collectives and projects. Parplume calls itself a cram school. Scattered in neighborhoods of generic sprawl in Sagamihara, Parplume utilizes social media such as Twitter to try to redefine the borders between education and expression, presentation and living, collectively and conjointly. It is an unparalleled project of separation, gathering, and dispersal, in the reciprocation between conventional and non-conventional art, and art and non-art.

Generally speaking, such aggregated and/or collective art activities continued intermittently throughout the Heisei Period. The differences in tendencies often correspond to the differences in social backgrounds. Today, it's becoming increasingly difficult for art to be produced by individuals — we are even losing sight of the conceptual outline of what an individual is — and it's likely that artistic practice will further be generated and transformed within collectives and projects. It bears repeating that the words "collective," and "project," are only used as tentative placeholders. New practices must not be shackled within old conceptual frameworks, and we need to remain vigilant about continuously renewing and substituting conceptual models. After all, we may still be intellectually sheltering in temporary evacuation facilities of outdated construction. Looking around, I find a landscape of "lounges," "terraces," and "workshops." Analogies of small but mobile huts (*hojo*?) are ubiquitous. And that could be a sign of what's coming, for this exhibition/catalogue which references "bubbles" from the second sentence of *Hojoki* by Kamo no Chomei.

Referring to "bubbles" and "debris," the art of the Heisei Period, or the "Heisei art," the lingering after-effect of "bubbles" in the first half, and a projected scenery of "debris" scattered in the second half.

Note: As you view the artists and the works in each of the three chapters here, you may imagine that the installation is similarly divided into three sections, organized in chronological order. In reality, the curation is instead deliberately integrated according to a reading of bubbles and debris. This catalogue has been edited as a companion which can be used for each individual to reimagine, re-assemble, and reconstruct for themselves. For that reason this catalogue places emphasis on the chronological record — and a corresponding the "Heisei Wall" at the venue — as a wall diagram, but on reflection, this organizing principle demonstrated that Heisei actually began with the dissolution of walls = ever-accelerating flows of capital and information, etc, and ending with the rebuilding of walls = division. In a broad sense, the exhibition extrudes the Heisei, a generation, into space. We find "*hojo* (huts)" and "roads, or alleyways," in highly granular "neighborhoods" of minimal connection. This virtual "neighborhood" is a landscape of Heisei art.

* Sawaragi Noi, "Criticism and Assessment: Concerning Art Concerning Disability", March 9 2019, *ART iT*.

(Sawaragi Noi)

パープルーム　Parplume

2013　Heisei 25 ―　相模原（神奈川）｜Kanagawa

パープルームのアー写
Promotion photo of Parplume
2020

パープルーム

美術家・梅津庸一（1982-）が 2013 年に設立。パープルームは、梅津自身の自宅兼アトリエに、「予備校」を中心に「ギャラリー」などが組み込まれた空間で展開される、生活と制作が渾然一体となった運動体である。そのモデルのひとつは黒田清輝が主宰した天真道場であり、近代絵画史の末尾に自分を位置づけている梅津個人の活動とも連続性が見出せる。パープルームは美術をめぐる教育の制度がもつ諸問題を俎上に載せながら、集団・共同体の在り方をめぐって実験的な創作活動を実践している。その実践はパープルーム TV、パープルームギャラリー、パープルクッキング、パープルミーティングなど多岐にわたる。パープルームが通常の予備校と著しく異なるのは、大学進学ではなくアート界に直接参画することを目標としている点である。また、固定化した師弟関係にまつわる諸問題には敏感に反応を示してきた。主宰の梅津が、介護に長く携わった経験も大きいだろう。なお各作家は「予備校生」と呼ばれてきたが、本展の出展者である安藤裕美（1994-）、アラン（1991-）、わきもとさき（1994-）、シエニーチュアン（1994-）については、2020 年から「メンバー」となっている。

Parplume

Parplume was founded by artist Umetsu Yoichi (1982-) in 2013. Parplume embodies a movement based on the idea of life and artistic production being all in one. Its activities are based in a space that is integrated into Umetsu's home and studio, consisting mainly of a preparatory school, but also incorporating a gallery and other functions. One of its models is the Tenshin Dojo that was led by Kuroda Seiki, and it can be seen as continuous with Umetsu's own practice, which he locates, in terms of art history, at the tail end of modern painting. Parplume instigates debate on the challenges of educational systems associated with art, but at the same time, it is involved in experimental artistic practice to explore the ideal forms of groups and communities. That practice is diverse, and includes Parplume TV, Parplume Gallery, Parpl Cooking, and Parpl Meeting. Where Parplume most obviously differs from regular preparatory schools is in aiming for its graduates to head straight into the art world instead of going to university first. It is also sensitive to the various issues that can occur in an entrenched student-teacher relationship. Umetsu's involvement in nursing care for many years has a substantial influence on his work. The Artists in this preparatory school had long been called "students," but those participating in this exhibition—Ando Yumi (1994-), Alan (1991-), Wakimoto Saki (1994-), and Shieneychuan (1994-)— were designated "members" in 2020.

[左上｜above left]
アラン
コムニカチオ
Alan
Communicatio
2018

[右上｜above right]
アラン
ゾンビマスター
Alan
Zombie Master
2017

梅津庸一
フロレアル －汚い光に混じった大きな花粉－
Umetsu Yoichi
*Floreal - Big pollen intermingled
with dirty light*
2012–2014

シエニーチュアン
私はそのような性質を見たことがありませんが、
あなたがゆっくりと反対側から近づいているようです
Shieneychuan
*I've never seen such a personality, but I think
you're slowly approaching from the other side*
2019

安藤裕美
見晴らし小屋に帰るアラン
Ando Yumi
*Alan Returns to the
Parplume Vantage Point*
2019

安藤裕美
光のサイコロジー
Ando Yumi
Psychology of Light
2019–2020

わきもとさき
ひとりくらし
Wakimoto Saki
Living Alone
2019–

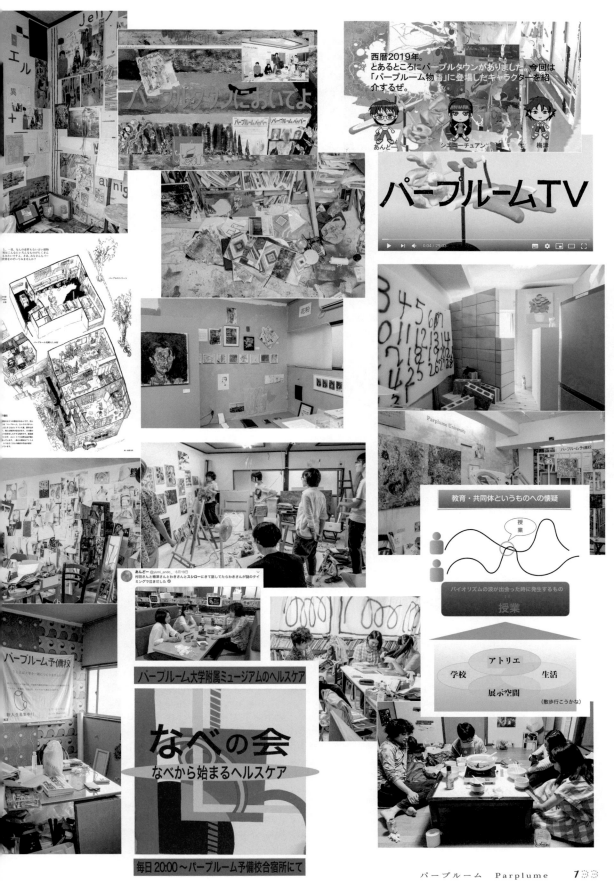

本展には「花粉の王国」と題されたインスタレーションが展示される。「花粉」は梅津とパープルームにとってしばしば言及される重要なキーワードである。「花粉」とは、性格、癖、生活様式や創作行為など、個々人にまつわる多様な要素を意味し、それらがさまざまな場で「受粉」されて結実することにより生まれる新たな美術のあり方を示唆している。とはいえ、日々展開される上述のような制作と発表、生活がさまざまな位相で分かち難く連結している活動を一元的に集約することは困難である。したがって本展での展示は、その多様な活動のなかから一部の物的要素の構成でみる、パープルームという運動体の素描ということになる。

　中央に馬蹄形の構造物があり、その上に黒田清輝の《智・感・情》（1899 年）からインスパイアされた梅津の連作《フル・フロンタル》（7点組、2018 年 –）を扇型に展示する。これに加えて、フランスのナビ派に強い関心を持つ安藤によるパープルームの日常を描いたアニメーション《光のサイコロジー》（2019–2020 年）が上映され、ゲームデザイナーとしても活躍するアランによるオリジナルボードゲーム《ゾンビマスター》（2017 年）や鳥が生み出す魔力の源を図解した作品《マナ・バード》（2017 年）他が展示される。また生活と制作の一体化を体現するわきもとのドローイング、コラージュ、そしてインスタレーション《ひとりくらし》（2019 年 –）。シュルレアリスムの作家が試みたオートマティスムを援用しながら、「ポスト・キャラアイコン絵画」を追求するシエニーチュアンのペインティングなどが展示の構成要素となる。

　こうしたかれらの作品群は、梅津の言を借りれば、パープルームによる「貧しい総合芸術」の展開である。「貧しい芸術」といえばイタリアの 1960 年代前衛美術アルテ・ポーヴェラを連想するが、ここでは演劇・映画に替わる新しい「総合芸術」として、自らの創造活動を位置づけている。この新しい運動体には現代美術の枠組みをさらに押し広げるもうひとつの可能性が開かれている。[NM]

Parplume presents an installation entitled *Kingdom of Pollen*. Pollen is an important keyword for Umetsu and Parplume, appearing from time to time in works and statements. Pollen signifies a diversity of elements associated with individuals—such as character, habits, way of life, and creative acts. It indicates a new approach to art that emerges from the fruits of pollination by such elements in a variety of scenes and situations. Despite this derivation, it is not easy to produce a single coherent exhibit by consolidating the day-to-day production and exhibition activities with the interlinked, hard-to-separate activities of the various phases of everyday life. Consequently, the installation is an attempt to sketch Parplume as an operational entity consisting of some of the physical elements that are a part of the group's multivariate activities.

The installation uses a horseshoe-shaped structure in the center of the space. On the structure—inspired by Kuroda Seiki's *WISDOM, IMPRESSION, SENTIMENT* (1899)— is Umetsu's multi-part work *Full Frontal* (7 panels, 2018–), arranged so as to be fanned out in an arc. There is also a screening of the *Psychology of Light* (2019–2020) animation depicting a regular day at Parplume by Ando, who has a keen interest in the French artists known as the Nabis. Alan, who is also a game designer, provides works including an original board game *Zombie Master* (2017) and *Mana Bird* (2017), which illustrates the source of the magic that a bird produces. There are also drawings and collages by Wakimoto, embodying a unification of life and art production, together with her installation *Living Alone* (2019–). Shieneychuan exhibits predominantly paintings, invoking the surrealists' experiments in automatism as she explores post-character icon painting.

According to Umetsu, the group of works by these artists is a development from Parplume's "general arte povera." The term recalls the avant-garde Arte Povera artists of 1960s Italy, but here it is used for a new general art classification that, in Parplume's creative activities, takes the place of theater and film. This new movement has the potential to further extend the envelope of contemporary art. [NM]

10

本書カバーを切り取り該当する図版をお貼りください

Please detach the corresponding plate from the cover and paste it here.

「平成美術：うたかたと瓦礫（デブリ） 1989−2019」展示風景
京都市京セラ美術館、2021年

Installation view of *Bubbles/Debris: Art of the Heisei Period 1989−2019*
Kyoto City KYOCERA Museum of Art, 2021

突然、目の前がひらけて
Suddenly, the view spreads out before us.

2015　Heisei 27 —　　小平（東京）| Tokyo

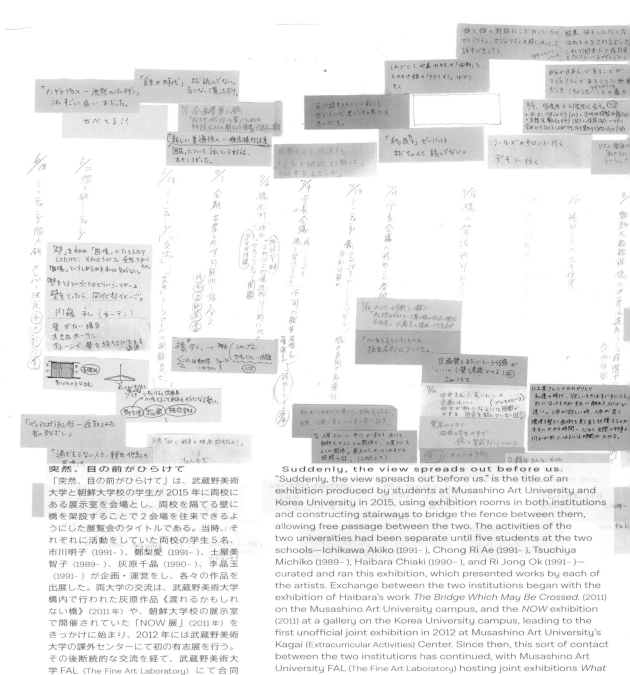

突然、目の前がひらけて

「突然、目の前がひらけて」は、武蔵野美術大学と朝鮮大学校の学生が 2015 年に両校にある展示室を会場とし、両校を隔てる壁に橋を架設することで 2 会場を往来できるようにした展覧会のタイトルである。当時、それぞれに活動をしていた両校の学生 5 名、市川明子（1991–）、鄭梨愛（1991–）、土屋美智子（1989–）、灰原千晶（1990–）、李晶玉（1991–）が企画・運営をし、各々の作品を出展した。両大学の交流は、武蔵野美術大学構内で行われた灰原作品《渡れるかもしれない橋》（2011 年）や、朝鮮大学校の展示室で開催されていた「NOW 展」（2011 年）をきっかけに始まり、2012 年には武蔵野美術大学の課外センターにて初の有志展を行う。その後断続的な交流を経て、武蔵野美術大学 FAL（The Fine Art Laboratory）にて合同展「この場所にいるということ」（2013 年）、「孤独なアトリエ」（2014 年）が開催され、後者は朝鮮大学校美術科のギャラリーにも巡回した。2017 年には「第 6 回都美セレクショングループ展」（東京都美術館）にて同メンバーで「境界を跨ぐと、」を開催。以来、本展で 3 度目の集結となる。

Suddenly, the view spreads out before us.

"Suddenly, the view spreads out before us." is the title of an exhibition produced by students at Musashino Art University and Korea University in 2015, using exhibition rooms in both institutions and constructing stairways to bridge the fence between them, allowing free passage between the two. The activities of the two universities had been separate until five students at the two schools—Ichikawa Akiko (1991–), Chong Ri Ae (1991–), Tsuchiya Michiko (1989–), Haibara Chiaki (1990–), and Ri Jong Ok (1991–)—curated and ran this exhibition, which presented works by each of the artists. Exchange between the two institutions began with the exhibition of Haibara's work *The Bridge Which May Be Crossed.* (2011) on the Musashino Art University campus, and the *NOW* exhibition (2011) at a gallery on the Korea University campus, leading to the first unofficial joint exhibition in 2012 at Musashino Art University's Kagai (Extracurricular Activities) Center. Since then, this sort of contact between the two institutions has continued, with Musashino Art University FAL (The Fine Art Laboratory) hosting joint exhibitions *What brings you here and where'd you go?* (2013) and *Return to the studio alone* (2014), with the latter exhibition followed by a run at the Korea University art department's gallery. In 2017, the same artists joined together to participate in the Tokyo Metropolitan Art Museum's *Group Show of Contemporary Artists 2017*, where they presented *To the other side of the boundaries,*. Their work for *Bubbles/Debris* is their third project together.

[上 | above]
区画壁を跨ぐ橋のタイムライン（アーカイブ資料）
Timeline for "A Bridge Striding over a Fence" (archival material)
2014-2015

[右上 | upper right]
灰原千晶、李晶玉
区画壁を跨ぐ橋のドローイング
Haibara Chiaki, Ri Jong Ok
Drawing for "A Bridge Striding over a Fence"
2015

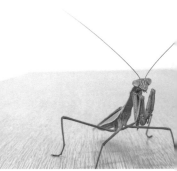

土屋美智子　　　　　　　　　　　Tsuchiya Michiko
昨日以前と明日以降の距離　　　　*Distance Between "Before Yesterday" and "After Tomorrow"*
映像　　　　　　　　　　　　　　Video 2017

　本展では、市川明子、鄭梨愛、土屋美智子、灰原千晶、李晶玉の5人が、2015年の展覧会「突然、目の前がひらけて」を再構成する。当時出展した作品、資料、プロジェクトから着想を得た作品の展示に加え、武蔵野美術大学と朝鮮大学校の敷地を跨いで設置された橋を再現する。

　2015年の展覧会は、隣接する両校の境界にある壁に橋を架ける試みから始まった。その過程で重ねられた5人の対話は、展覧会や橋の制作に関することにとどまらず、各自のアイデンティティやそれを取り巻くイデオロギー、歴史観にまで及ぶこともあった。異なる環境で育った同年代の作家たちが各々の視点に基づき行うこの対話は、しかしひとつの結論を目指すものではなかった。むしろ、各自の見解を尊重し、理解できないこともまた前提とした内省的なやりとりであり、それは多様な解釈を可能にするゆるやかな連帯と見ることもできる。

　当時は、ちょうど安保関連法案（2015年成立）を巡る世論の分裂が激しく、ヘイトスピーチが問題となっていた時期だったこともあり、日本人と在日朝鮮人の非対称な構図が背景にあったとも考えられる*。しかし、5人の対話の記録をたどっていくと、その構図を「マイノリティ／マジョリティ」という括りへ落とし込む姿勢自体の見直しも確認できる**。その点で、この展覧会は地理的に孤立した日本において、日本人がマジョリティとして自覚的に多文化主義を認めることの困難さを炙り出すとともに、「民族的な差異という単純な構図に括れるものでもない〔……〕アイデンティティ」***の複雑さや解釈の幅をも提示している。

　本展では、2015年に制作された高さ約2メートルの橋を会場の中央に架設する。かつての展覧会で架けられた橋では、両校に跨がる共生への強い意志が見られたが、本展の橋がひらく視界の先には一体何が見えるだろうか。5人の問いかけは、場所と時間、そして彼女たちの対話を超えて、橋を渡る鑑賞者へと投げかけられているのである。[TA]

鄭梨愛　　　　　　　　　　　　　　　　　　　Chong Ri Ae
ある所のある時におけるある一人の話と語り聞かせ　　*The Story of One Person at a Time in a Place and Its Narrative*
映像　　　　　　　　　　　　　　　　　　　　Video 2015

灰原千晶　渡れるかもしれない橋　朝鮮大学校の寮に塀越しに接する武蔵野美術大学の端にて
Haibara Chiaki　*The Bridge Which May Be Crossed.*
Campus of Musashino Art University adjacent dormitory of Korea University across the fence.　　2011

民族も国家も共同体幻想も幻滅は

作り出した幻滅とメンタルに変化ます

作り出した幻滅とは異います か

＊ 椹木野衣「この橋に両端（はし）はある
か」『美術手帖』68 巻 1032 号、美術
出版社、2016 年、210 頁。
＊＊「「マイノリティー／マジョリティー」
という言葉は、このミーティングの中
の相関図じゃないですけどそういうも
のを表す時に使った言葉でした。それ
ぞれの存在を表すのであれば、「マイノ
リティー／マジョリティー」で表すの
はざっくりすぎるのは勿論で、〔……〕
空気を分けたらという例えで言ってい
た〔……〕」（鄭）や「ひとまとめにし
ようとすると、ばらけているものが一
緒に映ってしまう感じがする」（土屋）
などといった発言は、この構図が結論
にはならないことを示している。「武蔵
美×朝鮮大　突然、目の前がひらけて」
制作委員会編『武蔵美×朝鮮大　突然、
目の前がひらけて』展覧会カタログ、
30 頁。
＊＊＊ 石川卓磨「協働と攪乱の中で」「突然、
目の前がひらけて」制作委員会編『境
界を跨ぐと、』展覧会カタログ、13 頁。

突然、目の前がひらけて　Suddenly, the view spreads out before us.

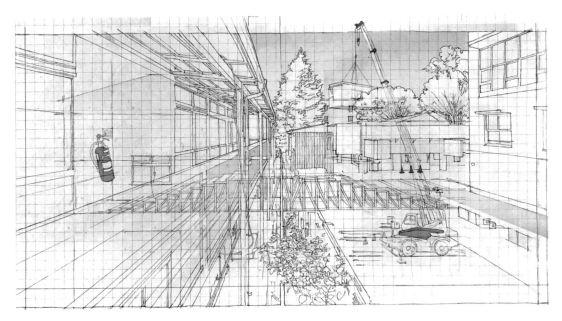

李晶玉　　橋 2021（エスキース）
Ri Jong Ok　　*The Bridge 2021 (Esquisse)*　　2015-2020

For *Bubbles/Debris*, the five artists—Ichikawa Akiko, Chong Ri Ae, Tsuchiya Michiko, Haibara Chiaki, and Ri Jong Ok—reprise and reconfigure their 2015 exhibition *Suddenly, the view spreads out before us*. In addition to exhibiting the works presented in 2015, along with related articles and works inspired by that project, they reproduce the bridge that they created between the neighboring campuses of Musashino Art University and Korea University in Tokyo.

　　The 2015 exhibition began with the attempt to build a bridge over the fence between the universities. The dialogue between the five students as part of that process extended beyond the exhibition and the fabrication of the bridge, encompassing each artist's identity, the ideology that formed part of the context, and views of history. The dialogue was based on the individual perspectives of each of the students, who were of the same generation, but were brought up in very different environments. Reaching a single conclusion was not the objective. Rather, it was an introspective affair, respecting each other's opinions and assuming from the start that there would be times when mutual understanding would not be possible. This could be seen as a moderate coalition facilitating a diversity of interpretation.

　　The original exhibition was held at a time of fierce public debate and division of opinion regarding legislation (passed in 2015) about the role of the Japanese military. The hate speech issue also gained public attention at this time. Part of the background to the exhibition was the unequal status of the majority Japanese population and the ethnic Korean (*Zainichi*) community associated with North Korea.* Nevertheless, examining the records of the dialogue between the students shows their attempts to refactor their approach to avoid categorization along minority/majority lines.** On that point, this 2015 exhibition reveals how difficult it is for the ethnic-Japanese population, as a majority, to consciously admit the existence of multiculturalism in a country which is physically isolated by its geography. The exhibition also attempts to show the breadth of interpretation and the complexity of "identity that cannot be categorized simply in terms of ethnic differences."***

　　The two-meter-high bridge fabricated in 2015 is installed in the current exhibition in Kyoto in the center of the venue. In the earlier exhibition, the bridge straddled the two universities as a powerful assertion of coexistence, but in the 2021 exhibition, it raises the question of what comes into view from the bridge. This question raised by the five artists transcends place, time, and the minutiae of their dialogue, and is directed squarely at the viewers who cross the bridge. [TA]

* Sawaragi Noi, "Kono Hashi ni Ryohashi wa Aruka (Does This Bridge Have Ends?)," *Bijutsu Techo* vol. 68 no. 1032, 2016: 210.
** Comments such as "'Minority/majority' is not one of the relationships that we were actively mapping in the meeting, but we used the phrase when we needed to describe that sort of thing. Of course, 'minority/majority' is of course too rough a category for defining an individual's identity, ... but I used it as an example of a potential dichotomy," (Chong) and "when you try to simplify things by grouping them together, too broad a category can make very disparate things look as if they are the same" (Tsuchiya) show that this categorization was not part of the final composition. Translated from records in "MAU & KU Suddenly, the view spreads out before us." planning committee (eds.), in *MAU & KU Suddenly, the view spreads out before us.* (exhibition catalogue), p. 30.
*** Ishikawa Takuma, "Kyodo to Kakuran no Naka de" (Amid collaboration and disturbance), in "MAU & KU Suddenly, the view spreads out before us." planning committee (eds.), *To the other side of the boundaries*, (exhibition catalogue), p. 13.

「平成美術：うたかたと瓦礫（デブリ）1989–2019」展示風景
京都市京セラ美術館、2021年

Installation view of *Bubbles/Debris: Art of the Heisei Period 1989–2019*
Kyoto City KYOCERA Museum of Art, 2021

11

本書カバーを切り取り該当する図版をお貼りください

Please detach the corresponding plate from the cover and paste it here.

クシノテラス Kushino Terrace

2016 Heisei 28 — 広島 | Hiroshima

櫛野展正　クシノテラスにて（2016年撮影）
Kushino Nobumasa at Kushino Terrace art space, 2016

クシノテラス

2016年、櫛野展正（1976-）が広島県福山市にて設立したアートスペース。伝統的な美術教育を受けず、独学自習で制作を続ける表現者たちによるアウトサイダー・アートを専門に扱う。櫛野は2000年より知的障害者福祉施設職員として働く傍ら、アート活動の支援を行い、福山市の鞆の津ミュージアムにてキュレーターとしてアウトサイダー・アートの展覧会を担当する。その後、未だ世の中から正当な評価を受けていない表現を世に知らせるために、2016年に独立しクシノテラスを開設。自らを「アウトサイダー・キュレーター」と名乗り、障害者の表現活動にとどまらず、全国各地で既存のアートシーンとは異なるフィールドで制作を行うアーティストたちを紹介している。

Kushino Terrace

Kushino Terrace is an art space in Fukuyama, Hiroshima Prefecture, founded in 2016 by Kushino Nobumasa (1976-). It specializes in outsider art, art produced by artists who are self-taught and practice independently without a traditional art education. Kushino began supporting art activities in 2000 while he was working at a welfare facility for people with intellectual disabilities, and he curated exhibitions of outsider art at the Tomonotsu Museum in Fukuyama. In 2016 he established Kushino Terrace with the aim of bringing the world's attention to art that is not yet properly appreciated. Calling himself an "outsider curator," Kushino presents artists from around Japan who are working in fields outside the conventional art scene, including, but not limited to, artists with disabilities.

[上 | above]
ガタロ（2020年撮影）
Gataro, 2020

[右 | right]
ガタロ
雑巾の譜
Gataro
Chronicle of My Cleaning Rags
2018-2020

[上 | above]
稲村米治（2014 年撮影）
Inamura Yoneji, 2014

[右 | right]
稲村米治
昆虫千手観音像
Inamura Yoneji
The Statue of Thousand Armed
Kannon with Insects Inlaid
1975

[上｜above]
上林比東三（2020 年撮影）
Kanbayashi Hitomi, 2020

[右｜right]
上林比東三
未知の生物
Kanbayashi Hitomi
Unknown Creatures
2017-

[上｜above]
ストレンジナイト
無題（創作仮面館）
制作年不明
Strange Knight
Untitled (House of Creative Masks)
Year unknown

[左｜left]
ストレンジナイト（2016 年撮影）
Strange Knight, 2016

[右下 | below right]
スナックジルバ (2020 年撮影)
Snack Jiruba, 2020

[左下 | below left]
城田貞夫とカラクリ人形 (2013 年撮影)
Joden Sadao and his mechanical doll, 2013

クシノテラスは、本展において稲村米治、ガタロ、城田貞夫、上林比東三、ストレンジナイトの5作家を紹介する。

　稲村米治（1919–2017）は、群馬で家族を養いながら、息子の夏休みの宿題を手伝ううちに昆虫標本に熱中し、寝る間を惜しんで昆虫を用いた作品を制作するようになった。採集した昆虫を独自の手法でピンに留め、全身を昆虫が覆う《昆虫新田義貞像》（1970年）を制作した後、残った昆虫を供養する心持ちで《昆虫千手観音像》（1975年）を建立した。クワガタムシ、コガネムシなど、多様な2万匹以上の昆虫に覆われた千手観音像は、玉虫厨子を思わせる輝きを保ち、細やかな千手が昆虫の形体によって再現されている。

　ガタロ（1949–）は、「河童」や「くず拾い」を意味する言葉を自らに命名。広島市営基町アパートのショッピングセンターで30年以上清掃員として勤務する傍ら、日々使用する掃除道具に美しさを感じ、絵を描き始めた。《雑巾の譜》（2018–2020年）は、酷使される雑巾にさまざまな表情を見出し、そこに自らの姿や弱者の立場などを重ね合わせた自画像的な作品。ゴッホの《ジャガイモを食べる人々》の構図を踏襲した《川底の唄》（2019年）では、社会的弱者とされる境遇の人々が闇鍋を囲む様子が描かれている。

　城田貞夫（1940–）は、広島県福山市にある改修した倉庫で「スナックジルバ」を営む。地元の人々が集う場所であり、城田の作品を見ることができる場所でもある。スナックに設けられたステージでは、すべて手作りのカラクリひとり芝居が上演され、その脇には城田が手掛けた木彫りの作品などが陳列される。本展では、地元の人々を楽しませたいという一心で営まれる「スナックジルバ」が、自作のカラクリ人形とともに再現れる。

　上林比東三（1952–）は、京都府舞鶴市で自動車の鈑金塗装店「カーペイント・ヒトミ」を営む傍ら、空想の生き物を表す流木彫像をこれまで300体以上制作している。流木の形状から、宇宙人や妖精などをモチーフにすることで、自由な発想による独創的な表現を追求している。

　ストレンジナイト（生年非公開–2018）は、本名は非公開で「ストレンジナイト」の異名を取る、廃材から2万点以上の仮面やドローイングを制作するマスクマン。栃木の茂みに覆われた建物で、自作を展示する「創作仮面館」を開設した。当初、本人が語った半生は、幼少期に両親と死別し、新聞配達をしながら保護猫20匹以上と暮らすという孤独な生活だった。しかし死後それが偽りで、実は家庭があり、新聞配達をしていなかったことが明らかになる。自らの人生まで創作することでアウトサイダーであろうとする姿勢は、アウトサイダー・アートの評価基準を再考するきっかけとなるだろう。[TA]

In *Bubbles/Debris*, Kushino Terrace presents five artists: Inamura Yoneji, Gataro, Joden Sadao, Kanbayashi Hitomi, and Strange Knight.

Inamura Yoneji (1919–2017) lived in Gunma Prefecture, supporting his family, and gained a fervent interest in insect specimens after helping with his son's summer project for school. Inamura began making artworks that used beetles and other insects, and found himself cutting down on sleep to put more effort into this endeavor. Developing his own method of pinning the insects that he collected, he created *The Statue of Konchu Yoshisada Nitta* (1970), covered entirely with insects ("*konchu*" is the Japanese for "insects"). Then, as an act of consolation for the insects that remained unused, he erected *The Statue of Thousand Armed Kannon with Insects Inlaid* (1975), a thousand-armed Avalokiteshvara statue covered by over 20,000 stag beetles, goldbugs and other insects, making it shine like the Tamamushi Shrine, famed for its decoration of iridescent jewel beetle wings. The miniscule arms and hands on the statue are reproduced by the forms of the insects.

Gataro (1949–) chose his artist name to incorporate the meanings of "*kappa*" and "ragpicker." He worked for over thirty years as a cleaner at the shopping center in the Motomachi Apartments complex of high-rise municipal apartments in Hiroshima. Discovering beauty in the tools that he used each day, he started to draw and paint them. *Chronicle of My Cleaning Rags* (2018–2020) is a series of drawings bringing out the many 'faces' of worn out cleaning rags in a form of self-portraiture, associating them with the artist himself likened to his self-portraiture and with vulnerable members of society. *Song from the River Bottom* (2019), which follows the composition of Vincent van Gogh's *The Potato Eaters*, depicts a group of people labeled as vulnerable by society sharing a *yami-nabe* (a one-pot potluck eaten in the dark).

Joden Sadao (1940–) runs Snack Jiruba, a unique entertainment-focused bar in Fukuyama, Hiroshima Prefecture. It's a place where local people can gather, and also a place to see Joden's works. Inside is a stage where he performs, either alone or with his hand-made mechanical dolls. Alongside the stage are rows of wooden carvings and other creations by Joden. With the home-made mechanical dolls, Snack Jiruba is reproduced for this exhibition to introduce a unique operation dedicated to bringing fun to local people.

Kanbayashi Hitomi (1952–) runs the Car Paint Hitomi auto body and paint shop in Maizuru, Kyoto Prefecture, and has also created over three hundred sculptures of imaginary creatures out of driftwood. Letting his imagination run free, he produces distinctive sculptures of aliens, fairies, and other motifs inspired by the shapes of pieces of driftwood that he finds.

Strange Knight (d. 2018) was a masked man who never disclosed his real name or date of birth, but drew and created over 20,000 masks from offcuts and found materials. He set up the House of Creative Masks in a tree-covered building in Tochigi Prefecture. When he established the museum, he said that his parents had died while he was still a child, and described living alone with over twenty rescued cats, working as a newspaper delivery boy. After his death, it became clear that he still had a family and had not delivered newspapers, but the way that he created his own life story, positioning himself as an outsider, suggests that perhaps the criteria for considering something as outsider art need to be reconsidered. [TA]

「平成美術：うたかたと瓦礫 1989–2019」展示風景
京都市京セラ美術館、2021年

Installation view of *Bubbles/Debris: Art of the Heisei Period 1989–2019*
Kyoto City KYOCERA Museum of Art, 2021

12

本書カバーを切り取り該当する図版をお貼りください

Please detach the corresponding plate from the cover and paste it here.

國府理「水中エンジン」再制作プロジェクト
Kokufu Osamu's Engine in the Water re-creation project

2016-2017 Heisei 28-29　京都｜Kyoto

「國府理 水中エンジン redux」
（後期展）の展示風景
アートスペース虹（京都）、2017 年
Installation view of
Kokufu Osamu's Engine
in the Water redux, part 2
Art Space Niji, Kyoto, 2017

國府理「水中エンジン」再制作プロジェクト
國府（1970-2014、京都市立芸術大学美術研究科彫刻専攻
修了）による作品《水中エンジン》のコンセプトを再
生させるプロジェクトとして、2016 年、インディペン
デントキュレーターの遠藤水城（1975- ）によって企画
され、國府の存命中に《水中エンジン》の展示（アー
トスペース虹［京都］、2012 年）に友人として携わった
アーティストの白石晃一（1980- ）、京都市立芸術大学
芸術資源研究センター研究員の高嶋慈（1983- ）、アー
トメディエーターのはがみちこ（1985- ）ら 4 人が参
加する。高嶋の言葉を借りると、國府は、自作した空
想の乗り物やクルマを素材に用いた立体作品などを通
して、自然とテクノロジー、生態系とエネルギーの循
環といった問題を提起してきた美術作家であった。学
生のときに発表した《自動杭打ち機》（1990 年）、ソー
ラーカーによるアートプロジェクト「Solar Power
Lab.」への参加（1993 年 -）、「KOKUFUMOBIL」シ
リーズ（1994 年 - ）をはじめ、次々と注目を集める作
品が発表される最中、国際芸術センター青森での個展
「相対温室」（2014 年）の作品調整中に事故で還らぬ
人となった。

Kokufu Osamu's Engine in the Water re-creation project
The project to recreate the *Engine in the Water* concept by
Kokufu Osamu (1970-2014, MFA in sculpture from Kyoto City University
of Arts) was first planned by independent curator Endo Mizuki
(1975-) in 2016. The project included the following members:
Shiraishi Koichi (1980-), who, as a friend of Kokufu, had been
involved in the exhibition of *Engine in the Water* when Kokufu was
still alive (Art Space Niji, Kyoto, 2012); Kyoto City University of Arts
Archival Research Center researcher Takashima Megumi (1983-);
and art mediator Haga Michiko (1985-). According to Takashima,
Kokufu was an artist concerned about nature and technology,
and about ecology and the circulation of energy, who addressed
these issues through projects such as three-dimensional works
incorporating imaginary vehicles and cars of his own creation.
Beginning with *Self Driller* (1990) when he was still a student, his
contribution to the *Solar Power Lab.* art project involving solar
cars (1993-), and his *KOKUFUMOBIL* series (1994-), he produced
a succession of attention-grabbing works. In 2014, when making
adjustments to a work that was part of his *Floating Conservatory*
solo exhibition at the Aomori Contemporary Art Centre, Kokufu
collapsed inside the work and never regained consciousness.

冷やし続けなければ暴走してしまうエネルギーの存在、そして最先端と言われた科学技術で稼働させていたシステムを止めるものが唯一まったく私たちに身近な普通の水であるという事実、そして汚染された水を貯蔵するタンクが為すすべなく増えていく光景。それらのすべてが、そこから作り出されていたエネルギーの上に暮らしている私たちの日常感覚に与えた影響は計り知れない。

——國府理「水中エンジン」展（アートスペース虹、2012年）の「展示趣旨」より抜粋

The existence of energy that will run out of control if it were not kept cold, and the fact that only ordinary water, which we are familiar with, can shut down systems that were running on cutting-edge science and technology. And without doing any kind of effort, there is the sight of tanks storing polluted water that is increasing. All of them, the impact on our everyday senses of living on the energy generated there is immeasurable.

—The extract from the statement of Kokufu Osamu, *Engine in the Water*, Art Space Niji, 2012

[左 | right]
國府理
《水中エンジン》ドローイング
Kokufu Osamu
Drawing for Engine in the Water
2012

[右 | far right]
國府理
《「未来のいえ」ドローイング
—水中エンジン—》
Kokufu Osamu
*Drawing for
"Cosmosphere"
—Engine in the Water—*
2013

[下 | below]
國府理
《水中エンジン—貯蔵》
Kokufu Osamu
Engine in the Water—Storage
ca. 2012–ca. 2013

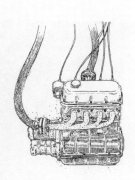

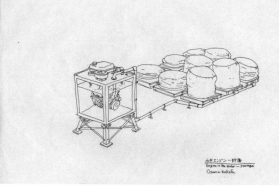

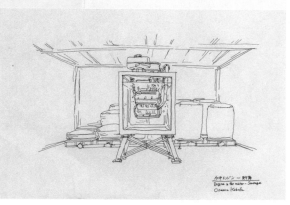

1　2012 年　國府理「水中エンジン」展、アートスペー
　　ス虹（京都）
　　エンジン 1 号機（展示後廃棄）：國府が愛用した軽トラ
　　ックの 550cc エンジン（スバル　サンバー EK23 型）を水
　　に沈め稼働させた。

2　2013 年　「國府理　未来のいえ」展、西宮市大谷記念
　　美術館（兵庫）
　　エンジン 2 号機（展示後廃棄）

1　2012: *Engine in the Water* exhibition (Art Space Niji, Kyoto)
　　Engine No. 1 (destroyed after exhibition): 550cc engine
　　from Kokufu's own truck (Type EK23 engine from a SUBARU
　　SAMBAR) run by Kokufu while submerged in the water.

2　2013: *Osamu Kokufu: Cosmosphere* exhibition
　　(Nishinomiya Otani Memorial Museum, Hyogo)
　　Engine No. 2 (destroyed after exhibition)

1

2

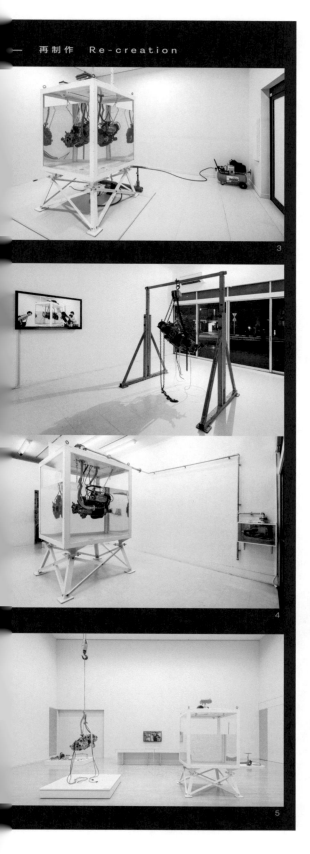

— 再制作 Re-creation

3

4

5

3　2017年　「裏声で歌へ」展、小山市立車屋美術館（栃木）
　　エンジン3号機：再制作プロジェクトによって再現さ
　　れ、会期中に計34回、約5分間の水中稼働を行った。

4　2017年　「國府理 水中エンジン redux」展、アート
　　スペース虹（京都）
　　前期展：「損傷・劣化した」エンジン3号機を水槽に
　　は入れずに、吊って展示した。
　　後期展：エンジン4号機を水中に沈めて、会期中の計
　　7日間、数回にわたり約5分間稼働させた。

5　2017年　兵庫県立美術館でのシンポジウム「過去の
　　現在の未来2」の関連資料として、水を張った水槽と、
　　水槽の外にエンジン4号機を並べて展示した。

3　2017: *Singing in Falsetto* exhibition (Oyama City Kurumaya
　　Museum of Art, Tochigi)
　　Engine No. 3: Reproduced by the Kokufu Osamu's Engine
　　in the Water re-creation project team, and run for about
　　5 minutes while submerged in the water on a total of 34
　　occasions during the exhibition period.

4　2017: *Kokufu Osamu's Engine in the Water redux*
　　exhibition (Art Space Niji, Kyoto)
　　Part 1: Damaged and degraded Engine No. 3 displayed
　　suspended in the gallery (instead of in a tank of water).
　　Part 2: Engine No. 4 submerged in the water and run for
　　about 5 minutes several times each day for 7 days during
　　the exhibition period.

5　2017: For "The Future of the Present of the Past 2"
　　symposium at the Hyogo Prefectural Museum of Art,
　　Hyogo, the water-filled tank and Engine No. 4 (not
　　submerged) were exhibited next to each other as reference.

京都造形芸術大学（現・京都芸術大学）ULTRA FACTORY
での再制作の作業風景、2017年

Recreation in progress at ULTRA FACTORY,
Kyoto University of Art and Design; now Kyoto
University of the Arts, 2017

2012 年、若手美術作家として注目を集めていた國府理は、京都のギャラリー、アートスペース虹にて《水中エンジン》を発表したが、２年後に急逝した。その後、福島第一原発事故に対してこの作品が示した態度に誘発されたという遠藤水城を中心に、再制作プロジェクトが始まった。

2017 年、ふたたびアートスペース虹にて展示することをめざし、メンバーは《水中エンジン》の構成要素を丁寧に確認した。たとえば水槽のなかに吊るされたエンジンが物理的には長持ちせず、生前の展示でもそうであったように――生前と死後では作家本人による指示の有無という違いはあれども――、メンバーによって都度差し替えられることは、はたして國府の作品の「保存」と言えるのか。会期中にエンジンを動かしたりメンテナンスしたり、いわば作家自身の行為が伴うかたちで「作品」もしくは「展示」としての体裁が保たれていたが、本人不在となった今、そのコンセプトを踏襲したと言えるのか。そもそも「未完成作」だったのではないか。遺族の話に耳を傾け、メカニックの専門家を呼び、「作品」の「再制作」とは何なのかという分析を積み上げた。

初期の國府は「心だけでもどこかに行った気持ちになれる」と乗り物をモチーフとした作品を多く作っていたが、次第に作品との関係性において自分を「外」へ置くようになったという。その心境をこう書き残す。「どこかへ行くためではなく、作品の中に私自身がいない世界を想像するようになった」* と――文字通り國府がいなくなった世界が到来してしまった今、この《水中エンジン》において、再制作メンバーは國府の想像する世界にどう応えていくのであろうか。

作品そのものだけでなく、作家の抱いた想像も瑕疵なく保存の対象としなければ補完できない作品。それをメンバーらは「新陳代謝的に継続する「システム」として再構築した」** という。重要なキーワードとなった「再制作」や「保存」、「アーカイブ」に関する議論もまた、平成の時代に認められるようになった現代美術の一面である。［IM］

＊　國府理著、國府理作品集出版委員会企画・編集『KOKUFUBOOK』青幻舎、2016 年。
＊＊　高嶋慈「國府理「水中エンジン」再制作プロジェクト――「キュラトリアルな実践としての再制作」が発する問い」
　　『artscape』（Web マガジン）2017 年 10 月 15 日号、https://artscape.jp/focus/10139881_1635.html（最終閲覧日：2021 年 1 月 5 日）

Kokufu Osamu, who had already built a reputation as a promising artist, presented *Engine in the Water* at Art Space Niji in Kyoto in 2012, but passed away suddenly only two years afterwards. Later, a project to re-create this work began, led by Endo Mizuki, who was motivated by the stance of *Engine in the Water* as a response to the Fukushima Daiichi Nuclear Power Plant accident.

Working towards an exhibition of the re-created work in 2017, also at Art Space Niji, the project team carefully checked out the elements that comprised *Engine in the Water*. If the engine that had been suspended in the water were in a physical state that would not last long, they faced the question of whether making replacements could be justified in terms of conservation of Kokufu's work. That question would have still arisen if the artist had been alive, but became even more acute with the artist no longer available to give instructions. Also, at the original exhibition, the engine was sustained as a work or as an exhibit by acts undertaken by the artist himself, such as running the engine and performing maintenance, but with the artist absent, there arose the question of whether the artist's concept could really be followed. Apart from everything else, this was arguably an unfinished work. The team steadily conducted an analysis of what the re-creation of this work would signify, listening to what his family had to say, and calling in an expert mechanic.

A large number of Kokufu's early works took vehicles as their motif. He explained that they gave him a sense of having gone somewhere, even if only in his mind. From there, his relationship with his works gradually changed, to become one in which he placed himself outside the work. He explained that feeling in the following way: "instead of going somewhere, I started to imagine a world inside the work in which I was not present."* With Kokufu literally no longer in this world, for this redux of *Engine in the Water*, the re-creation team had to consider what to do about the world that he imagined.

The work itself is not the only issue. The complementary aspects associated with this work cannot be re-created unless the conservation process flawlessly incorporates the artist's imagination. For that reason, the members "reconstructed a 'system' that continues to run, metabolically."** Their debate concerning the important keywords for this project—recreation, conservation, and archive—is another new aspect of contemporary art that started in the Heisei Period. [IM]

＊ Kokufu Osamu, Osamu Kokufu Book Publication Committee (ed.), *KOKUFUBOOK*, Seigensha Art Publishing, 2016.
＊＊ Takashima Megumi. "Kokufu Osamu 'Engine in the Water' Re-creation Project: Questions Raised by Re-creation as Curatorial Practice," in *Artscape* (October 15, 2017 edition). https://artscape.jp/focus/10139881_1635.html

13

本書カバーを切り取り該当する図版をお貼りください

Please detach the corresponding plate from the cover and paste it here.

「平成美術：うたかたと瓦礫（デブリ）1989－2019」展示風景　京都市京セラ美術館、2021年

Installation view of *Bubbles/Debris: Art of the Heisei Period 1989–2019*　Kyoto City KYOCERA Museum of Art, 2021

-本展では、作品の完全な再現展示について、展示室内でのエンジン稼働と水の持ち込みができないこと、およびアクリル水槽の保存の観点から、実現することができないため、オリジナルと再制作の両方が展示されたアートスペース虹の空間を忠実に再現し、そこにあるべき「作品」の不在を想起させる展示を試みる。
-In this exhibition, a full exhibit of the recreated work was not possible because of constraints on the use of water and on running an engine in the exhibition space, and because of conservation issues regarding the acrylic panel water tank. Instead, the exhibit attempts an accurate reproduction of the space at Art Space Niji where both the original and the re-created work were exhibited, in order to convey the absence of the "work" that should be there.

-再制作は、進行状況を公開しながら進められた。
-Progress reports on the recreation work (2017) were published here.
https://engineinthewater.tumblr.com

-本展の展示の一部として、プロジェクトの詳細なドキュメントを京都市立芸術大学芸術資源研究センターのウェブサイトで公開している。
-As part of this exhibition, new information about the project will be published on website of The Archival Research Center of Kyoto City University of Arts.
http://www.kcua.ac.jp/arc/

人工知能美学芸術研究会（AI美芸研）
Artificial Intelligence Art and Aesthetics Research Group

2016 Heisei 28 — 東京 | Tokyo

人工知能美学芸術研究会 （AI美芸研）
人工知能と美学・芸術に関する領域横断的なテーマを追究する研究会であり、その成果を作品として発表するアーティスト・グループでもある。美術家の中ザワヒデキ（1963–）と草刈ミカ（1976–）を中心に、総勢29名の発起人が集い、「人工知能美学芸術宣言」をもって2016年5月に発足した。公開の研究会やシンポジウムを継続的に開催しつつ、展覧会、コンサートなども行っている。2017–2018年には沖縄科学技術大学院大学にて「人工知能美学芸術展」を開催した。中ザワヒデキはインターネットが主流になる以前からCGを用いて作品制作を行い、「方法主義宣言」（2000年）を発表するなど、日本におけるコンセプチュアル・アートのなかで特異な位置を示す。草刈ミカは「凹凸絵画」（2002年–）といった作品シリーズを展開する美術家である。人工知能は独自の美学を持ちうるか、芸術の創作をしうるかというシンギュラリティ（技術的特異点）の問題にも絡む問いを起点に、美学や芸術、人間存在の本質を再考する。

Artificial Intelligence Art and Aesthetics Research Group
The Artificial Intelligence Art and Aesthetics Research Group (AIAARG) investigates cross-genre themes combining artificial intelligence with art and aesthetics. At the same time, it is an artist collective that produces works as its research output. Led by artists Nakazawa Hideki (1963–) and Kusakari Mika (1976–), it was launched in May 2016 with a total of 29 founders being motivated by the "Manifesto of Artificial Intelligence Art and Aesthetics." Its research meetings and symposiums are open to the public, and it also produces exhibitions and concerts. It organized the *Artificial Intelligence Art and Aesthetics Exhibition* at Okinawa Institute of Science and Technology Graduate University (2017–2018). Nakazawa used CG in his works even before the internet became mainstream, and published the "Methodicist Manifesto" (2000). He is a singular presence in conceptual art in Japan. Kusakari is known as an artist for her *Uneven Painting* series (2002–), among other works. Commencing from issues involving the singularity, such as whether artificial intelligence can have its own aesthetics and whether it can create art, AIAARG focuses on art and aesthetics, and on the essence of human existence.

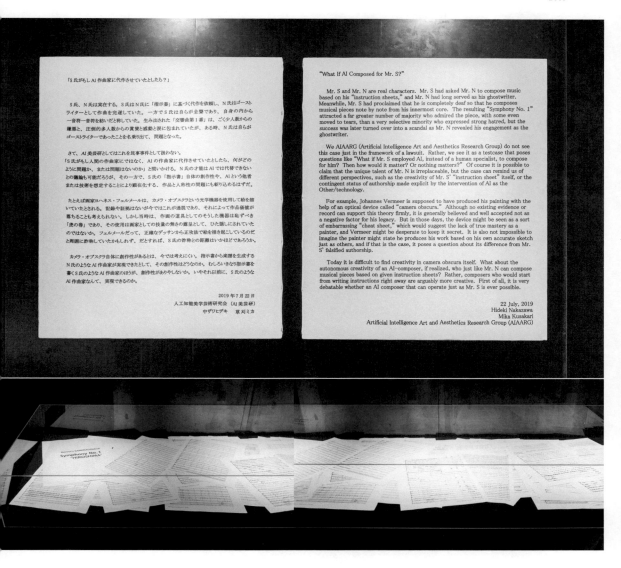

作品 -J（左）作品 -E（右）
Work-J (left) and *Work-E* (right)
2019

N 氏が S 氏に代作した交響曲の楽譜（展示風景）
2001 年暮れ（推定）から 2003 年初頭にかけて新垣隆氏が指示書を参照して佐村河内守氏に代作した
「交響曲第 1 番」の楽譜（総譜）（2011.04.11 版）。

Installation view of symphony score ghostwritten by Mr. N for Mr. S
The entire score of "Symphony No. 1," ghostwritten for Samuragochi Mamoru by Niigaki Takashi,
referencing Samuragochi's instruction sheet, from late 2001 (estimated) to early 2003.
April 11, 2011 edition.

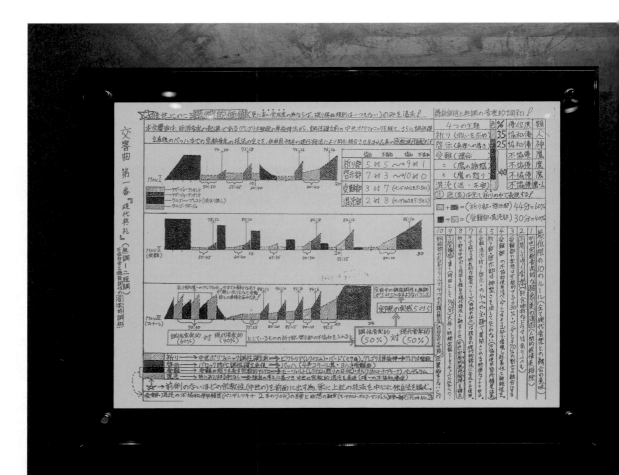

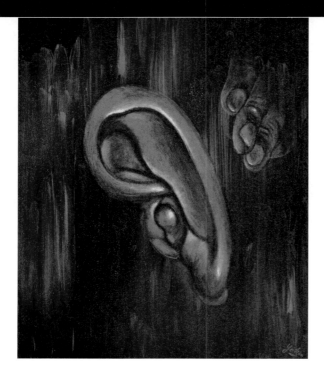

S 氏から N 氏への指示書
2001 年暮れ（推定）、佐村河内守氏が新垣隆氏に渡した「交響曲第 1 番」の指示書の複製。2014 年 2 月 6 日、ホテルニュオータニの edo ROOM で開催された記者会見にて、新垣氏が配布した複製物の現物。

Instruction sheet given to Mr. N by Mr. S
A reproduction of the "Symphony No. 1" instruction sheet that Mr. Samuragochi Mamoru gave to Mr. Niigaki Takashi at the end of 2001 (estimated); one of the actual copies distributed by Niigaki at a press conference held on February 6, 2014, in the Edo Room of the Hotel New Otani.
2014

横尾忠則
赤い耳
Yokoo Tadanori
Red Ear
2000

指示書の何よりもの特徴は、一瞥してそれとわかるグラフのような図形である。濃淡・面積・斜線・角度・反復・緩急等の各種パラメータにより、佐村河内が意図する楽曲の構成は一目瞭然だ。楽曲とは、すなわち感情の質と量の時間的制御であり、序破急や起承転結はこの通り図示できるのだ。これが実現できたらさぞかし感動的なのに違いないという、佐村河内の熱量も充満している。一見、図形楽譜のようでもあるが、作曲家から演奏家への指示ではなく、音符を書かない作曲家から音符を書く作曲家への指示であり、新しい。とはいえ図形楽譜も、音符では表せない感情の質や量の制御として書かれる場合もあるだろうから、遠すぎるわけでもない。

芸術至上主義は、この指示書の冒頭の一文に言語で記述されている。「☆後世に残る芸術的価値（更に高い完成度の為ならば、破り得ぬ規則は一つもない）のみを追求！」*1。この文章全体に下線が引かれ、点線と実線の四角枠に囲まれた「芸術的価値」の語は文字サイズが一回り大きく*2、「高い完成度」の5文字には傍点が振られている。こうした装飾が施された主張内容は、芸術をともかく最優先せよというもので、「芸術の為の芸術」と同義のこうした感覚は、真の芸術家なら多かれ少なかれ身に覚えがあるはずだ。ともかくここからだけでも、いよいよ芸術音楽の本丸である交響曲に取りかかるのだという、佐村河内の熱い意気込みが伝わってくる。実際、その当時は経済的に困窮していたにも拘わらず、なんとか200万円を工面して100万円ずつ2回に分けて新垣に渡し、作曲完成までの1年間は新垣への連絡も控えたというから半端ない。佐村河内は、新垣という才能を見つけたことを神にも感謝する気持ちだったろう。新垣ならば「後世に残る芸術的価値」が達成できると信じた。新垣の述懐中の言葉を使うなら、新垣に「賭けた」のだ。

*1 丸括弧内は、ベートーヴェンの言葉として知られる「"さらに美しい"ためならば、破り得ぬ（芸術的）規則は一つもない」を踏まえたものと考えられる。思想においても「現代のベートーヴェン」を自演し同化しようとする意気込みの顕れとも解釈できる。
*2 記者会見で配布された指示書では、実線の四角枠は認められるが点線の四角枠については上辺が認められない。複写の際に切れてしまった可能性がある。

The most striking feature of the instructions is the graph-like figure, which can be recognized at a glance. The composition of the music that Samuragochi intended is clearly visible through various parameters such as shading, area, oblique lines, angles, repetition, slow and rapid, etc. The music is the temporal control of the quality and quantity of emotions, and Jo-ha-kyu [introduction – development – climax] and Kishoutenketsu [introduction – development – turn – conclusion] can be illustrated in this way. It is filled with Samuragochi's enthusiasm that if this could be realized, it must be very moving. At first glance, it looks like a graphic score, but it is not an instruction from a composer to a performer, but from a composer who does not write notes to a composer who writes notes; thus this is new. However, graphic notation may also be written to control the quality and quantity of emotions that cannot be expressed by notes, so it is not far off.

The supremacy of art is described in language in the first sentence of this instruction. "☆Pursuing only 'Artistic value' for posterity! (for greater perfection, there is no rule that cannot be broken)" [1]. This entire sentence is underlined, and the words "Artistic value" surrounded by dotted and solid squares have a larger font size [2], and the words "greater perfection" are marked with side dots. The message of this decorated statement is that art should always come first, and this sense of "art for art's sake" is one that true artists should be more or less familiar with. At any rate, from this point alone, we can feel Samuragochi's passionate enthusiasm to finally take on the challenge of a symphony, the mainstay of art music. In fact, even though he was in financial trouble at the time, he managed to come up with 2 million yen and gave it to Niigaki in two installments of 1 million yen each, and even refrained from contacting him for a year until the composition was completed. This is not a half-hearted attitude. Samuragochi must have felt grateful to God for finding the talent that is Niigaki. He believed that Niigaki would be able to achieve "Artistic value for posterity." To use a phrase from Niigaki's reminiscences, he "bet" on Niigaki.

[1] The words in parentheses seem to be based on Beethoven's famous words, "There is no rule (in art) that cannot be broken for the sake of more beauty." It can be interpreted as a sign of his enthusiasm to act as a "modern Beethoven" and assimilate him also in thought.
[2] In the instruction handed out at the press conference, the solid square frame is visible, but the dotted square frame is not visible to have a top edge. It is possible that it was cut off during the copying process.

「S氏がもしAI作曲家に代作させていたとしたら」展の展覧会図録より抜粋
藤井麻利・藤井雅実＝訳
Excerpt from exhibition catalogue of *What If AI Composed for Mr. S?*
Translated by Fujii Mari & Fujii Masami

本展では、人工知能美学芸術研究会（以下、AI 美芸研）が 2019 年に東京・中目黒のギャラリーで発表した展覧会「S 氏がもし AI 作曲家に代作させていたとしたら」（The Container［東京］）を再現する。S 氏とは、自称耳の聞こえない作曲家（佐村河内守）であり、交響曲等の作品で広く世に知られたが、実は N 氏という現代音楽作曲家（新垣隆）を雇い、ゴーストライティングをさせていたことで名声を失った実在の人物（事件となったのは 2014 年）。ただし、S 氏による N 氏への「指示書」は、交響曲の世界観と音楽性を詳細に図示する独特なチャートとなっており、その指示書に基づき、N 氏は作曲家のプロフェッショナリティを発揮して作曲をし「譜面」に起こしたのであった。

　さて、これら「指示書」と「譜面」を見たときに、どちらがこの交響曲の実体としてオリジナリティを支えるものであろうか。真の「創作」はどの場面で起きていたのであろうか。さらに、もし「S 氏が AI 作曲家に代作をさせていたとしたら」、事後にこれほどのスキャンダルとなったであろうか。もし、S 氏の構想が「創作」ではなく、AI の作曲にこそ真の「創作性」があるとされるならば、そのとき、AI は人の持つ創造力を超えたものとして認知されるであろう。さもなければ、AI は単に道具として機能したのであり、芸術創造の源は S 氏にあり、社会的に抹消されることはなかっただろう。

　本展では AI 美芸研によるステートメントをキャンバスにプリントした 2 点の作品、および資料展示として S 氏による「指示書」のコピー＊、N 氏による「譜面」＊＊、そして CD に収録された演奏の再生を展示し、そこに横尾忠則による S 氏の肖像としての作品《赤い耳》（2000 年／2020 年［再制作］）が添えられる。

　《赤い耳》は、事件よりはるか以前に、S 氏が聴力を失った自身の肖像として横尾に依頼し描かれたもので、オリジナル作品はすでに作家の手元にないことから、本展を機に再制作された。［NM］

＊　N 氏による記者会見で配布されたもの（2014 年 2 月）。
＊＊ 楽譜作成ソフトで浄書され出力された譜面（2011.04.11 版。N 氏の手書きによる実際の作曲は 2002 年）。

Bubbles/Debris reprises *What If AI Composed for Mr. S?* (The Container, Tokyo, 2019), an exhibition by the Artificial Intelligence Art and Aesthetics Research Group (AIAARG) at a gallery in Nakameguro, Tokyo. Mr. S is the composer Samuragochi Mamoru, who professed to be deaf. He was widely known for his symphony and other compositions, but fell from grace in 2014 when it was revealed that he had employed contemporary music composer Mr. N (Niigaki Takashi) as a ghostwriter. To produce his symphony, Mr. S had given Mr. N an instruction sheet in the form of a distinctive chart with detailed instructions on the nature of the symphony and the perspective of the world that he was attempting to create. Mr. N used his professional skills to compose and create the score for the symphony on the basis of these instructions.

Looking at the instruction sheet and score raises the question of which of these two documents actually underlies the originality of the symphony. Where in the process did the actual creative work take place? Moreover, if Mr. S had instead used an AI composer to ghostwrite his work, would such a large scandal have resulted? And if the creative element came not from the imagination of Mr. S, but from the composition by the AI, would the AI be recognized as attaining or surpassing human creativity? If not, the AI would simply be functioning as a tool. In that case, Mr. S would be considered the source of all the artistic creativity, and he would not have faced such social opprobrium.

The exhibition presents two works by AIAARG in the form of statements printed on canvas. These works are accompanied by a copy of the instruction sheet produced by Mr. S* and the score produced by Mr. N.** A recording of the symphony on CD is played at the venue, and *Red Ear*, a portrait of Mr. S painted by Yokoo Tadanori (2000/2020) is also exhibited.

Red Ear was commissioned by Mr. S as a portrait after he lost his hearing, and was executed long before the scandal emerged. The artist no longer has access to the original painting, so he created a reproduction for the exhibition. [NM]

* Handouts from a press conference given by Mr. N. (February 2014)
** Copy of score (April 11, 2011 edition) output by music notation software. Mr. N's handwritten score was actually produced in 2002.

14

本書カバーを切り取り該当する図版をお貼りください

Please detach the corresponding plate from the cover and paste it here.

「平成美術：うたかたと瓦礫（デブリ） 1989–2019」展示風景
京都市京セラ美術館、2021年

Installation view of *Bubbles/Debris: Art of the Heisei Period 1989–2019*
Kyoto City KYOCERA Museum of Art, 2021

第 II 部
３つの平成論

Part II ,

an Introduction and

Three Essays

元号とそれなりに一体化できた、おそらく最後の時代の国風文化

赤坂真理

民と天皇の一体感

平成とは、昭和の残務処理の時空間であった。

昭和に時間がなかったというよりは、昭和が続きすぎたがために長らく処理できずにたまったことを、次の天皇が処理しようとした約30年、50代からの営為、それが平成。

そして平成の天皇（2020年現在、上皇明仁）が、ほぼ、その思うかたちの戦後処理を「象徴」でき、また自らの限界をも感じたときに、その役が次代に引き継がれることを期して、近代天皇制史上はじめて自ら退位することを決めて退位した、そんな時空間であった。

「平成アート」の話をするのになぜ天皇から始めるかというと、「平成」をふり返るという想像力と時間感覚じしんが、近代天皇制の想像力の中にあるものだからだ。

「一世一元の制」は、明治以来の近代天皇制の一つの根幹をなす決まり事である。

一人の、即位した天皇の肉体の現前と、一つの元号とが、ぴったりと重なること。

しかし、現実的に考えてみると、これは制度自体がかなりのあやうさを抱えている。

一人の人間がふつうに寿命をまっとうするとすると、次世代もそれなりの年齢となるということ。

特に寿命が長くなった現在では、一人の人間が天寿をまっとうするとは、親子ともに高齢となり、ことによれば、子が親に先立つ可能性も低くない。まるで老老介護の図のようで、若くぱりっとした王子（皇太子）が即位することなどは、かなわない。となると、人々の「天皇への「一体感（unity of the people）」」というものは薄れてゆく。

ちなみに、日本国憲法はGHQ草案がほぼそのまま残っているので、原文が英語と考えたほうがいい気がするが、日本語では「統合」と訳されている"unity"は、「一体感」と訳したほうがわたしはしっくりくる。一体型ユニットバスの、ユニット、と同じ語源である。天皇や元号の代替わりに、なんとなくの一体感を持てる人々、というのが、この一体感の表すところかなと思う。

こう考えると、「皇太子の恋のゆくえとご成婚フィーバー」というのは、若い時代にぱっとした出番のない皇太子の救済策だったようにも思える。それが、テレビという新メディアもあいまって、「天皇が民と一体感をつくる仕掛け」の見世物だったのだ。そこが現代においての、若き天皇（天皇じゃないけど）のクライマックスであり、巡幸行幸のような役割を果たす。これは現上皇（平成の天皇）から始まった。そして今上（令和）天皇においても、いちばん記憶されているのは、花嫁探しと、ご成婚だろう。それはほとんどパフォーマンスアート行為だったと思う。

わたしは、記憶の中で、現上皇の「皇太子ご成婚」「ミッチー（美智子妃殿下）ブーム」の映像を、天皇としての即位儀礼の一環のように感じていた。それは誤認というよりは、興行主の思惑通りなのだろう。みなが、頭の中に、「王子から王へ」「王の即位」とは、そのようなものであるという幻想がある。若き王が立ち、世を刷新してゆく。そして、およそ「王の即位」などというものは、生身の人間が幻想のほうに合わせるものなのである。

　じっさいの平成の天皇即位関連儀式というのは、わたしは見たはずだが、記憶にない。昭和天皇の大喪の礼のほうが記憶がある。そのほうが肌身に感じた重さであり、厳粛さであり、ある種の荘厳さであった。象徴的な死であった。その後にあった「新王」の即位は、やはりそれなりにぱっとしなかったわけだ、と思う。記憶に残らないのだから。

　明治、大正、昭和と、最初の三代——なんだってキモは最初の三代だと思うのだが——の近代天皇制の天皇たちが、若いうちから皇位につき、輝かしい若き王のように見えたのは、親の早い崩御という、ただの偶然によるものであった。偶然が続いたため、うかつにもそのことを誰も考えなかった。その意味がわかったのが、昭和の終わりで、さらに平成が終わるまで、誰も疑問視しなかったのだ。当の天皇を除いて。

　近代天皇制においては、ただのラッキーによって本質的な議論が行われなくなることが、よく起きる。側室制度を廃止したら皇位継承候補者が少なくなることも、原理的には大正時代からわかっていた。が、大正天皇に正室との間の男子が5人もいたため、議論されなかった（明治天皇は、側室の子15人の子女を持ち、男子が5人のうち、成人したのは大正天皇のみだった）。平成には、皇統に男児がたった一人生まれただけで、瞬時に女性天皇の議論がふっとぶということがあった。

　明治天皇はそもそも、その即位によって「明治」という西欧化をめざす新時代が始まった人物である。父親の孝明天皇は35歳で崩御。明治天皇は時代の転換期そのもののように、14歳で践祚（せんそ）した。平安京で生涯を過ごした皇子が、江戸に連れてこられて、乗ったこともない乗り物（馬、馬車）に乗せられ戦いの実権と象徴を担うという、アニメの『新世紀エヴァンゲリオン』さながらである。

　その孫の昭和天皇がやはり若くして即位したのは、父の大正天皇が病弱で早く崩御したためである。ちなみに大正天皇の即位は36歳。

　近代天皇制を象徴する三代の天皇、とりわけ明治と昭和の二代の天皇が、若くして即位し、長く在位したのは、第二次世界大戦に負けた今の目で見れば悲劇的な偶然のようであるし、その当時の多くの人々にとっては、希望の象徴であったろう。

　そして昭和天皇は医療に助けられつつ「戦後」を長生きし、平成の天皇が即位したのは55歳である。そして今もご健在の彼を見れば、もしもその崩御を待ったのなら、今上天皇の即位は、還暦をゆうに過ぎてのこととなったはずだ。ここには、それなりに遅かった自分の即位と同じくらいの年齢には、皇太子を天皇にしたいという、前天皇の個人的な想いがあったような気が、一人の人間としては、する。

平 成 の 母 胎

　平成という、昭和の残務処理とは、端的に言えば、敗戦の残務処理である。

天皇を研究する者たちが異口同音に言うのは、天皇研究が進んだのは、平成に入ってから、ということ。

　昭和に天皇研究がしにくかったのは、どうしても昭和天皇の戦争責任を避けては通れないからで、それは昭和天皇の肉体があったからである。制度と生身の、矛盾した質を持つ天皇。利用された無力の存在に見えて、実権もたしかに持ち行使した、という矛盾した存在。それをヒトラーのように弾劾することは、日本人には、しかねた。対戦国から見れば日本軍とは「皇軍」にほかならなかったわけだが、アメリカは政治判断で、その大元帥の罪を問わなかった。

　天皇は、「残務」そのものの「象徴」のように、残ったのである。

　原理的に考えれば、天皇に戦争責任は在る。ないはずはない、と考えるのが論理的に妥当である。

　それを考えずにいると、日本人の心に空白のスポットが生じる。見ないことにするスポットが生じてしまう。見たくない。だから、やってきた経済繁栄など、享楽的なことにはなんでも乗ってしまう。

　天皇の戦争責任を問わなかった米ソ冷戦下でのアメリカの判断、そしてそれを使った占領統治がなぜかとてもうまくいき、アメリカが解放軍にさえ見えた日本に、特異な戦後と自由がやってきた。そんな単なるラッキーを抱きしめつつ、それが冷戦下の単なるラッキーであったことを知っているのに知らないふりして、アメリカの傘下にどっぷり入り、恩恵をときに狂ったように享受しながら、日本人は恩恵と裏腹のアメリカへの鬱屈はもちろん持った。バブルとバブル崩壊は、「戦争２回戦」の顛末なのだ。それは経済戦争であり、また結局は、マネー敗戦という敗戦をした。

　日本の中で何かがわだかまり続ける、そして、戦後やアメリカ追従への異議申し立てや抗議を思わせることのすべては鎮圧され、暴力的な管理社会、監視社会が完成しようとする。暴力的なまでの安全社会。小説家の伊藤計劃が『ハーモニー』で描いたような安全社会。それが、1945年（昭和20年）以降の昭和という時代だった。

　それが、平成の直接の母胎である。

　それ（現上皇）が、平成が、処理すべく持ち越した案件である。

　息子が引き受けた、父（昭和天皇）の幸運と悲惨とである。

　であるからゆえ、平成が遠くに持っている原風景的青写真は、軍隊と瓦礫なのである。

　もっと遠くに探すと、昭和天皇が皇太子時代にその目で見た第一次世界大戦の焦土と瓦礫、関東大震災の瓦礫、即位後の世界金融大恐慌のデブリ化した証券や貨幣。

　同じ青写真からときおり自動再生産されてくるような風景を、日本人は繰り返し見た。たとえその原風景を、知らなくても。

　平成。

　阪神・淡路大震災、オウム地下鉄サリン事件──自衛隊と戒厳令と死の感じ──、東日本大震災、福島第一原子力発電所事故。

　その全てに出てくるカードは、軍隊と、大量死と、デブリ。

　デブリとは、サリンを入れたビニール袋の残骸から、地震と津波によるありとあらゆる瓦礫、ビニール袋いっぱいに詰め込まれた放射性物質に汚染された土、そして千年も万年も国土を汚し続ける核廃棄物まで。

　また、世界的にもそれは、第二次世界大戦後の処理の時空間だった。

ベルリンの壁崩壊（破壊と言ったほうがいいと思うが、ひとりでに壊れた「崩壊」と言うのが通例である）が1989年。いわば、壁が瓦礫になった。冷戦終結も1989年、ソヴィエト連邦の終わりが1991年。

そして平成を象徴するもう一つのキーワード、「バブル」とは、貨幣が「デブリ」と化す直前にまで膨れ上がった様である。

いつどの瞬間をとっても、貨幣も証券もデブリと化すことがありえたから、人々は狂って刹那的に楽しもうとした。享楽をあますまいと。いったい何が楽しいのか自分にもわからなくても。

しかし、あの程度のぜいたくに狂乱できたのは、やはり、瓦礫を知っている世代がいたからだと思う。バブルが華やかな時代だったという幻想を持つ人がいるが、あれは、あまりの貧しさと惨めさのコントラストがあっての狂乱で、ゆえに、いつも破滅と死の匂いがしていた。また、あのくらいの贅沢に狂乱できたのは、やはり圧倒的な貧しさ惨めさを知っている人々がいたからだ。あるいは、その第二世代が、親の惨めさ悲しさを、どこかで知っていたからである。

そして光には同じだけの影がなければ、エネルギーが釣り合わない。

バブルの「同期」は、オウムである。そして対消滅するように、どちらも潰える。

富士山麓のオウム施設サティアンは、原発事故時に失言した議員の言うとおり、実のところ福島第一原発の建屋そっくりであった。粗末なプレハブづくり。サリンや核燃料といった危険きわまりないものを、どうしてあんな粗末な施設で扱えるのか、わからないような。

そして、サティアンは原発に先駆けてデブリとなった。富士山麓にはその痕跡は、ただ「慰霊碑」と刻んだ石碑ひとつ以外にはなにもない。

福島第一原発は、安全のため解体はできず、壊れかけのままデブリと化している。

国 の か た ち と 象 徴

平成の天皇は、戦争の慰霊をして回った。それが、彼が「全身全霊」でした、「象徴」としての行為だと彼みずからが国民に直接語りかけた。中には、その親が行こうとして果たせなかった、悲願の場所もあった。

しかし、よくよく見ると、それは「太平洋戦争まわり」なのだ。アメリカによって、負けが決定している場所をなぞっていた。それは、平成なりに国のかたちを定める、天皇の「国見」であったようにも思える。天皇は国のかたちを定めたのだ。

平成から令和の、天皇の交代劇は、人間としてはやむないものだ。

が、権威という観点から見るならば、ダメージとなる。

近代天皇制は、「王の肉体は同時に二つはない」という原則に貫かれていた。それが一世一元の制であった。

最高権威は、一時代に一人と決まっていて、ブレがない。仮に戦争指揮官だとしたら、命令系統に、原理的にはブレがない。

対して、今、天皇を語るときに、わたしたちは惑う。

誰を何と呼んでいいか、誰の位が上なのか、よくわからない。平成時代をつとめた天皇を、諡で

ある平成天皇と呼ぶことができず、平成を過去にもできない。

　平成から令和とは、いわば、天皇みずからがバブル現象を起こした時代である。

　バブルはデブリとなっていくのか、他に解決法はあるのか、それを決めるのは、実は国民である。
　なぜなら、天皇が本当に国民統合の象徴であるとするなら、象徴のかたちは、国民の反映であり、決してその逆ではありはしない。
　近代天皇たちは、よくも悪くも、日本人の時代精神と時代の空気を左右してきた。平成展という回顧展が行われることも、レトロな何かを見て思わず「昭和だね」と言ってしまうことも、わたしたちにそれが根付いていることの証である。
　わたしたちはまだ近代天皇制の体感の中に生きている。

　ここ数年で、いちばん有名だったアート作品を挙げるならば、「あいちトリエンナーレ2019」の、抗議でいったん閉鎖された「表現の不自由展・その後」における「燃やされた天皇の肖像」と、「従軍慰安婦像」だろう。
　せっかく天皇が「国のかたちと象徴」を完成させた矢先の出来事だったので、これは「不敬」とされたのだろう。
　国のかたちと、せっかく天皇が最終的に終結させた戦争のかたちを、疑ってはいけなかったのである。その意味で言えば、広島は、どんなに悲惨でも美しくても、表現OKであり、推奨コンテンツですらあるかもしれない。わたしたちはまだ、表現に「不敬罪」がある国と時代に住んでいたのだ。
　この出来事は、時代の節目に出てきて、その閉鎖自体が、いちばんアートパフォーマンスじみた行為のようだった。
　これが、近年、一般に最も知られたアート作品でありアート展だったのは、やはりブラックジョークじみているとしか言いようがない。
　が、それはわたしたちに、平成が何であったかを、振り返ってみる必要を教えているのだ。

　すべての矛盾はすでにバブル状態になっている。
　と、平成は無言で教えている。

　わたしたちはそれを読み解かなければならない。
　アーティストというヴィジョナリーの力を借りて。

平成のアート

　アートの本質とは、時代の本質、文化の本質を直観し、それを超えることにある。
　それを超えること、あるいは元型的な質にアクセスすること。
　今、平成のアートを見ていると、その社会や自然現象への予感や予言に満ちているのに驚く。

　戦争や死や、津波や大量の瓦礫。もちろん、大衆の深層心理であったり、社会への風刺。焦土を破って出てくるような、新しいヴィジョン。

　そこには、現実の大津波に先立って大津波が描かれているし（池田学《予兆》2008 年）、9.11 ニューヨークへのテロに先立って、零戦がニューヨークを空爆する図がある（会田誠《紐育空爆之図（戦争画 RETURNS）》1996 年、本書 40–41 頁参照）。零戦がニューヨークを空爆する想像も、旅客機で世界貿易センタービルに突っ込もうとするのも、どちらも、かつてやられたことへの意趣返しである。きょうび言ってはいけないことになっているが、誰でも、戦争には勝ちたかったのである。負けたくはなかった。完膚無きまでにやられたままをよしとするのは、それこそが合理化である。それはどこかで精神の補償作業を意識的に必要とする。アートにはそれが出るし、できる。

　平成のアートを見ていると、「独特の国風文化」の開花、という感じがしてくる。

　平成は、漫画やアニメで育った世代が、それをメインカルチャーのほうへ持ってきた時代であり、今やそれはサブカルチャーとは言えずメインカルチャーとなっているが、平成にその営みがなされた頃はまだ、「これはもはやサブカルチャーではない」と、アーティストや評論家が、意識的に発信する必要があった。

　平成でおそらく最もよく知られた日本の現代アーティスト、村上隆の一連の仕事などを見ているとそういう感じがする。そして「マンガ」「アニメ」や「カワイイ」は世界に知られ、村上隆はルイ・ヴィトンとコラボをした。商業的大成功もおさめた。このあたりと、きゃりーぱみゅぱみゅのカワイイや、アニキャラ少女を逆に三次元化したような AKB48 は同一線上にある。

　日本画の影響や、日本画的なものへの、意識的、無意識的な回帰も感じる。

　それこそ村上隆が言ったように「スーパーフラット」。

　「二次元」。

　絵画という二次元のものを、無理やり三次元的に見せる必要はなく、立体感やパースなど教育で

すりこまれたことは忘れて、スーパーフラットでよい。日本人はもとからその感性を持ち合わせていた。かつて西欧人が、梱包の包装紙などに使われた日本の浮世絵を見て衝撃を受け、影響を受けたように、わたしたちはわたしたちの文化のルーツを再発見する必要がある、と。アニキャラなどへの「二次元萌え」の感性は、これと、相互に影響しあっていたのだろう。

　これは、教育などによってぬぐいがたく刷り込まれた、明治以来の西欧中心主義からの、意識的な、あるいは無意識的な、離脱でもあった。

　ここで、近代天皇制の問題が出てくる。日本文化と呪術・芸能の草の根の中心のようなところから出て、西欧的シンボルにされた、近代天皇というものと、近現代の「アート」とは似ていた。

　明治とは、西洋建築、西洋画を文化・教育の中心にすえた文化だった。

　このことは近年まで続き、かなり西欧教条主義だったが（いやいまだに、学校教育では、美大にでも行かない限り美術の授業で日本画は習わない）、日本人は、一見忘れ去られたルーツを持っていた。

　天皇も、中国の皇帝を下敷きにつくられた存在であった。が、藤原氏など「キング・メーカー（王をつくりそれを利用することで栄えた人たち）」の存在もあいまって、独自の国風の進化を遂げた。日本独自の存在であり、天皇家には易姓革命（王朝の交代）が起きていないのだから、尊い血統である、という、幕末に天皇を神聖化した論理だった。

　天皇自体のルーツに帰っていこうとすると、中国の皇帝とは似ても似つかないものになる。わたしたちは、いまだに天皇をうまく語れない。かなり意識的になってみないと、その存在は説明不能のものである。

天皇を「国風化」する

　平成のアートが、平安文化に接続したのは、当然だったかもしれない。独自性を、ハイブリッドに求めたのだ。平成のアーティストたちは、日本のルーツを求めて悩んだ先達、岡本太郎のように、奈良も弥生さえも遡って縄文にまで接続することはできなかった。彼らは、すでにインターネットにも否応なく接続されていたし、ハイブリッドな存在だったからだ。西洋風も、普通のことになりすぎていた。

　平安時代の「国風文化」とは、奈良の中国風に対して、「天皇」を「国風化」して、周りが天皇を利用し始め独自の貴族文化を築いた時代である。この頃の天皇を見ると、雅の総代のようである。天皇自身が簒奪戦を繰り広げたりしない（たぶん、できない）という意味でも、雅である。

　藤原氏から近現代に至るまで、日本史は、「天皇の利用の歴史」と言っても過言ではない。戦国武将や征夷大将軍といえども、天皇は討たなかった。天皇を討って自分が天皇になりかわるより、天皇はいつか自分に権威を付与する役にとっておいたほうが、利用価値があると踏んでいた。明治維新という武士階級内のクーデターは、それをして、まんまと成功した。

　天皇になりかわろうとしたのは（妄想の中で、そして実行もした）、オウム真理教の教祖、麻原彰晃なのではないかとわたしは思っている。ミニチュアでずさんなつくりの、神聖帝国を造った。オウム真理教広報だった上祐史浩は、地下鉄サリン事件を、テロではなくクーデター（政権転覆）の企てだったと言っている。ちょうど明治維新のようにだ。昭和維新を謳った二・二六事件のようにだ。

まあ、ずさんなつくりと言ったら大日本帝国もかなりずさんで、ずさんな計画で天皇を利用し、ずさんな作戦で補給も考えないずさんな戦争をした。その意味でそっくりだ。わたしたちは今でも大日本帝国の顛末を生きている。清算できていないと言えば、そのへんから、清算などできていない。

　アーティストの山口晃はこう語っている。
　「"自分の中の日本"という内発性で、油絵を国風化しようともくろんだものの」失敗し、画材と呼ばれるようなものさえすべていったん捨てて、安いクラフト紙にサインペンで"お絵かき"を始めた。「フィレンツェのポンテベッキオという石造三階建ての橋を日本式木造で描いたらおもしろかろう」と、描いてみたときに嘘のように筆が進んだのがターニングポイントだった。
　折しもその頃、古典と出会い直した。京都・奈良の神社仏閣を2週間にわたってめぐる機会があり、狩野永徳や長谷川等伯の襖絵、障壁画などを、本来の場所と光で見る。また、東京国立博物館で「やまと絵展」があり、平安以来の国風の画風に触れた。
　そして山口にとっては「かつて奇妙・不自然の感しか抱けなかった」日本画だったが、そのとき、人生が変わるほど心を動かされた。それは「油絵を習ったがゆえの気がします」と彼は言う。油絵偏重の「正統な」美術教育という、外側から見てショックを受けたわけだ。
　かつて外国文化だったものが、文化の「中心」とされるようになってしまい、「その中心」から「かつての自文化の中心」を「辺縁」として発見しなおしてショックを受けたことになる。ごく自然のように、何重にもねじれが入った歴史をわたしたちは生きている。
　日本画の画材は中国絵画と同じであるが、外来の技法を学びつつも、やむにやまれぬ内発性が、それを「誤読」のような結果に導く。そこにこそしびれてしまう、とも山口は語っている。「誤読」に見えることの中に見える、やむにやまれぬ内発性。それこそが、日本性であり、「私」としか言いようのないものであると*。

「誤読」の身悶えから生まれる日本文化

　漫画も、もうひとつの「国風文化」かもしれない。
　直接の祖型はたぶん戦後に入ってきたアメリカのディズニーやカトゥーンなのだろうが、そこに独特のコマ割りやデザインセンスや台詞やモノローグやナレーションや効果表現、擬音表現をつけて、独自の進化、独自としか言いようのない進化を遂げた。
　世界を見渡してみて、日本以上に、漫画が独特の進化を遂げた土地はない。まさに世界のMANGAである。MANGAは、描きこんであっても、圧倒的に線画であり、輪郭線であり、白と黒であり、同じく白黒の線である文字テキストと一緒に視覚処理しやすいのではないか。
　今日本に憧れる若い外国人の多くは、MANGAとANIMEで日本文化に触れている。そのことをもってクールジャパンを国策にするようなキャンペーンも検討されていたわけだが。しかしそれはやはり「誤読するときの身悶え」のようなものから、いやおうなしに生成されたものかもしれない。そういうところを忘れて、これがまさに日本オリジナル文化、などと言い出すと、つまらないものができていくようにも思う。読み込むうちに生成されてくる「萌え」、それこそ萌えとしか言いようのないものが、日本文化生成の切っ先にはあったのかもしれない。

漫画がどうして日本で独特の進化を遂げたのかは、わからない。外来象形文字である漢字を崩して仮名をつくり、象形文字と表音文字の両方をひとつのテキストの中に持って、絵と文字を同列に扱える脳を育てた、からなのかもしれないし、日本画や浮世絵はすでに輪郭線重視で漫画的、戯画的であったから、と言えるかもしれない。

海外のコミックスやフランスのバンドデシネなどを見ると、絵が妙に立体的で、文字と乖離した感がある。読者が、テキストはテキストで、絵は絵で、別に処理しなければいけない感じ。

平成のアートは、漫画やアニメの成長とともにあった作者たちになされたと同時に、漫画家の絵がアートとして大きく取り上げられはじめた時代でもあった。荒木飛呂彦、井上雄彦、岡崎京子、しりあがり寿、などなど。

アニメオタク層をそのままスライドさせてファン層にとりこんだ、秋元康プロデュースのAKB48 は、そういうことの「国内輸入現象」のようにわたしには見える。生身の人間がアニキャラのような格好で、歌い踊るばかりか、一人ひとりのファンの要望に応じてくれ、好みの人格を演じてくれる（という幻想をくれる）。アイドルであると同時に新しい接客業と言いたくもなるが、これもまた、平成生まれならではの表現と言えるだろう。

個人的に大好きなバンドである女王蜂は、天災続きで人災と天災の区別がつかなくなる、いかにも日本的な平成の風景から生まれた。どこかカタストロフと再生を感じさせるヴィジュアルと、ポップな音。女王蜂のコアメンバーは、阪神・淡路大震災を幼少期に生身で体験した神戸出身の兄妹である。瞳のどこかが、その風景を今も映している。ヴォーカルのアヴちゃんはトランスジェンダー。トランスジェンダーであることが普通のことである表現も、普通になっていくだろう。と同時に、ヘテロもまた一つのマイノリティととらえられなければならない。

ニコニコ動画のクリエイターだったミュージシャンの米津玄師は、ミュージシャンの枠を最初から超えている、というか、それを持たない。インターネットその他は、もはやごく普通の地面と同じで、その地面から、自分と同形の叫びを求めて叫んでいた。その叫びには、どこか懐かしいほど、文学少年の匂いがする。

アートがこれからどこへ行こうとしているかなんてわからない。

真に新しいものはリサーチやマーケティングからは生まれてこない。と同時に、本当に新しい何かを嗅ぎ取れるのは、過去のエッセンスを血肉にできた者だろう。何もかもを呑み込んで消費し、独自に解釈し、吐き出す日本。ありそうでなく、なさそうである、場所の影響、時代の影響。

それでも、新しい表現は、いつでも、たった一人の、やむにやまれぬことから出てくる。それがやむにやまれぬものであるほど、不思議なことに、他者の求めるものでもあり、どういう規模であれ、集合性も高いのだ。

（あかさか・まり／作家、パフォーマー）

* 山口晃「私と日本美術」『日本美術全集』第 20 巻所収、小学館、2016 年、201–203 頁。

と く だ ん か わ っ た こ と は な に も

立 岩 真 也

何 も な か っ た

　社会は変わらない、同じ社会が続いているのだと言おうと思っている。すると平成、1989 年から 2019 年にかけても、1990 年から 2020 年まででもよいのだが、自然の災厄はあったし、これからもあるだろうが、社会には何も変わったことは起こらなかった。あえてそのように見ようとも思うし、実際そのようにしか思えないとも思っている。

　みなが知っていることだが、業界によって新しさ・変化を求め言い表すその度合い等は同じではない。「学問」という領域では、僅かでもなにか新しいことがないと論文・業績とは言われない。そこで多くの場合、普通の学問では、まったく微々たる何かが加わることになる。ときには大きめな新しい見立てが示されることがある。いつのころからか新しいことを言うのが「思想」だということにもなっているから、なかにはその業界でもそこそこ受けたりするものもある。1990 年の前、おおむね 1980 年代、「ポストモダン」とか「消費社会」などと呼ばれるものが流行った。ただその頃大学院生などをしていた私はあまりおもしろいと思えなかった。その後のことになるが、「再帰性」がどうとか言われたこともあるし、「監視社会」だとか「リスク社会」が言われたこともあった。やはりみな間違ってはいない。しかしやはりそれほど新しいことと思えなかった。あるいは、新しいとされているものがどうということはない型にはまったものに見えた。

　「報道」の類も、論文のように小さく加えるというのとは違う基準で、新規なものを求める。毎日同じでは仕方がない。加えて情動に訴えるものが採用される。目立つ度合いの小さい出来事のほうがかえってそうだ。美しいあるいは悲しい物語が語られることになる。だったら報道なんかしないほうがよいと思うこともなくはない。しかし私だって、見るとすれば、そういう画像・映像であったりする。あまりに紋切型だとさすがにこの頃は人にうんざりされることもあるが、非難するつもりはない。ほぼ、仕方がないとは思っている。

　こうして各々の業界の事情は理解できるが、それで社会がわかる気はしない。まったく古典的な図式のほうがまだこの社会に起こっていることを説明できると、私は考えている。人々に存するべつだんこの社会・時代に限らない利害と、そのたんなる利害をそれ以上のものに押し上げ強くする方向に作用する規則、価値、観念とによってこの社会は構成されていると捉える。

　人は利を得ようとし面倒なことを避けようとする。それはとくによいことでもないが、わるいことでもない。そのうえで、この社会にあるのは、一つ、生産者が生産物を取得できるという私的所有の体制であり、それを正当とする価値・信仰である。そして一つ、それを支える方向に作用する

人間についての価値がある。つまり、作ることによって人の存在の価値が示されると信じられている。能産的で自律的であるのが人間であり、人間の価値であるとされる。この社会はまずそのような社会である。

　そして以上に関わり、また加えて生産に関わる変化がある。誰もが知るように、技術・産業の高度化があり、生産性の向上、生産の拡大、グローバリゼーションの進展がある。そして金融。今に始まったわけではないが、おおまかには現物をやりとりするわけでない経済の不安定性があって、危機が起こると大きくなる事情がある。それがときに現実化する。1990年代の「ショック」はそういうものだった。ただそれに対して結局はいくらかのことがなされ、経済の崩壊に至ることにもならない。

　基本は以上だが、それに、いろいろな具合に社会に存在する集まりや、内部や相互の利害が加わり、壁ができ、高くされたりする。おおまかには、自分たちが得ている利益を護ろうとする方向で動き、既に多くを得ている側はさらに拡大しようとする。

　生産力の上昇によって労働人口の過剰が生ずる。それは、人がもうあまり働かなくてもよいということなのだから、本来はたいへんよいことだが、我々の社会にあっては、失業に結びつく。他方で、途上国と呼ばれた地域にも生活が楽になった人たちはいる、と同時に、格差の拡大がある。それは誰でも理解できる理由によっている。普通に人を雇うことによる利潤以外に、複製が容易な商品、さらに追加費用なしで複製し配達できる商品がたくさんある。もちろんプログラムの類がそうだが、テレビや画像で拡散される試合や催にもそのことは言える。

　楽観的な近代主義者があまり計算にいれなかったのは、地域内・地域間での紛争民族や宗教の間の争いが広がったことだが、これにしても、グローバリゼーションに伴う攻防、としてだいたいは説明できる。まず、多くやむをえず流入してくる人がいる。それほどよい目を見てはこなかったが仕事には就けていた人たちには、流入する人たちは脅威と捉えられる。他方、単純労働でない仕事をしていたりして文化障壁を利用できるため、移民・難民の流入が直接の脅威でない層はリベラルでいられる。すると自国第一を言う人が、その人はもっとずっと儲かっていることを恨まれてよいような人であっても、恨んでよいはずの人たちに支持されてしまう。テレビをつけるとまったく不要にも毎日出てくる米国の（2020年10月における）大統領の画像を見るまでもなくわかることだ。

　そんな状態は変えたほうがよいし、それは可能だ。ないものを求めているのではない。すでにあるもの、むしろ余っているものの処分の仕方を考えればよいだけだからだ。しかしそれをしたくない人たちがいる。その時、この社会に「危機」があることにされる。それを意図的な策略とだけ考える必要はない。金（税）のとり方を間違えると実際に国に金はなくなる。国の金の出入りに関わる人たちが、それを少子高齢化による財政難だと言う。まじめにそう信じてしまっているふしがある。そうした「世界観」が世を覆い前提にされることになる。生産や生産力は足りているのだが、分けないことを、少ないこと、少なくなることのせいにすることになる。そうして足りないことが現実だとされる。それが現実だと本当に思っている人たちが再生産される。そして、すべきことできることをさぼっているから当然なのだが、局所的にはたしかに現実の不足は生じてしまっている。

　そうしたところをほぐしながら、変えていく根拠、道筋、方法を示す仕事がある。これはまずは

地味な仕事だ。革命にもいろいろあって、例えばゲバラが活躍できるためには、例えば中南米の山岳地帯のような条件が好適だし、明らかに悪徳な人々とそうでない人たちがはっきり分かれていると、すべきこともすっきり決まってくる。しかしそうでないこともあるということだ。

　仕方なくやっかいに社会はできているから、その社会をどうにかする時にも、仕方なく面倒なことを考えねばならない。だから仕方なくわくわくしない部分を含むことになる。また、理由は言わないが、派手な催として、例えば誰かが象徴する存在となるような行動はすくなくとも長く続かないし、むしろ続けないほうがよい。そして、全体としては地道な仕事であっても、ときどきは十分にわくわくするようなこともできるから、退屈なばかりでもない。楽しめもする。

　構想され目指される社会の具体的な仕組みは、みかけ上、今あるものと大きくは違わないものになるだろう。私はそれでよいのだと考える。社会なんていうものがそう面倒な具合にできていたら面倒だ。退屈に対して別の退屈を対置することになる。しかし構えは異なる。

　こうして、今のそしてこれからの社会を描くことが必要で、それが私の仕事であると思ってきた。ただ、これから記すようにその時々の出来事を追い、そのつど仕方なく言うことにずいぶんな時間をとられた。これからは、社会の大きな見立てについて短めにまとめ、もっと伝えねばと思っている。

生の浮き出し方隠され方

　こうして、そのときどきのことについて何かを言おうという積極的な気持ちは私には少ない。所有のあり方、お金の使い方であったり労働や所得の分配のあり方について基本的なことを考え書こうと思ってきた。しかし、にもかかわらず、書籍の場合もあり、またサイトの更新によってといった場合もあったが、そのときどきのことを記録し、公開してきた。サイトは http://www.arsvi.com/、「arsvi」は「生の技法」といった意味のラテン語「ars vivendi」の略。「生存学」で検索してください。

　多く、身体・生命・生死に関わることについて書くことになってしまった。人間やその身体に関心があるわけではないし、生死にしても、みなそのうちに死ぬという以外のことを言いようがないと思う。ただ、そうロマン的になれないから、かえってよいこともあると思っている。

　多くのことは画像にも文字にもならない。人々がなんとか持ちこたえているぶんには、多くはそのままにされる。あまりに大きく、手をおえないものも、そのままにされる。あるいは、大きなことが起こると、大きなことだからと後回しにされる部分がある。地震も感染症も、そのときどきのことへの対応の仕方が下手で、例えば停電になると冷蔵庫が動かなくて困るのだが、人工呼吸器が動かない人はもっと困る。代わりに発電機を使うが、それをどのように行き渡らせるか、置き場をどこにするか、室内では危険だといった、わかりやすいが、人々があたふたしていると忘れることの多いことを伝える。こういう「その他」の、そのように残される仕事をする。

　他方、そこそこに大きく報じられることもある。死、とくに殺し殺されたり、また自らが死を選んで人に殺させたりするとすこし騒がれる。それは扇情的な出来事でもあって、生死の選択だと

か、決意の死だとか、言われる。そして、その死を悲しむ人たちが対置するのは、輝いて生きている人もいるとか、そういう話だ。

　そんなことではない、余計なことを言ってほしくないし、してほしくないと思う。だから、取材があれば受けるし、苦労して短文を書いたりする。まったくうっとうしいことだが、仕方がない。

　実際には、平凡な社会の平凡なあり方が、死において現れる。一つには、生きていくのに必要なもの、金や人手が足りないという身も蓋もない状況のもとで、あるいはそれを予測して、死ぬことだ。身体が弱ったりして動けなければ働けず、稼ぎなく、そしてさらに追加して必要なもの例えば人手がいるが、それもない。さきほど述べたわかりやすすぎる社会のあり方によって、そうなる。

　そして一つには、陳腐ではあるが強固でもある人間のあり方についての信仰のもとで、人がたくさん死んでいく。生きるために生産物が必要で、そのために生産があるのだが、できることが生きる価値であるという倒錯した価値を受け入れたままだと、死ぬことになる。この国の人たちは、そんな価値をそう強く信じてはいないのかもしれない。間違ったことを信じているよりはよいから、信じていないことはわるいことではないと私は思う。しかしいざという時に、まじめになり潔くなってしまう人も現れてしまう。自分の生命や生命の終わりは自分で決めねばと思ってしまう。

　さらに一つ、危機・不足というお話がそれを後押しする。全般的に既に足りないあるいはこれから足りなくなるからと思い、そして既に自分については確かに足りないから、そして、自分の価値を測り、退場する。たいがいはそのままにされているが、ときに目立つ事件になる。そうすると、それは美しくされたりする。例えば、平成の後に感染症をめぐる様々が今起こっているのだが、医療機器が足りなくなるかもという認識のもとで、それを使える人の順番を決めようということになる。例えばいま人工呼吸器を使っている人が自分はもういらないと言ったらその意志を尊重しようという話が現れる。その人の思いに敬意を表してよいと思う。しかしそのことと、それを社会のきまりとして採用し実行するのとはまったく異なる。

　しかし、普段は気の利いたこと新しいことを言っている（と自分のことを思っている）人、能天気に技術や未来を語ったりする口説の徒たちが、いつからどのように信じることになったのか、危機や不足のお話をそのままに受け入れ、ひどくつまらないことを言う。それはとてもだめだと思う。だから、平凡だが間違ってはいないことを言い続けることになる。

　実際は、空間はおおく普通に閉ざされていたり、時間は停滞したりしている。例えば一度、未来がつらいと思うまったく当然の家族の心性とそれに涙する人々の善意とが集まり合わさり、治癒の期待も加わり、病院に収容された人たちがいる。やがてその病院がどんな病院であるかも周囲に知られないまま、そこに入ることになった人たちは、その後静まりかえったその場所において、死ぬまでの 30 年とか 40 年とかの長い時間を過ごすことになる。

　そうしてなにもなく続いている日常が、天変地異をきっかけにして一時的に別の場に現れることもある。東日本大震災のときの福島での原発事故で人々が避難せざるをえないということがあって、施設が閉鎖されたりした。精神病院にもそんなことが起こった。すると初めて、そこに長く、40 年だったか、いてしまった人がいることがわかった。その人は病院から出て暮らすようになり、今年になって、そんな空間と時間に生きさせられたことについての裁判が始まった。すこしだけ報じられた。

そんな具合に社会は作られ維持され、そして表され、そして隠されている。だからその様をまず記述する。そういう退屈な仕事を言葉を使う仕事をする人たちはやるしかない。

受 動 す る こ と

それと「アート」——さきに「学問」「思想」「報道」と括弧をつけた——がどう関わるのか私にはわからない。何も知らない私が無理にアートに言及することはないのだろうとも思う。映画や音楽、その他からもまったく遠ざかったのはもう40年ほど前で、その後のことはまったく知らない。

新しいもの、新しいことに応ずることは、この世界でも求められているのだろう。そして、それはこの国に限ったことでもないのだろう。とすれば、同じように、とにかく目立つとか、新しいとされているものに飛びつくとか、そんなことはありそうだしあってわるいわけでもない。そして、時代との関係、あるいは関係のなさは、様々あってきただろうし、社会をしかじかの方向に向かわせるにあたっての情動を喚起する役割を果たしてきたこともいろいろとあった。それでも私は、かなり信用している。

まずまったく素朴に、私たちの多くは理屈を間違える、例えば社会を理解したりこれからのことを考える上での道筋を誤つのだが、アートはそれと直接には関係のないところで成立しているということがあるだろう。

たぶんそのことと関係して、一つ、それはつまらない、と言う力がそこにはあると思う。私の場合には、音楽であることが多かったが、実際社会の多くの部分はつまらないし、つまらないと思ってよいのだと思った。

無駄なことを気にするようにこの社会はできているが、ほんとうはなんでもよい、なんでもよいという言い方が間違っているなら、それでよい。そのことを受け取った。「現代思想」もそのようなことを言いたいのだと解することはできるが、しかしそのことを言うためなら余計な言葉を重ねているし、ここにある社会を記述するためには言葉と理屈が足りない。そう思ってきたから、そちらの仕事をしてきた。その私に気持ちをくれた側に対しては、へんな理屈や理論に惑わされないようにという以外に言うことはない。

そしてアートは、人が受動的であってよいことを示している。私がどうであるかということと別に、私が何であるか、何を作るかと別に、世界はよいものであることを伝えているし、またその世界の一部でもある。世界は受け取ればよい、世界にはそれだけのものがあり、そして、もっとゆっくりでよいと思うほどだが、さらに人々がなぜだか加えてしまうものの数は日々増えてもいるということだ。

しかし、アートはまず創造の行為である、と言われるかもしれない。そのことについて補足しよう。

一つ、生産されることは肯定するし、ある人が何かが上手であるということもまたまったく否定せず、褒め称えよう。そしてなぜか表現したい人はやまほどいる。なかには、自己実現や存在証明

のために作っている人たちもいるだろうし、そんな人たちもいてよいだろう。しかし、そういう成分よりたくさんのものがある。世界全般が過剰であるというのと同じく、またそれ以上に、作品はたくさん作られ、堆積されている。そしていくらかのものは複製され再生もされる。

　そうすると、一つ、十分にたくさんあるので、私たちの多くは、何もせず、受け取ればよい。そしてそれはよいことだ。そのことを言うのは、ときに、非生産的であるとされる人たちを救おうと、皆が創造的であるとしようとされることがあるからだ。もちろん、事実、どんな人も何かを生産し発信しているのだと言うことはできる。ただ私はそういうことをがんばって言いたくはない種類の人間だ。いや、私の趣味が、というのと別に、なにかその人が創造的であることを求められ、周囲はそれを頑張って探してきて取り出してほめたりしなければならないのは、双方が疲れ、双方にとってよくないと思うからだ。そして、生産しようとする人は過剰なほどいて、多くの人たちは受けるだけで十分だという世界はわるくない。

　ずっと以前に、身体がまったく動かなくなったらどうするかと、そんな人（ALS＝筋萎縮性側索硬化症の人）を家族にもつ人に聞かれたことがある。そういう人たちのことを書いた本『ALS──不動の身体と息する機械』（医学書院、2004年）を刊行する2年前、2002年のことだった。仕方がないから1日中音楽を聞いていると答えた。それは当時なかなか困難だった。LPの時代は終わりCDはあったが、連続演奏ができる再生機でも一度に5枚ぐらいまでだったかと思う。それが今はPCやスマホを使っていくらでも貯めることができる。プレイリストをランダム再生すれば、1度始まれば48時間分の音源が再生され続けていくものが今は私にもある。以前に比べたらもっとなんとかなる、と思う。

　建築であるとか、空間の感覚に関わる技能についても、関わる部分があるだろう。ずっと昔、吉本隆明という人が、建築家は奇抜な大きな施設を設計したりなんかするより普通の人のためのもっとちゃんとした家を作るべきなのだと言ったことがあって、その時には狭量なことを言う人だと思った。私は奇妙に大きなものもきらいではないからだ。ただその小言もいくらかは当たっていると思う。アートは、世界が受け取るだけで十分であることを示す。さらに少し加えると、うまいこと受動的でいられる空間・時間はどんなものだろう、そのとき身体や身体が纏うものはどんなものだろう。そんなことも少し思う。

（たていわ・しんや／社会学者）

恐 る べ き 平 成 元 年

平らかになり、泡沫のように消えて行き、
瓦礫のように砕け散って行く時代のはじまりを巡って

片 山 杜 秀

予兆

平成元年は不思議な年であった。生死の境を彷徨っていた昭和天皇は昭和 63（1988）年を乗り越え、昭和 64 年を迎えたが、そこで長い命もついに尽きた。崩御は 1 月 7 日。ただちに皇太子が即位し、新元号は平成と発表された。

天皇は崩御するまで必ず在位し、代替わりは崩御と同時に行われ、元号もそのとき変わる。明治政府が定めた一世一元の制である。天皇が存命しているのに急に退位するなどと言い出せば、それは天皇が為政者に不満を抱いているせいであると解釈されやすい。事実、幕末の孝明天皇は、たびたび退位の意思を示して公卿や幕府を脅迫した。同じ手を明治天皇に用いられることを明治政府は警戒し、天皇の自由意思による退位を封ずることにしたのだろう。また、改元を江戸時代までのように、吉事や凶事に合わせて自由に行うことを続ければ、近代国家として正式に元号を使いながら政治を行うのに不都合を生じやすい。年の勘定が煩雑化する。改元が政治的意味を持ちすぎる可能性も高まる。たとえば、凶事が頻繁に起こるから気分を変えたいと望んで改元しても、なお凶事が絶えなければ、そこで国家の正統性を疑う者も出よう。主にそうした理由で、一世一元の制が創出されたと考えてよい。それはつまり、天皇の在位とそのときの元号の通用する期間を、共に天皇の寿命へと帰し、統一する仕掛けであった。忠君愛国の観念が国民道徳の基調として要求される時代には、天皇の命とそれに紐づけられた元号によって、国民の時間感覚が支配されるのは、国家にとってまことに好ましくもあった。こうして、天皇という一個の人間の生によって時代を区切る独特の制度が、ひとつの近代国家に与えられた。その区分は、寿命に左右されるのだから、多分に偶然的であって、歴史の大事とは、天皇崩御以外のことでそうそうリンクするものでなく、事実、明治天皇の崩御した明治 45 年改め大正元（1912）年も、大正天皇の崩御した大正 15 年改め昭和元（1926）年も、日本史や世界史に大きな出来事のあった年では必ずしもなかった。

ところが、昭和 64 年改め平成元年に関しては、そうでもない。歴史の大事が目白押しと言ってもよい。それ自体としては小事かもしれないが、後の大事の伏線や予兆と見られることも、幾つもあった。それらの殆どは昭和天皇の崩御とは常識的に考えれば関係がない。しかし、30 年以上続くことになる平成やその先の令和まで引きずられる事柄の、初発点や結節点と認め得る出来事が、

やはりとても多い。泡沫や瓦礫を生むのにつながるタネがちりばめられている。ゆえに平成元年は不思議なのである。一種の特異年なのか。いや、歴史の重要な転換期のど真ん中の年に昭和天皇が崩御したと言うべきだろうか。

転 換 期 と し て の 平 成 元 年

その年を甚だ粗雑ながら振り返ってみよう。まず2月。ソ連軍がアフガニスタンから撤退した。前後の経過のあることで、いきなり2月に俄かにまとめて撤退したわけではない。だが、1989年における一連の東側世界の激動を予告するような事象であったには違いない。1985（昭和60）年、ミハイル・ゴルバチョフがソ連共産党の指導者になって、ペレストロイカと呼ばれるソ連の大規模構造改革に着手した。そうしたらすぐ翌年がチェルノブイリの原発事故である。この巨大な原子力災害は、ソ連の諸側面での制度疲労の端的象徴とみなされ、ゴルバチョフはチェルノブイリをペレストロイカの梃子にできると錯覚し、今こそソ連を多年にわたって支配してきた秘密主義からの脱却のときであり、原発事故関係の情報を積極公開すべきだと、グラスノスチ、すなわち情報公開を政治スローガンとして掲げた。ゴルバチョフは原発事故を改革プロセスの伸長の道具にすることに懸けたのだが、グラスノスチは反体制派を勢いづかせて百家争鳴状態を生み出すばかりだった。チェルノブイリをきっかけにソ連の衰退に歯止めが利かなくなっていったというのがひとつの観方であろう（チェルノブイリ事故とソ連衰退史の重なりは、平成における福島の原発事故と“日本衰退史”への教訓を含むとは言うまでもない）。1989年のアフガニスタンからのソ連軍の撤退は、そんなソ連国家の衰弱情況を可視化するものであった。世界規模の軍事的覇権を目指し、米国と張り合ってきたソ連は急激に萎み始めていた。

そこにはソ連の競争相手の米国のアフガニスタンに対する工作も功を奏していた。米国はソ連のアフガニスタン侵攻、ひいてはインド洋への南進を阻止しようとして、米国の得意とする代理戦争の手法を用いた。アフガニスタンのイスラム原理主義勢力、タリバン等に武器や資金を供与し、組織を育て、ソ連と戦わせた。後に米国にとってこそ手ごわくなるというところまでの計算はあまりなかったようだ。2001（平成13）年9月11日の同時多発テロ事件につながる。“テロとの戦い”の時代は、ソ連のアフガニスタン侵攻史とリンクさせなければ見えてこず、その大きな節目は平成の頭にあった。

ついで4月1日。日本で消費税法が施行された。1988（昭和63）年の暮れに国会を通った。税率は3％から始まった。直接税から間接税へ。経済成長著しく右肩上がりの経済が続く時代なら儲けている産業から優先的に税を取れば財政も回って行くものだが、成長がなだらかになり一種の極相を呈し始めると、税金の取り立て先もめぼしい箇所がなくなり、広く薄く全階層・全領域から取る方向に転換する。時代に見合ったことがちょうど平成元年に起きた。

そして6月3日。竹下登内閣が総辞職した。1月には小渕恵三官房長官が新元号を発表したりもし、新時代にもそれなりの政治力を発揮していくだろうとも思われた政権の退場だった。原因はいわゆるリクルート疑獄である。多数の政治家がリクルート・コスモスの未公開株を譲渡されていた

問題が昭和の終わりから尾を引いていた。竹下内閣の主要閣僚では例えば宮澤喜一蔵相はいちはやく退任に追い込まれていた。それでも幕引きは出来ず、首相退陣にまで至った。こうした政治とお金の問題は、戦後政治でも昭電疑獄、造船疑獄、ロッキード事件などと、執拗に繰り返されてきた。与党の歴史はすなわち疑獄史であった。自民党長期支配は、戦後日本に繁栄と安定を齎してきたという言い方もできるけれど、ずっと同じ政党が政権を握り、与党が交代せず、当選回数を増やしてベテラン化する与党議員も多いとなれば、政治家たちは特定の官僚と長く密につながり、得意分野に利権を持ち、何らかの業界と金脈で結ばれ、どうしても腐敗が進行する。

　実はこの構図は戦後長く日本資本主義を擁護する立場の人々からは必要悪と考えられていた。保守党の堕落を攻撃し、政権から追い落とそうとすれば、オルタナティヴとして浮上するのは革新・中道政党になる。日本が東側陣営に引き込まれるきっかけになりかねない。だから腐っても自民党。しかし、平成元年に様子は違ってくる。東側は派手に躓いている。リクルート疑獄の後にいよいよ本格化してくる東側世界の崩壊を目の当たりにすれば、日本に革新政党の存在価値はもはやなく、社会党や共産党の時代は終わったと、たちまち観念されるようになる。そうして東西冷戦が終わり、米国流の資本主義と民主主義が世界の勝者になるならば、日本の政党も米国のように二大保守政党が相応しいという議論が巻き起こるだろう。二大政党がともに保守ならば、政権交代によって経済体制に混乱の生ずる心配もないし、周期的に与党が入れ替われば、水の濁る暇はなくなり、政治腐敗も起きにくくなるだろう。リクルート疑獄に端を発する政界の騒動に、崩壊に向かう東側世界の様相が相俟ると、小沢一郎等が主導した、自民党のオルタナティヴとしての新保守政党を作る構想につながってゆく。平成日本の政治的エネルギーのかなりは、二大保守政党の確立こそ日本の未来の理想という方向に動員された。マスコミも学者もそれを煽った。しかし、不毛に終わった。イデオロギー無き技術的政治は、技術の優劣以外に評価のしどころのない政治状況を生み、多少のドラマはあったにせよ、ついには、経験豊富でテクニカルな対応に優れる既成保守政党が、経験貧困な新規保守政党よりも国民から高く支持されるという"政権交代なき時代"に回帰し、保守長期政権の腐敗は反復され、しかも対抗勢力に思想的な差異が十分に認められないので、歴史意識や目的意識も希薄となり、選択肢の幅もあまりなく、縮み切った政治状況が現出して今日に及んでいる。政党の対立の構図から選挙の仕組みまでを破壊したら、そこから新しい芽は育たず、泡沫と瓦礫が積みあがるばかりとなったのが、平成の政治改革と称されるものであったろう。

「歴史の終焉」という幻影

　日本の政治から思想までの長期にわたる混乱の大きな具体的きっかけを作った竹下内閣の倒壊の翌日、平成元年こと1989年はまたも大事を呼び込む。6月4日の天安門事件である。中国で鄧小平の政権が改革・開放路線に舵を切って、「豊かになれる者から豊かになれ」とのスローガンのもと、社会主義計画経済の国に自由市場経済を導入しだした。近代思想史の常識からすれば、経済だけを自由にし、政治を自由にしない社会はあり得ない。でも中国共産党は一党独裁を続けようとしている。これは無理筋だ。自由を求める市民や学生の力を押しとどめることはできない。いったん

弾圧されても、ソ連や東欧諸国の 1989 年の情況を見れば、それで終わるはずはあるまい。中国の政治も複数政党制や民主主義的選挙を認める方向へと変わってゆくだろう。西側の多くの識者はそう予測した。日本における社会主義政党の退潮は、ソ連の衰退とその果ての崩壊のみならず、天安門事件にも影響されて起こったことだろう。

　ところが、事件から 30 年以上経ってみると、当初の予想とまったく違っている。経済生活での自由の追求と政治生活での不自由の甘受が、とりあえず両立しうることを、天安門事件以来の中国史は証明しているかのようだ。中国の政治権力は、ソ連の失敗に深く学んでその轍を踏まないようにし、天安門事件から 30 年以上経っても揺らいでいない。それどころか大国化の道を弛みなく歩んでいる。

　思い起こせば、1989 年の諸事象を大きなきっかけとし、1992（平成 4）年に刊行されたフランシス・フクヤマの『歴史の終わり』でひとつの定式化を観る "歴史の終焉テーゼ" とでも呼ぶべきものがあった。それはイデオロギー無き時代の唯一のイデオロギーであったのだろう。社会主義の崩壊とは冷戦構造とイデオロギー対立の終わりを意味し、それに伴ってイデオロギー闘争としての歴史も終焉し、イデオロギーの終わりとは即ちユートピアの始まりで、そのユートピアとは即ち米国型の自由主義と民主主義のグローバル化によって完成するものであり、したがってたとえば日本も米国を真似て保守二大政党の国になるべき。1989 年から数年のうちの世界の諸経験から編み出された、そんな考え方が "歴史の終焉テーゼ" であったろう。しかし、このテーゼは天安門事件やベルリンの壁の崩壊やソ連の崩壊の熱に浮かされた一時の幻影であって、決して真理でも正解でもなかった。中国には中国の、ソ連崩壊後のロシアにはロシアの、アフガニスタンやイランやイラクにもそれぞれの真実があって、世界が米国型の自由主義と民主主義で一元化するなどという物語は妄想の域を出ず、むしろ世界が、イデオロギー闘争による二極か三極への凝集作用さえ失って、宗教や民族やもっと小さなセクトに切り刻まれ、多元化と分裂の道を進んでいると明らかになったのが、この約 30 年であったろう。それはつまり共鳴し合えないノイズが増えるということで、瓦礫化していくとも形容されうる経過であったろう。

　だが、それにもかかわらず、たとえばこの国は間違ってしまい、"歴史の終焉テーゼ" こそが本当であると長いこと思い続けて、迷走を重ね、泡沫を実体と見、破壊と瓦礫のあとに戦後復興をしのぐ新しい希望の現実をすぐ立ち現わせられると錯覚した。気が付けば、泡沫はすぐ消え、瓦礫は瓦礫のままである。世界を分断する多元化は国家間の水準でも、国内の水準でも容赦なく進行し、香港のような西側の自由な社会のありようを長年味わってきた場所も、中国流の別の価値観と統制のシステムに呑みこまれようとしている。そこから迸るのは難民であり政治亡命者であろう。とにかく、歴史の終わりとはまるで違う、中国の新しい道が 1989 年 6 月 4 日から始まっていたことを、我々は改めて思い知らねばならない。

揺れる日本列島

この天安門事件の翌月の 7 月 13 日、日本列島にひとつの変化があった。静岡県の伊東市の沖で

海底噴火が起きた。伊東の港のすぐ目の前で大きな水柱が上がった。その後、大きな被害を生み出すには至らず、終息していったが、翌1990（平成2）年からの雲仙普賢岳の噴火、1995（平成7）年の阪神・淡路大震災、2011（平成23）年の東日本大震災、その他、風水害を含む多くの自然災害が連なって行く、平成の31年間のひとつの徴候として現れていたのが、伊東沖の噴火であったとは言えるだろう。いついかなる大災害が襲うか分からない。特に日本列島は変動期に入っており、未曽有の地震や津波がいつ来ても不思議ではなく、火山の大噴火もありうるという言説の広がりは、刹那主義や虚無主義とリンクして、平成から令和への、この国の気分を決定している。あまり先のことを真面目に考えてもしようがないということである。

　翌月の8月26日には日本国内に慶事があった。礼宮文仁親王と川嶋紀子との婚約が発表された。秋篠宮家の誕生につながる。平成から令和にかけては、皇族の人数という即物的な問題もあれば、昭和が遠くなってゆき、皇族も国民も世代交代してゆくので、先の戦争への反省と平和への祈りということばかりでは、皇室に求められる価値も賄いきれなくなる状況も生じ、時代相が泡沫と瓦礫に特徴づけられるのに見合うかのように、皇室もまた揺動化し不安定化する時期を迎えているとも考えられる。秋篠宮家はそんな時代をどう転ばせて行くかに重要な役割を果たす家であり、その誕生の起源が平成元年に求められることは注意されてよい。

　それから11月4日である。オウム真理教が坂本弁護士一家を殺害した。同教団は阪神・淡路大震災の直後に、毒ガスを使った大規模な都市型のテロを為すことにもなる。それは、2001年の米国での旅客機を用いたテロに優るとも劣らず、しかも6年先駆ける、新しいテロの時代の到来を告げる大事件であり、そのことが日本で、しかも国際的な勢力などによってではなく、国内のカルト宗教団体によって引き起こされ、その目的となれば国家の転覆であった。それまでの常識では、その種の大規模なテロは、少なくとも近現代の世においては、共産主義でも民族主義でも、言わばより広く流通可能な思想、それによって過激な行動に走るか走らないかはともかく、思想自体としては政治思想なり社会思想なり経済思想なりとして社会的影響力を持ちうるものによって惹起されるものであったかと思う。ところが、オウム真理教が信者以外にまで強く訴える力を有していたかとなると疑問であろう。ところがそのような組織が大規模なテロを起こせるだけの資金力や技術力を有するに至った。国家や大企業でなくとも、強力な毒ガスのような大量殺戮兵器を製造し、使用することが可能であると世界に証明した。決して大げさでなく、世界史に否定的な意味での画期を成す出来事であろう。狂信家たちの小集団がカタストロフを導きうる時代に入ったということだ。

　そんな教団の外部に対する本格的かつ直接的な破壊行動の発端が坂本弁護士一家殺害事件なのであろう。しかもこの事件は天安門事件やリクルート疑獄などと違い、昭和天皇崩御と関係づけられなくもない。オウム真理教の麻原彰晃は、カルト教団の教祖に典型的な世界観を展開していた。自らの健康状態の悪化を、日本の滅亡や世界の破滅の予感と結びつける。麻原が自らにも世界にも危機が迫っていると側近たちに積極的に言い出したのは1988（昭和63）年の秋とされる。教団の行動が急進化するきっかけになったと言われる、いわゆるオウム真理教在家信者死亡事件が起きたのは同年9月22日。その3日前の9月19日には、昭和天皇が吹上御所で吐血し重体となって、世間に昭和の終わりが強く意識されはじめた。そこに意味があるとも推測できよう。麻原の危機意識の亢進は昭和天皇が重体になったこととダブっている。昭和から平成へ移り変わるのと、オウム真

理教の行動パターンが過激化するのとが重なる。そういう時間経過になると観察できる。昭和天皇の崩御と平成の新天皇の即位による時間の区切り目が、オウム真理教内部の歴史感覚としては、教団による世の中の建て替えに相応しい時期とイメージされたということではないのか。教祖とは教団の天皇であり、教祖の健康問題が本物の天皇のそれと相乗りすれば、少なくとも教団内部では危機の想像力が高まり行動にも激しく影響しうるということを、昭和 63 年から平成 7 年までのオウム真理教の歴史はよく示しているのではあるまいか。

平 成 元 年 の 正 体

　坂本弁護士一家が殺害された 5 日後になる、11 月 9 日の夜から 10 日にかけて、東西ベルリンを隔てていたベルリンの壁の通行が自由になり、10 日、11 日ぐらいからは実際に壁が壊され、瓦礫になり始める。社会主義がいよいよ風前の灯になったかのように思え、"歴史の終焉テーゼ"の真実味がいよいよ高まった時期である。瓦礫という言葉も肯定的に使えた。このタイミングに合わせるかのように、11 月 21 日には日本労働組合総連合会（連合）が結成される。社会党系で労使対立を基調とする日本労働組合総評議会（総評）、民社党系で労使協調を基調とする全日本労働総同盟（同盟）等が大同団結し、ほとんど大政翼賛会化して、社会主義の退潮の時代にフィットし、階級対立路線よりも融和路線にシフトした巨大労組である。平らかに成ると読める平成という元号の創案者は安岡正篤だとは、改元時の首相、竹下登が広めたのだが、信憑性の不十分なひとつの説だけれども、安岡は右翼運動家として、戦前に労使協調こそが大いなる和を重んじる日本に相応しい労働運動の極致であると説き、戦後も一貫してそういう主張を為し続けた人で、その意味では連合の誕生ほど平成の時代に相応しい出来事もなかった。脱イデオロギー時代を象徴する連合は、自民党に対抗可能な新しい保守・中道の大同団結的勢力を育て、この国に保守二大政党制を定着させようと大胆に振る舞うが、それは結局、うたかたの夢に終わったのであろう。しかも、資本家に対して労働者階級の権利を擁護するイデオロギー闘争を忘れ気味になった連合の時代は、正規雇用から非正規雇用への労働者の比重の転換を抑制する役割を十分に果たせなかったろう。"歴史の終焉テーゼ"というバスに乗り遅れないようにと多くの労組指導者が先走った結果、平成のあいだ、働く者の権利は徐々に損なわれ、国民多数の収入の基盤が砕けて弱くなっていったのだと思っている。

　このあと、ベルリンの壁の崩壊に連動した出来事が続く。11 月 17 日、チェコスロバキアでビロード革命が起き、12 月 3 日には米国のジョージ・H・W・ブッシュ大統領とソ連のゴルバチョフ書記長が地中海のマルタ島で会談し、冷戦終結を宣言して、平和のユートピアがついに到来したかのように思われ、12 月 22 日にはルーマニアでチャウシェスクの政権が倒れた。

　そして 12 月 29 日は東京証券取引所の「大納会」。日経平均の終値は史上最高値の 3 万 8,915 円 87 銭を付けた。これ即ちバブル経済の絶頂であり、翌年の「大発会」から下落に転ずる。株価の泡沫時代は平成元年と共に去った。

　平成元年に触れるべき物事はまだあるだろう。だが、とりあえずは以上の出来事が物語り、推し

量らせ、兆しを示すことで、平成から令和まで、1990年代から2020年代までのかなりが見通されてくるだろう。相反する点もそこにはいろいろと見いだされるが、大ざっぱな傾向としては以下の諸点を挙げてみてもよいかもしれない。（1）ソ連の退潮を主たる理由として資本主義と社会主義とのイデオロギー対立が無効になって行く。（2）歴史から方向性が特に（1）に関連して失われてゆく。（3）時間意識が特に（2）に関連して前後の脈絡を失いがちになり刹那化してゆく。（4）価値意識がやはり特に（2）に関連して序列を失ってゆき、物事が容易に泡沫化したり瓦礫化したりする。（5）文化芸術からは、特に（2）（3）（4）に関係して、真正なもの、真の未来を探究しようという意欲が消滅してゆかざるを得ず、その必然の結果として作品がキッチュ化する。（6）イデオロギーの無効化がユートピアの到来と錯覚される傾向にあったので、（1）から（5）はどれもネガティヴにとらえられるものでもあるはずなのに、脱歴史化と中性化と技術化の鼎立によって、時間も空間も価値も何もかも、引き出しに整理して収められた収蔵品のように管理可能だという幻想が、過渡的現象に過ぎないとはいえ、一旦は蔓延るようになる。（7）人間の知恵を超越した自然の摂理も絡むことなので、（1）〜（6）には必ずしも関係しないことを含め、カタストロフの様々な予兆が認められる。

　胎児よ、胎児よ、何故躍る。平成元年の正体がわかって、おそろしいのか。

（かたやま・もりひで／政治学者、音楽評論家）

Bubbles / Debris: Art of the Heisei Period 1989 – 2019
Sawaragi Noi

Framing Eras in Art

Time frames. Humanity has developed many conventions to organizing time. Japan uses a mix of the Gregorian calendar, which describes an epoch which began with the birth of the Christ, moving towards the eschaton, and Japanese Imperial eras, each of which presume a new beginning, in a theoretically eternal series of renewals. Somehow, recently the national arts community has been focused on exhibitions framing in Gregorian decades, "art of the 80s," and now already rushing towards retrospectives of "art of the 90s." This begs the question of what critical validity can be found in framing art movements in either device? How can we resolve cultural issues according to anything but life as lived?

As the massive global disruptions of this on-going pandemic and societal malaise have clearly shown us, only trivial time moves in convenient increments. Surely nothing could be clearer now than how external forces may intervene and uproot our sense of continuity. External impacts rupture our lifestyles, perceived time splits into before and after, and irreconcilable, incomparable distinctions are created. Demarcations are evident. In disaster sites like the 2011 Great East Japan Earthquake and Tsunami, images of clocks, stopped at the moment of the event, become iconic. These mechanical devices were stopped, jarred by the physics of the impact, but the images gain their resonance because those ruptures were also recorded within the meta-physics of our inner selves.

The linguistic origin of trauma is the Greek word for "wound." The trauma of profound loss, for example a family member, severs our sense of interior and exterior time, its fabric ceases to extend into the future as before. There, in the aftershock, an alternate arrangement takes form, which de-conditions our former sense of the passing of hours and days, it invalidates time's seeming uni-directional flow, even the sense that time is formally measurable. We begin again, as individuals, as a society; we enter a subjective "traumatic" period of viscerally shared experience, until a new normal may form.

Traumatic times, times of highly subjective destabilizing experiences, initiate a cycle of nausea and healing in search of a new equilibrium. Time is experienced more consequentially. We sense our environments more acutely, we are in an agitated state antithetical to the calming, consistent and rational sense of time which clocks exist to facilitate. Anyone who attempts to manage the framing of an era is a participant in an attempt to create a fiction of time moving coherently forward. To frame "art of the 80s" or "art of the 90s" is to make oneself complicit in neglecting or worse, negating, the context of expressive activities of those enduring passages through trauma, and possibly healing. Here I will disregard the general theory that "time" acts on human beings, and instead claim it as a cultural activity, a context for existence, and therein seek the fundamental influence of art in time(s).

The Post-War Ended in 1989, the 1st Year of Heisei

We can point to the familiar habit of framing aesthetic questions in terms of decades as a by-product of the fortunate coincidence of having lived several essentially in-consequential decades.

Free from "traumatic time," society was made capable of rallying its artifacts, its debris, around this "decades" perspective. And this convenience was afforded by the larger context of a "post-war" era.

The framing of a "post-war" era insists on convenient ambiguities, in that, until the next big war re-traumatizes our sense of time and space, rips and fragments our continuum, this "post-war" era will carry the comforting appearance of assured renewability. All we need is inertia. 2020 was the 75th anniversary of the cessation of hostilities in WWII. Even the blows of historic tragedies such as Hiroshima and Nagasaki are softened in being commemorated by such geometric "round" numbers. Thus we are able to distance ourselves, brace our trauma for certain key commemorations, and calm the depressing nightmares within a reliably recurring cycle, and imagine that they will fade over time. Such mechanical assurances that we are moving away from trauma is a compelling argument for remaining in a contiguous "post-war" period.

The post-war frame basically consists of first, recovering from the smoldering rubble of war and re-establishing the economy, second, extraordinary growth within rebuilding which accelerated middle class consumption, and third, inertia. These phases are easy to measure, assuring to promote. Yet while events which distress this narrative have continued to take place, including various unreasonable incidents among marginalized elements of society, unresolved issues from the war, and post-war development issues, including large-scale environmental contamination incidents, each was successfully overwritten by national celebratory events such as the 1964 Tokyo Olympics, the 1970 Osaka Expo, etc, which reclaiming the framing back from the threat of traumatic discontinuity. Such was the victory of the "post-war" reconstruction and high growth narrative. But today, 25 years into a "lost decade," it has long lost all sense of credulity. In this Japan of diminishing expectations, we are simply not moving forward according to "post war" criteria. What, then, causes the trauma which weighs on our post-war hearts?

I would argue that the point these various factors align is 1989, the 1st year of Heisei. Emperor Hirohito died, the "post war" Showa ended, the Heisei era began, and the smoothness of post-war reconstruction, high growth, and middle-class creation experienced a criticality event, melting down, producing severe trauma. This happened in the absence of ameliorating national=citizens' bonding events to absorb the shock and restore status quo. The promise of triviality was betrayed. Fissures appeared, intermittent traumatic exposure became the norm. The viability of framing cultural expression into decades evaporated. And from this point, a fission-fusion (division of one into two/the aggregating of two into a larger one) of artistic practices emerged, rising and dispersing as much like bubbles as acts of individual expression. Dense and decentralized aggregates of practice (formerly known as "art work"), left debris in their wake.

Each Era Resets Our Sense of Accumulated Time

The Heisei Period was when the poles of temporal continuity became distraught. While framing the art of the 1950s or 1960s provides a common precedent to examinations of the art of the 80s or 90s, nobody attempts surveys of "the art of the 40s." And just as "the art of the 20s," or 30s, makes some sense, "Japanese art of the 1880s," or 1890s, does not, because traumatic incidents took place in the 1940s and 1880s and 1890s which rendered conceptions of historical continuity pointless, namely the Greater East Asia (=Pacific) War, and the Meiji Restoration.

In these cases, Imperial era names prove useful. Each emperor does imprint upon their era, and so their name can provide sufficient context to the traumas and banalities of their reign. "Art of the Meiji," "Art of the Taisho," and "Art of the Showa," each make sense because of their Imperial/historical framework. An "Art of the Meiji" survey would carry expectations of reviewing the influences of the Meiji Restoration, the emperor returning to power over the shogunate, and the nation opening its doors to industrialization and international exchange. "Art of the Taisho" would be expected to review the short-lived Taisho democratic reforms before and after the monumental impact of the Great Kanto Earthquake. "Art of the Showa," would usually be divided into pre-war, wartime, and post-war phases, each reviewing the various kinds of trauma and oblivescence that the War brought to cultural activity.

The framework of post-war art existed as a part of the "latter Showa" timeline, sharing the premise of the "reconstruction, high growth, and middle-class creation" temporal regime being implemented. When that model has run its course, conceptions of "post-war," "the art of the post-war," and more importantly the calming sense of progress (that is, after all, what Fordist time is attempting with its post-war decades) all collapse together.

Therefore, while this exhibition/catalogue proposes a review of "the art of the Heisei" it should not be taken as a definitive statement, or an assertion that the Heisei was anything but a series of fragmented temporalities, like the art of the Meiji or Showa Periods. Our aim is contrary. Each imperial transition assumes a trauma of grief and prayer for the departed emperor, which ruptures chronological sequentiality. Each cycle of return and rejuvenation of the Imperial calendar dispels all accumulated energy of disasters and misadventures, and likewise, begins with a celebration of continuity ("The Emperor is Dead! Long live the Emperor!"). The beginning of Reiwa was exceptional in that the previous emperor abdicated while healthy. Nevertheless, right after the era change, we were visited by an alternative mourning period (a cyclical turn-over) due to the COVID-19 pandemic.

Our aim is to look back on "Art of the Heisei" and examine the detritus of how the period was artistically lived. Our point of departure was the "Ground Zero Japan" exhibition I organized at the end of the millennium (Art Tower Mito, 1999). "Ground Zero Japan" was an attempt to "reset" Japanese art, bringing post-war Japanese art not towards accumulation and development, but rather by making explicit its stumbling blocks — its lack of historical context, its lack of viable market, its lack of critical frameworks — not to impose order upon it but rather allow it to exist more on its own terms. Let it collapse once, so as to more appropriately restructure, free from unwarranted expectations. Ironically, the fact of the Gregorian *fin de millénaire* seemed a legitimate opportunity to take stock. In Japan, *Les Prophéties* by Nostradamus enjoys extraordinary popularity, and this helped provide a kitsch prophetic symbolism, an amusing context foretelling humanity's ruin. Cutting an epoch into decades makes about as much sense as a 16C prophet, but the turn of the millennium gave me a pretty large target to aim at. After all, time is tilted here and there and reveals odd angles in unexpected places.

What Happened in Art of the Heisei

At the end of the Heisei era, the literary journal *Shincho* asked me for a top 10 list. My response is as follows, with some new notes.

1. The Heisei eve face-off between mainstream acceptance of "post-Mono-ha" over "Mono-ha" (which began circa 1968/Showa 43), and the emergence of a new generation of artists, born in the later Showa 30s/the early 1960s, with no connection to either. The latter are rather a TV-influenced generation, collective audio-visual media culture people, as exemplified by the 1964/Showa 39 Tokyo Olympics, which everyone in Japan experienced simultaneously. The stage for this changing of the guard was the Roentgen Kunst Institut, which opened in 1991/Heisei 3, in a large renovated warehouse in Omori Higashi, Tokyo. Artists including Ameya Norimizu, Takashi Murakami, Yanobe Kenji, Aida Makoto, Ozawa Tsuyoshi, Hachiya Kazuhiko, Sone Yutaka, and Nakayama Daisuke all launched their careers here, each incredibly releasing representative works from the start of their careers, and in the process erasing the borders between academia, the avant-garde art, and pop culture.

2. A rush of new contemporary museum architecture opening across Japan, in a Keynesian aftermath of the 1991/Heisei 3 asset bubble economy collapse. Art institutions such as Contemporary Art Gallery, Art Tower Mito (Arata Isozaki & Associates, 1990/Heisei 2), the Museum of Contemporary Art Tokyo (Takahiko Yanagisawa + TAK Architects INC, 1995/Heisei 7), the Mori Art Museum (Gluckman Tang Architects, 2003/Heisei 15), the 21st Century Museum of Contemporary Art, Kanazawa (Kazuyo Sejima + Ryue Nishizawa/SANAA, 2004/Heisei 16), and Aomori Museum of Art (Jun Aoki & Associates, 2006/Heisei 18), each focused on contemporary art, which demanded new forms and functions, resulting in the role of post-modern architects being given greater prominence, and in giving architecture a more central role in art practice.

3. The ascendance of curators and gallerists. In response to these new contemporary art museums, and the influence of the global art market, curators transitioned from academic or administrative museum bureaucrats to art-world opinion-makers. From Heisei, curators not only surveyed and researched art practices but increasingly became the jet-setting protagonists reporting from the global art world front lines, responsible for formulating exhibition concepts, working with artists, attending global conferences, writing and editing bilingual catalogues, some even serving as commissioners of international biennale and triennale festivals. In 1998/Heisei 10, nine galleries held *G9*, a new Tokyo art fair as de facto manifesto, at Spiral Hall, Tokyo. They differentiated themselves from dealers, focused on sales, instead highlighting on the exhibition as phenomenon, and they grew to exert enormous traction among the new generation of Japanese creators, and within the international market. Today, co-operation with gallerists is essential for museums.

4. The increased acceptance of photography and moving image work. Both of these forms had previously been considered sub-fields of painting and sculpture, rarely subjects of museum exhibitions or collection activity, but in Heisei both came to play increasingly central roles in art. Photography, in particular, which used to be primarily experienced in publications (reproductions, in other words), came to be considered exhibition-worthy for galleries and museums. The most notable examples being Araki Nobuyoshi and Moriyama Daido, both considered only photographers in Japan, while internationally evaluated as artists. Morimura Yasumasa and Hiroshi Sugimoto are both artists who use photography to produce art, and who similarly rose in critical artistic acclaim. It was during the Heisei Period that both the Tokyo Photographic Art Museum (Nonaka Shigeru, Kume Sekkei Co. Ltd, partially opened in 1990/Heisei 2, completed in 1995/Heisei 7) which focuses on photography and moving image, and the NTT InterCommunication Center (Takahiko Yanagisawa + TAK Architects INC, established in 1990/Heisei 2, facility opened in 1997/Heisei 9), which features emerging media art, were inaugurated.

5. The success of regional art festivals. The Echigo-Tsumari Art Triennale started in the year 2000/Heisei 12, in the mountains of Niigata Prefecture. The festival took place across a broad area of mountain farming hamlets and forests. The strength of the organization's work in community building, and excellent curation, defied all barriers to its improbable venues in difficult-to-access locations, resulting in both expanding the art market, and revolutionizing options for art tourism in Japan. Its potential for continuity an open question from the outset, still, the extraordinary experiences available elevated the dis-reality of the art, and with each presentation, it has managed to dramatically increase the number of visitors, becoming one of the biggest success models for contemporary art in the Heisei Period. The Setouchi Triennale, begun in 2010/Heisei 22, similarly connected the islands of Setouchi which, like the Niigata mountains, were another poor rural area suffering depopulation. Combined with the launch of a suite of spectacular museums and facilities by Benesse Art Site Naoshima, and open all year round (unlike Echigo which is primarily visited every third summer) this art site has become a must-visit destination for global art tourists. Kitagawa Fram serves as the general director for both festivals. Of particular note in the Setouchi program is the Teshima Art Museum (building design by Nishizawa Ryue, art by Naito Rei, 2010/Heisei 22), which ranks among the top contemporary art installations globally. It's installation on Teshima island, provided a dramatic turn-around for an island which had previously been in the news because of illegal industrial waste disposal.

6. The globalization of the art world. After the "end of the Cold War" in 1989/Heisei 1, American-led globalization swept the globe. Artists and galleries sought opportunities in new markets, switching their focus from local to global. In Japan, the first notable shifts were re-evaluations of Kusama Yayoi and Ono Yoko, whose domestic recognition had lagged behind that of their male contemporaries, with international blockbuster shows by both catapulting them into a new level of respect and serious study in Japan. Of course artists such as Kawamata Tadashi, Miyajima Tatsuo, Ohtake Shinro, Nara Yoshitomo, and Takashi Murakami also received renewed appreciation abroad. In particular, *the Superflat* exhibition (trilogy), curated by Takashi Murakami, created a global cultural phenomenon.

7. The resuscitated reputations of Foujita Tsuguharu and Okamoto Taro. Foujita was a star of the École de Paris, uniting the techniques and sensibilities of Japanese painting and Western painting in his own unique style. His later cooperation with the Imperial army during WWII, however, and his work glorifying the Imperial Japanese military, were criticized in the post-war period. Feeling abandoned by Japan, he expatriated to Paris, changed his faith, and changed his name to Léonard Foujita. He passed away never seeing his motherland again. During the post-war period few surveys or exhibitions featured his work. During the Heisei, however, his indispensability to early Showa art came to be appreciated, and with it a more nuanced appraisal of his body of work. In 2006/Heisei 18, a Foujita retrospective was held to commemorate the 120th anniversary of his birth, including his military art, at the National Museum of Modern Art, Tokyo. Okamoto, who passed away in 1996/Heisei 8, lost his reputation in the art world by seeking mass media fame, as a TV entertainer. Due to the efforts of Toshiko Okamoto, who served as his secretary, and eventually became his adopted daughter, Taro's reputation has been much restored. His *Tower of the Sun*, from Osaka Expo '70, has become only more iconic over time. His *Myth of Tomorrow* large-scale wall mural, long thought lost in Mexico, was rediscovered, repaired, and installed prominently in Shibuya station, one of Japan's largest rail hubs. Okamoto was also an important advocate of Jomon pottery from Okinawa and Tohoku, and notably one of the first artists to challenge the subject of the nuclear age. Both proved influential to artists who flourished in the Heisei Period.

8. Japanese art=a genealogy of playfulness. It might seem unbelievable today but through much of modernity, exhibitions of Japanese traditional art, with the possible exception of ukiyo-e, weren't able to attract visitors, and magazines which covered it floundered. Then came Tsuji Nobuo's *Lineage of Eccentrics: The Miraculous World of Edo Painting* (first published in *Bijutsu Techo*, 1968/Showa 43), which focused on "eccentric" artists such as Ito Jakuchu, Soga Shouhaku, Nagasawa Rosetsu, and Iwasa Matabee, and gradually lead to greater awareness, and popularity. Also the dedication and promotional activity of *Nihon Bijutsu Ouendan*, a unique collaboration between art historian Yamashita Yuji and avant-garde artist Akasegawa Genpei in 1996/Heisei 8, rallied a common sense of urgency about the Japanese people becoming ignorant of their own culture. Late in the Heisei, museums started to see the queues return for traditional art and artists.

9. Outsiders and art. The Los Angeles County Museum of Art's *Parallel vision: Modern Artists and Outsider Art* was presented at the Setagaya Art Museum in 1993/Heisei 5. The powerful and aberrational artworks and expressions, works by eccentrics and lunatics, illiterates and prophets, brought an impact unseen in other forms of art. Originating in the post-WWII Art Brut movement, founded by Jean Dubuffet, outsider art was not even considered in Japan, where the expressions by those without proper art education had been limited, and drawings by the mentally ill might have been produced as part of welfare programs perhaps, but never allowed within fundamental discussions about the nature of art, or what it is for. With the new Tokyo Olympics at hand, Art Brut is interpreted as Para-art, serving national policy. Today the outsider art boom is being co-opted, but it will eventually regain its power, and once again detonate a hole in conceptions of Heisei expression.

10. Disasters and art. Despite its linguistic roots as a great "leveling" (becoming super flat?), the Heisei was a decidedly bumpy period. It may not have had major wars like Showa, but disasters continued unabated. Starting with a record-setting, famine-level rice crop failure due to a cold summer in 1993/Heisei 5, and followed by two great disasters, the Great Hanshin Earthquake of 1995/Heisei 7, and the Great East Japan Earthquake and Tsunami of 2011/Heisei 23, as well as multiple major earthquakes on Kyushu and Hokkaido islands, accompanied by downpours and massive mudslides, and numerous occasions when many Japanese were forced to relocate, throughout Heisei Japan remained a disaster site. Everyone knew that no one was safe. Furthermore, one of the historically worst nuclear disasters occurred at the Fukushima Daiichi Nuclear Power Plant, and it remains in critical condition, under a declared state of emergency, even today. The non-conventional collective and cooperative activities by artist groups such as Chim↑Pom, formed in 2005/Heisei 17, were powerfully resonant responses to this condition. Autonomous and independent of pre-existing art systems or museums or festival success models, their multi-faceted collaborative approach of employing multiple strategies for surviving unstable and unknown circumstances, and nimble sense of self-organization and self-production saw them creating their own opportunities time and again, as admirably lithe innovators. This manner or practice is symbolic of Heisei art, and I expect it to only increase in the next generation.

The *Shincho* request was to 10 but were I to revisit it today I would dial it up to 11, adding the influence of social media (the contagious power of SNS, Twitter and Facebook in society).

11. Social media and art. Social networking services such as Twitter played outsized roles in emergency information sharing, i.e. to rescue victims, to confirm survivors, to source requisite materials, etc in the Great East Japan Earthquake and Tsunami disasters. While centralized bureaucracies repeatedly failed, decentralized networks proved their resilience time and again. The growth and viability of these information platforms has augmented exponentially since the Great Hanshin Earthquake of 1995/Heisei 7, when the rapid adoption of Windows 95, along with early cell phones, were seen as key, and accelerated the development of smart phones. Today, they are essential social infrastructure. The diffusion of IT based communication has also introduced considerable innovation into the art world. Art has traditionally relied on exhibitions of unique items, making it an exceptionally analog business. Thus, for long, it was difficult for art to engage online environments like the music industry did. But since just before the Great East Japan Earthquake and Tsunami, new art forms which consider online and offline environment equally, and enable discourses between particular physical exhibition places and virtual non-sites, began to flourish in Japan. A typical example was *The Manifesto of CHAOS*LOUNGE 2010*, announced in 2010/Heisei 22 by Chaos*Lounge, a unit comprised of Kurose Yohei, Umezawa Kazuki, and Fujishiro Uso. [Sawaragi 2016]

Disasters Becoming Flat

The events of the Heisei happened neither orderly nor evenly. We see them as organized only because the Heisei Period ended, somehow, and the Reiwa Period began. Organizing art as being of the Heisei implicitly presumes an importance in the arrival of the Reiwa Period, just as it presumes a meaning distinct to the Showa Period. And this method similarly leaves us clueless about where we are now, in the Reiwa Period, because we will only understand the art of the Reiwa after it's over. Our rescue from this temporal limbo is what I call Japan's status as a "bad place" (in my book *Japan, Modernity, and Art*, published in 1998/Heisei 10), namely, the extreme geological instability of the Japanese archipelago, providing a near-constant punctuation of these Imperial eras with violent existential crises. The two, Imperial and geological, are in fact intimately connected through oblivion and repetition. The imprint each emperor makes on the nation integrates its crises and provides an embodiment for each era. I just listed the top 11 arts of the Heisei Period. But in reality, if we are to claim them for Heisei art, then we are also obliged to claim them as commonly equipped with a Heisei-inherent aspect, in their backgrounds, and at their root.

I was born in 1962/Showa 37, two years before the 1964/Showa 39 Tokyo Summer Olympics. I barely remember it. But six years later, with the opening ceremony of the Osaka Expo, I experienced my first indelible impression of the Showa emperor, delivered from the family TV screen. When I think back about the Showa emperor, my associations are almost always of such celebratory events, if not major national enterprises such as Expos. In my mind I see a throng of Japanese gathered in some location, a ceremony, and the emperor raising his hand, responding to their adoration. The figure of the Showa emperor, together with these celebratory ceremonies symbolize the development of Japan, the peace of its people, and everyone's efforts to achieve them, but is at the same time, a scene which symbolizes the post-war, the bright latter Showa Period. To phrase it another way, these scenes are inextricably linked to the existence of the emperor as living god in the genesis, prosecution, and recovery from the war. The Showa Period included the most horrible war Japan has known and this adds complexity and nuance, light and darkness, to all art of the Showa Period: no matter how expressed, nothing from this era can ever not be informed by its many paradoxes.

What, then, about the Heisei? The reign of the Heisei emperor had none of this national ostentation, no Tokyo Summer Olympics, or Osaka Expo like the Showa. The Chinese logograms of its name mean "leveling," but the Heisei was not a time of national unification or mobilization. It lacked the Showa drama of light and darkness, of peace contrasted with war. In that sense we can, for now, follow the lead of the artist Takashi Murakami, and claim that Heisei was Superflat. To me, the indelible image of the Heisei era was the emperor and empresses' bearing when visiting Heisei's many ongoing sites of devastation. The Heisei emperor presented an utmost contrast to the Showa emperor's pageantry. The Heisei emperor typically appeared to the public when providing emergency care for Japanese citizenry displaced from their homes by large-scale disasters, lost refugees, resting on blue tarps laid out in school gymnasiums, temporary partitions providing whatever sense of privacy and solace, while they learned to cope with their immediate difficulties. And in these scenes, the emperor with his wife, the commoner empress, at his side, always humble in aspect, in support of these citizens, face-to-face, importantly bending down to eye level. That Heisei disasters levelled the emperor's gaze, such that he was never looking down upon them, but rather seeing them eye to eye, was no small feat for either emperor or citizen.

The nation-building events of the Heisei were incidents, accidents, and catastrophes unparalleled since the war. But unlike the war there was no drumbeat to announce their approach. There were no clear meta-narratives of Showa causes and effects of war. Heisei was a time of a normalization (leveling=arising) and learning to coexist with an unpredictability and enormity of violence, but without even a reason to look for cause or effect. In disasters the extraordinary becomes ordinary, the new normal, nothing special. The speed with which we forget accelerates. It can appear almost as though nothing is happening, but numerous sudden, "bad times" created fissures in the Heisei, and revealed how vast our vulnerability, and required protracted aftermaths. These traumatic episodes, sewn together, make up the fabric of the Heisei.

1989/Heisei 1

The Heisei began in 1989. The Showa emperor, whose glorious figure had disappeared from public view since the previous year was replaced by physiological indices such as body temperature, heart rate, and melena count, before he passed away at the beginning of the New Year. The whole nation went into mourning, and a new emperor ascended. But we were quickly shaken out of that circumstance by a series of revolutions in Poland, Hungary, East Germany, Bulgaria, Czechoslovakia, and Romania in the European "east," as well as the Tiananmen Square incident in China. And of course the sequence of events which led to the fall of the Berlin Wall.

The fall of the Berlin Wall was a turning point of such magnitude that we still feel its aftershocks even now, in Reiwa, with the Covid-19 pandemic. It's not just that the physical barrier separating East and West Berlin was broken, allowing the free traffic of goods and services. It hadn't the catastrophic proportion of the disasters of 1995/Heisei 7, 2001/Heisei 13, or 2011/Heisei 23. But the fact that the Berlin Wall was brought down by the citizenry, meant that the iron curtain, a defense of one of the two superpowers which had carved the world up and controlled it since WWII, could be forfeited so easily. The speed with which the Cold War ended made an impression which, I think, no-one had imagined. And driven by this, the a-ideological mechanism known as globalism (in cold war terms of being neither capitalism nor communism) began to sweep across the planet. This acceleration, aggregating the world into a single market, mobilizing people, things, and events, was so antithetical to the previous containment of walls and the "curtain." The consolidation of the super-national EU, with its rationalization of borders (people) and currency (things) was the epitome of this movement. Of course the explosive growth of the Internet, unbound by time, space, or taxation, staged the biggest tipping point to raise mobility and aggregation. From then on, the world became increasingly subsumed into mass mobilization, delirium and desire, and profit at dizzying scale.

Until then Japan had been a "post-War miracle" economy under the protection of the U.S. nuclear umbrella and trade agreements. Then as the U.S. faltered, Japan expanded into an unprecedented bubble economy, in fact a culmination of the Cold War domestic boom, in the context of a rapidly globalizing new world order, before collapsing in on itself. When that bubble burst in 1990/Heisei 2, Japan slid into a form of perpetual recession-as-economy. Blue-chip financial institutions and large corporations fell like dominos. Mergers and takeovers rewrote the economy. Foreign capital came to feed on the remains. And so it remains to this day.

Of course not everything was destroyed. But the bubble economy completely rewrote everything, like a war or disaster might, and rapidly installed a regime of quick-buck scrap and build short-term thinking. In that sense, it was a new form of catastrophe. Not just the economy, but rather the bankrupt rot it ushered in leered at and imposed upon art like a new parasitic superstructure.

The Japanese art world protected itself by shutting down and turning inward, rapidly losing global relevance. Artists fled overseas to try make a living or even continue producing. New gallerists emerged, connecting to the world's art markets, to support them. Of course this drastic transition happened in all Japanese industries at once. Since 1989/Heisei 1, the planet began a massive unravelling of people, things, and events. It's conceivable that a contributing factor to climate change, evidently the greatest issue facing us today, as well as for repeatedly epidemiological outbreaks of unknown viruses (new types of pneumonia, such as SARS and MERS) during the Heisei Period, are because of this explosive level of exchange, and the rapid development of lands previously unexploited. The trigger was the collapse of the Berlin Wall, and the fall of global ideological polarity: ripples from 1989, Heisei year 1, still felt today.

1995/Heisei 7   50th Anniversary of the End of the War

1995/Heisei 7 was the year that post-Cold War globalism first started to impact Japan. It coincided with the milestone 50th year anniversary of the end of WWII hostilities. It was supposed to be a rare festive Heisei stage, for the nation to celebrate with the Heisei emperor, half a century removed from defeat and occupation, half a century of economic prosperity, now seeking its place in an integrated new global order. But the Great Hanshin Earthquake struck in January. Having been born after the war, I'd never experienced anything like that before, except in the abstract; in films, comic books, or on TV. A disaster of that scale, leveling Kobe one of the great modern metropolises of Japan to rubble and ash in a matter of minutes, was new to most who experienced it. This was the beginning of the 50th year anniversary of the end of the war. And in an instant, we were all transported right back to the destruction of wartime and defeat. Kobe was devastated. Fires burned on, unabated. People rushed to evacuation centers, lining up for food and warmth in order to survive. It was a scene that refused to heal, followed by richter-scale 7 aftershocks reverberating across Japan for days. The figure of the Heisei emperor, quietly consoling survivors in the evacuation centers, began to carry profound symbolic meaning in this vortex of vulnerability.

A scant two months later, in March of the same year, radical followers of the cult Aum Shinrikyo released the chemical weapon sarin nerve gas on a crowded morning commuter train. The mastermind was identified as the guru Asahara Shoko. Leaders of the cult all became death-row prisoners, and were later executed during Heisei. According to their testimony they were planning to spray sarin from above the capital city using helicopters to better perpetrate mass murder and subvert the nation through a coup d'etat. It was a horrible token for art — an early apparition of visualizing the invisible, the unspoken surfacing, like scum bubbles forming and rising, incrementally aggregating into form... from sarin to radiation, from radiation to coronavirus, globalization permeating a ring of porus gateways into the Heisei era.

1995/Heisei 7 was the year when the negative aspects of globalism rose to the surface in Japan. The technology, the knowledge, and the funding which enabled the Aum Shinrikyo cult to arm and refine chemical weapons was secretly procured at their base "Satian," at the foot of Mt. Fuji, through underground networks tied to the now-dismantled former Soviet Union. The dissolution of the Cold War resulted in a vast surplus of weapons, traded through global networks, later provoking America's "war on terror." This germination took place in Japan, one of the safest places in the world, in the Heisei Period, in the form of Japanese killing Japanese, releasing unheard-of chemical weapons inside trains filled with completely innocent people, on one of the world's busiest inner-city subway networks. It is still hard to imagine it, as I write this. But in the wake of this incident, "security" surveillance systems, which were still unfamiliar to Japan — again visualizing the invisible — were rapidly implemented throughout the cities. Inevitably, this narrowed the opportunities for the new generation artists, who had actively used public spaces to wage collective guerrilla activities, because now they could be constantly monitored.

2001/Heisei 13   9.11

In 2001/Heisei 13. Four passenger jets, laden with fuel, vanished from their flight paths. Two careened into the twin-towers of the World Trade Center, a symbol of the global economy, designed by Japanese-American architect Minoru Yamasaki, in the heart of Manhattan's financial district. Broadcast all over the world, the buildings spewed flame and black smoke. As we all watched on TV, the twin-towers collapsed to the ground. I was by chance watching news on TV. Suddenly the screen switched to the feed from New York. I witnessed the whole story unfolding in near real time. Then came the unconfirmed information that another jet had crashed into the headquarters of the U.S. Department of Defense, the Pentagon. Washington D.C. had been another target as well. All suicide attacks. I had no idea what was going on. But I felt a clenched sense of urgency, and knew that something unbelievable was happening in front of my eyes.

The incidents were soon identified as anti-American terrorist attacks by Islamic fundamentalists. Within a month this led to aerial bombings in Afghanistan, where the Taliban, the suspected assailants, were based. Down the road, al-Qaeda, a network of international terrorists came to be regarded as the enemy. A new war (but was it?) began to unfold around the world, between the U.S. and its allies, and invisible "terrorist cells." This mutated into the Iraq War, in the name of which the historic capital of Baghdad was assaulted, and destroyed. Retaliatory terror strikes expanded into towns that weren't even identified as battlefields. Suicide bombers and vehicular assaults increased. "Soft targets," such as concert halls, stadiums, and restaurants eventually became battlefields. The bizarre "war on terror" destabilized the world such that any site could be considered a latent battlefield at any time. We can say that the terrorists willingly became collectives, as opposed to traditional centralized armies. We can dress it up to call it the multitude-ification of terrorists. There is much we could say about it, but this is not the time or place.

This new state of war can also be traced back to 1989, Heisei year 1. In a sense, we might even say that the Heisei era opened a path for the seeds sown in 1989/Heisei 1 to sprout, quickly growing strange brambles, and transforming into a jungle the likes of which we'd never seen. The collapse of the Berlin Wall, the symbol of the Cold War, and the remarkable dismantling of the superpower Soviet Union, soon thereafter, was read as an American ideological victory, of liberal democracy finally defeating the Soviet Union's socialist ideal. Except that since the ideology was now no longer constrained by an alternative, the ideological aspects of the struggle vanished and advocates of liberal democracy simply pretended to represent justice.

With the East/West dichotomy gone, the axis shifted and less evident ideological battles emerged, plunging the world into new forms of turmoil. Fundamentalist Abrahamics faced off. The first concrete exposition was the Gulf War, in 1991/Heisei 3, the first declared war for the U.S since Viet Nam. The Gulf War became a foreshadowing of the 9/11 attacks, or rather initiated the friction with Saddam Hussein that later drew the U.S. into the Iraq War — or rather, compelled the U.S. to reiterate the Gulf War, on an expanded scale. The Gulf War also introduced new technologies. The attacks on Baghdad were broadcasted to the world on CNN. Again a foreshadowing of the broadcasts I witnessed of the collapsing WTC on 9.11.

In fact, after being put into action in the Gulf War, mobile technology rapidly improved, and soon evolved into products which have captured our everyday desires. Today's information technologies, including for example social (or socially engaged?) media, is designed to keep the user constantly accumulating messages and responses, and inculcates a battlefield psychology of confirming and sharing one's location, in order to commence operations immediately. There, we are endlessly stressed, tethered to the anxiety of incoming calls and responses. Our ordinary lives have become battlefield where we're exposed and unarmed. There are no "ordinary" options left for us anymore, even if we want them. Our ordinary has become the Operation Desert Storm of information saturation.

The 9/11 attacks of 2001/Heisei 13 were the moment, the anti-globalism flash point, which had begun to seethe under the surface since 1989/Heisei 1. There, in the radiant blue NY sky, black pillars of smoke and fiery plumes were dutifully transmitted to every corner of the planet via global information distribution networks. This traumatic moment in 2001/Heisei 13 visualized the invisible, and a merging of daily life and battlefield logic levelled daily life. Our "everyday" lives were marched to into an endless war of attrition.

2011/Heisei 23　3.11

10 years later, at 2:46PM, on March 11th, 2011/Heisei 23, an unprecedented magnitude 9.0 undersea megathrust earthquake hit off the Tohoku coast of East Japan. Hundreds of kilometers of Japan's Pacific coast was flooded by the resulting tsunami. Countless people became victims, some of them still missing today. Many who survived lost their family homes and towns, and were left no choice but to become domestic refugees. On top of which, the effects of the tsunami caused the Fukushima Daiichi nuclear power plant to lose connection with its external power supply, making the pressure vessels lose coolant and dry-boil from nuclear fuel decay, resulting in three reactors melting down. We will never reclaim or contain all of the nuclear fuel that left those reactors that day, carried by the wind, contaminating eastern Japan. Other materials continue to be leaked into the oceans. There still remain areas where the radiation levels haven't decreased enough for residents to return home, creating literal point-of-no-return evacuation zones.

Our level of technological sophistication, and reliance, means that we can't clearly separate natural disasters from man-made disasters. True, earthquakes are an unavoidable and productive part of the Earth's natural physiology, but nuclear power generation is a product of human ingenuity. The combination can be lethal. Behind each nuclear plant, so many built along Japan's coasts, there was always an excuse, an extension of the post-war thinking, that we were in control, that the goal was to sustainably reduce carbon dioxide emissions for the sake of our rapidly warming planet. "Eco-friendly" is something we're all familiar with. But in post 1989/Heisei 1 globalism, a decidedly "eco-unfriendly" warming of the planet is accelerating. Heisei era leaders were proud to discuss reduction targets at international conferences (and develop models like the Kyoto Protocol) and sign agreements, but as long as globalism kept accelerating, and more and more large and small airplanes were launched, their models were confounded and their targets mocked. And the drastic, even violent climate change of recent years is the result. It is also, no doubt a contributing factor to the diffusion of new undiscovered viruses from previously unexploited lands (AIDS, SARS, MERS, Zika, dengue, Ebola, etc). There's no doubt that out lack of consideration about our stewardship of the planet has created multiple situations where our actions magnify the resulting ecological damage. In this exhibition we built a huge chronological record board that we named the "Heisei Wall" on-site. As you will see on the chronological table printed in this catalogue, right after the beginning of the Heisei Period, things like volcanic eruptions, and bad crops due to fickle weather (1993/Heisei 5), and unprecedented nuclear power and processing plant accidents have continued across Japan. The Tokaimura nuclear accident (1999/Heisei 11), was a serious criticality accident, which resulted in two fatalities, the first post-war death caused by a domestic nuclear complex. The 2011 Great East Japan Earthquake and Tsunami (2011/Heisei 23) was a massive and composite disaster unique in human history. There have been many portentous events, and inobvious social after-effects, as well as projections of more disasters in the future. Scenes of mass victims, domestic refugees, evacuees sitting on the floors of public facilities, gymnasium halls and such, has become a common part of the news. It could happen anywhere, at any time in Japan.

Since 2011/Heisei 23, we've been living in a period of accidents and disasters and constant ambient anxiety. Needless to say this novel coronavirus pandemic, delivered at the close of the Heisei and start of Reiwa, is the extension of these natural and man-made accidents. Except this time, unlike in the Heisei Period, it doesn't work for the present emperor to pay visits to the affected areas, because of the risks to both parties. March 11, 2011/Heisei 23 was a dolorous beginning of the end of the Heisei Period, but it also carries a signal to be heeded lest we repeat our mistakes in the Reiwa.

Disaster Literature/Against-Architecture Essay *Hojoki*

To discuss the role of the endless cycle of disasters and the endurance of unsettled time in Japan, it's instructive to return to what we might call the first Japanese disaster essay, the critically acclaimed *Hojoki*, or *An Account of a Ten-Foot-Square Hut*, written in March 1212 by Kamo no Chomei, a 12–13C hermit who lived during the politically tumultuous transition from the end of the classical era of the Heian imperial court, to the beginning of the first feudal military Kamakura Shogunate.

The pivotal event of Chomei's youth would have been the struggles between the Minamoto and the Taira clans. Both families were of divine Imperial lineage, the bloodline which had ruled Japan since the time of myth and legend. Both Minamoto and Taira family branches had been demoted from the line of succession, and into the ranks of the nobility, but both then over generations worked to amass regional military power and mount their returns to capture the court. The nadir came on April 25, 1185, when a 6 year-old Taira emperor who held no actual power in life, but rather existed as a proxy for his grandfather's rule, was drowned by his own grandmother to evade capture in the battle of Dan-no-ura. Thus the Taira were overthrown, and the path to military rule in Japan was cleared.

The opening lines of *Hojoki* are known to all Japanese: "The current of the flowing river does not cease, and yet the water is not the same water as before. The foam that floats on stagnant pools, now vanishing, now forming, never stays the same for long. So, too, it is with the people and dwellings of the world." Like Heraclitus before him, Chomei portrays the vicissitudes of time using the metaphor of a river, but here with a decidedly darker tone. The changes of power, the ruins of the formerly-admirable families, the dignity of the capital and its court, as a melee of disasters scattered and resurfaced, whether great conflagrations, tornados, famine, epidemic, an earthquake, the relocation of the capital itself, all serving to empty once-prosperous Kyoto into something helpless and desolate and vaguely ill, just like the accumulated roil of scum bubbles on the surface on an otherwise beautiful river.

"Impermanence," the first of the three marks of existence in Buddhist thought, is traditionally used to describe *Hojoki*. To me Chomei's sense of impermanence seems born rather more from a profound sense of alienation, a self-evacuation, an internal flight and refuge from an outer reality of disaster and betrayal. Chomei abandoned Kyoto in the late stages of its slow creeping malaise, but instead of entering a monastery, he became a hermit in the mountains of Hino, and lived in a kind of mobile hut (=*hojo* approx. 3.03m x 3.03m) which could easily be unbound from the earth, carried off and reassembled in case of impending crisis. A *hojo* is a retreat in form and in function, a formal appreciation of the banality of impermanence, a pragmatic immersion in traumatic time, an antithesis to the idea of an eternal capital of the gods which had been the presumption of Kyoto. The word *hojo* sounds quaint today, but in retrospect, it was a form of temporary disaster shelter. *Hojoki* is not only an excellent vividly written essay of turbulent late classical Japan, but it's also a literature which could be born only from an evacuee, a literature from impermanent shelter (decisively NOT a work of permanent architecture or statement), a literature as impermanent shelter.

In the preface of the Chikuma Gakugei Bunko edition of *Hojoki*, Asami Kazuhiko's revised translation states that "In the history of Japanese literature, the first work which featured disaster head on was probably *Hojoki*" (page 8). In the preceding chapter, "Japanese and buildings," you'll find the following linguistic history of architecture and the state:

"The Chinese character for 'dai-jin (minister)' can also be read as 'oto-do.' The origin of the word 'oto-do' is said to be 'oho-tono,' which means both, minister, and palace.

The emperor is called 'ten-no,' but also 'mikado,' in Japanese. 'Mikado' also means grand gate. Today, we use honorific title of 'hei-ka' for emperors. 'Hei' also means grand stairs to ascend into the palace. Another, similar word 'kakka,' as in 'ka(ku),' is used in words like 'tenshu-kaku (tower keep),' which indicates prestigious tall buildings.

Each of these words were used to directly and indirectly describe grand, strong architecture, and gradually each was subverted to mean those grand buildings' inhabitants.

Grand architecture immediately symbolizes the status and power of its owners and inhabitants. Small houses and shabby buildings specifically represent the absence of status and power. This is why Japanese people are self-conscious about public buildings, and often cleave to private home ownership.

Chomei, on the other hand, was wary of big houses. He was a man without connection to status, power, or wealth, quietly observing a time and its society from a small mountain hut, and writing his thoughts. And from this outline comes *Hojoki*" (page 6–7).

Hojoki can therefore be read as a kind of against-architecture book, in a context where architecture symbolizes power, with ministers and emperors at its apex. It's clear that Chomei understood this relationship. He had originally been of a family associated with the prestigious Shimogamo shrine, involved in those same power games, but Chomei lost those games, and his place at the shrine, and so escaped to become a mountain hermit. No matter the cause, it seems clear that he hated ostentatious architecture and the status and power of those who inhabited them, and that is where the design conception for his "*hojo,*" the most minimal of huts, emerged, in order to maintain critical distance in every sense. *Hojoki* should be read as more than classic literature, rather we should let it speak directly to us, to all who have lost their palaces, their big and robust buildings, their nuclear power plants, returned once again to a more restless existence, whether in evacuation centers or temporary houses, or other anti-palaces, to live life in uncertainty, in anxiety, as we have since 2011. Perhaps by daring to choose small houses, tentative buildings, and temporary shelters, we can position ourselves within an attitude fit to survive this world, and avoid falling prey to the games, the status, the power, the over-reaching architecture, infrastructure, and technology of our time.

It's easy to confirm that this thinking is not just about architecture. Where in politics you have a "minister" in art you have "master," an author of a masterpiece to be emulated across generations, something that young talent will be raised on, bridging the turbulence generations. But are "masters" even possible in contemporary society? Instead of simply adding more architectural tissue, more masters and ministers and larger narratives authorizing monolithic Heisei-era authority, people instead opted for small *hojos*, repeated tentative gatherings and dispersions, efficiently eluding "stagnation" while collectively challenging life within provisional bubbles, not really even art "works" or "projects." The "art of the Heisei Period" might better be described as a zigzag path trod between collapsing structures in traumatic times, than a chronology of monuments, buildings, or decades.

What we should note in this exhibition is the fact that many people — not just artists — managed to assemble in each *hojo* when needed, consciously or unconsciously rebelling against Heisei historicization, against master's pieces, against symbolizing the period, and continued each with their own sustainable and matter-of-fact activities as though submerged from view. They are not to be found via the search terms "collaboration" or "borderless-ness" from early Heisei, or "collective" or "socially engaged" from late Heisei. Artists (and everyone else on the Internet) hasn't had a choice but to evade and regroup, and rely on one another, creating opportunities for face to face engagement, and new forms of exchange. Today our forms of assembly reflect a time with no other options but to mirror the mirrors.

Debris Are the Future of Our City

They, lilting lightly like bubbles on the surface, rapidly and repeatedly coming and going, gradually accumulating around the debris of unrelenting emergency. Debris is a ghastly word that every Japanese has been assailed by with since the detritus of tens of thousands lost to the 2011 Great East Japan Earthquake and Tsunami. It was the word used again for the refuse from the nuclear melt-downs of the Fukushima Daiichi Nuclear Power Plant accident. The violence of torrential rains and flooding inevitably creates a lot of debris. It is the material opposite of the immaterial river scum which flits among and evades massive structures, but whether by froth or debris, what the two forms share in common is that they both emerge from the massive structures our civilization used to inhabit and occupy, and are in ascendance in the collapse of the post-war socio-economic structure. This collapse, aided by the great disasters, generates a portrait of us as a frenzy which forms and dissolves in liminal spaces, paired with debris (again!) in phase between times and places. Calling this exhibition *Bubbles/Debris* pays reference to the book *the Future* of *Debris* published in 2019/Reiwa 1 by Isozaki Arata, architect — or perhaps more appropriately anti-architect — another inspiration worthy to seat alongside Kamo no Chomei.

Isozaki the architect/anti-architect has in fact a deeper connection with Kamo no Chomei which warrants exploration. His *Contingency Manual — What made the issue of the plan for the new national stadium of Japan going sideways* was published in 2016/Heisei 28, before *the Future of Debris*. The book included a newly re-written chapter 3, titled "Debris and ranks" under Part 1, as well as a "Personal chronology of Isozaki Arata" suffix in place of a postscript. In the chronology we find disasters of war, turmoil earthquakes and such, alongside his biological decades, starting from 1931 (age 0) when the Mukden Incident took place (an event staged by Japanese militarists as a pretext for the invasion of Manchuria), until 2011 (age 80) when the Great East Japan Earthquake and Tsunami, and meltdown, occurred.

According to his notes, "Ever since I was old enough to understand, I have been told that my ancestors were washed ashore from Uryu island, which reportedly sank in Beppu Bay, during the 1596 Keicho earthquake." In 1951 (age 20), in the middle of the Korean war, "I lost my parents. My house burnt. All of our household articles were disposed, and I moved to Tokyo. I moved around, becoming a displaced Tokyoite." In 1961 (age 30), approaching the Cuban Crisis, he recollects, "I left for a trip around the world, my Grand Tour. I realized that to think about buildings you need to be at the actual sites. I started to call my workplace my atelier. I emulated traveling craftsmen, who migrate from site to site." Reminiscent of Kamo no Chomei, these also represent the accounts of a young Isozaki, who sank in the sea, burnt in the fire, ultimately abandoned the ordinariness of home, distanced himself from monolithic architecture, and chose to become a nomad as a vocation. In notes for 1971 (age 40) he mentions the Cultural Revolution. His resonance with Kamo no Chomei is actualized when he says "I read *Hojoki* in English translation while traveling, and realized for the first time that this was a disaster book. A temporary hut may be the most precise definition of architecture." This is likely the formation of architectural=temporality for the anti-architect Isozaki.

Isozaki's personal record follows the turmoil and earthquakes which demarcate each decade. In 1981 (age 50) remarking on the Iranian Revolution, "Finding a clue in the words of the 13th century Japanese Buddhist priest Dogen, 'Time comes and goes,' I found the concept of the tea house, Uji-an. At this time my temporary homes were hotels in Manhattan and Santa Monica." In 1991 (age 60), he comments on the collapse of the Soviet Union, "Turning sixty, I decided the motto of my life shall be to remain a vagrant." In 2001 (age 70) commenting on 9.11, he looks back, "I selected 12 great works and published *12 homes*, a selection of modern homes, as mail art. None of them were built by architects. All of them were vagabonds. I'm a parasite, so to speak."

In 2011 (age 80) on 3.11, "The idea of the mobile concert hall Ark Nova was conceived from a folk story, in which a spiritual or deity-like being pays visit in a floating vessel, an *Utsufune*. Just like the *hojo* could be transported by a two-wheeled cart, so can this hall can be folded and put in a container to seek its next point of anchorage." Here the *hojo* of Chomei's *Hojoki* comes from the sea, a drifting construction on the surface of the sea, without any Earthly foundations. The *hojo* for Isozaki, he of the hut or boat, is the architectural opposite of the palace. It doesn't just echo the thesis of architecture=anti-architecture, but also the layers of the thesis. "A ruin is the future of our city," campaigned Isozaki, against the Japan-US Security Treaty of 1960. Today, this ruin is transformed by earthquakes and nuclear accidents, fulfilling his prediction that "debris are the future of our city." The froth scum on the water's surface gradually aggregates over repeated incidents, accidents, and earthquakes, now so thick as to be almost one with the debris. Each of the palaces=masters, once the symbols of power, have turned into "oversized garbage/debris" ("oversized garbage" is a category of trash disposal which requires payment and reservations to be taken away. The presumption is something that will require specialized handling to remove), hard to dispose of, or disappearing into the landscape of other accumulated wreckage.

Museums are no exceptions. In 2019/Reiwa 1 a typhoon flood submerged nine of the Kawasaki City Museum's storage houses, damaging a total of 229,000 archival documents. If a museum shuts down, does it re-emerge as a massive "oversized garbage/debris"? In this world where anything can disappear into the bubble froth and debris, museums cease to be grounded palaces. Instead they are more like arks, setting sail for the unknown, in a vast stormy sea of heaving white waves and the sailor's imminent crisis of wreckage or sinking (presaging their conversion to debris).

Bubbles and Debris

And thus a collection of promising artists, cross-disciplinary, cross-boundary, collaborative, collective, socially engaged, scattered throughout the Heisei Period, are like drifting bubbles of potentiality within museums/palaces, for now their secure gates selectively revealing future debris. Today, in this beautiful newly renovated museum in Kyoto, a passage of situational Heisei transition from "bubbles to debris" is on view, a review of encounters and dispersions, of aggregations of artists, and this divides this Heisei Period into three traumatic epochs, in order to make explicit the "Art of the Heisei Period" as a proper signifier, ambivalent chronology and all, organizing these "bubbles and debris" of autonomous *hojo* clusters, rich with latency — an "art of density" (refusing to obey rules against closed spaces, large gatherings, social distancing) presaging their own future banning as outcasts.

It's worth noting that the site of this exhibition, the Kyoto City KYOCERA Museum of Art (also known as the Kyoto City Museum of Art), opened in 1933/Showa 8, is the oldest surviving public art museum in Japan. Inaugurated to commemorate Emperor Showa's Ceremony of Accession, in 1928/Showa 3, it was initially called the Kyoto Enthronement Memorial Museum of Art, and renamed the Kyoto City Museum of Art in the post-war occupation force withdrawal, de-emphasizing state Shinto for civic society. In other words, the museum was originally founded as imperial era transition celebratory culture. Given that this exhibition deals with the theme of imperial eras, Showa to Heisei, and Heisei to Reiwa, the exhibition's curation finds resonance in the continuity/discontinuity of the venue itself.

An era name is a designation of the reign of an individual emperor. The Chinese character for se/yo, "one generation," is composed of three tens = "thirty." The Heisei era lasted 30 years, one generation (This is exceptional because over 10% of Imperial eras have lasted less than a year, and the longest was Showa, which preceded it, at just over 62 years). Inside "The Art of Heisei" is therefore the corpus of Japanese art world creativity from the Heisei reign, while outside of the exhibition venue unfolds a world already inscribing the space-time and creativity of the Reiwa reign. The Showa venue therefore, houses the three chapters of this exhibition — the gatherings and dispersions of artists, the bubbles, and the debris — describe the Heisei art corpus, while providing bridges to whatever manner of gatherings and dispersions, and still unformed aesthetics of "The Art of Reiwa" to come, just outside.

Note 1: *The 1973 Kyoto Biennale* was held at the the present venue, the Kyoto City KYOCERA Museum of Art (then the Kyoto City Museum of Art) in 1973/Showa 48, as a group show featuring the art of six collectives: The Group of Five's Photobook Revolution Editorial Committee +5, Equivalent Cinema, Acquaintance + acquaintance + acquaintance, Nirvana accumulated materials — research station for ultimate expression, The Play, and Japan Kobe Zero. According to the official introduction, the show dealt "not with the art by each art group or individual collaboration, but rather with the art by temporary collectives which repeatedly face and engage new challenges," and serve "to question what manner and function art might play in the future, and in the process concretely illuminating the complexity and difficulty of what <contemporary art> is facing." Hirano Shigemitsu contributed an essay to that catalogue entitled "What is <art by collectives>?" for which he asked each of the six collectives "What does collective mean to you?" So this is not the first time for an exhibition focused on art groups "facing and engaging" (= *Utakata*/rubble?) to be held at the Kyoto City KYOCERA Museum of Art. This is not an exhibition with a focus on genealogy. And yet I feel the need to add this note, to point out that there could be another potential meaning for the fact that The Play, a collective which participated in the mentioned Biennale, installed a suspension bridge as its work titled *BRIDGE* on site, might coincidently "bridge" to "Suddenly, the view spreads out before us." presented in this exhibition.

Note 2: In this exhibition/catalogue, the *1973 Kyoto Biennale* "art of collectives" corresponds to "collective activity by artists." In this text we'd like to make a distinction with the thinking of that time. The 14 "collectives" participating in *Bubbles/Debris* are sets of entities who share common interests for a given moment, rather than any kind of fixed "grouping" attempting to share or exercise power. Debris arriving and dispersing as a function of chaotic forces is our metaphor of association, each member/entity is a constituent element of that set, as seen at that moment, from that perspective. The "collectives" generally refer to associations of two or more members, but do not exclude one or no elements, in the case of a collective in dissolution. In that sense, the *utakata*/debris conceptual model in this exhibition/catalogue forms another kind of set. Furthermore, "Heisei Art" as an organizing principle in this exhibition/catalogue is the sum of activities of these various "sets," and "sets of sets" from throughout the Heisei era (1989–2019).

[References]
Isozaki Arata, *Contingency Manual — What made the issue of the plan for the new national stadium of Japan going sideways*, Seidosha, 2016.
Isozaki Arata, *The Future of Debris*, Seidosha, 2019.
Kamo no Chomei, *Hojoki*, or *An Account of a Ten-Foot-Square Hut*, (emendated and translated by Asami Kazuhiko), Chikuma Gakugei Bunko, 2011.
Sawaragi Noi, "Personal=Historical Depiction 1999–2015," text included in the vol. 20 of *Nihon Bijutsu Zenshu*, Shogakukan, 2016, pp. 177–185.
Sawaragi Noi, "Art of the Heisei Period 1989–2019," *AICA* (= International Association of Art Critics Japanese Section) *Journal* vol. 19, released in November 9 2018, on AICA website. https://www.aicajapan.com/ja/no19sawaragi01/
Sawaragi Noi, "Best 10 of Heisei Art," published in June 16 2019, *Kangaeruhito webmagazine* (first released in *Shincho* magazine vol. 116 May issue, Shinchosha, 2019, pp. 164–166). https://kangaeruhito.jp/article/7711

The National Culture of an Era That Was Likely the Last to Experience a Sense of Unity in Accordance with the Japanese Imperial Era System

Akasaka Mari

The Unity of the People with the Emperor

The Heisei era belonged to a space and time devoted to clearing the backlog of unfinished business from the Showa era.

It's not so much that there wasn't enough time during this era, but rather that it lasted so long that the next Emperor tried to deal with a whole host of issues that had piled up for almost 30 years that couldn't be dealt with for the longest time, starting in his 50s. That was the fate of the Heisei era.

This was a space and time where the Emperor during the Heisei era (the retired Emperor Akihito, as of 2020) was able to "symbolize" this postwar process the way he wanted. When he realized his own limitations, he decided to abdicate for the first time in the history of the modern Imperial system, in the hope that the next generation would take over the role.

Why does this discussion of Heisei-era art begin with the figure of the Emperor? The reason is that the imagination and sense of time involved in the act of looking back on Heisei itself can be found in the imagination that gave birth to the modern Imperial system.

The "one reign, one era name" principle has been one of the fundamental pillars of the modern Imperial system since the Meiji era.

The physical presence of an enthroned Emperor must coincide exactly with the name of an era.

In reality, however, this only goes to show that the system itself is extremely fragile and tenuous.

If one person can make it through a normal lifespan, it means that the next generation will also come of a certain age.

Particularly now that life expectancy is getting longer, it is not unlikely that a person will live a full natural lifespan, with both parent and child becoming old, and the child even possibly passing on before his or her parents. This is a world in which the elderly become caregivers to the elderly. There would be no fresh young prince (Crown Prince) to ascend the throne. Under this scenario, the "unity of the people" with the Emperor will diminish.

As the version of the Japanese Constitution drafted by General Headquarters of the Supreme Commander for the Allied Powers remains to us almost in its original form, it seems to me that we ought to think of the Constitution as an English-language document. The word "unity" has been translated into Japanese as *togo*, but personally I would be more inclined to use the term *ittaikan*. "Unity" has the same etymology as the "unit" in "unit bath" (a Japanese term for a single, prefabricated bathroom module, or unit). To me, it's those people who feel a certain sense of unity in the Emperor, the name of the era, and all the other elements that accompany the transition to a new era, who best embody this "unity of the people."

In this sense, "The Crown Prince's Quest for Love and Marriage Fever" seems to have been devised as a way to bring about the salvation of a prince who did not have much of a presence during his younger days. Coupled with the new medium of television, this was a sort of pageant that was designed as a mechanism through which the Emperor might foster a sense of unity with his people. This was the modern-day climax of the young Emperor's — although he was not actually the Emperor — activities, and fulfilled the role of a kind of pilgrimage. It began with the current retired Emperor (the Emperor during the Heisei era). In Emperor Naruhito's case, it was probably his search for a bride and his actual marriage that is most clearly remembered — something that almost approached a work of performance art.

As far as I recall, the images of the "Crown Prince's marriage" and "Micchi (Princess Michiko) Boom" of the current retired Emperor seemed to me to be part of his enthronement rituals. Rather than being some kind of misconception, it was probably just what the impresarios wanted. Everyone has the illusion in their minds that this is what the transition from "prince to king" or "the enthronement of the king" is all about. The young king will rise and rejuvenate this world. The "enthronement of the king" is something that those who are alive tailor to suit their illusions.

I believe that I saw the actual ceremonies related to the accession to the throne of the Emperor during the Heisei era, but I don't remember them. I have a better memory of Emperor Showa's Great Mourning Ceremony, which had a visceral sort of weight, solemnity, and majesty to it. It was a symbolic death. To me, the enthronement of the "New King" that followed was not so satisfying for what it was, because it did not leave much of an impression.

The first three Emperors of the modern Imperial system during the Meiji, Taisho, and Showa eras — and I think the heart of the matter lies with these first three generations — took up the throne at a young age and came across as these brilliant young kings because of the early demise of their parents, something that was a mere coincidence. As these coincidences persisted, nobody gave even a cursory thought to them. Their significance was realized only at the close of the Showa era, and nobody questioned it again until the Heisei era came to an end — except the Emperor himself.

In the modern Imperial system, it often happens that mere chance prevents essential discussions from taking place. It has been known since the Taisho era that the abolition of the concubine system would reduce the number of candidates to the throne. This option, however, was not discussed, because Emperor Taisho had four boys with his legal wife (Emperor Meiji had fifteen children from his concubines, and while there were five boys, only Emperor Taisho reached adulthood). During the Heisei era, the discussion of a female Emperor was instantly brushed aside as soon as a single boy was born to the Imperial family.

The Meiji Emperor was the one whose accession to the throne initiated the new Meiji era that aspired towards Westernization. His father, Emperor Komei, passed away at the age of 35. Emperor Meiji ascended the throne at the age of 14, just as if he were a turning point in time. This is just like the anime *Neon Genesis Evangelion*, in which a prince who spent his life in Heian-kyo was brought to Edo (now Tokyo) and made to ride a horse and carriage that he had never even been on before, in order to take on a symbolic role of authority in battle.

His grandson, the Emperor Showa, ascended the throne at a young age because his father, the Emperor Taisho, was weak from illness and died at an early age. Incidentally, Emperor Taisho acceded to the throne at the age of 36.

The accession to the throne at such a young age and the long reign of the three Emperors of the modern Imperial system, especially the two Emperors of the Meiji and Showa eras, seems to be a tragic coincidence from today's perspective, with Japan having lost World War II. For many people at the time, these ascensions would have been a symbol of hope.

Aided by medical care, Emperor Showa lived a long life throughout the "postwar" period, and the Emperor during the Heisei era did not ascend the throne until he was 55 years old. If he had waited for his predecessor's death, the current Emperor would not have taken to the throne until well past his 60th birthday. It seems to me, as a human being, that the former Emperor had a personal desire to have the Crown Prince become Emperor when he was about the same age as he was at the time of his own belated accession.

Incubating the Heisei Era

The clearing of the backlog of unfinished Showa business known as Heisei was, to put it quite simply, a matter of cleaning up after Japan's defeat in the war.

Those who study the Emperor are all unanimous in their opinion that this field of Imperial studies only made progress since the dawn of Heisei.

What made it difficult to study the Emperor during the Showa era was the fact that it was simply impossible to dodge the issue of the Emperor Showa's responsibility for the war, seeing as how the physical being of this Emperor was still present. This was an Emperor that embodied a contradiction: he was both an institution and a living being. He was a paradoxical entity, a seemingly powerless being that had been made use of, but who also had real power and exercised it. The Japanese could not, however, impeach him in the same way that Hitler had been. From the point of view of the opposing country, the Japanese military was nothing other than the "Imperial Army," but the United States made a political decision not to impeach their commander-in-chief.

The Emperor remained, like a symbol of the unfinished business itself.

In principle, the Emperor is responsible for the war. It is logically reasonable to think that there is no reason that he is not.

If we go without thinking about it, a blank spot will emerge in the Japanese mind — a spot in their hearts that they will choose not to look at. Nobody wants to confront it. So we embrace the economic prosperity and other pleasures that come our way.

Somehow, the American decision not to hold the Emperor accountable for the war against the backdrop of the US-Soviet Cold War and the occupied rule that made use of this fact worked so well that Japan almost came to see the Americans as some kind of liberation army, ringing in a peculiar postwar era and freedom. Even as they continued to embrace this sheer luck, the Japanese pretended not to realize how fortuitous this state of Cold War affairs was even though they were quite aware, coming fully under the umbrella of the US and enjoying all the benefits, sometimes as if in a crazed trance. Of course, on the flip side of these favors, the Japanese deeply resented the Americans. The bubble and its collapse marked the end of the "second round of the War." It was an economic war and, in the final analysis, a monetary defeat.

Something continues to rumble in Japan. All acts that appear to be objections and protests against the postwar situation and compliance with American policy will be quashed, and a violent society of surveillance and control is trying to consummate itself. A society so safe that it is violent — much like the one described by the novelist Ito Keikaku in his book *Harmony*. This is what it was like during the post-1945 Showa era.

This safe society was what directly incubated the Heisei era, the case carried forward (the current retired Emperor) that Heisei had to deal with.

The good fortune and misery of the father (Emperor Showa) that the son has inherited.

As such, the blueprint depicting the originary landscape that Heisei has held on to in the distance is that of the Army, and rubble.

Look further afield and you'll find the scorched earth and rubble of World War I that Emperor Showa saw with his own eyes when he was the Crown Prince, the rubble of the Great Kanto Earthquake, and stocks and currencies that were turned into debris during the global financial crisis that followed his accession to the throne.

The Japanese have repeatedly been faced with scenes that sometimes appear to be automatically reproduced from the same blueprint, even if we do not know what the original landscape looks like.

Heisei.

The Great Hanshin Earthquake, the Aum Shinrikyo Tokyo subway sarin attack — the Self-Defense Forces, martial law, and the feeling of death — the Great East Japan Earthquake, the Fukushima Daiichi nuclear disaster.

The recurring elements in all of these incidents are the Army, mass casualties, and debris. This debris ranges from the remains of plastic bags filled with sarin to all sorts of rubble created by earthquakes and tsunamis, plastic bags filled with radioactive soil, and nuclear waste that will continue to contaminate the country for thousands or tens of thousands of years.

Globally, it was also a space and time of processing the aftermath of World War II.

The fall of the Berlin Wall (I think it ought to be called "destruction," but custom dictates that the wall "collapsed" by itself) happened in 1989 — that is, the wall was reduced to rubble. The Cold War also ended in 1989, and the end of the Soviet Union came in 1991.

The "bubble" that symbolized the Heisei era seems to have swelled up until the moment that the money turned into "debris."

Since it was possible that money and stocks might turn into debris at any moment, people went crazy and tried to seek pleasure in the moment. They wanted enjoyment and hedonism — even if they didn't quite know what was so fun about it.

The reason we were able to work ourselves up to that level of frenzied (but ultimately modest) luxury, however, is because there was a generation of people who knew the rubble, after all. Some people have this illusion that the bubble was an era of extravagance and glamor, when in fact it was a frenzy of contrasts involving extremes of poverty and misery, with a miasma of doom and death hanging overhead. Another reason that we were able to indulge in this crazy modicum of consumption was because there were still people around us who had known crushing poverty and misery, or because the generation that followed had glimpsed, somewhere along the line, the misery and grief of their parents.

The light always needs an equivalent amount of shadow in order to balance the energy.

Contemporaneous with the bubble was the cult of Aum Shinrikyo. They would annihilate each other, and both would be destroyed.

The Aum facility called Satyam (Sanskrit for "truth") located at the foot of Mount Fuji, just as a Diet member awkwardly pointed out during the Fukushima nuclear disaster, looked exactly like the building at the Fukushima Dai-ichi nuclear power plant — shoddy prefab construction. So drab looking that one has trouble understanding how such a clunky building managed to handle such deadly substances as sarin and nuclear fuel.

Satyam was the first instance of debris before Fukushima. At the foot of Mount Fuji, there is no other remnant of this facility to be seen except a stone monument inscribed with the word "cenotaph."

The Fukushima Dai-ichi nuclear power plant, which cannot be dismantled for safety reasons, has been reduced to a half-destroyed pile of debris.

The Shapes and Symbols of Japan

The Emperor during the Heisei era went around memorializing the war. He himself told the people directly that this was a "symbolic" act that he had performed with "all his might." Some of them were places that his parents had longed to visit, but been unable to.

On closer inspection, however, the Emperor's trails were based "around the Pacific War." They traced a path where Japan's defeat by the United States had already been determined: the Emperor's "view of the nation" that would decide the shape of Japan particular to Heisei. It was the Emperor who determined the shape of the country.

The drama that accompanied the changing of Emperors from Heisei to Reiwa is an unavoidable event as a human being.

From the perspective of power and authority, however, it is damaging.

The modern Imperial system was based on the principle that the corporeal form of the king can never have two bodies at once. This was the basis of "one reign, one era name."

Supreme authority can only be vested in one person per era, with no deviations. If the Emperor were to become the commander in a war, for instance, there would be in principle no deviation from the chain of command.

In contrast, when we speak of the Emperor today, there is some confusion.
We do not know whom to refer to and what to call him, or who is higher in rank. The Emperor who served during the Heisei era cannot be called "Emperor Heisei," as this is a posthumous title, nor can Heisei be referred to in the past.

The period from Heisei to Reiwa was an era in which the Emperor himself created the phenomenon of the bubble.

It is actually the people who will decide whether the bubble will become debris, or whether there is another solution.

This is because if the Emperor were truly the symbol of national unity, then the form of the symbol is a reflection of the people, and never the other way around.

Modern emperors, for better or worse, have influenced the Japanese spirit and temperature of the times. The fact that a retrospective exhibition called "Heisei Exhibition" is being held, or that when we see something retro, we blurt out "how Showa!" demonstrates that this fact runs through the very fiber of our being.

We are still living as if we were experiencing the modern Imperial system.

The most famous artworks of the past few years were *Holding Perspective Part II*, which depicted portraits of the Emperor being burned, and *Statue of Peace*, which depicted a comfort woman, both shown at the "After 'Freedom of Expression?'" exhibition at the Aichi Triennale 2019, which was temporarily shut down due to protests.

This must have been considered "disrespectful," because the incident occurred just as the Emperor was putting the finishing touches to "the shapes and symbols" of Japan.

The shape of the nation and the war that the Emperor had finally brought to an end should not have been questioned. In that sense, it is considered acceptable to depict Hiroshima through art, no matter how tragic or beautiful. Doing so might even be looked upon favorably. We had been living in a country and era where the concept of *lèse-majesté* still existed in the realm of artistic expression.

This event came at a historical juncture, and the shutting down of the exhibition itself came across as the most performance art-like gesture of all.

One can only conclude that the fact that these artworks and this exhibition were the most well-known to the general public is nothing other than black humor.

It also tells us, though, that we need to look back to examine what the Heisei era was all about.

All contradictions are already a bubble. This is what Heisei silently teaches us.

This is something we must decipher, with the help of these visionaries called artists.

The Art of Heisei

The essence of art is to grasp intuitively the spirit of an era, the nature of the culture, and to go beyond it.

It consists in going beyond that, or offering access to some sort of archetypal quality.

Looking at the art of the Heisei era today, I am amazed at how much it is filled with premonitions and prophecies about society and natural phenomena.

War and death, tsunamis and massive amounts of debris. Of course, there is also the deep psychology of the masses, and social satire. New visions that seem to break out of the scorched earth.

A huge tsunami was depicted in advance of a real tsunami of equivalent magnitude (Ikeda Manabu, *Foretoken*, 2008), and a painting of a Zero fighter bombing New York City was made prior to the 9/11 terrorist attacks (Aida Makoto, *A Picture of an Air Raid on New York City (War Picture Returns)*, 1996). Both the imagined Zero fighter bombing of New York City and the attempt to fly a passenger plane into the World Trade Center are reprisals for what was done to them in the past. Everyone wanted to win the war, even though they are not supposed to say so today. We did not want to be defeated. To somehow see being roundly beaten as a desirable outcome is a true act of rationalization. It requires conscious, compensatory gestures to be made in our hearts and minds. This is something that art can do, and does.

When we look at the art of the Heisei era, we understand that it represents the flowering of a "unique national culture."

Heisei was the era in which the generation that grew up with manga and anime brought it into the main culture, so that it is now no longer a subculture, but part of the mainstream. At the time that this was achieved in the Heisei era, it was still necessary for artists and critics to make a conscious effort to communicate that this was no longer a subculture.

This is the feeling I get when I look at the works of perhaps the best-known contemporary Japanese artist of the Heisei era, Takashi Murakami. Manga, anime, and *kawaii* culture became known around the world, and Murakami collaborated with Louis Vuitton, which resulted in his career achieving huge commercial success. This is on the same level as Kyary Pamyu Pamyu's *kawaii* cuteness and groups like AKB48, which represent three-dimensional versions of young anime girl characters.

I also feel the influence of Japanese *nihonga* painting, and a conscious or unconscious return to things that resemble Japanese paintings.

That's exactly what Takashi Murakami said: "Superflat."

"Two-dimensional."

According to Murakami, there is no need to take a two-dimensional painting and force it to look three-dimensional: we should forget about the sense of three-dimensionality and perspective that was inculcated in us, and just let everything be "Superflat." The Japanese have always had this sensibility. Japan needs to rediscover the roots of our culture in the same way that the Westerners of times past were shocked and influenced by the Japanese *ukiyo-e* graphics that were used on wrapping paper and other packaging. The two-dimensional *moe* sensibility with regard to anime characters and this Superflat sensibility must have exerted a reciprocal influence on each other.

This was also a conscious or unconscious departure from the Eurocentrism that had been firmly instilled in us through education and other means ever since the Meiji era.

Here is where the problem of the modern Imperial system comes into play. The figure of the modern Emperor, who emerged from a sort of grassroots center of Japanese culture and magic/performing arts and became transformed into a Western symbol, was somewhat analogous to modern and contemporary "art."

The Meiji era was based on a culture that placed Western architecture and Western painting at the center of its culture and education.

Although this tendency persisted until quite recently and was effectively a form of Western dogmatism (no, we still don't learn about Japanese *nihonga* painting during art classes at school, unless we are actually attending an art college), the Japanese had roots that seemed at first glance to have been forgotten.

The Emperor was also a figure that had been created under the Chinese Emperors. Coupled with "king-makers" (those who prospered by creating and using such rulers) such as the Fujiwara clan, the Emperor successfully evolved a unique national style. As the Imperial family that was unique to Japan had never been faced with the kind of dynastic revolution that accompanied the change of dynasties in China, for instance, the logic that prevailed in the late Edo Period was that the Emperor had become sanctified because he came from noble lineage.

If we try to go back to the roots of the Emperor himself, he bears little resemblance to the figure of the Chinese Emperor. We find ourselves still unable to talk adequately about the Emperor. Unless we become quite acutely conscious of it, it is practically impossible to explain the nature of this figure.

"Nationalizing" the Emperor

It may have been a foregone conclusion that the art of the Heisei era would establish a connection with Heian culture, as the result of a search for uniqueness in a hybrid manner. Artists of the Heisei era could not connect to the Jomon Period, and not even to the Nara Period, unlike predecessors like Okamoto Taro who had struggled to find their Japanese roots. They were already connected to the internet, and had become a sort of hybrid entity. Western style had also become far too common.

During the Heian Period, the "national culture" was based on how the figure of the Emperor became "nationalized": those around him began using him in order to construct a unique aristocratic culture, in contrast to the Chinese style of the Nara or Yayoi Periods. When one looks at the Emperor during this time, he seems to be a kind of Imperial envoy or representative of *miyabi* (an idealized longing to transcend secular power and politics in favor of beauty and aesthetics). This Emperor was also *miyabi* in the sense that he did not, or could not, wage a war of usurpation.

It would not be an exaggeration to say that Japanese history, from the Fujiwara clan up until the modern and contemporary age, is the history of how the Emperor has been made use of. Even warlords and shoguns did not seek to subjugate their Emperors. Rather than force the Emperor into submission and take his place, they decided that the Emperor would be more valuable to them if they kept him in this role that would one day confer more power and authority on them. The *coup d'état* within the warrior class that was the Meiji Restoration did just that, with a fair amount of success.

To my mind, the person who tried to take the place of the Emperor — in his deluded imagination, but also in terms of actual action — was Asahara Shoko, the leader of Aum Shinrikyo. Asahara created a miniature, sloppily constructed Holy Empire. Joyu Fumihiro, a former spokesman for Aum Shinrikyo, claimed that the sarin gas attack on the Tokyo subway was not a terrorist attack, but an attempted *coup d'état* (overthrow of the government) — just like the Meiji Restoration, or the February 26 Incident (attempted *coup d'état* of February 26, 1936) that exalted the Showa Restoration. Speaking of sloppy construction, the Empire of Japan was pretty slapdash, too, in how it made use of the Emperor with plans hastily cobbled together, waging sloppy wars using haphazard strategies without even thinking about how supplies would be replenished. In that sense, the two were exactly alike. We are still living out the aftermath of the Empire of Japan. If it seems as if this aftermath has not been accounted for or reckoned with, then it is from this perspective that none of this has been settled.

The artist Yamaguchi Akira puts it in the following way.

"I tried to nationalize oil painting with a spontaneous, internal sense of what 'Japan' meant to me but failed, so I threw away all of my painting materials and began making sketches with a felt-tip pen on cheap Kraft paper. The turning point came when it occurred to me that it might be interesting to depict the Ponte Vecchio, a three-story stone bridge in Florence, as if it were a Japanese-style wooden structure. When I tried, my pen flew all across the paper with an incredible speed and power."

It was around this time that Yamaguchi became reacquainted with the classics. He had the opportunity to visit shrines and temples in Kyoto and Nara over a period of two weeks, where he saw the paper sliding door and screen paintings of artists like Kano Eitoku and Hasegawa Tohaku in their original locations and light. At the *Yamato-e Painting* exhibition at the Tokyo National Museum, he was exposed to Japanese styles of painting since the Heian Period.

For Yamaguchi, Japanese painting once evoked "nothing but a strange and unnatural feeling," but this was a deeply moving, life-changing encounter. "I think it was because I studied oil painting." This was the shock of someone from the outside looking in, someone who had received an "orthodox" art education that privileged oil painting.

What was once a foreign culture has now come to be considered the "center" of culture, and we are shocked to rediscover the "former center of our own culture" as something "marginal" to that "center." We are living out a history that is riddled with multiple twists and turns as if it were perfectly natural.

The materials used in Japanese painting are the same as those found in Chinese painting. Even as they learn and acquire foreign techniques, however, certain intrinsic traits of Japanese artists ineluctably lead them to produce a "misreading" of them. This, according to Yamaguchi, is what left him perplexed and numb. An unavoidable intrinsic quality that can be seen in what appears to be a "misreading." This is what it means to be "Japanese" — something that can only be described as "I." *

Japanese Culture, Born out of These Contorted "Misreadings"

Manga, too, might be said to be another form of "national culture."

The direct prototypes for manga were probably the Disney characters and cartoons from America that were imported into Japan after WWII. With the addition of a unique panel layout, design sensibility, dialogue, monologues, narration, effects, and onomatopoeic expressions, manga evolved in a way that was unique, that can only be described as such.

There is nowhere else in the world where manga has evolved in a more unique way than Japan. Japanese manga belongs to the world. Even when it is depicted with a painterly density, manga is overwhelmingly an art of line drawings, of contours and outlines, black and white, and easy to process visually, together with words and text that are also made up of black and white lines.

Many young people from abroad with a penchant for Japan these days are exposed to Japanese culture through manga and anime. As such, the government considered launching a campaign that would make "Cool Japan" a national policy. This, however, may be a phenomenon that originated from the "contortions" that accompanied the "misreadings." If we forget about this aspect of the whole affair and declare this a culture unique to Japan, my feeling is that we will end up with something quite dull and boring. The *moe* (strong feeling of affection) generated as you read and digest the manga — or that which can only be called "*moe*" — may have occupied the forefront of the creation of Japanese culture.

Nobody really knows why manga managed to evolve in such a unique manner in Japan. It may have been due to how the Japanese took apart the foreign hieroglyphic Chinese characters of *kanji* to create the kana syllabary, so that we could have both hieroglyphic and phonetic characters in a single text, thereby cultivating a brain that is capable of dealing with both pictures and characters within the same line. Or perhaps it's because Japanese *nihonga* painting and *ukiyo-e* graphics were already cartoonish and caricature-like with their emphasis on contours and outlines.

If you look at foreign comics and French *bandes dessinées*, the pictures are strangely three-dimensional and feel disconnected from the text. Text is text and pictures are pictures, and readers feel as if they have to be handled separately.

The art of the Heisei era was made by the creators who coincided with the growth of manga and anime. At the same time, it was a time when the drawings of manga artists like Araki Hirohiko, Inoue Takehiko, Okazaki Kyoko, Shiriagari Kotobuki and many others began to be widely taken up as art.

AKB48, produced by Akimoto Yasushi, seems to me to be representative of the "phenomenon of domestic imports," where the anime and otaku demographic segues directly into the fan base. Not only do these flesh-and-blood humans sing and dance like anime characters, they also respond to the requests of their individual fans and give us the illusion that they are playing the role of our preferred persona. It's tempting to say that AKB48 are both idols and a new kind of customer service. In any case, one might say that they could only have been born in the Heisei era.

My personal favorite band, Queen Bee, emerged out of a very Japanese, Heisei-era landscape, during which a string of disasters and catastrophes had made it hard to distinguish between which were human-made and which were natural. The band's visuals evoke a sense of catastrophe and rebirth, and their sound is pop. The core members of Queen Bee are a brother and sister from Kobe who experienced the Great Hanshin Earthquake in their childhood. To this day, there is something in their eyes that still reflects the scene of that disaster. The vocalist, Avu-chan, is transgender. Perhaps there will come a day when it will become normal to say that being transgender is normal — and at the same time, heterosexuals will have to be seen as a minority.

The musician Yonezu Kenshi, a creator of the video content site Niconico, has always transcended the framework of a musician. Or rather, he never had it in him. The internet and other things are no longer the same as the mundane ground on which we stand, and from that ground, he screamed out because he was seeking out a scream that was identical to his own. Yonezu's protest has the whiff of a literary, artistic youth that is almost reminiscent of a past age.
One never knows where art is going to go in the future.

Something that is truly new doesn't come from research or marketing. At the same time, however, the only people who are able to sniff out something new are those who have managed to turn the essence of the past into something real and concrete. Japan is a country that swallows everything, consumes it, interprets it in its own way, and then spits it out. The influences of these places and times seem both plausible and unlikely.

And yet, new art always emerges out of some single, unavoidable factor stemming from one individual. Strangely enough, the more unavoidable it is, the more others want it. No matter what scale it is on, it also has a strong sense of collectivity.

Akasaka Mari, writer and performer

* Yamaguchi Akira, "Japanese Art and I," *Nihon Bijutsu Zenshu* vol. 20, Shogakukan, 2016, pp. 201–203.

Nothing Much Has Changed

Tateiwa Shinya

Same as It Ever Was

I want to argue that society hasn't changed, that the same society has continued more or less as it was. It doesn't matter whether we view the Heisei era as being from 1989 to 2019 or 1990 to 2020 – while natural disasters have occurred, and will presumably continue to occur in the future, there has been no change in our society. This is how I choose to look at things, and I think it is in fact the only reasonable view to take.

As everyone knows, the degree of novelty or innovation required in different industries or fields is not the same. In the domain of "academic inquiry" for example, if you don't offer something at least a little bit new, your work and writings won't be considered worthwhile. In most cases, therefore, little things are constantly being added in mainstream academia. Sometimes a major new idea is put forward. At some point "thought" became saying something new, and since then various ideas have been facilely adopted in this domain. Before 1990 and mainly in the 1980s, what is referred to as "post-modernism" and the idea of the "consumer society" were in vogue. I was a graduate student during this period, but I didn't find these approaches very interesting. After that much was made of the idea of "recursiveness," and there was discussion of the "surveillance society" and "risk society." None of these approaches was wrong. But neither did they seem all that novel. What was considered new seemed to fit a certain mold and not be anything special.

The field of "news reporting," too, demands new things, albeit with different criteria from the incremental additions found in academic papers. The same thing day after day won't do. Things that appeal to the emotions get brought in. This is especially the case with events that don't stand out very much. They end up getting turned into a sad or beautiful story. If this is how it has to be, I think there are some things that shouldn't be reported. But when looking at the news, even I tend to look at photographs or videos like this. Nowadays there are things that bore people if they are too clichéd, but I do not mean to criticize this. There's not much to be done about it.

We can understand individual industries or fields in this way, but I don't get the feeling we understand society. I think what is happening in this society can be explained better using a completely classical schema. This society can be viewed as being composed of the interests existing in people that are not limited to this particular society or era, and the rules, values, and concepts that function to strengthen these interests and push them above anything else.

People seek to obtain benefits and avoid things that are burdensome. This is not a particularly good thing, nor is it particularly bad. On this basis, what we have in this society is a system of private property in which those who produce obtain what is produced, and the values and beliefs that justify this system. There is a value concerning human beings that serves to support this system: it is believed that the value of a person's existence is demonstrated by making things. To be a human being is to be productive and independent, and these qualities are seen as determining a person's value. This is the kind of society in which we live.

In relation to the above, there are also changes that occur concerning production. As everyone knows, technology and industry are advancing, productivity is improving, production is expanding, and globalization is progressing. So is finance. This is not something that has just started today, but there is instability caused by an economy not mainly comprised of the exchange of real goods, and circumstances that can balloon when a crisis occurs. This sometimes actually happens. The economic "shock" of the 1990s was an example of this. But in the end several things were done in response, and the economy did not reach the point of collapse.

This is what is most fundamental, but groupings that exist in society under various conditions and their internal or reciprocal interests are added on top of this foundation, and walls are erected and made higher. Broadly speaking, people move in the direction of trying to protect the benefits they have obtained, and those who have already obtained more try to expand their holdings even further.

An increase in productivity gives rise to an excess of workers. This means people don't have to work as much, so it ought to be a very good thing, but in our society it leads to unemployment. On the other hand, while there are people in the so-called "developing world" whose lives are becoming more comfortable, at the same time economic disparity is growing. The reason for this is something anyone can understand. Apart from the profits made by employing people normally, there are many products that can be easily reproduced, and indeed reproduced and delivered without any additional cost. Software is of course one example of this, but it can also be said of sports and events broadcast on television or streamed as video.

What optimistic modernists have not often included in their calculations is the spread of intraregional and interregional ethnic and religious conflicts, and these too can largely be explained as disputes accompanying globalization. To begin with, there are many people who have no choice but to move into a new country or region. The people already living there who had not enjoyed the best circumstances but were at least able to find employment view this influx of people as a threat. Those in the strata who do not view migrants and refugees as a threat because their work is not simple labor and they can use cultural barriers to protect themselves, on the other hand, can afford to be liberal. People who say, "Our country first," even though they ought to be resented for having much more money, thus end up being supported by those who ought to resent them. This would be obvious even without the excessive coverage of the president of the United States (as of October 2020) we see every day when we turn on the television.

This state of affairs should be changed, and changing it is possible. It is possible because to do so does not require something that doesn't exist. All that is necessary is to think about a way of handling what already exists, and indeed in surplus amounts. But there are some people who do not want to do this. Because of them, this society is viewed as being in a "crisis." But it is not necessary to only think of this as an intentional strategy. If mistakes are made in the collecting of money (taxes), the country can in fact run out of funds. People concerned with the government's inflow and outflow of money talk about financial difficulties caused by a decreasing number of children and an aging population. There are some who genuinely believe this is a problem. This kind of "worldview" becomes a broadly accepted premise. There is sufficient production and production capacity, but inability to divide and distribute resources is blamed on scarcity or decreasing quantities. Insufficiency is taken to be a reality. People who truly believe this is a reality are reproduced. There is thus a shirking of what should and could be done, and this inevitably leads to scarcity actually arising in certain places.

Presenting the grounds, processes, and methods for change while remedying this kind of misunderstanding is a task to be undertaken. It is, to begin with, a plain, unprepossessing task. There are all kinds of revolutions. For example, it was amenable conditions in the mountainous regions of South and Central America that made it possible for Che Guevara to carry out his activities, and when a clear line can be drawn between those who are corrupt or immoral and those who are not, what needs to be done becomes starkly apparent. But it is not always like this.

Society is full of unavoidable difficulties, so when it comes to making society better, too, we must inevitably consider tiresome details. Our work must therefore include some elements that are not so fun or exciting. Without getting into why this is the case, showy, ostentatious undertakings, such as movements where someone becomes a symbol of what is being advocated, do not last long, or indeed should not last long. And while on the whole ours is steady, painstaking work, it still has its moments of excitement from time to time, so it is not always boring. We can also enjoy ourselves.

In terms of how they appear, the concrete systems of the kind of society we are imagining and aiming at do not differ greatly from what exists today. I think this is a good thing. If society is made of tiresome details, then so be it. We contrast one version of boring with another. But the structure is different.

There is thus a need to depict the society of today and of the future, and I have come to think of this as my job. Covering individual events or incidents of the kind I will discuss here, however, has in each case taken up quite a bit of my time. Going forward I think I should do more to communicate an overall diagnosis of society in a shorter, more concise form.

Ways of Bringing Life to the Surface and Ways of Hiding It

With this aim in mind, I don't have much desire to say something about the individual incidents and situations that arise from time to time. I want to think and write about more fundamental things regarding the nature of private property, how money is used, and how labor and income are to be distributed. Nevertheless, whether in books or through updates on a website, there are cases in which I have documented and discussed particular situations. The website is www.arsvi.com. "Arsvi" is an abbreviation of "*ars vivendi*," Latin for "techniques for living." You should be able to find it by searching for "arsvi" on the Internet.

I've ended up writing mostly about things related to the body, life, and death. It is not that I have a particular interest in human beings or our bodies, nor do I have much to say about life and death apart from the fact sooner or later we all die. But I think that being incapable of being more romantic has its good points.

Most things are not put into words or images. The things people can endure are mostly left as they are. Things that are too big and seem beyond our control are also left untouched. When something big happens, there are things that are put off because of the scale of what is happening. The response to particular incidents like earthquakes and epidemics can be poor; for example, it is a problem for us when our refrigerators stop working because of a blackout, but people whose mechanical ventilators stop working have a much bigger problem. Generators can be used instead, but questions such as how they are to be distributed, where they are to be kept, and whether it is dangerous for them to be inside a patient's room, while not difficult to understand, are often overlooked when people are very busy, and I try to convey this fact that such things are often overlooked. I do the work of documenting these "miscellaneous" issues.

On the other hand, there are some things that are quite widely reported. Death, particularly when someone kills or is killed, or cases in which someone chooses to die and has someone kill them, causes quite a stir. It is presented as a sensational event, and phrases like "choosing between life and death" or "death by choice" are used. There are stories that juxtapose people saddened by this death with those who go on living with a positive attitude, that sort of thing.

I don't want people to do or say things that are excessive or aren't true. When there are requests from the media I therefore accept them, and put considerable effort into writing short statements. It's a real pain, but it cannot be helped.

In reality, the ordinary state of ordinary society is manifested in death. People die under the stark circumstances of not having what they need to go on living, such as money or the assistance of other people, or in anticipation of such circumstances. If your body is weakened and you cannot move, then you cannot work and have no earnings, and additional things you need, like the assistance of other people, are also lacking. Because of the very straightforward state of society I have just described, this is what happens.

In addition, many people die because of an antiquated yet stubborn belief about how human beings ought to be. In order to live we need goods that are produced, and to this end there is production, but accepting a perverted idea of value in which the value of being alive is determined by what you are able to do or produce results in people dying. People in this country perhaps do not believe very strongly in these sorts of values. Since it is better than a mistaken belief, I think this lack of belief is not a bad thing. In moments of crisis, however, some people start to take this view seriously. They end up thinking that they themselves must decide on their own life or its end.

Another issue is the fact that talk of crisis or scarcity pushes this view forward. Believing that overall there already isn't enough, or there won't be enough in the future, some people who are indeed already suffering shortages when it comes to their own needs then measure their own value and decide to make their exit. This is usually allowed to occur without intervention, but in particularly visible cases it becomes an incident. When this happens, it is glamorized. For example, after the Heisei Period various things have occurred surrounding the current infectious disease pandemic, and based on the idea that there will be a shortage of medical devices there has been an effort to decide the order of people who will be allowed to use them. It has been suggested, for instance, that we should respect the will of those who are currently using mechanical ventilators who have offered to give them up. I think it is right to express respect for these people's intentions. But this is very different from adopting and implementing their wishes as a decision of society.

However, people who normally say clever, novel things (at least in their own opinion), the kind of people who like to expound upon technology and the future, unquestioningly accept the idea of crisis and scarcity, having at some point somehow come to believe in it, and say things that are truly inane. I think this is very bad, so I keep saying things that are prosaic but not mistaken.

In practice, space is often greatly restricted, and time frozen in place. For example, there are people who are admitted to hospital out of their family's understandable belief that their future will be difficult, the gathering of well-intentioned people who shed tears over this, and the expectation of medical treatment. Without the people around them ever knowing what sort of hospital it is, these people end up spending a very long time, thirty or forty years in some cases, silently living out their lives in an institution.

There are cases in which this uneventful daily life is temporarily shifted to a different place as a result of a natural disaster. When the Fukushima nuclear power plant accident occurred following the 2011 Great East Japan Earthquake, people were forced to evacuate the area and several institutions were closed, including a mental hospital. Only then was it revealed that someone had been living there for a very long time, perhaps forty years. This person then left the hospital, and this year a court case began over his having been made to live in such a space for such a long time. It has received only a little coverage in the news media.

Society is constructed and maintained by these sorts of conditions, and is both revealed and hidden by them. Their nature must therefore be documented. People who work with words have no choice but to take up this tedious task.

Being Passive

How this relates to "art" — I have already put quotation marks around "academic inquiry," "thought," and "news reporting" — I myself do not know. As someone who knows nothing about it, I don't see how I can comment on art. I moved away from movies, music, and other forms of art forty years ago, and I don't know anything about what has happened since then.

The world presumably demands new things, and responses to new realities. This is not only the case in Japan. If so, then in the same way we will presumably jump at what stands out, or what is seen as new; this does in fact seem to occur, and it is not a bad thing. Works of art can be said to have various connections (or lack of connection) to their era, and stir up passions that lead society in various different directions. That said, I put quite a lot of faith in art.

To begin with, most of us, in a completely straightforward sense, are mistaken in our reasoning, taking erroneous paths when thinking about society or the future, for example, and art has elements that are formed in a place that is not directly connected to this kind of thought.

Perhaps owing to these elements, art has the capacity to say, "That's boring." In my case, I thought mostly about music, but in fact I considered most parts of society boring, or not worthy of being considered interesting.

This society is constructed to make us care about things that are a waste of time, but if it is wrong to say, "Anything goes, anything is fine," then this is a good thing. I have received this from art. "Modern thought" can be interpreted as trying to say this kind of thing, but it uses too many words to do so, and not enough words and reasoning are devoted to describing the society that exists here and now. Having come to this conclusion, I made this my job. To those who gave me this sense, I can say only that they should try not get confused by strange reasoning or theories.

Art also shows that it is fine for people to be passive. It communicates that separate and apart from how I am, what I am, and what I make, the world is good, and art is itself a part of the world. We should receive the world. There are many things in it, and every day, to the degree that I wish I could slow it down, the number of things people are adding to it is increasing.

It may be said, however, that art is a creative act. Let me add a few words on this point.

To begin with, things being produced is to be affirmed, and we should praise someone being very good at something without in any sense rejecting or negating this achievement. And there are a great number of people who want to express something. Among them there are presumably those who create for the sake of self-realization or proof of their own existence, and this is not a bad thing. However, there are more things created than only those made up of these components. Just like the world in general is full of excess, many extra works are made and accumulate. Some of them are then copied and played over and over again.

This being the case, one fact to be noted is that there is already enough, so most of us can simply receive these works without doing anything ourselves. This is a good thing. I say this because in order to help those who are seen as non-productive it is sometimes asserted that everyone is creative. Of course, it can in fact be said that every human being produces or puts out something. But I'm the sort of person who does not want to make a point of saying this. Quite apart from my own preferences, however, I also take this approach because requiring that such people be creative, and that the people around them make an effort to search for, draw out, and praise this creativity, is tiring for everyone involved and does no one any good. And having a world in which there is a surplus of people trying to produce and most people need only receive is not a bad thing.

Many years ago, I was asked what I would do if I could no longer move my body at all by someone with a family member in such a condition (they had ALS). This was in 2002, two years before I wrote *ALS: Immobile Bodies and Machines that Breathe* (Igaku Shoin, 2004), a book about people with this disease. I replied that I would listen to music all day as I couldn't think of anything else to do. At the time this would have been quite difficult. Vinyl records had been replaced by CDs, but even stereos designed for continuous play could only hold around five discs at a time. Today's computers and smartphones can store an endless amount of music. I myself have a device that can provide forty-eight hours of music if you set the playlist on random. I think listening to music all day is much more feasible than in the past.

When it comes to architecture or the skills related to the perception of space, too, there are presumably elements related to this way of thinking. A long time ago a man named Yoshimoto Takaaki said that architects should build proper houses for ordinary people rather than focus on innovative designs for large structures, and at the time I thought he was being narrow-minded. I was not averse to things that are unusually large. But I think his assertion is correct in some ways. Art demonstrates that it is enough for the world to simply be received. To expand on this a little, what would the kind of space and time that would allow us to do a good job of being passive look like? In such circumstances, what becomes of the body or what wraps around the body? I also sometimes think about these sorts of things.

Tateiwa Shinya, sociologist

1989: The Terrible Dawn of Heisei

— The beginning of an era that started peacefully before disappearing like a wave of bubbly froth, and crumbling like a pile of debris

Katayama Morihide

Signs and Omens

The first year of the Heisei era was a strange year. Emperor Showa, who had been teetering on the border between life and death, got through Showa 63 (1988) and lived to see the start of Showa 64 (1989), but that was when his long life finally came to an end. He passed on January 7. The Crown Prince ascended the throne immediately, and it was announced that the new era was to be called Heisei.

The reign of an Emperor always lasts up until his death. The transition to a new era occurs simultaneously with his passing, at which point the name of the era also changes. This is the "one reign, one era name" principle that was established by the Meiji government. If the Emperor is still alive and suddenly announces his abdication, for example, this might easily be interpreted as evidence that he is dissatisfied with his rulers. In fact, during the last years of the Tokugawa Shogunate, Emperor Komei often threatened the nobles and shoguns by expressing his intention to abdicate. It was quite likely that the Meiji government was wary of Emperor Meiji using the same tactic, and therefore decided to block the Emperor from abdicating of his own free will. Moreover, if the government continued to change the name of the era freely depending on whether it was auspicious or not to do so, as it had done up until the Edo Period, this would quite easily obstruct the practice of politics while having official recourse to the name of the era as a modern nation. Keeping tabs on the calendars would become complicated, and there would also be a higher possibility that the changing of the era would acquire too much political significance. For example, if one wanted to produce a shift in the tone of the times by changing the name of the era because too many unfortunate incidents were occurring, but the streak of bad luck continued even then, people would start to question the legitimacy of the state. This was the primary reason that the "one reign, one era name" system was created. In short, this was a mechanism that sought to unify the reign of the Emperor and the period during which the name of that era would apply, by attributing both to the Emperor's lifespan. At a time when notions of loyalty and patriotism were demanded as cornerstones of the sense of national morality, it became quite desirable for the nation to be able to control the people's sense of time through the lifespan of the Emperor and the name of the era associated with it. Thus a unique system of marking the passage of eras through the life of the Emperor as a single, human individual was given to a modern nation. This act of division was certainly accidental, as it depended on the lifespan of the Emperor in question. Historical importance was not linked to anything other than the death of the Emperor. In fact, neither 1912, when Emperor Meiji died, nor 1926, when Emperor Taisho passed on, were necessarily years that saw significant events unfold in terms of Japanese or world history.

However, this was not the case for Showa 64, or Heisei 1 (1989), which was practically filled to the brim with major historical events. While they may have been minor occurrences in and of themselves, there were a number of things that could have been seen as signs or omens of future events. Most of them had nothing to do with the demise of Emperor Showa, if you think about them in terms of common sense, but there were many that could be seen as starting points, or nodes of a sort, that would drag on over the more than 30 years that the Heisei era spanned, or even the Reiwa era that lay beyond. Scattered here are the seeds that would lead to all the bubble and debris. This is why the first year of the Heisei era was so mysterious and baffling. Was it a singular, unprecedented year? Or rather, was it that Emperor Showa passed on in the middle of an important turning point in history?

The First Year of the Heisei Era as a Turning Point

Let us take a very rough look back at that year, starting with February. Soviet troops withdrew from Afghanistan. This was not a sudden, comprehensive withdrawal that occurred in February, as there was a back-and-forth process involved. There is little doubt, however, that this incident foretold the string of turbulent upheavals that would erupt across the Eastern Bloc in 1989. In 1985, Mikhail Gorbachev became leader of the Communist Party of the Soviet Union and initiated large-scale structural reforms known as *perestroika*. The year right after that saw the Chernobyl nuclear accident. This massive nuclear disaster was seen as a symbol of institutional fatigue concerning various aspects of the Soviet Union, and Gorbachev, who was under the illusion that Chernobyl could be used as leverage for *perestroika*, declared that now was the time to break free from the secrecy that had ruled the Soviet Union for so many years, and actively disclose information related to the nuclear accident. This stance was promoted under the political slogan of *glasnost*, or openness of information. While Gorbachev was determined to use the nuclear accident as a tool for extending the reform process, *glasnost* only served to embolden dissidents and set in motion a hundred different schools of political thought. (It goes without saying that the overlap between the Chernobyl disaster and the history of the decline of the Soviet Union contains lessons for the Fukushima nuclear accident and the history of Japan's own decline during the Heisei era.) The withdrawal of Soviet troops from Afghanistan in 1989 was a visual manifestation of the decline of the Soviet state. The Soviet Union, which had been competing with the United States for global military hegemony, had begun to fade rapidly.

The Soviet Union's competitor, the United States, also succeeded in its efforts against Afghanistan. In an attempt to prevent the Soviet Union from invading Afghanistan and eventually advancing southward towards the Indian Ocean, the U.S. deployed proxy warfare, one of its particular specialties, providing arms and funds to the Taliban and other Islamic fundamentalist groups in Afghanistan, nurturing their organizations, and having them fight against the Soviet Union. They did not seem to have calculated, however, that the Taliban would later become a formidable force for the U.S. to deal with, something that eventually led to the terrorist attacks of September 11, 2001. The era centered on the "war on terror" cannot be read without linking it to the history of the Soviet Union's invasion of Afghanistan — and the major milestone in this war was to be found at the beginning of the Heisei era.

Next: April 1. The Japan Consumption Tax Act went into effect, having been passed by the Diet towards the end of Showa 63 (1988). The rate started at 3%, heralding a shift from direct to indirect taxation. In a time of rapid economic growth and continuous upward mobility, public finances would remain liquid as long as profitable businesses were taxed as a priority. As growth began to slow and a kind of polarity emerged, however, obvious sources of taxation began to dwindle, and so the tax system shifted to skimming a thin margin from a broad swathe at all levels, and from all domains. This shift that was perfectly suited to the times occurred exactly in the first year of the Heisei era.

June 3. The cabinet of Takeshita Noboru resigned. In January, Chief Cabinet Secretary Obuchi Keizo announced the name of the new era, and an administration that had promised to wield a certain amount of political power in the new era departed. The reason for this was the so-called Recruit scandal, in which the problem of numerous politicians that had been given private shares of Recruit Cosmos stock had persisted since the end of the Showa era. Among the main figures of the Takeshita cabinet, finance minister Miyazawa Kiichi, for example, was forced to resign at once. Even then, the issue could not be resolved, and the situation became exacerbated to the point where the Prime Minister himself was forced to step down. These problems revolving around politics and money, including the Showa Denko corruption scandal, the so-called "shipbuilding scandal" involving bribery concerning a petition designed to supplement profits in the industry, and the Lockheed bribery scandal, recurred persistently in postwar politics. The history of the ruling party, in short, has been a history of scandal. It can be said that the long-term rule of the Liberal Democratic Party (LDP) has brought prosperity and stability to postwar Japan. When the same party is in power for a long time, the ruling party does not change, and many members of the ruling party become veterans as the number of times they are elected increases, however, politicians cultivate long and close ties with particular bureaucrats, acquire an interest in their field of specialty, and become linked to certain industries through financial connections, and corruption inevitably runs rampant.

In fact, this arrangement was considered a necessary evil by the defenders of Japanese capitalism for a long time after the war. If they attacked the corruption of the conservative parties and tried to oust them from power, it would have been the reform and centrist parties that would emerge as alternatives. This might well have dragged Japan into the Eastern Bloc. So the LDP it would be, even if it was corrupt. All of this changed in the first year of the Heisei era, however. The Eastern Bloc crumbled spectacularly. This collapse, which had finally been building to a climax after the time of the Recruit scandal, meant that all at once, there was no longer any value to be found in Japan's reform parties, and the era of the Socialist Party and Communist Party had come to a close. In this sense, if the Cold War between East and West ended and American-style capitalism and democracy won a global victory, there would then be a debate over the desirability of two conservative political parties in Japan, just like in the United States. If the two major parties are both conservative, there would be no need to worry about the economic system being disrupted by a change of government. And if the ruling party is replaced periodically, there would no longer be time for the water to become muddied, and political corruption would be less likely to occur. The political turmoil triggered by the Recruit scandal, combined with the collapse of the Eastern Bloc, led to the idea of creating a new conservative political party as an alternative to the LDP, championed by Ozawa Ichiro among others. A great deal of the political energy of Heisei Japan had been mobilized in the service of ideals pertaining to the future of the country, which involved the establishment of two major conservative parties. The mass media and various academics encouraged this. This initiative, however, was utterly unproductive. A technocratic brand of politics without ideology had created a political arena in which there was no way to evaluate anything other than through the quality of one's technical knowhow. In spite of a certain degree of drama, we have finally returned to an "era without regime change" where established conservative parties, with their wealth of experience and technical expertise, win more popular support than newly founded greenhorn conservative parties, and the corruption of the longstanding conservative party returns. Since there is no substantive ideological difference to be seen between these opposing forces, their sense of history or purpose becomes tenuous, leading to a shrunken and atrophied political situation with a dearth of options that persists to this day. It was the "political reforms" of the Heisei era, as they were called, that showed that if you destroy everything from the structure of the rivalry between political parties to the framework of elections, no new shoots will grow — only a heap of bubbly froth and debris.

The Illusion of the "End of History"

The day after the deposition of the Takeshita cabinet, which triggered long-term confusion in everything from Japanese politics to ideology in a major and substantive manner, 1989 brought with it another major event: the Tiananmen Square incident of June 4. In China, Deng Xiaoping's administration took a reformist and open-door policy, introducing elements of a free market economy into a country with a socialist planned economy under the slogan "let some people get rich first." The common consensus in the history of modern thought holds that it is impossible to have a society in which only the economy is made free, while politics is not. The Chinese Communist Party, however, is trying to continue its one-party dictatorship, which defies reason. It is impossible to stifle the power of citizens and students who seek freedom. Even if these movements are suppressed, it will not be the end of the world, as we saw in the Soviet Union and Eastern Europe in 1989. China's politics will likely move towards recognizing a multi-party system and allowing democratic elections. Many Western pundits have predicted this. The retreat of socialist parties in Japan was probably influenced not only by the decline and eventual collapse of the Soviet Union, but also the Tiananmen Square incident.

However, more than thirty years have passed since Tiananmen, and things have turned out quite differently from what was anticipated at the time. The history of China since Tiananmen seems to prove that the pursuit of freedom in economic life and the tolerance of some degree of inconvenience in political life can be compatible, at least for the time being. China's political elite has learned deeply from the failure of the Soviet Union in order to avoid making the same mistakes, and it has not wavered even more than 30 years after Tiananmen. On the contrary, it is hurtling steadily down the path towards becoming a great power.

Let us look back for a moment and recall what I would term the "end of history thesis," which was largely triggered by the manifold events of 1989 and formulated in Francis Fukuyama's *The End of History and the Last Man*, published in 1992. This was perhaps the only ideology that existed in an age without ideologies. The collapse of socialism meant the end of the Cold War structure and its ideological confrontations, which in turn meant the end of history as an ideological struggle. The end of ideology meant the beginning of utopia, a process that would be completed by the globalization of American-style liberalism and democracy. As such, Japan should imitate the U.S. and become a country with two major conservative parties, for instance. This line of thinking, which emerged from various world events and experiences within a few years of 1989, is what is known as the "end of history thesis." However, this thesis was merely a temporary illusion that was borne aloft by the fever of Tiananmen Square, the fall of the Berlin Wall, and the collapse of the Soviet Union: it neither contained the truth nor constituted any sort of correct answer or response. China has its own truth, Russia after the collapse of the Soviet Union has its own truth, and Afghanistan, Iran, and Iraq each have their own truths. The narrative that the world would be unified by American-style liberalism and democracy has hardly risen above the level of a delusion. Rather, what has become clear over the past 30 years or so is that the world has lost its sense of cohesion by which countries concentrate around two or three poles as the result of ideological struggles: it has been chopped up into smaller sects that revolve around religion or ethnicity, and is headed down the path of pluralization and division. In other words, the number of noises that are unable to resonate with each other is increasing — a process that might be described as "turning to rubble."

In spite of this, however, Japan was mistaken in continuing to think for a long time that the "end of history thesis" was valid: it went repeatedly astray, treated the bubbly froth as something of real substance, and deluded itself into believing that a new reality of hope that would surpass the level reached by the country's postwar reconstruction would soon emerge in the wake of the destruction and rubble. Before one realizes it, the froth has quickly dissipated, and the rubble is still rubble. The pluralization that enforces divisions around the world is relentless, both domestically and between nations, and even places like Hong Kong, which has long enjoyed a taste of the free society of the West, is being co-opted by another, Chinese-style system of values and control. From this, there will be a surge of fugitives and political refugees. Whatever the case, we must remind ourselves that this is the beginning of a new path for China that began on June 4, 1989, something that is quite different from the "end of history."

The Swaying Japanese Archipelago

On July 13, a month after the Tiananmen Square incident, there was a shift in the Japanese archipelago. An underwater eruption occurred off the coast of the city of Ito, in Shizuoka Prefecture, and a large column of water rose right in front of its port. Although the eruption then died down without causing any serious damage, a succession of catastrophes followed — the eruption of Mount Unzen the following year in 1990 (Heisei 2), the Great Hanshin-Awaji Earthquake in 1995 (Heisei 7), the Great East Japan Earthquake in 2011 (Heisei 23), and a string of numerous other natural disasters, including wind and flood-related incidents. The Ito underwater eruption might be said to have been a kind of symptom of the 31 years of the Heisei era. One never knows when a major disaster will strike, and what form it will take. The Japanese archipelago, in particular, seems to have entered a period of transition. We should not be surprised if an earthquake or tsunami of unprecedented magnitude were to strike. The widespread theory that a major volcanic eruption might also occur can be linked to a sense of nihilism, or a certain principle of living only for the moment, setting the tone for the mood of this country from Heisei up until Reiwa. In short, there is little point in thinking too seriously about the future.

The following month, on August 26, there was a celebratory event in Japan: the announcement of then Imperial Prince Fumihito (Crown Prince Akishino)'s engagement to Kawashima Kiko, which led to the birth of the Akishino family. From the Heisei through to the Reiwa era, there was the immediate and practical problem of the number of members in the Imperial Family, but also the fact that the Showa era was fading into the distance, as well as the generational shift in the Imperial Family and Japanese citizenry alike. This gave rise to a situation in which reflections on the past war and prayers for peace alone were not enough to cover the values required of the Imperial Family: it seemed as if they had entered a period of turbulence and instability, as if to correspond with how the phase of that particular era was characterized by bubbles and debris. It should be noted that the Akishino family will play an important role in determining how to turn such an era around, and that its birth can be traced back to the first year of the Heisei era.

Next was November 4. Members of the Aum Shinrikyo cult murdered the lawyer Sakamoto Tsutsumi and his family. This was the same cult that went on to perpetrate large-scale terror attacks in urban centers using poisonous gas right after the Great Hanshin Earthquake. These acts, which rivaled the scale and atrocity of the 2001 terrorist acts using passenger planes in the U.S., happened six years earlier, and were significant in how they heralded the arrival of a new era of terrorism. They were carried out in Japan, not by an international force, but a domestic religious cult whose goal was to overthrow the state of Japan itself. Up until then, it had been widely accepted that large-scale terrorism of this kind, at least in the modern world, was caused by communism, nationalism, or any other ideology that could be widely circulated — ideologies that may or may not result in radical actions, but that are capable of wielding some kind of social influence as a political, social, or economic way of thinking. While it is doubtful that Aum had the ability to appeal to anyone other than its followers, such an organization had the financial and technological resources to carry out such large-scale terrorist attacks. Aum proved to the world that it was possible to manufacture and deploy weapons of mass murder, such as potent poisonous gas, without being a state or a large corporation. It would certainly not be an exaggeration to say that this was an epochal milestone in the history of the world in a negative sense: we had entered an era in which a small group of fanatics was capable of bringing on a catastrophe.

The murder of the lawyer Sakamoto and his family was a full-scale and direct act of subversion perpetrated against the outside world by this cult. Moreover, unlike the Tiananmen Square incident or the Recruit scandal, this particular case was perhaps not entirely unconnected to the demise of Emperor Showa. Asahara Shoko of Aum cultivated a worldview typical of cult leaders, drawing a link between the deterioration of his own health to his premonition of the downfall of Japan and the destruction of the world. In the fall of 1988 (Showa 63), Asahara apparently came out and declared to his aides that a crisis would soon threaten both himself and the world. The so-called Aum Shinrikyo deaths, which are said to have triggered the radicalization of the cult, occurred on September 22 that same year. Three days before that, on September 19, Emperor Showa vomited blood at the Fukiage Palace and became critically ill, and it began to dawn quite obviously on the world that the end of the Showa era might be near. We can assume that there was some deeper meaning to this. Asahara's heightened sense of crisis overlapped with Emperor Showa's critical condition. The transition from the Showa to Heisei eras coincided with the radicalization of Aum's behavioral patterns. This is what we can observe with the passage of time. It is possible that the historical sensibility that presided within Aum saw this temporal turning point represented by the demise of Emperor Showa and the accession to the throne of the new Emperor in the Heisei era as a suitable time for the cult to rebuild the world. The guru is the Emperor of the cult, and if the guru's health problems are shared by the real Emperor, there would be a heightened imagination of a crisis at least within the cult itself, possibly leading its actions to become more radical. This is what the history of Aum Shinrikyo from 1988 to 1995 clearly shows.

The True Meaning of the First Year of the Heisei Era

From the night of November 9 through November 10, five days after the murder of the Sakamoto family, the Berlin Wall separating East and West Berlin was opened to traffic. At some point around November 10 or 11, the wall actually started to be torn down and reduced to rubble. It was a time when socialism seemed to be on the verge of being extinguished, and the "end of history thesis" was ringing truer and truer. The term "rubble" was also being used in a positive sense. As if timed to coincide with this, the Japanese Trade Union Confederation (abbreviated as *Rengo* in Japanese) was formed on November 21. Formed through an alliance of the General Council of Trade Unions of Japan (*Sohyo*), a socialist-oriented organization based on labor-management conflict, and the Japanese Confederation of Labor (*Domei*), a democratic-socialist organization based on labor-management cooperation, Rengo was a huge labor union that had shifted from a path of class confrontation to one of reconciliation, in keeping with an era where socialism had gone into retreat. Takeshita Noboru, who was Prime Minister at the time that the era changed, popularized the idea that it was Yasuoka Masahiro who had come up with the name of Heisei, which can be read to mean "may peace prevail." While this is only one theory, which does not have sufficient credibility, as a right-wing activist Yasuoka had argued before the war that labor-management cooperation was the ultimate labor movement that was appropriate for a country like Japan that values great harmony, and he continued to make this argument consistently after the war. In this sense, then, no other event was as befitting of the Heisei era as the birth of Rengo. This organization, which symbolized the post-ideological era, made a bold attempt to establish a conservative two-party system in this country by fostering a new conservative and middle-of-the-road united coalition that could stand up to the LDP, but this ended up as nothing more than a pipe dream. Moreover, the era of Rengo, which seemed to have forgotten the ideological struggle to protect the rights of the working class against the capitalists, was unable to satisfactorily fulfill its function of curbing the shift in the proportion of workers who had gone from formal to informal employment. In my view, because many labor leaders were hastily preoccupied with not missing the bus when it came to the "end of history thesis," the Heisei era saw the rights of working people gradually undermined, and the foundation of the income of the majority of people shattered and weakened.

This was followed by a series of events linked to the fall of the Berlin Wall. The Velvet Revolution took place in Czechoslovakia on November 17, while U.S. President George W. Bush and General Secretary of the Soviet Union Mikhail Gorbachev met on the Mediterranean island of Malta to declare the end of the Cold War on December 3, and it seemed that the peaceful utopia had finally arrived. On December 22, Ceaușescu's regime fell in Romania.

December 29 was the Tokyo Stock Exchange's last trading session for the year. The closing price of the Nikkei hit an all-time high of 38,915.87 yen. This was the peak of the bubble economy, and the first trading session the following year marked the beginning of the decline. The bubble era of stock prices ended with the first year of the Heisei era.

There are probably other things that happened in the first year of the Heisei era that warrant our attention. For now, however, the events described above tell a story, put forward a hypothesis, and point to various signs that help us project much of the future from the Heisei through Reiwa eras, from the 1990s up until the 2020s. While there are various points of conflict to be found here, the following general trends seem evident.

(1) The ideological confrontation between capitalism and socialism would be nullified, mainly because of the retreat of the Soviet Union.

(2) History would lose its sense of directionality, especially in relation to (1).

(3) One's consciousness of time tends to lose its context and become ephemeral, especially in relation to (2).

(4) One's sense of value, especially in relation to (2), is thrown into disorder, and things can easily turn into bubbles and debris.

(5) The will to seek out the authentic, and a real future, must necessarily disappear from culture and art, especially in relation to (2), (3), and (4). The inevitable result is that works of art will become kitsch.

(6) Since the nullification of ideology tended to be perceived as the arrival of a utopia, (1) through (5) should all have been viewed negatively. The illusion that time, space, value, and everything else could all be managed as if they were collectibles to be stowed away in a drawer, brought about by the trifecta of dehistoricization, neutralization, and technologization, will prevail for a time, even if it is nothing more than a transient phenomenon.

(7) Various signs and omens of catastrophe can be discerned, including those not necessarily related to (1) through (6), because they involve a kind of providential nature that transcends the realm of human wisdom.

O unborn children, why do you stir so? Are you terrified to learn the true meaning of the first year of the Heisei era?

Katayama Morihide, political scientist and music critic

A Short History of Heisei (1989–2019) Bubbles/Debris

·Natural and man-made disasters, including war, appear in bold white type.

1989 / Showa 64, Heisei 1

Jan **Emperor Showa (Hirohito) dies. Akihito, his son, succeeds to Chrysanthemum Throne. Era name changes to "Heisei" on January 8.**

Apr Japanese government introduces consumption tax.

May Hiroshima City Museum of Contemporary Art opens.

Jun Tiananmen Square Incident

Jul **Earthquakes off Izu Peninsula, Shizuoka**

Sep Sony announces its acquisition of Columbia Pictures Entertainment.

Oct Mitsubishi Estate buys majority stake in Rockefeller Center in New York.

Nov Yokohama Museum of Art opens.

Fall of Berlin Wall

Dec Summit talks between United States and Soviet Union, leading to end of Cold War

Nikkei 225 closed at all-time high of 38,915 yen.

1990 / Heisei 2

Jan Japan's stock prices plummet, following burst of bubble economy.

Mar Art Tower Mito opens.

Aug Iraq invades Kuwait.

Oct Reunification of Germany

Nov Nintendo releases Super Famicom (known as "Super Nintendo Entertainment System" in United States and Europe).

1991 / Heisei 3

Jan **Gulf War breaks out. Japan donates 13 billion dollars in support.**

Apr Japan's Self-Defense Force dispatches minesweepers to Persian Gulf (first SDF deployment overseas).

Jun **Eruption with pyroclastic flows at Mount Unzen's Fugendake, Nagasaki.**

Dec Dissolution of Soviet Union and establishment of Russian Federation

1992 / Heisei 4

Jun Act on Cooperation for United Nations Peacekeeping Operations (PKOs) passes, paving way for Self-Defense Forces to be dispatched overseas.

Oct Emperor and Empress visit China for the first time in history.

1993 / Heisei 5

Jan **Hokkaido Earthquake off Kushiro**

Jun Crown Prince Naruhito marries Owada Masako.

Jul G7 Summit Meeting in Tokyo

Hokkaido Nansei-oki Earthquake near Okushiri Island

Aug **Catastrophic flooding in Kagoshima caused by heavy rain**

Sep **Emergency import of rice from Thailand due to poor crop caused by exceptionally cold summer**

Nov European Union (EU) established.

1994 / Heisei 6

Oct **Kuril Islands Earthquake in Hokkaido**

Dec Sony Computer Entertainment releases PlayStation.

Offshore Sanriku (*Sanriku Haruka-oki*) Earthquake off Aomori

1995 / Heisei 7

Jan **Great Hanshin-Awaji Earthquake hits Kobe.**

Mar **Tokyo subway sarin gas attack by cult group Aum Shinrikyo**

Museum of Contemporary Art Tokyo (MOT) opens.

Nov Microsoft releases Japanese edition of Windows 95.

Toyota Municipal Museum of Art opens.

Dec **Sodium leak accident at Monju, Japanese sodium-cooled fast reactor in Fukui**

1996/Heisei 8

Feb Nintendo releases Pokémon Red and Pokémon Green for Game Boy.

Jul Roslin Institute in UK successfully clones female sheep, Dolly, in historic first.

1997/Heisei 9

Mar Nuclear accident at JCO Co., Ltd. plant, Tokaimura, Ibaraki

Jul Asian financial crisis

Nov Failure of major financial corporations, such as Sanyo Securities, Hokkaido Takushoku Bank, and Yamaichi Securities

Dec Kyoto Protocol adopted with the aim of preventing global warming.

1998/Heisei 10

Feb Winter Olympics in Nagano

Mar Act on Promotion of Specified Non-profit Activities ("NPO Law") passes.

Jun Financial Services Agency established.

Sep Heavy rain in Kochi

Oct Long-Term Credit Bank of Japan fails, is put under temporary state control, and subsequently sold.

Dec Nippon Credit Bank fails, is put under temporary state control, and subsequently sold.

1999/Heisei 11

Jan Euro adopted as new single currency by 11 member states of European Union.

Jun Basic Act for Gender Equal Society takes effect.

Heavy rain in western Japan in Hiroshima and Fukuoka

Sep First criticality accident in Japan at Tokaimura plant in Ibaraki

Nov Exhibition, *Ground Zero Japan*, curated and supervised by Sawaragi Noi at Art Tower Mito, Ibaraki.

2000/Heisei 12

Mar Eruption of Mount Usu in Hokkaido

Jul G8 Summit Meeting in Kyushu-Okinawa

Eruption of Mount Oyama on Miyakejima Island

Sep Heavy rain in Tokai region

Oct Tottori Earthquake in western Tottori

2001/Heisei 13

Mar Geiyo Earthquake near Hiroshima

Sep 9/11 Attacks in United States

First Yokohama Triennale

2002/Heisei 14

Jun 2002 FIFA World Cup Football (soccer) co-hosted with South Korea

Sep Japan-DPRK Pyongyang Declaration. Abduction of Japanese citizens by DPRK officially acknowledged.

Oct Contemporary Art Museum, Kumamoto opens.

Nov First case of SARS (severe acute respiratory syndrome) found in Guangdong province in southern China. Disease spreads globally.

2003/Heisei 15

Mar Iraq War begins.

May Act on the Protection of Personal Information passes.

Sep Hokkaido Earthquake off Tokachi

Oct Mori Art Museum opens.

Nov Yamaguchi Center for Arts and Media (YCAM) opens.

2004/Heisei 16

Sep Medium-scale eruption of Mount Asama in Nagano (first eruption in 21 years)

Oct Typhoon Tokage causes damage in multiple regions of Japan.

Chuetsu Earthquake in Niigata

21st Century Museum of Contemporary Art, Kanazawa opens.

Nov National Museum of Art, Osaka relocates and opens in central Osaka.

Dec Indian Ocean Earthquake and Tsunami (Sumatra, Indonesia)

2005/Heisei 17

Mar Fukuoka (*Fukuoka-ken Seiho-oki*) Earthquake

Apr Derailment accident on JR West's Fukuchiyama Line

Jul Terrorist bombings in London

Dec Number of newborns falls below deaths for the first time in Japan, causing net decline in population.

2006/Heisei 18

Jan Heavy snow of 2006

Jul Heavy rain in Nagano, Shimane, Kagoshima, and other prefectures

Aomori Museum of Art opens.

2007/Heisei 19

Jan National Art Center, Tokyo opens.

Mar Noto Earthquake in Ishikawa

Jul Chuetsu Offshore Earthquake in Niigata

2008/Heisei 20

Jun Iwate-Miyagi Nairiku Earthquake in Tohoku region

Jul G8 Summit Meeting in Toyako, Hokkaido

Sep Global financial crisis. Leads to bankruptcy of Lehman Brothers.

2009/Heisei 21

Jan Bitcoin invented.

May Swine flu pandemic

Sep Inauguration of Hatoyama Yukio Cabinet following victory of Democratic Party of Japan (*Minshu-to*) in lower house election.

2010/Heisei 22

Jan Japan Airlines files for bankruptcy.

Feb Massive earthquake in Chile

Sep Chinese fishing trawler collides with Japanese Coast Guard patrol boats in waters near Senkaku Islands.

Oct Heavy rain in Amami Oshima Island, Kagoshima

Nov WikiLeaks publishes diplomatic cables of United States.

2011/Heisei 23

Jan GDP of China exceeds that of Japan, making it the world's second-largest economy.

Volcano eruption of Mount Kirishima (Shinmoedake) in Kagoshima

Mar Great East Japan Earthquake

Fukushima Daiichi Nuclear Power Plant reactor cooling systems fail. Hydrogen explosions occur in Units 1, 3, and 4.

Jun Anti-nuclear power rallies across Japan

Sep Typhoon Talas causes large-scale flood damage in Kii Peninsula, Wakayama.

2012/Heisei 24

May Tokyo Skytree, the world's tallest tower, opens.

Tornado in northern Kanto region

Dec Abe Shinzo returns as prime minister, following Liberal Democratic Party's major victory in lower house election.

⬤⬤⬤/Heisei 25

Jun First case of MERS (Middle East respiratory syndrome) in Saudi Arabia causes subsequent global outbreak.

Sep Tokyo selected as host city for 2020 Olympics and Paralympics.

Oct Typhoon Wipha hits Izu-Oshima, east of Izu Peninsula, causing landslides and debris flows.

Dec Act on the Protection of Specially Designated Secrets ("State Secrecy Law") passes.

2014/Heisei 26

Apr Consumption tax raised to 8%.

Aug Heavy rain in Hiroshima causes massive mudslides.

Sep Volcanic eruption of Mount Ontake

20.15/Heisei 27

Mar Same-sex partnership recognized in Shibuya Ward, Tokyo.

Sep Japanese government forces passage of security legislation (known as "war bills").

Heavy rain in Kanto and Tohoku regions

Nov Terror attacks in Paris

2016/Heisei 28

Jan Japanese government introduces Individual Number system (widely known as "My Number" system) for administering social security and taxation.

Apr Kumamoto Earthquakes

May Barack Obama first sitting U.S. President to make visit to Hiroshima.

Jun United Kingdom votes to leave European Union in referendum.

Jul Nintendo releases Pokémon GO.

Mass murder of disabled people at care home in Sagamihara, Kanagawa

Aug Emperor expresses intention to abdicate in coming years.

2017/Heisei 29

Jan Donald Trump assumes presidency of United States.

Jul Heavy rain in northern Kyushu

2018/Heisei 30

Jun First summit meeting between United States and North Korea

Northern Osaka Earthquake

Jul Execution of 13 sarin terror attack perpetrators, including Matsumoto Chizuo.

Heavy rain in western Japan, including Kansai, Chugoku, Shikoku and Kyushu regions

Sep Typhoon Jebi hits Kansai region.

Hokkaido Eastern Iburi Earthquake

Oct Diplomatic relations between Tokyo and Seoul worsen over wartime labor issue.

Nov Osaka chosen as host city for 2025 World Expo.

Dec Annual number of inbound visitors to Japan, increasing rapidly since 2012, surpasses 30 million.

2019/Heisei 31, Reiwa 1

Feb U.S. President Trump declares national emergency to secure funds to build wall on border with Mexico.

Apr Massive fire in Notre-Dame de Paris cathedral, France

May Era name changes to "Reiwa" (beautiful harmony), and Crown Prince Naruhito succeeds to throne.

平成美術ブックリスト

・書誌情報は刊行年順に初版のみ記載した。

平成をより深く知るために

平成論

與那覇潤『知性は死なない——平成の鬱をこえて』
文藝春秋、2018 年

佐藤優、片山杜秀『平成史』小学館、2018 年

片山杜秀『平成精神史——天皇・災害・ナショナ
リズム』幻冬舎新書、2018 年

原武史『平成の終焉——退位と天皇・皇后』
岩波新書、2019 年

福嶋亮大『らせん状想像力——平成デモクラシー文
学論』新潮社、2020 年

平成の思想／批評／美術

大塚英志『物語消費論——「ビックリマン」の神
話学』（ノマド叢書）、新曜社、1989 年

上野千鶴子『家父長制と資本制——マルクス主義
フェミニズムの地平』岩波書店、1990 年

伊藤俊治『機械美術論——もうひとつの 20 世紀美
術史』岩波書店、1991 年

福田和也『日本の家郷』新潮社、1993 年

鶴見済『完全自殺マニュアル』太田出版、1993 年

宮台真司『制服少女たちの選択』講談社、1994 年

小熊英二『単一民族神話の起源——〈日本人〉の
自画像の系譜』新曜社、1995 年

宮台真司『終わりなき日常を生きろ——オウム完
全克服マニュアル』筑摩書房、1995 年

酒井直樹『死産される日本語・日本人——「日本」
の歴史 - 地政的配置』新曜社、1996 年

岡田斗司夫『オタク学入門』太田出版、1996 年

大澤真幸『虚構の時代の果て——オウムと世界最
終戦争』ちくま新書、1996 年

見田宗介『現代社会の理論——情報化・消費化社
会の現在と未来』岩波新書、1996 年

加藤典洋『敗戦後論』講談社、1997 年

中沢新一『ポケットの中の野生』（今ここに生きる
子ども）、岩波書店、1997 年

港千尋『映像論——「光の世紀」から「記憶の世紀」
へ』NHK ブックス、1998 年

東浩紀『存在論的、郵便的——ジャック・デリダ
について』新潮社、1998 年

熊倉敬聡、千野香織編『女？日本？美？——新た
なジェンダー批評に向けて』
慶應義塾大学出版会、1999 年

渡部直己『不敬文学論序説』（批評空間叢書 17）、
太田出版、1999 年

高橋哲哉『戦後責任論』講談社、1999 年

斎藤環『戦闘美少女の精神分析』太田出版、2000 年

吉見俊哉『カルチュラル・スタディーズ』（思考の
フロンティア）、岩波書店、2000 年

大塚英志『物語の体操——みるみる小説が書ける
6 つのレッスン』朝日新聞社、2000 年

五十嵐太郎『終わりの建築／始まりの建築——
ポスト・ラディカリズムの建築と言説』（10+1

series）、INAX 出版、2001 年

酒井隆史『自由論——現在性の系譜学』
青土社、2001 年

岡崎乾二郎『ルネサンス 経験の条件』
筑摩書房、2001 年

柄谷行人『トランスクリティーク——カントとマ
ルクス』批評空間、2001 年

東浩紀『動物化するポストモダン——オタクから
見た日本社会』講談社現代新書、2001 年

五十嵐太郎『新宗教と巨大建築』
講談社現代新書、2001 年

中沢新一『緑の資本論』集英社、2002 年

香山リカ『ぷちナショナリズム症候群——若者た
ちのニッポン主義』中公新書ラクレ、2002 年

小熊英二『〈民主〉と〈愛国〉——戦後日本のナショ
ナリズムと公共性』新曜社、2002 年

養老孟司『バカの壁』新潮新書、2003 年

坂口恭平、佐藤直子英訳『0 円ハウス』
リトル・モア、2004 年

中沢新一『アースダイバー』講談社、2005 年

保坂和志『小説の自由』新潮社、2005 年

三浦展『下流社会——新たな階層集団の出現』
光文社新書、2005 年

杉田俊介『フリーターにとって「自由」とは何か』
人文書院、2005 年

藤原正彦『国家の品格』新潮新書、2005 年

本田由紀、内藤朝雄、後藤和智『「ニート」って言
うな！』光文社新書、2006 年

佐藤優『自壊する帝国』新潮社、2006 年

雨宮処凛『生きさせろ！——難民化する若者たち』
太田出版、2007 年

湯浅誠『反貧困——「すべり台社会」からの脱出』
岩波新書、2008 年

宇野常寛『ゼロ年代の想像力』早川書房、2008 年

濱野智史『アーキテクチャの生態系——情報環境
はいかに設計されてきたか』NTT 出版、2008 年

水村美苗『日本語が亡びるとき——英語の世紀の
中で』筑摩書房、2008 年

佐々木敦『ニッポンの思想』講談社現代新書、2009 年

毛利嘉孝『ストリートの思想——転換期としての
1990 年代』NHK ブックス、2009 年

内田樹『日本辺境論』新潮新書、2009 年

柄谷行人『世界史の構造』岩波書店、2010 年

佐々木中『切りとれ、あの祈る手を——〈本〉と〈革
命〉をめぐる五つの夜話』河出書房新社、2010 年

開沼博『「フクシマ」論——原子力ムラはなぜ生ま
れたのか』青土社、2011 年

上野千鶴子『ケアの社会学——当事者主権の福祉
社会へ』太田出版、2011 年

古市憲寿『絶望の国の幸福な若者たち』
講談社、2011 年

與那覇潤『中国化する日本——日中「文明の衝突」

一千年史』文藝春秋、2011 年

坂口恭平『独立国家のつくりかた』
講談社現代新書、2012 年

片山杜秀『未完のファシズム——「持たざる国」
日本の運命』（新潮選書）、新潮社、2012 年

白井聡『永続敗戦論——戦後日本の核心』（at プラ
ス叢書）、太田出版、2013 年

大澤聡『批評メディア論——戦前期日本の論壇と
文壇』岩波書店、2015 年

内田樹編『日本の反知性主義』（犀の教室）、
晶文社、2015 年

特集「絵描きと戦争」『美術手帖』67 巻 1026 号、
美術出版社、2015 年

高橋源一郎、SEALDs『民主主義ってなんだ？』
河出書房新社、2015 年

大塚英志『感情化する社会』太田出版、2016 年

立岩真也、杉田俊介『相模原障害者殺傷事件——
優生思想とヘイトクライム』青土社、2016 年

特集「アウトサイダー・アート——描かずには生
きられない！ 境界線上の表現者たち」『美術手帖』
69 巻 1049 号、美術出版社、2017 年

東浩紀編『観光客の哲学』（ゲンロン 0）、
ゲンロン、2017 年

國分功一郎『中動態の世界——意志と責任の考古
学』（シリーズ ケアをひらく）、医学書院、2017 年

千葉雅也『勉強の哲学——来たるべきバカのために』
文藝春秋、2017 年

山田昌弘『底辺への競争——格差放置社会ニッポ
ンの末路』朝日新書、2017 年

笠原美智子『ジェンダー写真論 1991–2017』
里山社、2018 年

特集「ART COLLECTIVE——アート・コレクティ
ブが時代を拓く」『美術手帖』70 巻 1066 号、
美術出版社、2018 年

立岩真也『病者障害者の戦後——生政治史点描』
青土社、2018 年

平成の文学／詩

吉本ばなな『TUGUMI つぐみ』
中央公論社、1989 年

岡崎京子『pink』マガジンハウス、1989 年

松浦理英子『親指 P の修業時代』（上下）、
河出書房新社、1993 年

奥泉光『石の来歴』文藝春秋、1994 年

岡崎京子『リバーズ・エッジ』宝島社、1994 年

笙野頼子『タイムスリップ・コンビナート』
文藝春秋、1994 年

村上春樹『ねじまき鳥クロニクル』（全 3 巻）、
新潮社、1994–1995 年

保坂和志『この人の閾（いき）』新潮社、1995 年

水村美苗『私小説——From left to right』
新潮社、1995 年

柳美里『フルハウス』文藝春秋、1996 年

渡辺淳一『失楽園』（上下）、講談社、1997 年

村上春樹『アンダーグラウンド』講談社、1997年
阿部和重『インディヴィジュアル・プロジェクション』新潮社、1997年
車谷長吉『赤目四十八瀧心中未遂』文藝春秋、1998年
川上弘美『神様』中央公論社、1989年
村上春樹『約束された場所で──underground 2』文藝春秋、1998年
村上春樹『神の子どもたちはみな踊る』新潮社、2000年
村上龍『希望の国のエクソダス』文藝春秋、2000年
高橋源一郎『日本文学盛衰史』講談社、2001年
村上春樹『海辺のカフカ』（上下）、新潮社、2002年
舞城王太郎『九十九十九』講談社ノベルス、2003年
阿部和重『シンセミア』（上下）、朝日新聞社、2003年
村上龍、はまのゆか絵『13歳のハローワーク』幻冬舎、2003年
恩田陸『夜のピクニック』新潮社、2004年
町田康『告白』中央公論社、2005年
イシグロ、カズオ『わたしを離さないで』土屋政雄訳、早川書房、2006年
川上弘美『真鶴』文藝春秋、2006年
平野啓一郎『決壊』（上下）、新潮社、2008年
川上未映子『ヘヴン』講談社、2009年
村上春樹『1Q84』（全3巻）、新潮社、2009–2010年
朝吹真理子『きことわ』新潮社、2011年
西村賢太『苦役列車』新潮社、2011年
多和田葉子『雪の練習生』新潮社、2011年
高橋源一郎『恋する原発』講談社、2011年
水村美苗『母の遺産──新聞小説』中央公論社、2012年
赤坂真理『東京プリズン』河出書房新社、2012年
小川洋子『ことり』朝日新聞出版、2012年
いとうせいこう『想像ラジオ』河出書房新社、2013年
姜尚中『心』集英社、2013年
加藤智大『東拘永夜抄』批評社、2014年
柳美里『JR上野駅公園口』河出書房新社、2014年
最果タヒ『死んでしまう系のぼくらに』リトルモア、2014年
又吉直樹『火花』文藝春秋、2015年
元少年A『絶歌──神戸連続児童殺傷事件』太田出版、2015年
村田沙耶香『コンビニ人間』文藝春秋、2016年
吉増剛造『怪物君』みすず書房、2016年
赤坂真理『箱の中の天皇』河出書房新社、2019年

参 加 作 家 を よ り 深 く 知 る た め に

Complesso Plastico

Complesso Plastico「Project for BT by CP」『美術手帖』40巻601号、602号、41巻604号、美術出版社、1988–1989年

篠原資明「光と生のトランスアート」『メタリズム』展覧会カタログ、ワコールアートセンター、1989年

水戸芸術館現代美術ギャラリー編『脱走する写真──11の新しい表現』展覧会カタログ、水戸芸術館現代美術ギャラリー、1990年

インタビュー「花形文化通信」42巻、1992年11月号、繁昌花形本舗、https://hanabun.press/2019/10/01/complessoplastico/（最終閲覧日：2021年1月5日）

IDEAL COPY

水戸芸術館現代美術ギャラリー編『脱走する写真──11の新しい表現』展覧会カタログ、水戸芸術館現代美術ギャラリー、1990年

セゾン美術館、アイディアル・コピー編『21世紀・的・空間 現代美術と民俗的空間の出会い──日本の眼と空間III』セゾン美術館、1994年

東京都写真美術館、IDEAL COPY編『IDEAL COPY個展 Channel: Documents』（映像工夫館作品展 時と空間の記憶3）、東京都写真美術館、1997年

フランス国立高等美術学校編『どないやねん！Donai yanen! 現代日本の創造力』フランス国立高等美術学校、1998年

熊倉敬聡『脱芸術／脱資本主義論──来るべき〈幸福学〉のために』慶應義塾大学出版会、2000年

テクノクラート

南條史生ほか『人間の条件展──私たちは、どこへ向かうのか。』展覧会カタログ、ワコールアートセンター、1994年

南條史生ほか編『Trans culture: la Biennale di Venezia 1995 トランスカルチャー』展覧会カタログ、国際交流基金、1995年

飴屋法水『キミは動物と暮らせるか？』（にこにこブックス）、筑摩書房、1997年

椹木野衣監修『日本ゼロ年』展覧会カタログ、水戸芸術館現代美術センター、2000年

飴屋法水『夜想2-：＋ vol.1 飴屋法水 ボディ感覚』ステュディオ・パラボリカ、2001年

飴屋法水『ブルーシート』白水社、2014年

DIVINA COMMEDIA

椹木野衣「無重力の美学」『STUDIO VOICE』流行通信社、1991年

「ディヴィナ・コメディア──死のプラクシス」『美術手帖』44巻649号、美術出版社、1992年

『MITO ANNUAL '93 ANOTHER WORLD 2 ドキュメント編 アナザーワールド・異世界への旅あるいはヴァーチャル・リアリティからの逃走』水戸芸術館現代美術ギャラリー、1992年

砥綿正之＋松本泰章、白井雅人「トランスグレッション 砥綿正之＋松本泰章」、NTTインターコミュニケーション・センター（ICC）企画「ICCコンセプト・ブック──想像力の未来を予告するミュージアム」NTT出版、1997年

岩城覚久「イメージ・プロセッサとしての身体──「ディヴィナ・コメディア」（1991）」『映像学』88号、日本映像学会、2012年

作家関連ウェブサイト、http://towata-matsumoto.net（最終閲覧日：2021年1月5日）

GEISAI

村上隆『召喚するかドアを開けるか回復するか全滅するか』展覧会カタログ、東京都現代美術館、2001年

村上隆企画『THE ★ GEISAI──アートを発見する場所』カイカイキキ、2005年

村上隆「格闘技バトルトーク21世紀アート"ガチンコ"宣言 村上隆vsホンマタカシ」「原宿フラット全記録 浅田彰×岡崎乾二郎×椹木野衣×村上隆」「東京都現代美術館個展『召喚するかドアを開けるか回復するか全滅するか』」「東京芸術館夏祭り」「芸術道場GP」「対談：辻惟雄、浅田彰」「カイカイキキ設立」ほか、『村上隆完全読本──美術手帖全記事1992–2012』美術出版社、2012年

「GEISAI#20」GEISAI実行委員会、2013年、http://www.geisai.net/g20/（最終閲覧日：2021年1月5日）

Chim↑Pom

Chim↑Pom、阿部謙一編『なぜ広島の空をピカッとさせてはいけないのか』無人島プロダクション、2009年

Chim↑Pom『芸術実行犯』朝日出版社、2012年

Chim↑Pom『エリイはいつも気持ち悪い──エリイ写真集』朝日出版社、2014年

Chim↑Pom、椹木野衣編『Don't Follow the Wind』河出書房新社、2015年

Chim↑Pom『都市は人なり Sukurappu ando Birudo プロジェクト全記録』LIXIL出版、2017年

Chim↑Pom ほか編著『We Don't Know God: Chim↑Pom 2005–2019』ユナイテッドヴァガボンズ、2019年

卯城竜太、松田修『公の時代』朝日出版社、2019年

Chim↑Pom公式ウェブサイト、chimpom.jp（最終

閲覧日：2021 年 1 月 5 日)

contact Gonzo

『contact Gonzo magazine 001: The Weather Report Issue』2009 年

『contact Gonzo magazine 002: Sate Kambing Issue』2015 年

「contact Gonzo（コンタクト・ゴンゾ）／咲くやこの花インタビュー vol. 8」2017 年 3 月 4 日、https://ameblo.jp/sakuya-art/entry-12253286411.html（最終閲覧日：2021 年 1 月 5 日）

三ケ尻敬悟、吉崎和彦編『wow, see you in the next life. / 過去と未来、不確かな情報についての考察』山口情報芸術センター（YCAM）、2019 年

Vimeo、YouTube にて各パフォーマンス映像を随時公開中

東北画は可能か？

赤坂憲雄『東北学へ 1──もうひとつの東北から』作品社、1996 年

『三瀬夏之介──日本の絵』展覧会カタログ、青幻社、2013 年

三瀬夏之介、鴻崎正武監修『東北画は可能か？：2009-』東北芸術工科大学、2015 年

真室佳武「東北画は可能か？─地方之国構想博物館─」──未来への歩みに向けて『第 4 回都美セレクション グループ展 記録集』東京都美術館、2016 年

カオス*ラウンジ

椹木野衣「美術と時評 6：カオス*ラウンジ──萌えいづる自由・平等とその行方」『ART iT』2010 年 4 月 28 日、https://www.art-it.asia/u/admin_columns/4a3tyg6zdlvuecumtrbq（最終閲覧日：2021 年 1 月 5 日）

黒瀬陽平『情報社会の情念──クリエイティブの条件を問う』NHK ブックス、2013 年

「対談：卯城竜太（Chim↑Pom）×黒瀬陽平（カオス*ラウンジ）福島からもうひとつのアートワールドをつくる」『美術手帖』67 巻 1031 号、美術出版社、2015 年

黒瀬陽平「カオス*ラウンジ新芸術祭 2017 市街劇「百五〇年の孤独」」2017 年 12 月 19 日、http://chaosxlounge.com/wp/archives/2157（最終閲覧日：2021 年 1 月 5 日）

カオス*ラウンジ 公式ウェブサイト、http://chaosxlounge.com（最終閲覧日：2021 年 1 月 5 日）

DOMMUNE

DOMMUNE『DOMMUNE OFFICIAL GUIDE BOOK -1ST』幻冬舎、2011 年

宇川直宏『@DOMMUNE──FINAL MEDIA が伝授するライブストリーミングの超魔術 !!!!!!!!』河出書房新社、2011 年

磯部涼『プロジェクト FUKUSHIMA!──2011/3.11-8.15 いま文化に何ができるか』K&B パブリッシャーズ、2011 年

菊地成孔、大谷能生、DOMMUNE『JAZZDOMMUNE』メディア総合研究所、2012 年

「ARTIST INTERVIEW 宇川直宏──ファイナルメディア DOMMUNE とは何か？」、特集「Chim↑Pom プレゼンツ REAL TIMES」『美術手帖』64 巻 964 号、美術出版社、2012 年

パープルーム

梅津庸一「パープルームの条件」『芸術批評誌 REAR』36 号、リア制作室、2016 年

梅津庸一「Interview パープルーム──美術の制度をいかに侵食し続けるか？」、特集「ART COLLECTIVE──アート・コレクティブが時代を拓く」『美術手帖』70 巻 1066 号、美術出版社、2018 年

「interview 梅津庸一／パープルーム──日常を観察し、生活とアートのあわいをつくる（聞き手：中尾拓哉）」『美術手帖』71 巻 1075 号、美術出版社、2019 年

梅津庸一「展評──尖端から末端をめぐって 第 10 回 コロナ禍と「常設展」」『ゲンロン β』51 号、ゲンロン、2020 年

梅津庸一監修、特集「絵画の見かた──自分にとって良い絵とは何か？」『美術手帖』72 巻 1085 号、美術出版社、2020 年

突然、目の前がひらけて

「武蔵美×朝鮮大 突然、目の前がひらけて」制作委員会編『武蔵美×朝鮮大 突然、目の前がひらけて』展覧会カタログ、『武蔵美×朝鮮大 突然、目の前がひらけて』制作委員会、2015 年

韓東賢「武蔵美×朝鮮大「突然、目の前がひらけて」展に思うこと──ただぼんやりしていても共にはいられない時代に」Yahoo! JAPAN ニュース、2015 年 11 月 16 日、https://news.yahoo.co.jp/byline/hantonghyon/20151116-00051523（最終閲覧日：2021 年 1 月 5 日）

椹木野衣「この橋に両端（はし）はあるか」『美術手帖』68 巻 1032 号、美術出版社、2016 年

「突然、目の前がひらけて」制作委員会編『境界を跨ぐと、』展覧会カタログ、「突然、目の前がひらけて」制作委員会、2017 年

クシノテラス

櫛野展正編著『極限芸術──死刑囚は描く』クシノテラス、2016 年

櫛野展正『アウトサイドで生きている』タバブックス、2017 年

櫛野展正『アウトサイド・ジャパン──日本のアウトサイダー・アート』イースト・プレス、2018 年

國府理「水中エンジン」再制作プロジェクト

遠藤水城編『裏声で歌へ』展覧会カタログ、裏声で歌へ実行委員会、2017 年

高嶋慈、はがみちこ、白石晃一、遠藤水城「國府理「水中エンジン」再制作プロジェクトについて」『AMeeT』（Web マガジン）、一般財団法人ニッシャ印刷文化振興財団、2017 年 7-8 月（全 4 回）、第 1 回：https://www.ameet.jp/digital-archives/1170/、第 2 回：https://www.ameet.jp/digital-archives/1205/4/、第 3 回：https://www.ameet.jp/digital-archives/1219/、第 4 回：https://www.ameet.jp/digital-archives/1237/2/（最終閲覧日：2021 年 1 月 5 日）

高嶋慈「國府理「水中エンジン」再制作プロジェクト──「キュラトリアルな実践としての再制作」が発する問い」『artscape』（Web マガジン）、2017 年 10 月 15 日号、https://artscape.jp/focus/10139881_1635.html（最終閲覧日：2021 年 1 月 5 日）

小林公「國府理《水中エンジン》試論 その 1」「國府理《水中エンジン》試論 その 2」『ART RAMBLE』vol. 58、59、兵庫県立美術館、2018 年

小林公「國府理《水中エンジン》試論 その 3」『兵庫県立美術館 研究紀要 No. 14』2020 年

國府理「水中エンジン」再制作プロジェクト実行委員会「國府理 水中エンジン redux ──國府理「水中エンジン」再制作プロジェクト」、https://engineinthewater.tumblr.com（最終閲覧日：2021 年 1 月 5 日）

人工知能美学芸術研究会（AI 美芸研）

人工知能美学芸術研究会『S 氏がもし AI 作曲家に代作させていたとしたら』展覧会カタログ、The Container、2019 年

椹木野衣「美術と時評 86：歴史の遠近をすり抜けて──「S 氏がもし AI 作曲家に代作させていたとしたら」展からの考察」『ART iT』2019 年 9 月 5 日、https://www.art-it.asia/top/contributertop/203132（最終閲覧日：2021 年 1 月 5 日）

人工知能美学芸術研究会編著『人工知能美学芸術展 記録集』展覧会カタログ、人工知能美学芸術研究会、2019 年

人工知能美学芸術研究会編著『S/N：S 氏がもし AI 作曲家に代作させていたとしたら』人工知能美学芸術研究会、2021 年（特別協力：ゲーテ・インスティトゥート大阪・京都）

人工知能美学芸術研究会 公式ウェブサイト、https://www.aibigeiken.com（最終閲覧日：2021 年 1 月 5 日）

作品リスト
List of works

凡例

・作品リストは本展を構成する3つの時代区分ごとに、参加作家の活動開始年や結成年の順に記載した。ただし、その始まりにおいて時期（開始・結成年）を同じくするものについては、作家名の五十音順に従った。

・同一グループに属する個人作家の各作品の掲載順については、基本的に作家名の五十音順に従った。

・作品リストは出展作品と参考資料等から構成されている。

・作品の情報は、アーティストグループ、個人作家名、作品タイトル（資料名）、制作年、素材（形状、技法）、サイズ（cm）（映像の場合は尺［分をmin.、秒をsec.と表記]）、所蔵、クレジット（写真が含まれる場合の撮影者、物品・技術協力者等）の順に記載した。ただし、当該アーティストグループの作品群のなかで出展作品すべてが同一グループによる制作である場合は、個々の作品における作家名を省略した。

・和文タイトルが欧文表記されており欧文タイトルと同一の場合は、欧文タイトルのみを記載した。

・作品は作家や所蔵者の都合により、不出品または変更となる場合がある。

Notes

· The List of Works follows the exhibition's rough division of the Heisei Period into three periods. Within each of these periods, works are presented in order of the start of the artist group's career (or date of formation). Where a number of artist groups started at about the same time (year), they are ordered according to the Japanese phonetic order for their group names.

· Works by individual artists belonging to the same group are basically ordered according to the Japanese phonetic order for the artist names.

· The List of Works consists of exhibited works and reference materials.

· Artwork data is presented in the following order: the name of the artist group, name of the individual artists, title of the work (title of reference material), date of execution, materials (shape, technique), size (in centimeters) (for video, length in minutes and seconds), collection, and credits (photographer credits when photographs are included, lender/donor credits, collaborator credits). When all the artist group's works exhibited were made by the same group, artist names are omitted for individual works.

· If a work has a Roman script title that is used unchanged as the Japanese title, the Japanese title is omitted.

· Works listed may be withdrawn from the exhibition or substituted in accordance with the artist or owner's wishes.

Complesso Plastico

C+P 2020
2020（再制作｜Re-creation）
インスタレーション（1988–1990 年の初
期作《Love and Gold》、《Live Together》、
《Everybody knows NEW LIFE》ほかの部分
の再制作、映像、記録写真による再構成）
Installation (Re-creation of parts, videos,
archival photos of the early works from
1988–1990, including *Love and Gold*, *Live
Together*, *Everybody knows NEW LIFE* and
other works)
十字架に組んだブラウン管モニター4 台、ブラウ
ン管モニター4 台、金色のレンガ、バーミキュライト、
植木鉢に十字架、インクジェットプリント、映像、
音楽
Cross made with 4 CRT monitors, 4 CRT
monitors, golden-colored bricks, vermiculite,
flowerpot with a cross, inkjet prints, videos,
music
サイズ可変
Dimensions variable
作家蔵｜Collection of the artists
撮影：小熊栄（《Love and Gold》）
Photo: Oguma Sakae (*Love and Gold*)
協力：名古屋芸術大学　先端メディア表現コース
Support: New Media Design Course, Nagoya
University of the Arts

IDEAL COPY

Channel: Peace Cards
1990/2020（再制作｜Re-creation）
スライド、プロジェクター、トランプ
Slide projectors, playing cards
作家蔵｜Collection of the artists

機材協力：豊浦英明、中山博喜、八木良太、京都芸
術大学、成安造形大学、名古屋芸術大学
テクニカル・サポート：浅野豪
Equipment supported by Toyoura Hideaki,
Nakayama Hiroki, Yagi Lyota, Kyoto
University of the Arts, Seian University of Art
and Design, Nagoya University of the Arts
Technical support by Asano Takeshi

Channel: Exchange
1993–
インスタレーション
Installation
作家蔵｜Collection of the artists
テクニカル・サポート：真下武久（2021 年）
Technical support by Mashimo Takehisa (2021)

テクノクラート
TECHNOCRAT

Dutch Lives
2020
1990–2003 年に発表された以下のプロジェク
ト／パフォーマンス／作品を発掘し、その諸
要素、記録資料（写真、映像）等により構成
構成：飴屋法水、西島亜紀
Exhibition consisting of parts, archival
materials (photographs and videos) and
objects rediscovered from the following
projects/performances/artworks presented
from 1990 to 2003
Direction: Ameya Norimizu, Nishijima Aki

- テクノクラート《WAR BAR》（1990）より：
  24 都市の地図の版下、展示に使用した機械・
  展示風景の記録映像
- 飴屋法水《ジャパニーズソング》（1991）より：
  電話回線で収集した音声（部分）
- テクノクラート《Dutch Life vol. 1 コンタ
  ミネイテッド》（1992）より：
  菌・稲の培養等の記録写真の映像、展示風
  景の記録映像、人工呼吸器のポストカード
- テクノクラート《Dutch Special 私もかわ
  いいアライグマ》（1993）より：
  街中の幼女達を収めた映像（部分）
- テクノクラート《Dutch Special コロニー・
  イン・ザ・シティ》（1993）より：
  東京で採取した菌を可視化した映像（部分）
- テクノクラート《Dutch Life vol. 2 ジャン
  キーフード》（1993）より：
  食品をカプセル剤化した作品の記録映像
- テクノクラート《Dutch Life vol. 4 カミン
  グアウト》（1993）より：
  採血風景・展示風景の記録映像、血液提供の
  同意書類
- テクノクラート《Dutch Special 入れ墨・
  輸血パフォーマンス》（1994）より：
  日本の漫画キャラクターを入れ墨で入れる
  パフォーマンスの記録映像
- テクノクラート《Dutch Life vol. 5 セックス・
  アパルトヘイト》（1994）より：
  男女別のシール、パネル、展示風景の記録写真
- テクノクラート《Dutch Life Vol. 7/8 公衆
  精子計画》（1995）より：
  精子提供者のパネル、「公衆精子計画」パネ
  ル、「夫婦交換計画」パネル、「血液交換計画」
  パネル、輸送用木箱（以上ベネチア版）、精
  液採取の記録映像、精液凍結保存用タンク、
  精子提供同意書類等
- 飴屋法水《動物堂》（1995–2003）より：
  資料（輸入申請書類、検疫申請書類、海外取
  引書類ほか）
- テクノクラート《丸いジャングル》（1996）より：
  メキシコでの菌の採取・展示風景の記録映
  像、展示されたポラロイド写真
- 飴屋法水《インプリンツ・オブ・自分—あな
  たに対する100 の質問》（1999）より：
  展示参加者の回答による映像より椹木野衣
  氏の回答部分、アンケート回答書類
- ブラウン管テレビ 29 台（本展展示用）ほか
- From Technocrat, *WAR BAR*, 1990:
  Camera-ready copy of 24 city maps,
  documentary footage of equipment used in
  the exhibition/installation views
- From Ameya Norimizu, *Japanese Song*,
  1991:
  Audio recorded over the telephone (partial)
- From Technocrat, *Dutch Life vol. 1:
  CONTAMINATED*, 1992:
  Video of documentary photography of
  fungus/rice cultivation, etc.; documentary
  footage of installation; postcards of medical
  ventilator
- From Technocrat, *Dutch Special: I'm a
  Cute Racoon, Too*, 1993:
  Video of young girls in town (partial)
- From Technocrat, *Dutch Special: Colony
  in the City*, 1993:
  Video of visualization of microbes collected
  in Tokyo (partial)
- From Technocrat, *Dutch Life vol. 2:
  JUNKIE FOOD*, 1993:
  Documentary footage of work consisting of
  food in capsule form
- From Technocrat, *Dutch Life vol. 4:
  COMING OUT*, 1993:
  Documentary footage of blood collection/

exhibition, blood donation consent forms, etc.
- From Technocrat, *Dutch Special:
  TATOO & BLOOD TRANSFUSION
  PERFORMANCE*, 1994:
  Documentary footage of being tattooed with
  a Japanese manga character
- From Technocrat, *Dutch Life vol. 5: SEX
  APARTHEID*, 1994:
  Male/female segregation stickers, panels,
  documentary photographs of installation
- From Technocrat, *Dutch Life Vol. 7/8:
  PUBLIC SEMEN*, 1995:
  Panel of semen donors, panel of Public
  Semen Project, panel of Swapping Project,
  panel of Blood Exchange Project, crates
  (all from Venetian edition); documentary
  footage of semen collection; liquid nitrogen
  tank; semen donor consent forms, etc.
- From Ameya Norimizu, *Dobutsu-do*,
  1995–2003:
  Documents (import forms, quarantine
  forms, international transaction forms, etc.)
- From Technocrat, *Round Jungle*, 1996:
  Documentary footage of Mexico microbe
  collection and installation, Polaroid
  photographs exhibited in Mexico
- From Ameya Norimizu, *Imprints: 100
  Questions to You*, 1999:
  Sawaragi Noi's response (part of the
  video of responses by participants) and
  questionnaire response forms
- 29 CRT television sets (for *Bubbles/
  Debris*), and other objects

サイズ可変
Dimensions variable
作家蔵（ただし、《Dutch Life vol. 5 セックス・ア
パルトヘイト》のパネルは北見和義氏蔵）
Collection of the artist (except panels of
Dutch Life vol. 5 SEX APARTHEID, on loan from
Mr. Kitami Kazuyoshi)
--
註：
テクノクラートへの参加者：中山大介、石川成俊、浜
里堅太郎、田口和裕、古川明宏、川井千恵、国広美香、
三好愛、岸みどり、大沢直子、福島美紀

協力：池内務、椹木野衣、大友良英、宇川直宏、秋田
敬明、福居ショウジン、新川貴詩、吉根聡、南條史生

Note:
Participants in Technocrat: Nakayama
Daisuke, Ishikawa Narutoshi, Hamasato
Kentaro, Taguchi Kazuhiro, Furukawa Akihiro,
Kawai Chie, Kunihiro Mika, Miyoshi Ai, Kishi
Midori, Osawa Naoko, Fukushima Miki

Collaborators: Ikeuchi Tsutomu, Sawaragi
Noi, Otomo Yoshihide, Ukawa Naohiro, Akita
Takaaki, Fukui Shojin, Shinkawa Takashi,
Yoshine Satoshi, Nanjo Fumio

DIVINA COMMEDIA
(the council of divina commedia)

砥綿正之＋松本泰章
Towata Masayuki + Matsumoto Yasuaki
DIVINA COMMEDIA
1991
映像
Video
15 min.
作家蔵｜Collection of the artists

1991 年 神戸ジーベックホール
監督：巽直央
美術：砥綿正之、松本泰章
マネジメント：続木東作

2021 年 再構成インスタレーション（京都市京セラ美術館）
監督：松本泰章
映像テクニカル：岸本康
音響テクニカル：吹田哲二郎
展示協力：株式会社インターオフィス（MR バウハウスエディション：シェーズロング［ミース・ファン・デル・ローエ］、サイドテーブル E1027［アイリーン・グレイ］）

1991: Xebec Hall, Kobe
Director: Tatsumi Naohiro
Art: Towata Masayuki, Matsumoto Yasuaki
Management: Tsuzuki Tosaku

2021: Installation with recorded video (Kyoto City KYOCERA Museum of Art)
Director: Matsumoto Yasuaki
Video technical: Kishimoto Yasushi
Acoustic technical: Suita Tetsujiro
Support: inter office ltd. (MR Bauhaus edition – chaise longue [Mies van der Rohe], E1027 side table [Eileen Gray])
© TOWATA + MATSUMOTO

GEISAI

芸術道場 GP 2001 スライドショー
GEIJUTSU DOJO Grand Prix 2001 Slideshow
2020
スライドプロジェクション（記録画像、スライド約 390 枚）
Slide projection (archival photographs, approx. 390 slides)
approx.10 min.
GEISAI 実行委員会蔵
GEISAI Executive Committee
© Kaikai Kiki Co., Ltd. All Rights Reserved.

GEISAI#11　2008 スライドショー
GEISAI#11 2008 Slideshow
2020
スライドプロジェクション（記録画像、スライド約 200 枚）
Slide projection (archival photographs, approx. 200 slides)
approx.10 min.
GEISAI 実行委員会蔵
GEISAI Executive Committee
© Kaikai Kiki Co., Ltd. All Rights Reserved.

GEISAI#13　2009 スライドショー
GEISAI#13 2009 Slideshow
2020
スライドプロジェクション（記録画像、スライド約 160 枚）
Slide projection (archival photographs,approx. 160 slides)
approx. 6 min.
GEISAI 実行委員会蔵
GEISAI Executive Committee
© Kaikai Kiki Co., Ltd. All Rights Reserved.

Chim↑Pom

SUPER RAT -CHIBAOKAKUN-
2006
渋谷センター街で捕獲したネズミの剥製
A rat stuffed after being caught at Shibuya Center-gai Street
18.3×20×15
個人蔵｜Private collection

SUPER RAT ビデオ
SUPER RAT Video
2006/2011
映像（展覧会バージョン）
Video (edited for public exhibitions)
3 min. 13 sec.
作家蔵｜Collection of the artists

SUPER RAT -Scrap and Build-
2017
ミクストメディア（新宿で捕獲したネズミの剥製、解体された歌舞伎町のジオラマ、土、石膏、キタコレビルで発掘した猫の骨、塩ビ板、鉄製フレーム、ネズミの餌、水、コンクリートガラ、映像）
Mixed media (stuffed rats captured in Shinjuku, Kabukicho diorama demolished, soil, plaster, cat bones excavated in Kitakore Building, PVC sheet, iron frame, rat food, water, concrete fragments, video)
立体｜sculpture　高さ｜height: 147、直径｜diameter: 100
映像
Video
2 min. 40 sec.
作家蔵｜Collection of the artists
協力：西村健太、楊俊彦
In cooperation with: Nishimura Kenta, Yo Toshihiko

Sukurappu ando Birudo プロジェクト（資料映像）
Sukurappu ando Birudo Project (archival video)
2020
7 min. 54 sec.
作家蔵｜Collection of the artists

ビルバーガー
Build-Burger
2018
ミクストメディア（「にんげんレストラン」のビルから切り出された 3 階分のフロアの床、各階の残留物）
Mixed media (3 layers of concrete floors cropped from Ningen Restaurant, various furniture and objects from each floor of the building)
サイズ可変｜Dimensions variable
(400×360×280)
個人蔵｜Private collection
協力：三井孝明（2021 年）、にんげんレストラン、Smappa! Group、古藤寛也
In cooperation with: Mitsui Takaaki (2021), Ningen Restaurant, Smappa! Group, Koto Hiroya

ビルバーガー
Build-Burger
2018
ミクストメディア（「にんげんレストラン」のビルから切り出された 3 階分のフロアの床、各階の残留物）
Mixed media (3 layers of concrete floors cropped from Ningen Restaurant, various furniture and objects from each floor of the building)
サイズ可変｜Dimensions variable
(186×170×155)
作家蔵｜Collection of the artists

協力：三井孝明（2021 年）、にんげんレストラン、Smappa! Group、古藤寛也
In cooperation with: Mitsui Takaaki (2021), Ningen Restaurant, Smappa! Group, Koto Hiroya
協力：ANOMALY ／無人島プロダクション
Courtesy: ANOMALY and MUJIN-TO Production

contact Gonzo

公園
Koen (Park)
2005
映像
Video
52 min. 31 sec.（オリジナル｜original)
作家蔵｜Collection of the artists
--
出演：垣尾優
撮影・編集：塚原悠也
「泉北アートプロジェクト」より
Performance by Kakio Masaru
Filmed by Tsukahara Yuya
for "Senboku Art Project"

ヘルシンキにて
「the first man narrative」シリーズより
Helsinki
from the series, "the first man narrative"
2008/2021
ミクストメディア（ネガフィルム、インクジェットプリント）
Mixed media (negative film, inkjet prints)
サイズ可変
Dimensions variable
作家蔵｜Collection of the artists

Shelters
2009/2021
映像
Video
20 min.（オリジナル｜original)
作家蔵｜Collection of the artists

東北画は可能か？
Is Tohoku-ga possible?

東北画は可能か？
Is Tohoku-ga possible?
東北八重山景
Overlapped Tohoku Mountainscapes
2010
綿布にアクリル
Acrylic on cotton cloth
234×385.4
作家蔵｜Collection of the artists

東北画は可能か？
Is Tohoku-ga possible?
方舟計画
Ark Plan
2011
綿布にアクリル
Acrylic on cotton cloth
229.5×384
作家蔵｜Collection of the artists

東北画は可能か？
Is Tohoku-ga possible?
東北山水
Tohoku Mountain and Waterscapes
2011
綿布にアクリル
Acrylic on cotton cloth
229.5×410.2
作家蔵｜Collection of the artists

東北画は可能か？
Is Tohoku-ga possible?
しきおり絵詞
*Shikiori-Ekotoba −a Woven
Narrative of Seasons−*
2013-
着古した布、綿布、毛糸、蚊帳
Worn cloths, cotton cloth, yarn, mosquito net
サイズ可変
Dimensions variable
作家蔵｜Collection of the artists
制作協力：荒達宏
Production supported by Ara Tatsuhiro

石原葉
Ishihara Yo
sí
2011
和紙に岩絵具、水干絵具
Mineral pigments, water-dried paints on
Japanese paper
60.6×45.5
作家蔵｜Collection of the artist

近江谷沙里
Omiya Sari
強風ハローごはん
Gale Hello Meal
2011
キャンバスにパステル、水彩絵具、色鉛筆
Pastel, watercolors, colored pencils on
canvas
45.5×60.6
作家蔵｜Collection of the artist

海藤千紗音
Kaito Chisato
若木山縁起
Auspicious of Mt. OSANAGI
2010
紙にアクリル
Acrylic on paper
60.6×45.5
作家蔵｜Collection of the artist

狩野宏明
Kano Hiroaki
天狗飯七
Tengu's Spoon
2013
綿布に白亜下地、油彩
Chalk, oil painting on cotton cloth
50.0×60.6
作家蔵｜Collection of the artist

鴻崎正武
Kozaki Masatake
TOUGEN Tohoku
TOUGEN
2009
和紙に金箔、岩絵具、油彩、アクリル
Gold foil, mineral pigments, oil painting, and
acrylic on Japanese paper
60.6×45.5

作家蔵｜Collection of the artist

鴻崎正武
Kozaki Masatake
鴻草
Kono-kusa
2011
和紙に金箔、岩絵具、油彩、アクリル
Gold foil, mineral pigments, oil painting, and
acrylic on Japanese paper
45.5×60.6
作家蔵｜Collection of the artist

佐々木綾子
Sasaki Ayako
レイヤー
Layer
2011
和紙に墨、胡粉、水干絵具、アクリル、油性ペン
Ink, whitewash, water-dried paint, acrylic, oil-
based pen on wallpaper
60.6×50
作家蔵｜Collection of the artist

佐々木優衣
Sasaki Yui
東北遷都計画
New: Japanese Civil War（2012～）
2010
コラージュ、アクリル
Collage, acrylic
45.5×60.6
作家蔵｜Collection of the artist

多田さやか
Tada Sayaka
色即是空
Void
2011
新聞紙にアクリル、岩絵具
Acrylic, mineral pigments on newspaper
60.6×45.5
作家蔵｜Collection of the artist

久松知子
Hisamatsu Tomoko
ひと山むこうなまずが
The Catfish Raged Across the Mountain
2011
紙に水彩絵具
Watercolors on paper
45.5×60.6
作家蔵｜Collection of the artist

三瀬夏之介
Mise Natsunosuke
東北幻想
Illusion of Tohoku
2010
雲肌麻紙に墨、アクリル、金属粉
Ink, acrylic, metal on Kumohada hemp paper
60.6×45.5
作家蔵｜Collection of the artist

三瀬夏之介
Mise Natsunosuke
日本の絵
Painting of Japan
2017
雲肌麻紙に墨、胡粉、金箔
Ink, whitewash, gold leaf on Kumohada hemp
paper
サイズ可変
Dimensions variable

作家蔵｜Collection of the artist

渡辺綾
Watanabe Aya
山の神さま〜みちしるべ〜
Mountains of Prayer
2010
壁紙にアクリル、色鉛筆
Acrylic, colored pencils on wallpaper
65×50
作家蔵｜Collection of the artist

槇壽宏
Maki Toshihiro
ムカサリ絵馬
Mukasari Ema
2019
紙に水彩絵具
Watercolors on paper
57×42
黒鳥観音蔵
Collection of Kurotori Kannon

DOMMUNE

*THE 100 JAPANESE
CONTEMPORARY ARTISTS/season 6*
2020-2021
映像（#051 は本展のための再編集、#025 は 2015
年 9 月 3 日収録の season 3 より）
Video (Video #051 was edited for this
exhibition. Video #025 was originally recorded
on September 3, 2015 for *season 3*)
#040 TECHNOCRAT｜テクノクラート
#041 IS TOHOKU-GA POSSIBLE?｜東北
    画は可能か？
#042 PARPLUME｜パープルーム（Take 2）
#043 SUDDENLY, THE VIEW SPREADS OUT
    BEFORE US.｜突然、目の前がひらけて
#044 GEISAI
#045 KOKUFU OSAMU'S ENGINE IN THE
    WATER RE-CREATION PROJECT｜國
    府理「水中エンジン」再制作プロジェクト
#046 IDEAL COPY
#047 COMPLESSO PLASTICO
#048 DIVINA COMMEDIA
#049 CONTACT GONZO
#050 KUSHINO TERRACE｜クシノテラス
#051 ARTIFICIAL INTELLIGENCE ART AND
    AESTHETICS RESEARCH GROUP｜
    人工知能美学芸術研究会（AI 美芸研）
#052 CHIM↑POM（Chapter 2）
#053 DOMMUNE
#025 CHAOS*LOUNGE｜カオス*ラウンジ
approx. 120 min. each
--
© DOMMUNE、各出演アーティストグループ
© DOMMUNE, each of the participating artists
Courtesy of ANOMALY

カオス*ラウンジ
Chaos*Lounge

カオス*ラウンジ宣言 2010
*The Manifesto of CHAOS*LOUNGE
2010*
2010
© カオス*ラウンジ｜Chaos*Lounge

パープルーム
Parplume

パープルーム
Parplume
花粉の王国
Kingdom of Pollen
2020
インスタレーション（以下の作品により構成）
Installation (consisting of the following
works)

アラン
Alan
ゾンビマスター
Zombie Master
2017
木材、染料、インク、レジンキャスト
Wood, dye, ink, resin, casting
21×21.3×5
作家蔵｜Collection of the artist

アラン
Alan
パープルーム予備校の模型
The Model of Parplume Preparatory School
2017
木
Wood
178.5×79.7×30
みそにこみおでん氏蔵
Collection of Mr. Misonikomi Oden

アラン
Alan
マナ・バード
Mana Bird
2017
木材、染料、剥製、点滴スタンド
Wood, dye, stuffed bird, intravenous stand
高さ｜height: 220、直径｜diameter: 132
作家蔵｜Collection of the artist

安藤裕美
Ando Yumi
相模原の駐輪場にいる梅津さん
*Mr. Umetsu at the Bicycle Parking Lot in
Sagamihara*
2019
キャンバスに油彩
Oil on canvas
65×80.5
作家蔵｜Collection of the artist

安藤裕美
Ando Yumi
ジョナサンで談笑する3人（シエニーチュアン、
梅津庸一、安藤裕美）
*Three People Chatting at Jonathan
(Shieneychuan, Yoichi Umetsu, Yumi Ando)*
2019
キャンバスに油彩
Oil on canvas
54×65
みそにこみおでん氏蔵
Collection of Mr. Misonikomi Oden

安藤裕美
Ando Yumi
見晴らし小屋に帰るアラン
Alan Returns to the Parplume Vantage Point
2019
キャンバスに油彩
Oil on canvas

34×53
釣之郎氏蔵
Collection of Mr. Tsuri Shiro

安藤裕美
Ando Yumi
光のサイコロジー
Psychology of Light
2019–2020
映像
Video
17 min. 9 sec.
作家蔵｜Collection of the artist

梅津庸一
Umetsu Yoichi
フル・フロンタル
Full Frontal
2018–
パネルに油彩（7点組）
Oil on wooden panel (7 panels)
180.6×99.8 each
みそにこみおでん氏蔵
Collection of Mr. Misonikomi Oden

シエニーチュアン
Shieneychuan
私はそのような性質を見たことがありません
が、あなたがゆっくりと反対側から近づいてい
るようです
*I've never seen such a personality, but I
think you're slowly approaching from the
other side*
2019
布に油彩、木炭、スプレー
Oil, charcoal, spray on cloth
60.0×89.5
飯島モトハル氏蔵
Collection of Mr. Iijima Motoharu

わきもとさき
Wakimoto Saki
home bag
2018.8.7
紙、鉛筆、ビニール、ガムテープ、印刷物
Paper, pencil, vinyl, packing tape, printed
matters
22.3×27.7
みそにこみおでん氏蔵
Collection of Mr. Misonikomi Oden

わきもとさき
Wakimoto Saki
home bag
2018.8.13
紙、鉛筆、ビニール、ガムテープ、印刷物
Paper, pencil, vinyl, packing tape, printed
matters
22.3×27.7
作家蔵｜Collection of the artist

わきもとさき
Wakimoto Saki
ひとりくらし
Living Alone
2019–
ミクストメディア（布、アクリル、アルミホイル、
ペン、お風呂に入った紙、印刷物、ビニール、テープ、
油性塗料、塵）
Mixed media (cloth, acrylic, aluminum foil,
pen, paper, printed matters, vinyl, tape, oil-
based ink, dust)
182×182×190
作家蔵｜Collection of the artist

パープルーム
Parplume
パープルームTV（資料映像）
Parplume TV (archival video)
2019–2020
作家蔵｜Collection of the artists

突然、目の前がひらけて
S u d d e n l y , t h e v i e w
s p r e a d s o u t b e f o r e u s .

突然、目の前がひらけて
Suddenly, the view spreads out before us.
区画壁を跨ぐ橋のタイムライン（アーカイブ
資料）
Timeline for "A Bridge Striding
over a Fence" (archival material)
2014–2015
327×40
作家蔵｜Collection of the artists

突然、目の前がひらけて
Suddenly, the view spreads out before us.
アーカイブ資料：
・プロジェクトに関する自筆メモ等
・区画壁を跨ぐ橋の受付カード
・航空写真、プレスリリース
・記録写真（朝鮮大学校側）
・記録写真（武蔵野美術大学側）
・模型（初期スロープ案）
・模型（最終プラン）
Archival materials:
・Notes for "A Bridge Striding over a
 Fence"
・Entry Card for "A Bridge Striding over a
 Fence"
・Aerial photograph, press release
・Photo of the bridge from Korea
 University
・Photo of the bridge from Musashino Art
 University
・Maquette of a slope for an early plan
・Maquette for the final plan
2014–2015
作家蔵｜Collection of the artists
記録写真（2点とも）：加藤健
Photo of the bridge: Kato Ken

灰原千晶、李晶玉
Haibara Chiaki, Ri Jong Ok
区画壁を跨ぐ橋のドローイング
*Drawing for "A Bridge Striding over a
Fence"*
2015
紙にモノクロデジタルプリント、色鉛筆
Color pencil on B/W digital print
30.5×39.5
個人蔵｜Private collection

鄭梨愛
Chong Ri Ae
ある所のある時におけるある一人の話と語り聞
かせ
*The Story of One Person at a Time in a
Place and Its Narrative*
2015
映像
Video
20 min.
作家蔵｜Collection of the artist

土屋美智子
Tsuchiya Michiko
展示風景「「突然、目の前がひらけて」アンケート」
Installation view of "Questionnaire of
Suddenly, the view spreads out before us."
2015
インクジェットプリント
Inkjet print
70.2×130
作家蔵 | Collection of the artist
撮影：加藤健
Photo: Kato Ken

土屋美智子
Tsuchiya Michiko
「境界を跨ぐと、」アンケート
Questionnaire of *To the other side of the
boundaries,*
2015, 2017/2021
29.7×21.0
作家蔵 | Collection of the artist

土屋美智子
Tsuchiya Michiko
昨日以前と明日以降の距離―フォリャンテイ・
レーナの場合
*Distance Between "Before Yesterday" and
"After Tomorrow" ―Lena Foljanty's Case*
2017
映像
Video
19 min.
作家蔵 | Collection of the artist

土屋美智子
Tsuchiya Michiko
昨日以前と明日以降の距離―オオカマキリの場合
*Distance Between "Before Yesterday"
and "After Tomorrow" ―Japanese Giant
Mantis's Case*
2017
映像
Video
9 min. 50 sec.
作家蔵 | Collection of the artist

土屋美智子
Tsuchiya Michiko
memo:01~06
2020
紙に印刷
Printed on paper
33.7×33.7
作家蔵 | Collection of the artist

灰原千晶
Haibara Chiaki
展示風景「渡れるかもしれない橋」
Installation view of *The Bridge Which May
Be Crossed.*
2011
インクジェットプリント
Inkjet print
120×80
作家蔵 | Collection of the artist

灰原千晶
Haibara Chiaki
Playground
2015
映像
Video
7 min. 49 sec.
作家蔵 | Collection of the artist

李晶玉
Ri Jong Ok
橋　2021
The Bridge 2021
2015–2021
パネルに紙、デジタルプリント、鉛筆、墨、アクリ
ル
Paper, digital print, pencil, ink, acrylic on
panel
100×50
作家蔵 | Collection of the artist
--
「突然、目の前がひらけて」（京都市京セラ美
術館、2021 年）
技術協力：株式会社ジェネレーション・エックス
*"Suddenly, the view spreads out
before us."* (Kyoto City KYOCERA Museum of
Art, 2021)
Technical support: Generation-X Co., Ltd
※以上の作品および資料は、すべて下記のプ
ロジェクトに関するものである。
「突然、目の前がひらけて」（2015 年）
協力：袴田京太朗（武蔵野美術大学）、李鏞勲（朝鮮
大学校）、武蔵野美術大学、朝鮮大学校
※ The above works and archival materials
are all related to the following project:
"Suddenly, the view spreads out before us."
(2015)
Supported by Hakamata Kyotaro (Musashino
Art University) and Li Yong Hun (Korea
University), Musashino Art University, Korea
University

クシノテラス
K u s h i n o   T e r r a c e

稲村米治
Inamura Yoneji
昆虫千手観音像
*The Statue of Thousand Armed
Kannon with Insects Inlaid*
1975
昆虫（甲虫）、木、鉄芯、コルク、銅線、針金、布、テー
プ、針
Insects (beetles), wood, iron core, cork,
copper wire, wire, cloth, tape, needles
180×100×100
群馬県板倉町蔵
Collection of Itakura Town

上林比東三
Kanbayashi Hitomi
未知の生物
Unknown Creatures
2017–
流木、発砲スチロール
Driftwoods, styrofoams
作家蔵 | Collection of the artist
展示協力：いさざ会館
Installation assisted by Isaza Kaikan

ガタロ
Gataro
記憶の椅子
Stools for Remembering the Past
2016
27.5×20.0×24.0
作家蔵 | Collection of the artist

ガタロ
Gataro
雑巾の譜

Chronicle of My Cleaning Rags
2018–2020
紙に鉛筆（約 450 点）
Pencil on paper (approx. 450 pieces)
approx. 21.0×29.7 each
櫛野展正氏蔵
Collection of Mr. Kushino Nobumasa

ガタロ
Gataro
川底の唄
Songs from the River Bottom
2019
板にアクリル、ニス
Acrylic and varnish on panel
75.5×94
作家蔵 | Collection of the artist

Gataro, A Janitor Artist (資料映像 | documentary
video)
2020
映像
Video
5 min. 43 sec.
櫛野展正氏蔵
Collection of Mr. Kushino Nobumasa
編集：田頭潤一
撮影・ナレーション：櫛野展正
Edited by Tagashira Junichi
Filmed and narrated by Kushino Nobumasa

城田貞夫
Joden Sadao
無題（番場の忠太郎）
Untitled (Chutaro of Bamba)
ca. 2000
カラクリ芝居の舞台、人形、道具
Stage, dolls and tools for hand-made
mechanical doll theatre
舞台 | stage: 23×182×93
作家蔵 | Collection of the artist

スナックジルバ（城田貞夫 資料映像）
Snack Jiruba (documentary video on Joden
Sadao)
2019
映像
Video
3 min. 28 sec.
櫛野展正氏蔵
Collection of Mr. Kushino Nobumasa
編集：田頭潤一
Edited by Tagashira Junichi

ストレンジナイト
Strange Knight
無題（創作仮面館）
Untitled (House of Creative Masks)
制作年不明
Year unknown
インスタレーション（約 250 点の仮面、コラージュ、
立像など）
Installation (approx. 250 pieces of masks,
collage, standing figure)
クシノテラス蔵、個人蔵
Collection of Kushino Terrace, Private
collection
協力：創作仮面館
Courtesy of Sosaku Kamenkan (House of
Creative Masks)

國府理「水中エンジン」
再制作プロジェクト
Kokufu Osamu's
Engine in the Water
re-creation project

國府理「水中エンジン」再制作プロジェクト
Kokufu Osamu's Engine in the Water re-creation project
國府理「水中エンジン」redux
Kokufu Osamu's Engine in the Water redux
2021
國府《水中エンジン》（2012、2013）の水槽（鉄、アクリル）、軽トラック「スバルサンバー EK23 型 KT1」のエンジン（2017 年再制作）
Water tank of Kokufu Osamu *Engine in the Water* (2012, 2013) (iron, plexiglass), engine of a pickup truck "SUBARU SAMBAR EK23 KT1" (re-creation, 2017)
240×130×130
國府克治氏蔵
Collection of Mr. Kokufu Katsuya
制作協力：京都美術工房、京都芸術大学 ULTRA FACTORY（2017 年再制作）、京都市立芸術大学 芸術資源研究センター
Supported by Kyoto Bijutsu Kobo, ULTRA FACTORY of Kyoto University of the Arts (re-creation, 2017), The Archival Research Center of Kyoto City University of Arts
サウンドデザイン：シュヴァーブ・トム
グラフィックデザイン：中家寿之
Sound design: Tomas Svab
Graphic design: Nakaie Toshiyuki

展覧会案内ハガキ「國府理　水中エンジン」とサインスタンド（アートスペース虹）（資料）
Invitation card for the exhibition, Kokufu Osamu *Engine in the Water*, sign stand (Art Space Niji)
(referential material)
2012
印刷物、サインスタンド
Printed on paper, sign stand
14.8×10（ハガキ｜invitation card）
個人蔵｜Private collection
協力：アートスペース虹（サインスタンド）
Supported by Art Space Niji for the sign stand

「水中エンジン」再制作記録映像
Documentation of Engine in the Water re-creation
2017
映像
Video
approx. 3 min.
作家蔵｜Collection of the artists

國府理
Kokufu Osamu
水中エンジン―貯蔵
Engine in the Water − Storage
ca. 2012–ca. 2013
紙にインク（2 点）
Ink on paper (two drawings)
21×29.7
國府克治氏蔵
Collection of Mr. Kokufu Katsuya
協力：アートコートギャラリー
Courtesy of ARTCOURT Gallery

國府理
Kokufu Osamu
「未来のいえ」ドローイング―水中エンジン―
Drawing for "Cosmosphere" — Engine in the Water —
2013
紙にインク
Ink on paper
29×21
國府克治氏蔵
Collection of Mr. Kokufu Katsuya
協力：アートコートギャラリー
Courtesy of ARTCOURT Gallery

資料写真｜Archival photos:
・國府理「水中エンジン」展の展示風景、アートスペース虹（京都）
Installation view of Kokufu Osamu, *Engine in the Water*, Art Space Niji, Kyoto
2012
12.7×17.8
・《水中エンジン》のメンテナンス作業中の國府理のポートレート
A portrait of Kokufu Osamu in maintenance work of *Engine in the Water*
2013
8.9×12.7
・「國府理　水中エンジン redux」後期展の展示風景、アートスペース虹（京都）
Installation view of *Kokufu Osamu's Engine in the Water redux, part 2*, Art Space Niji, Kyoto
2017
12.7×17.8
撮影（以上 3 点）：シュヴァーブ・トム
Photos: Tomas Svab

人工知能美学芸術研究会
（AI 美芸研）
Artificial Intelligence
Art and Aesthetics
Research Group

人工知能美学芸術研究会
Artificial Intelligence Art and Aesthetics Research Group
作品 -J
Work-J
2019
キャンバスに UV プリント
UV print on canvas
45.5×38.0
みそにこみおでん氏蔵
Collection of Mr. Misonikomi Oden

人工知能美学芸術研究会
Artificial Intelligence Art and Aesthetics Research Group
作品 -E
Work-E
2019
キャンバスに UV プリント
UV print on canvas
45.5×38.0
個人蔵｜Private collection

S 氏から N 氏への指示書（資料）
Instruction sheet given to Mr. N by Mr. S (referential materials)
2014（公表｜public disclosure）
紙にコピー
Photocopy on paper

21.0×29.7
人工知能美学芸術研究会蔵
Collection of the Artificial Intelligence Art and Aesthetics Research Group

N 氏が S 氏に代作した交響曲の楽譜（資料）
Symphony score ghostwritten by Mr. N for Mr. S (referential materials)
2011
紙にコピー
Photocopy on paper
29.7×42.0（243 頁｜sheets）
人工知能美学芸術研究会蔵
Collection of the Artificial Intelligence Art and Aesthetics Research Group

N 氏が S 氏に代作した交響曲の演奏（資料）
CD performance of the symphony ghostwritten by Mr. N for Mr. S.
(referential materials)
発売｜Released: 2011/7/20
CD｜compact disc
人工知能美学芸術研究会蔵
Collection of the Artificial Intelligence Art and Aesthetics Research Group
註：
『佐村河内守：交響曲第 1 番《HIROSHIMA》』
DENON COCQ-84901
演奏：大友直人指揮、東京交響楽団
録音：2011 年 4 月 11–12 日、パルテノン多摩大ホール（世界初録音）
発売：2011 年 7 月 20 日、日本コロムビア株式会社
Note:
"Mamoru Samuragochi: Symphony No. 1 *Hiroshima*" DENON COCQ-84901
Naoto Otomo conducted Tokyo Symphony Orchestra.
Recorded on April 11–12, 2011 at Parthenon Tama Main Hall (World's first recording)
Released on July 20, 2011 by Nippon Columbia Co., Ltd.

横尾忠則
Yokoo Tadanori
赤い耳
Red Ear
2000/2020（再制作｜re-creation）
キャンバスに油彩
Oil on canvas
72.7×60.6
作家蔵｜Collection of the artist
--
特別協力：ゲーテ・インスティトゥート大阪・京都
In Collaboration with Goethe-Institut Osaka Kyoto

フォト・クレジット | Photo Credits

p. 68
Photo: Oguma Sakae

pp. 72, 73 [上 | top], p. 73 [左下 | bottom left], p. 74 [左下 | bottom left], p. 75 [上 | top]
Photo: Asano Takeshi

p. 73 [右下 | bottom right]
Photo: Tahara Motohiro

pp. 74, 75 [下段左から 2、3、5番目 | bottom, 2nd, 3rd, 5th from left]
Photo: Takashima Kiyotoshi

p. 78
© Sasaki Nakayuki

pp. 84, 85
Photo: Fukunaga Kazuo

pp. 84−87
© TOWATA + MATSUMOTO

pp. 94
Photo: GEISAI Photography Team
© Kaikai Kiki Co., Ltd. All Rights Reserved.

pp. 95−97 [上 | top]
Photo: Yagi Kenji
© Kaikai Kiki Co., Ltd. All Rights Reserved.

pp. 95−97 [中・下 | middle, bottom]
Photo: GEISAI Photography Team
© Kaikai Kiki Co., Ltd. All Rights Reserved.

pp. 100, 101 [左上、下 | upper left, bottom], 102, 103
Photo: Morita Kenji

pp. 100−103
Courtesy of the artist, ANOMALY and MUJIN-TO Production

p. 112, 113
Photo: Seno Hiromi (FLOT)

p. 113 [上 | top]
Photo: Omote Nobutada

p. 131 [右下 | bottom right]
Photo: Mishima Ichiro

p. 142
© Fujino Masaaki

p. 143 [右上 | upper right]
Photo: Tsuzuki Kyoichi

p. 144 [右上 | upper right]
Photo: Suzuki Hidenori

pp. 148, 150, 151 [左中、下 | middle and bottom left]
Photo: Tomas Svab

p. 151 [左上 | upper left]
Photo: Kioku Keizo

pp. 154, 155, 156 [上 | top]
Photo: Kaido Masaru

謝辞 ｜ Acknowledgments

本展開催および本書刊行にあたり、多大なご協力を賜りました作家、所蔵家の皆さまをはじめ下記の諸機関、関係者の方々に感謝の意を表します。
＊機関名、氏名は五十音順（和文）、アルファベット順（欧文）に掲載しています。（敬称略）

We would like to thank the following artists, lenders, institutions and individuals for their invaluable assistance to the realization of this exhibition and the publication.（Honorifics omitted）
＊ Institution and personal names are listed in kana order（Japanese）and alphabetical order（English）.

飴屋法水
市川明子
遠藤水城
ガタロ
上林比東三
クシノテラス
城田貞夫
白石晃一
人工知能美学芸術研究会
高嶋慈
鄭梨愛
土屋美智子
東北画は可能か？
灰原千晶
はがみちこ
パープルーム
平野治朗
松蔭浩之
松本泰章
有限会社カイカイキキ
李晶玉
Chim↑Pom
contact Gonzo
DOMMUNE
IDEAL COPY

飯島モトハル
稲村茂
梅沢和木
岡田伊代子

北見和義
熊谷寿美子
群馬県板倉町
黒鳥観音
國府克治
釣之郎
砥綿理恵
花牟禮有基
浜里堅太郎
原田崇人
みそにこみおでん
横尾忠則
吉野誠一

岩渕貞哉
楠見清
熊倉敬聡
黒澤伸
小金沢智
新藤淳
須藤絢乃
中尾拓哉
原久子
見増勇介
山本浩貴

秋田敬明
池内務
池田裕之
上田雄三
岡田勉
風元正
国広美香
小林公
小山登美夫
豊浦英明
中ザワヒデキ
中山ダイスケ
中山博喜
西島亜紀
袴田京太朗
藤城里香
松本吏樹郎
八木良太
矢野優
山本裕子
李鏞勲
ろくでなし子
David d'Heilly

アートコートギャラリー
いさざ会館
株式会社インターオフィス
京都芸術大学
京都市立芸術大学 芸術資源研究センター
成安造形大学
名古屋芸術大学 先端メディア表現コース
無人島プロダクション
明治クリックス
ANOMALY
CASHI
imura art gallery

本展準備中、参加作家の砥綿正之氏が逝去されました。謹んでご冥福をお祈りいたします。

編者
榑木野衣

美術批評家。1962 年秩父生まれ。京都の同志社で大学生
時代を過ごす。著書に、『シミュレーショニズム』（洋泉社）、
『日本・現代・美術』（新潮社）、『反アート入門』『アウトサ
イダーアート入門』（ともに幻冬舎）、『後美術論』『震美術論』
（ともに美術出版社）、『感性は感動しない』（世界思想社）など。
キュレーターとしての仕事に「日本ゼロ年」展（水戸芸術館、
1999–2000）など。多摩美術大学教授。

京都市京セラ美術館

1933 年開館。2020 年春、リニューアルオープン。
〒 606-8344 京都市左京区岡崎円勝寺町 124
kyotocity-kyocera.museum

Editor
Sawaragi Noi

Art critic. Born in Chichibu city, Saitama prefecture, in 1962. Studied at Dousisha
University, Kyoto. His writings include *Simulationism* (Yosensha Publishing),
Japan/Modern/Art (Shinchosha Publishing Co., Ltd.), *An Anti-Introduction to Art, An
Introduction to Outsider Art* (Both Gentosha Inc.), *Post-Art Theory, Earthquake Art
Theory* (Both Bijutsu Shuppan-sha), and *Sensitivities Aren't Impressions, but Rather
Revelations* (Sekaishisosha). His curatorial works include *Ground Zero Japan*
exhibition (Art Tower Mito, 1999–2000). Professor at Tama Art University.

Kyoto City KYOCERA Museum of Art

Opened in 1933, newly renovated in 2020.
124 Okazaki Enshoji-cho, Sakyo-ku, Kyoto 606-8344 Japan
kyotocity-kyocera.museum

平成美術：うたかたと瓦礫 1989–2019

［展覧会］
企画・監修：榑木野衣
制作統括：高橋信也、土屋隆英（京都市京セラ美術館）
学　芸：野崎昌弘、筒井彩（京都市京セラ美術館）、
　　　　泉川真紀
展示デザイン：前田尚武（京都市京セラ美術館）
会場グラフィックデザイン：松本弦人

［カタログ］
編集：
水野良美（京都市京セラ美術館）
望月幸治（世界思想社）

翻訳：
有限会社フォンテーヌ（pp. 3, 61, 66–88, 94–124, 130–154, 158, 223）
デイヴィッド・ディヒーリ（pp. 63, 65, 91, 93, 127, 129, 184–199）
ウィー・ジングウェン・ダーリル（pp. 200–206, 211–215）
ロバート・チャペスキー（pp. 207–210）
照山貴子（pp. 216–219）

デザイン：
松本弦人

Bubbles/Debris: Art of the Heisei Period 1989–2019

［**Exhibition**］
Curatorial Supervisor: Sawaragi Noi
Project Management: Takahashi Shinya, Tsuchiya Takahide（Kyoto City KYOCERA Museum of Art）
Curatorial Team: Nozaki Masahiro, Tsutsui Aya（Kyoto City KYOCERA Museum of Art），
　　　　Izumikawa Maki
Exhibition Design: Maeda Naotake（Kyoto City KYOCERA Museum of Art）
Graphic Design: Matsumoto Gento

［**Catalogue**］
Editors:
Mizuno Yoshimi（Kyoto City KYOCERA Museum of Art）
Mochizuki Koji（Sekaishisosha）

Translation:
Fontaine Limited, Kyoto（pp. 3, 61, 66–88, 94–124, 130–154, 158, 223）
David d'Heilly（pp. 63, 65, 91, 93, 127, 129, 184–199）
Wee Jingwen Darryl（pp. 200–206, 211–215）
Robert Chapeskie（pp. 207–210）
Teruyama Takako（pp. 216–219）

Design:
Matsumoto Gento

平成美術：うたかたと瓦礫 1989–2019
2021 年 2 月 28 日　初版第 1 刷発行

編者：
榑木野衣
京都市京セラ美術館

発　行：世界思想社
発行者：上原寿明
〒 606-0031 京都市左京区岩倉南桑原町 56
電話　075-721-6500
振替　01000-6-2908
http://sekaishisosha.jp/

印刷・製本：株式会社サンエムカラー

Bubbles/Debris: Art of the Heisei Period 1989–2019
First Edition: Febuary 28, 2021

Edited by Sawaragi Noi and Kyoto City KYOCERA Museum of Art

Published by Sekaishisosha,
an imprint of Sekaishisosha-Kyogakusha Co. Ltd.
56 Iwakura Minamikuwahara-cho, Sakyo-ku, Kyoto 606-0031 Japan
http://sekaishisosha.jp/

Printed and Bound by SunM Color Co., Ltd.

カバー｜Cover
Photo: Kioku Keizo